LIBRARY OF HEBREW BIBLE/
OLD TESTAMENT STUDIES

543

Formerly Journal for the Study of the Old Testament Supplement Series

EXCLUSIVE INCLUSIVITY

Identity Conflicts Between the Exiles and the People who Remained (6th–5th Centuries BCE)

Dalit Rom-Shiloni

B L O O M S B U R Y
NEW YORK · LONDON · NEW DELHI · SYDNEY

Bloomsbury T&T Clark

An imprint of Bloomsbury Publishing Inc

1385 Broadway	50 Bedford Square
New York	London
NY 10018	WC1B 3DP
USA	UK

www.bloomsbury.com

Bloomsbury is a registered trade mark of Bloomsbury Publishing Plc

First published 2013
Paperback edition first printed 2015

Library of Congress Cataloging-in-Publication Data
A catalog record for this book is available from the Library of Congress

ISBN: HB: 978-0-567-08006-6
       PB: 978-0-567-66150-0

Typeset by Forthcoming Publications Ltd (www.forthpub.com)
Printed and bound in the United States of America

To the families of the late Sula, Dvora, and Mina

CONTENTS

ABBREVIATIONS

AB	Anchor Bible
ABD	*Anchor Bible Dictionary.* Edited by D. N. Freedman. 6 vols. New York, 1992
AnBib	Analecta biblica
AOTC	Abingdon Old Testament Commentaries
AS	Assyriological Studies
ATD	Das Alte Testament Deutsch
BA	*Biblical Archaeologist*
BDB	Brown, F., S. R. Driver, and C. A. Briggs. *A Hebrew and English Lexicon of the Old Testament.* Oxford, 1907
BHS	*Biblia Hebraica Stuttgartensia.* Edited by K. Elliger and W. Rudolph. Stuttgart, 1983
Bib	*Biblica*
BibOr	Biblica et orientalia
BWANT	Beiträge zur Wissenschaft vom Alten und Neuen Testament
BZAW	Beihefte zur Zeitschrift für die alttestamentliche Wissenschaft
CAD	*The Assyrian Dictionary of the Oriental Institute of the University of Chicago.* Chicago, 1956–
CBC	Cambridge Bible Commentary
ErIs	*Eretz Israel*
ETSMS	Evangelical Theological Society Monograph Series
FAT	Forschungen zum Alten Testament
FRLANT	Forschungen zur Religion und Literatur des Alten und Neuen Testaments
GTA	Göttinger theologischer Arbeiten
HALAT	Koehler, L., W. Baumgartner, and J. J. Stamm. *Hebräisches und aramäisches Lexikon zum Alten Testament.* Fascicles 1–5, 1967–95 (KBL3). ET: *HALOT*
HAT	Handbuch zum Alten Testament
HBS	Herders biblische Studien
HDR	Harvard Dissertations in Religion
HKAT	Handkommentar zum Alten Testament
HSM	Harvard Semitic Monographs
HTR	*Harvard Theological Review*
HUCA	*Hebrew Union College Annual*
IB	*Interpreter's Bible.* Edited by G. A. Buttrick et al. 12 vols. New York, 1951–57
ICC	International Critical Commentary
IDBSup	*Interpreter's Dictionary of the Bible: Supplementary Volume.* Edited by K. Crim. Nashville, 1976
JANES	*Journal of the Ancient Near Eastern Society*

JAOS	*Journal of the American Oriental Society*
JBL	*Journal of Biblical Literature*
JCS	*Journal of Cuneiform Studies*
JJS	*Journal of Jewish Studies*
JNES	*Journal of Near Eastern Studies*
JSJSup	Journal for the Study of Judaism: Supplement Series
JSOT	*Journal for the Study of the Old Testament*
JSOTSup	Journal for the Study of the Old Testament: Supplement Series
JSPSup	Journal for the Study of the Pseudepigrapha: Supplement Series
JSS	*Journal of Semitic Studies*
JTS	*Journal of Theological Studies*
KAT	Kommentar zum Alten Testament
KBL[3]	Koehler, L., and W. Baumgartner, *Lexicon in Veteris Testamenti libros*. 3d ed. Leiden, 1997
LHBOTS	Library of Hebrew Bible/Old Testament Studies
LSTS	Library of Second Temple Studies
LXX	Septuagint
NCBC	New Century Bible Commentary
NICOT	New International Commentary on the Old Testament
NJPS	*Tanakh: The Holy Scriptures: The New JPS Translation according to the Traditional Hebrew Text*
OBT	Overtures to Biblical Theology
OLA	Orientalia lovaniensia analecta
OTG	Old Testament Guides
OTL	Old Testament Library
OTS	Old Testament Studies
PHSC	Perspectives on Hebrew Scriptures and Its Contexts
SAA	State Archives of Assyria
SBLDS	Society of Biblical Literature Dissertation Series
SBLMS	Society of Biblical Literature Monograph Series
SBLSymS	Society of Biblical Literature Symposium Series
SBT	Studies in Biblical Theology
ScrHier	Scripta hierosolymitana
SNTSMS	Society for New Testament Studies Monograph Series
SSN	Studia Semitica Neerlandica
SVTP	Studia in Veteris Testamenti pseudepigraphica
TDOT	*Theological Dictionary of the Old Testament.* Edited by G. J. Botterweck, H. Ringgren, and H.-J. Fabry. Translated by J. T. Willis, D. E. Green, and D. W. Stott. 14 vols. Vols. 1–2 revised. Grand Rapids, 1974–2004
TynBul	*Tyndale Bulletin*
VT	*Vetus Testamentum*
VTSup	Vetus Testamentum Supplements
WBC	Word Biblical Commentary
WMANT	Wissenschaftliche Monographien zum Alten und Neuen Testament
ZABR	*Zeitschrift für altorientalische und biblische Rechtgeschichte*
ZAW	*Zeitschrift für die alttestamentliche Wissenschaft*

PREFACE

My first attraction to the topic dealt with in this monograph was the seemingly great difference between current Jewish history and the biblical evidence concerning the relationships between the dispersed and homeland Judean communities, following the deportations from Judah in the early sixth century B.C.E.

Boronovitch, Byten, and finally Warsaw, were the places left behind by most of my family members between the two world wars. The first family member to immigrate to the land of Israel was my great-uncle, Ze'ev Kovensky, who by 1920 had arrived at Jaffa port as a *halutz* (pioneer), to help build Tel Aviv. At approximately the same time, Sula, his older sister, along with her husband Abraham Swetitsky (later shortened to Sweet) and their firstborn child, Betty, left for the United States and arrived in Kansas City. In the mid-1930s, the youngest of the Kovensky siblings, my grandmother Mina, with her husband David Rabinowitz and her one-and-a-half-year-old son, my father Joseph, accepted the certificates of immigration sent by her brother Ze'ev and headed to the land of Israel. The oldest Kovensky brother, Aaron, and his wife remained in Poland, along with their sister, Devorah, her husband Moshe Swetitsky (Sweet) and four of their five children (their older son, Zvi, immigrated alone to Israel); by the early 1940s they had all been massacred by the Nazis. This is the beginning of our family's modern-day Diaspora story: the story of two "family-tribes," one in the United States, the other in Israel.

This shorthand report is by no means exceptional. It is the very common story of, I would assume, many thousands of Jewish families in the twentieth century. Due not only to the two world wars in Europe, but also to other factors, such as the inspiration and activism of the Zionist movements that preceded them; ongoing antisemitism and persecution in the Soviet Union; periods of distress and persecution in the Arab countries of the Middle East; and so on, Jewish families the world over have been separated. Some members have immigrated to the land of Israel; others have found refuge in other Diaspora communities.

One clear common denominator has united us all—there was never a question that אנשים אחים אנחנו ("we are kinsmen," Gen 13:8)—whether in Israel or in the Diaspora, we were brothers or cousins, bound in genuine kinship relationships, connected by our religion, family histories, and national memories.

In the ancient Near East, exile was a military punishment forced upon individuals or groups of people as an aspect of the subjugation of territories won in war. From the point of view of the deported population, exile marks the last step of the defeat, the beginning of a long, dislocating journey, and then resettlement in a new and unknown land.

Although exile is a recognized phenomenon in the history of the ancient Near East already by the third millennium and increasingly during the second,[1] it had become an international imperial policy by the Neo-Assyrian period, and flourished under Tiglath-Pileser III (745–727 B.C.E.) and his successors. The Neo-Assyrian kings used exile as their most severe strategy to control rebellious territories that had previously been subjected, through vassal treaties, to the kings of Assyria. An Assyrian exile meant a massive two-way transfer of at least two subject populations and the establishment of an organized Assyrian bureaucracy in the peripheral provinces, supported by military forces.[2] The Neo-Babylonian Empire is considered to have carried on the Neo-Assyrian policy of exile, but the Babylonians differed from their predecessors in their interests and in their administrative organization. Thus, they did not bother to implement the two-way exile, and settled for bringing exiles to Babylon and its vicinity.[3]

In contrast to Assyrian propagandist formulae describing victory and exile as all-encompassing consequences of war, there are reasons to believe that exiles were always partial, dividing the subjugated peoples

1. Ignace J. Gelb, "Prisoners of War in Early Mesopotamia," *JNES* 32 (1973): 70–98; Jack M. Sasson, *The Military Establishments at Mari* (Studia Pohl 3; Rome: Pontifical Biblical Institute, 1969), 48–49; Shmuel Ahituv, "New Documents Pertaining to Deportation as a Political System in Ancient Egypt," *Beer-Sheva* 1 (1973): 87–89 (in Hebrew).

2. Bustenay Oded, *Mass Deportations and Deportees in the Neo-Assyrian Empire* (Wiesbaden: Reichert, 1979), 18–32, 41–74; Frederick M. Fales and J. N. Postgate, *Imperial Administrative Records, Part II: Provincial and Military Administration* (SAA 11; Helsinki: Helsinki University Press, 1995), xxviii–xxx, 91–119.

3. David S. Vanderhooft, *The Neo-Babylonian Empire and Babylon in the Latter Prophets* (HSM 59; Atlanta: Scholars Press, 1999), 81–114.

into exiles and those who remained in the homeland.[4] Deportations from Israel and Judah, reported in the biblical literature, accord with this international policy and with the overall experience of peoples in the ancient Near East over the course of the eighth to the sixth centuries B.C.E. (see, e.g., 2 Kgs 15–17, 24–25).[5] Indeed, the biblical evidence tells of several compulsory waves of Neo-Babylonian deportations (and one flight initiated by Judeans themselves: 2 Kgs 25:26; Jer 41:16–18; 43:1–7), which divided the Judean population and created one of the first, and certainly the major, internal separations between homeland and Diaspora.

4. In contrast to the impression conveyed by the "stereotyped scribal exaggeration" of the biblical accounts (Oded, *Mass Deportations*, 22), the partial character of the Neo-Assyrian deportations can be gathered from both literary and archaeological evidence (see, for instance, Arthur C. Piepkorn, *Historical Prism Inscriptions of Ashurbanipal* (AS 5; Chicago: University of Chicago Press, 1933), p. 70, ll. 37–38; and Oded, *Mass Deportations*, 21–25. In a recent study, Bustenay Oded considered both the imperial policies and the massive deportations from Judah, see *The Early History of the Babylonian Exile (8th–6th Centuries BCE)* (Haifa: Pardes, 2010 [in Hebrew]), 24–83, 99–124.

5. The Neo-Babylonian deportations were not the first to have separated the people of Israel into homeland and Diaspora communities. The first exiles had already taken place in the Neo-Assyrian period, first in waves of deportations from the Northern kingdom (733 and 722 B.C.E.), and then through the Assyrian deportation of 701 B.C.E. from Judah itself. See Israel Eph'al, "Assyrian Dominion in Palestine," in *The Age of the Monarchies*. Vol. 1, *Political History* (ed. A. Malamat and I. Eph'al; The World History of the Jewish People 4/1; Jerusalem: Massada, 1979), 276–89; Mordechai Cogan, "Judah Under Assyrian Hegemony: A Re-examination of Imperialism and Religion," *JBL* 112 (1993): 403–14; Peter Machinist, "Palestine, Administration of (Assyro-Babylonian)," *ABD* 5:69–81; Nadav Na'aman and Ran Zadok, "Sargon II's Deportations to Israel and Philistia (716–708 B.C.)," *JCS* 40 (1988): 36–46. For studies of Israelite and Judean existence in exile, see Israel Eph'al, "'The Samarian(s)' in the Assyrian Sources," *Ah, Assyria... Studies in Assyrian History and Ancient Near Eastern Historiography Presented to Hayim Tadmor* (ed. M. Cogan and I. Eph'al; ScrHier 33; Jerusalem: The Hebrew University/Magnes, 1992), 36–45; idem, "The Western Minorities in Babylonia in the 6th–5th Centuries: Maintenance and Cohesion," *Orientalia* 47 (1978): 74–90; Bustenay Oded, "Observations on the Israelite/Judaean Exiles in Mesopotamia During the Eighth-Sixth Centuries BCE," in *Immigration and Emigration within the Ancient Near East: Festschrift E. Lipiński* (ed. K. Van Lerberghe and A. Schoors; OLA 65; Leuven: Peeters, 1995), 205–12; and idem, *The Early History of the Babylonian Exile*, 85–97; Ran Zadok, *The Jews in Babylonia during the Chaldean and Achaemenian Periods according to the Babylonian Sources* (Studies in the History of the Jewish People and the Land of Israel Monograph Series 3; Haifa: University of Haifa Press, 1979; idem, *The Earliest Diaspora: Israelites and Judeans in Pre-Hellenistic Mesopotamia* (Tel Aviv: Tel Aviv University Press, 2002).

The year 597 B.C.E. is a landmark in the history of Judah. In the month of Adar, the Babylonians implemented the first exile from Jerusalem, the Jehoiachin exile (*Babylonian Chronicles* 5:11–13; 2 Kgs 24:8–17).[6] According to the biblical sources, this event divided the Judean people into two communities, the Exiles with King Jehoiachin in Babylon on the one hand, and "Those Who Remained" in the land under King Zedekiah, on the other (העם הנשארים בארץ, Jer 40:6). This division is our starting point, from which this separation has continued and was even intensified at the time of the partial return to Judah/Yehud by the early Persian period (שיבת ציון, Ps 137:1).[7]

The current study describes the ideological argumentations developed and constantly transformed in selected biblical sources, and it aims at highlighting two major points. First, the homeland–Diaspora relationships that obtained in the sixth and then fifth centuries B.C.E. These relationships seem to be extraordinary in comparison to both ancient and modern phenomena.[8] The topic known in contemporary Jewish circles as

6. Albert K. Grayson, *Assyrian and Babylonian Chronicles* (Winona Lake: Eisenbrauns, 1975; 2nd ed. 2000), 102. Bustenay Oded, "Judah and the Exile," in *Israelite and Judean History* (ed. J. H. Hayes and J. M. Miller; OTL; Philadelphia: Westminster, 1977), 469–88.

7. Theoretically, we should see evidence of conflict between homeland and exiled populations, initially within Israel itself (733 B.C.E.); after 722–720 B.C.E., between Israel and Judah, and so on. Remarkably, however, even the Judean exile of 701 B.C.E., reported only in Assyrian inscriptions, does not correlate with explicit biblical evidence for such a conflict. cf. Stephen C. Stohlmann, "The Judean Exile After 701 B.C.E.," in *Scripture in Context*. Vol. 2, *More Essays on the Comparative Method* (ed. W. W. Hallo, J. C. Moyer, and L. G. Perdue; Winona Lake: Eisenbrauns, 1983), 147–76. Rather, biblical sources focus on the Babylonian exiles, and hence scholars have concentrated on the different ideological reactions in that later era. See, for example, Peter R. Ackroyd, *Exile and Restoration: A Study of Hebrew Thought of the Sixth Century B.C.* (OTL; Philadelphia: Westminster, 1975); Ralph W. Klein, *Israel in Exile: A Theological Interpretation* (OBT 6; Philadelphia: Fortress, 1979).

8. Tensions between the Jewish Diaspora and Israel have been frequently noticed throughout the twentieth century. Yet, even at its toughest points, it has been clear that the Jewish people comprises both communities. I mention but a few of the retrospectives on the modern era: Ben Halpern and Israel Kolatt, *Changing Relations Between Israel and the Diaspora* (Study Circle on Diaspora Jewry in the Home of the President of Israel 3; Jerusalem: Hebrew University, The Institute of Contemporary Jewry, 1969 [in Hebrew]), 6–7); Eliezer Don-Yehiya (ed.), *Israel and Diaspora Jewry: Ideological and Political Perspectives* (Comparative Jewish Politics 3; Ramat Gan: Bar Ilan University Press, 1991 [in Hebrew]); Yossi Beilin, *His Brother's Keeper: Israel and Diaspora Jewry in the Twenty-first Century* (New York: Schocken, 2000); among many others.

"Israel–Diaspora relationships" has engendered lively and complicated discussions over the last hundred years. But, in fact, scholars have often traced back contemporary homeland–Diaspora conflicts to the division drawn between "Jerusalem" (i.e. the entire land of Israel) and "Babel" in rabbinic literature,[9] or even as far back as the conflicts of the Persian period.[10] The present study calls us to look even further back, to the early sixth century B.C.E., in order to discover the earliest stages of the Israel–Diaspora relationship, and follow its early transformational stages that could definitely be designated as formative for the later Israel–Diaspora conflict or conflicts.

Second, it is argued that biblical texts of the Neo-Babylonian and the early Persian periods show a fierce adversarial relationships between the Judean groups. We find no expressions of sympathy to the deported community for its dislocation, no empathic expressions toward the People Who Remained under Babylonian subjugation in Judah. The opposite is apparent: hostile, denigrating, and denunciating language characterizes the relationships between resident and exiled Judeans throughout the sixth and the fifth centuries.

When it comes to homeland–Diaspora relationships there seems to be no resemblance between the Hebrew Bible portrayals and modern situations. Babylonian economic documents of the Neo-Babylonian and Persian periods shed light on the economic and the sociological status of the deportees in their new settlements in Babylon.[11] Yet these sources cannot solve the riddle presented here: Why and how did this Babylonian Diaspora community develop such hostile relations with its homeland community? And vice-versa: Why and how did the homeland community left in Judah following the Babylonian deportations re-establish its

---

9. For references in rabbinic literature to Israel and Diaspora relationships, see, among others Isaiah M. Gafni, *Land, Center and Diaspora: Jewish Constructs in Late Antiquity* (JSPSup 21; Sheffield: Sheffield Academic, 1997); Erich S. Gruen, "Diaspora and Homeland," in *Diasporas and Exiles: Varieties of Jewish Identity* (ed. H. Wettstein; Berkeley: University of California Press, 2002), 18–46.

10. On the internal conflict during the Persian period, see Chapter 2 below, and the literature there.

11. For a recent discussions of Judean Exiles in Babylon, their status, and the signs of their social, economic, and political integration into Neo-Babylonian society, see F. Rachel Magdalene and Cornelia Wunsch, "Slavery Between Judah and Babylon: The Exilic Experience," in *Slaves and Households in the Near East* (ed. L. Culbertson; Oriental Institute Seminars 7; Chicago: The Oriental Institute of the University of Chicago, 2011), 113–34; Oded, *The Early History of the Babylonian Exile*, 125–96.

communal life by delegitimizing those Exiles that had been forced to leave their homeland? What needs and ends were served by such intra-community division and hostility?

This monograph brings to fruition several years of research, during which I have published five papers on various facets of this topic. I am grateful to the first publishers of these papers who graciously allowed me to rework these materials for this platform.[12] The present book adds discussions I had so far not gone into, portraying the picture in its full impact.

Over these years of research I have directly and indirectly benefited from the scholarly negotiation with teachers, colleagues, and students. I am genuinely indebted to what I have learnt (and continuously do), especially from Professor Sara Japhet and Professor Shalom M. Paul of the Hebrew University of Jerusalem; to my close colleagues of The Theological Perspectives on the Book of Ezekiel Section at the Society of Biblical Literature Annual Meeting; and to my colleagues and students at Tel Aviv University.

Thanks are due to the Hebrew Union College in Jerusalem for the award of the Dorot fellowships that supported this research in its earlier stages (2002–2004), and to the Israel Science Foundation (ISF) for its generous support in funding the English editing of this book.

This work has been carried on in three libraries: the Hebrew Union College Abramov Library in Jerusalem, the Israel National Library at Givat Ram, Jerusalem, and the Katz Center for Advanced Judaic Studies,

---

12. The papers and their original places of publication are: (1) "Ezekiel as the Voice of the Exiles and Constructor of Exilic Ideology," *HUCA* 76 (2005): 1–45; (2) "Exiles and Those Who Remained: Strategies of Exclusivity in the Early Sixth Century BCE," in *Shai le-Sara Japhet: Studies in the Bible, Its Exegesis, and Its Language Presented to Sara Japhet* (ed. M. Bar Asher et al.; Jerusalem: Bialik Institute, 2007), 119–38 (in Hebrew); (3) "Deuteronomic Concepts of Exile Interpreted in Jeremiah and Ezekiel," in *Birkat Shalom: Studies in the Bible, Ancient Near Eastern Literature, and Post-biblical Judaism Presented to Shalom M. Paul on the Occasion of His Seventieth Birthday* (ed. C. Cohen et al.; Winona Lake: Eisenbrauns, 2008), 101–23; (4) "Group-Identities in Jeremiah: Is It the Persian Period Conflict?," in *A Palimpsest: Rhetoric, Stylistics, and Language in Biblical Texts from the Persian and Hellenistic Periods* (ed. E. Ben Zvi, D. Edelman and F. Polak; PHSC 5; Piscataway, N.J.: Gorgias, 2009), 11–46; (5) "From Ezekiel to Ezra–Nehemiah: Shifts of Group-Identities within Babylonian Exilic Ideology," in *Judah and the Judeans in the Achaemenid Period: Negotiating Identity in an International Context* (ed. O. Lipschits, G. Knoppers, and M. Oeming; Winona Lake: Eisenbrauns, 2011), 127–51.

in Philadelphia, Pennsylvania. I whole-heartedly thank the librarians in each of these institutions for their actual assistance, and for the special atmosphere they have created to facilitate the work.

This book would not have seen the light of day without the initial invitation and the guidance of the LHBOTS academic editor, Dr. Andrew Mein. The ongoing assistance of Dr. Ruth Clements in editing my English, raising bothering questions and contributing insightful comments, has been of great value to me. At the final stage of production, Duncan Burns inexhaustibly guaranteed its precision.

Finally, but not the least important, I was able to carry on this research and writing work thanks to the ongoing support of my family—my friend and partner, Amnon, and our children: Eshel and his spouse Moran, Carmel and her husband Avidan, and Elad. This book is dedicated, however, to the larger family, to the many descendants of Sula and Mina, and to those of Devorah through her son Zvi. Twentieth-century circumstances separated the sisters, but did not diminish their love for each other nor did they untie the connections between their families, in Israel and in the Diaspora.

Chapter 1

INTRODUCTION

During four periods within the sixth and fifth centuries B.C.E., biblical sources reflect internal polemics between the Judean Exiles in Babylon and Those Who Remained in Judah. The first two junctures were times of exile within the Neo-Babylonian period, when Judah suffered several waves of deportation carried out by the Babylonian emperor Nebuchadrezzar II (605–562 B.C.E.). Biblical sources mention the Jehoiachin Exile (597 B.C.E.) as the event that formed a Judean community in Babylon, distinguished from and antagonistic to Those Who Remained behind in Judah and Jerusalem until its eventual destruction (586 B.C.E.). Hence, 597–586 B.C.E. is the earlier, formative period of this polemic. 586 and forward were years of additional waves of deportation from Judah to Babylon, which added new dimensions to this initial opposition; though the precise end date of this period is unknown, it is clearly prior to 539 B.C.E.[1] These compulsory exiles, which divided the Judean population, created one of the first, and certainly one of the major, separations between homeland and Diaspora communities.[2]

1. Jer 52:28–30 mentions three waves of deportation, in 597, 586, and 582 B.C.E., enumerated according to the regnal years of Nebuchadrezzar. For a thorough discussion of the sources and their evidence with regard to the dating of the waves of deportations and the numbers of deportees, see Rainer Albertz, *Israel in Exile: The History and Literature of the Sixth Century B.C.E.* (trans. David Green; SBL Studies in Biblical Literature 3; Atlanta: Society of Biblical Literature, 2003 [German original, 2001]), 70–90.

2. The Neo-Babylonian deportations were not the first to have created a division between homeland and Diaspora communities; see the Preface, pp. xiv–xv. This phenomenon of partial deportations has brought scholars to deny the very existence of the Babylonian Exile per se; cf. Philip R. Davies, "Exile! What Exile? Whose Exile?," in *Leading Captivity Captive: "The Exile" as History and Ideology* (ed. L. L. Grabbe; JSOTSup 278; Sheffield: Sheffield Academic, 1998), 128–38; and the careful reconsideration of Daniel L. Smith-Christopher, *A Biblical Theology of Exile* (OBT; Minneapolis: Augsburg Fortress, 2002), 27–73.

The historical circumstances of the final eleven years of Jerusalem and Judah (597–586 B.C.E.) challenged major Judean institutions and long-established conceptions. Preexilic Priestly and Deuteronomic conceptions of exile do not recognize the notion of partial deportation, and assume a linear sequence of (1) iniquity; (2) destruction/death in the land; and finally, (3) dispersion of all survivors from out of the land of Israel, to suffer further calamity in captivity.[3] The ongoing existence of the Temple, the royal court, and daily life in Jerusalem following the events of 597 stood in puzzling contrast to these traditional understandings. For the Jehoiachin Exiles, their own (partial) exile preceded—and saved them from—the destruction of the city left behind. On the other hand, for Those Who Remained in Judah, the expulsion of the Exiles meant their exclusion from the People of God whose national identity was tied to life in the land (as in Deut 28:36; 1 Sam 26:19, etc.).

Moreover, perceived as punishment for religious and moral sins, the early and partial exile from Judah raised questions for both communities with regard to their own respective responsibilities for their fortune and future existence.

Finally, understood as expulsion from God's land in retribution for violating his covenant, this partial exile presented fundamental questions of religious and national identity: Should exile actually signify the exclusion of the deportees from the people of God, and should Those Who Remained be considered *the* sole Remnant, or vice versa? Such questions had major implications for the two communities' hopes for restoration.

The two other points that gave rise to polemic were, paradoxically, times of return. The first occurred in the early Persian period, between the Edict of Cyrus and the dedication of the Second Temple—the days of Sheshbazzar, Zerubbabel son of Shealtiel, and Jeshua son of Yehozadaq (538–516 B.C.E.); the second spanned the days of Ezra and Nehemiah in Jerusalem (ca. 458–432 B.C.E.).[4] These two short eras, of approximately

---

3. See Deut 4:25–28; 8:19–20; Lev 18:24–30; 20:22–24; and the lists of curses in Lev 26:14–45; Deut 28:15–68. Return to the land from a place of exile (as in Lev 26:39–45; Deut 4:29–31 and 30:1–10) is a second, exilic layer added to the preexilic concept of exile in both the Deuteronomic and the Priestly traditions. On these earlier concepts of land and exile as reinterpreted in Jeremiah and Ezekiel, see Rom-Shiloni, "Deuteronomic Concepts of Exile Interpreted in Jeremiah and Ezekiel," 101–23 and see the discussion below, pp. 144–69, 204–19.

4. On the historical background, see J. Blenkinsopp, *Ezra–Nehemiah* (OTL; Philadelphia: Westminster, 1988), 60–70. Persian imperial policy has been discussed by Kenneth G. Hoglund, *Achaemenid Imperial Administration in Syria-Palestine and the Missions of Ezra and Nehemiah* (SBLDS 125; Atlanta: Scholars Press,

twenty years each, were times of restoration. Nevertheless, these were the occasions when the two divided Judean communities faced each other on Judean soil. The repatriated Babylonian Exiles, who are said to return each to his hometown (איש לעירו, Ezra 2:1; Neh 7:6), and Those Who Remained in Judah throughout the sixth century and on, found themselves once again in close proximity.[5]

Framing this time span and geographic arena, the literary sources that are the focus of this study comprise the major prophetic books stemming from the sixth (down to the early fifth) century B.C.E.: Jeremiah, Ezekiel, Deutero(/Trito)-Isaiah, Haggai, and Zechariah (1–8), along with the historiographical composition of Ezra–Nehemiah dating from the fifth and fourth centuries B.C.E.[6]

Historical data, sociological observations, archaeological evidences, and the study of the literary compositions have caused scholars to focus on the later eras. The Edict of Cyrus and the return of the first wave of Repatriates to Jerusalem, in order to rebuild Yahweh's Temple and to reinstitute its cult, were taken to designate the beginning of a new period in the history of the Judean/Jewish people. But, at least according to Ezra–Nehemiah, by the beginning of this period, distinctive barriers had already developed between the exiled and the non-exiled Judean communities, over questions of group/national identity: Who was entitled to participate in this restoration? Who was included within the restored community, and who was excluded from it?[7]

Scholars continue to debate the question of the exact period when this conflict emerged in Yehud. Sara Japhet and Peter R. Bedford are among those who sharply distinguish Haggai and Zechariah from Ezra–Nehemiah, and thus argue that the conflict in its most extremely exclusive form started only with the communities represented by the latter

1992); Oded Lipschits, "Achaemenid Imperial Policy, Settlement Processes in Palestine, and the Status of Jerusalem in the Middle of the Fifth Century B.C.E.," in *Judah and the Judeans in the Persian Period* (eds. O. Lipschits and M. Oeming; Winona Lake: Eisenbrauns, 2006), 19–52.

5. For the different groups in the land and in the Diaspora during the Persian period, see Sara Japhet, "People and Land in the Restoration Period," in *Das Land Israel im biblischer Zeit: Jerusalem-Symposium 1981 der Hebräischen Universität und der Georg-August-Universität* (ed. G. Strecker; GTA 25; Göttingen: Vandenhoeck & Ruprecht, 1983), 103–25.

6. Discussion of Zech 9–14 and of Malachi will await further study.

7. The exclusion of Those Who Remained in the Land from the new political entity is mentioned in connection with the reinstitution of the sanctuary (Ezra 3), the reconstruction of the Temple (Ezra 4–6), and the reconstruction of the walls of Jerusalem (Neh 2:19–20). See the discussion in Chapter 2.

compositions; that is, by the fifth and perhaps even the fourth centuries.[8] According to Bedford, the crucial conflict was that with the Samarians, in the fourth century B.C.E.; and this was anachronistically retrojected (in Ezra 3:1–4:5) into the early Persian period, to the time of Zerubbabel and Joshua; to the time of Zechariah the repatriate and Haggai the not-exiled.[9] However, John Kessler has argued that "burning questions" of geography and identity (including questions of homeland and Diaspora) had already been formulated in connection with "the officially authorized return"; that is, upon the earlier return, by the last decades of the sixth century (as illustrated in Ezra 4:1–5, in reference to the earlier reinstitution of the Jerusalem Temple).[10]

I would like, however, to problematize the notion that this intra-community conflict began only with the return to Yehud, whether early or late. Is this internal conflict really only a late sixth-, or even fifth- (or fourth-) century phenomenon? and did it emerge initially in Persian Yehud? Although scholars do in fact mention passages in Ezekiel and Jeremiah to show that deliberations over identity issues among Judean communities started at an earlier juncture, there is still a need for a thorough overview of these conflicts and their intra-connections, from the earliest stages to the latest attested forms in Ezra–Nehemiah.[11]

---

8. Japhet, "People and Land"; Peter R. Bedford, *Temple Restoration in Early Achaemenid Judah* (JSJSup 65; Leiden: Brill, 2001), 42–61; idem, "Diaspora: Homeland Relations in Ezra–Nehemiah," *VT* 52 (2002): 147–66, especially 150–51 n. 8. The present study challenges both this late time frame and the suggested perspectives; see below, pp. 62–74, 82–98, 135–36. Another approach was taken by H. G. M. Williamson ("The Concept of Israel in Transition," in *The World of Ancient Israel: Sociological, Anthropological, and Political Perspectives: Essays by Members of the Society for Old Testament Study* [ed. R. E. Clements; Cambridge: Cambridge University Press, 1989], 141–61), who found the first seeds of exilic exclusivity in Deutero-Isaiah (Isa 40–55; see especially pp. 146–47).

9. Bedford, *Temple Restoration*, 278–79.

10. John Kessler, "The Diaspora in Zechariah 1–8 and Ezra–Nehemiah: The Role of History, Social Location, and Tradition in the Formulation of Identity," in *Community Identity in Judean Historiography: Biblical and Comparative Perspectives* (ed. G. N. Knoppers and K. A. Ristau; Winona Lake: Eisenbrauns, 2009), 119–45. The scholarly notion that the Return would be the spur for conflict was already raised by Daniel L. Smith[-Christopher], *The Religion of the Landless: The Social Context of the Babylonian Exile* (Bloomington: Meyer Stone, 1989), 179.

11. Although she has put greater emphasis on Ezra–Nehemiah, Japhet ("People and Land") noted the earlier phases of internal debate over identity issues. In reference to Ezekiel (specifically Ezek 11:14–21), she aptly argued that "The issue, then, is not merely one of possession or dispossession of the land, although this is an important facet of it, but moreover, who are the people of God: the exiles or those

The present monograph explores these Judean (Yahwistic) internal identity conflicts over a span of more than 150 years, from the early years of the sixth century to the late decades of the fifth century B.C.E., arguing that this wide time span enables us more easily to follow the evolution of this internal debate over Judean identity and to trace its transformations. My goals are to present the biblical sources that testify to these long eras of continual redefinitions of identity, to examine the divisive strategies and argumentations that informed this ongoing process, and to follow through time the ideological transformations of these arguments. In this way, I hope to articulate the dynamics and transformations of the power relationships between the two (new) Judean communities, in Judah/Yehud and in Babylon.

The current discussion is focused on quite narrow themes, looked at through a fairly narrow lens—it is a literary-ideological study of group identity issues found in biblical texts, ones that are dominated by the concerns of Babylonian Exiles and Repatriates.[12] This specific, somewhat narrow, focus is governed by my interest in group identity argumentation and political strategies. Hence, this study does not pretend to be exhaustive in any way, as it leaves out of consideration extra-biblical

who remained in the land?" (108); this issue will be thoroughly discussed in Chapter 6 below. Compare to Bedford (*Temple Restoration*, 61–63), who claimed that attempts to substantiate the notion of an internal division by the time of the Neo-Babylonian period have been unsuccessful. The current study aims to prove the opposite.

12. Many other topics, such as the historical and archaeological evidence for this period, are beyond the scope of this monograph. Discussion of such contextual evidence may be found in the four volumes, wide-ranging in content and scope, emerging from an ongoing series of international conferences on this period: Oded Lipschits and Joseph Blenkinsopp, eds., *Judah and the Judeans in the Neo-Babylonian Period* (Winona Lake: Eisenbrauns, 2003); Lipschits and Oeming, eds., *Judah and the Judeans in the Persian Period*; Oded Lipschits, Gary N. Knoppers, and Rainer Albertz, eds., *Judah and the Judeans in the Fourth Century B.C.E.* (Winona Lake: Eisenbrauns, 2007); Oded Lipschits, G. N. Knoppers, and M. Oeming, eds., *Judah and the Judeans in the Achaemenid Period: Negotiating Identity in an International Context* (Winona lake: Eisenbrauns, 2011). Among other topics that will not be discussed here, I also want to highlight the historical-sociological issue of the transition from Yahwism to Judaism; see on this Joseph Blenkinsopp, *Judaism, The First Phase: The Place of Ezra–Nehemiah in the Origins of Judaism* (Grand Rapids: Eerdmans, 2009). Likewise important are recent efforts towards reconstructing a trans-Yahwistic sociological picture; as has been done, for example, by John Kessler, "Persia's Loyal Yahwists: Power Identity and Ethnicity in Achaemenid Yehud," in Lipschits and Oeming, eds., *Judah and the Judeans in the Persian Period*, 92–121.

sources that shed light on Yahwistic communities during the Persian period. This focus is, however, justified by the biblical evidence itself.[13] It is of significant importance that while there are reasons (and actual data) to assume the existence of at least six Yahwistic communities during the Persian period, the biblically represented negotiations over identity issues are limited to only two of these communities: the Babylonian Judean community and Those Who Remained in Judah/Yehud.[14] Hence, this somewhat schematic division serves for both the Neo-Babylonian and the Persian periods. These two communities are the focus of the present study. By the early phase, the Babylonian Judean community comprises the Jehoiachin Exiles, and later on, the 586 Exiles in addition. Those Who Remained are the people left in Jerusalem and Judah under Zedekiah (Jer 27–29; 37–39), who following the Destruction remained in Mizpah under Gedaliah (Jer 40–41), and after his murder all flew to Egypt (41:16–18; 43:1–7), yet assumedly, even this voluntary flight left a remnant in the land. It is, therefore, just as important to notice that by the Persian period, two different circles of conflict had developed between Babylon and Judah/Yehud. The one pertained to relationships among the Babylonian Exiles and Babylonian Repatriates to Judah, the second to relationships between Repatriates and Those Who Remained in Judah/Yehud.[15]

The intra-relationships among Judean Yahwistic groups, mostly dated to the Persian period, has captured vast interest in the last few decades. Special attention has indeed been given to the relationship between the Babylonian Diaspora community and the Repatriate community that

13. This somewhat simplistic dichotomy suggested by the biblical sources demands this schematic division. There is no question that the Judean society had kept its class ranks in both centers, but it is of interest that this social diversity hardly shows in the texts. Thus, I would refute Gary Knoppers's criticism in his paper "Exile, Return, and Diaspora: Expatriates and Repatriates in Late Biblical Literature," in *Texts, Contexts and Readings in Postexilic Literature: Explorations into Historiography and Identity Negotiation in Hebrew Bible and Related Texts* (ed. L. Jonker; FAT 2/53; Tübingen: Mohr Siebeck, 2011), 29–61, especially pp. 41–42 (and n. 44).

14. Kessler ("Persia's Loyal Yahwists," 92–98) mentions six different Yahwistic communities of this time: "(1) Golah returnees; (2) Golah remainees in Babylonia; (3) Yehudite remainees; (4) Egyptian Yahwists; (5) Samarian Yahwists; (6) other Yahwists in the Levant."

15. R. J. Coggins, *Haggai, Zechariah, Malachi* (OTG; Sheffield: JSOT, 1987), 57, correctly states that "we should probably be wise enough to admit that we have insufficient evidence to enable us to spell out the detailed structure of the community"; and see Kessler, "Persia's Loyal Yahwists," 93–96.

returned from Babylon to Persian Yehud.[16] However, the ongoing relationship between the two groups is often seen too simplistically: once
they have come back to Yehud, the Repatriates are often understood to
have become enfolded into the homeland community(/ies) of Those Who
Remained (though they are said to be leading the entire community,
based on Hag 1:1, 12–14, etc.); and the conflict between the two Babylonian groups is understood to have been transformed into a conflict
between homeland (Yehud) and Diaspora.[17]

My study of the unfolding of these internal conflicts over time challenges this assumption and points to the need to keep the two circles of
conflict apart. The overarching conflict between the two geographical
realms of Babylon and Yehud does not exclude the possibility of further
internal divisions within each of the two Judean communities: (1) among
the Exiles, who constantly distinguish between those in the Diaspora and
those who have been repatriated; (2) and among those in Yehud, between
those long-settled and those recently resettled in Yehud.[18]

Hence, these two areas, Babylon and Judah/Yehud, form the geographical boundaries of the present study, although my main focus is on
the second circle of group identity conflicts: those between the Babylonian Repatriates and Those Who Remained in Judah/Yehud. The attempt
to address these issues brings to the fore both literary and socio-historical
methodological considerations.

16. Fairly recent studies include Peter R. Bedford, in both his book, *Temple
Restoration*, and his paper, "Diaspora: Homeland Relations"; Gary N. Knoppers,
"Ethnicity, Genealogy, Geography, and Change: The Judean Communities of Babylon and Jerusalem in the Story of Ezra," in Knoppers and Ristau, eds., *Community
Identity in Judean Historiography*, 147–71; see especially 161–63, where Knoppers
identified the two Judean groups as (1) those centered in Mesopotamia, and (2) those
settled in Jerusalem. While geographically separated, he noted, they operate according to similar social-religious structures, kinship structures, ethnic markers (such as
language, etc.), and community names. Knoppers focused only on the Babylonian
Repatriates (in their several waves of return), looking at what he termed the
"transtemporal and international nature of the Israelite people" (p. 168). The current
study argues that Knoppers's observation demonstrates only the exclusive perspective of this community of Babylonian returnees.

17. This scholarly perception is mostly apparent in reference to studies on the
Repatriate spokespersons Haggai, Zachariah, as well as Deutero-Isaiah; see the
discussion below, in Chapters 3, 4, and 5.

18. Compare to Kessler ("The Diaspora in Zechariah 1–8 and Ezra–Nehemiah"),
who described Zech 1–8 as addressing "two primary geographical realms: people
who had already returned to the homeland and those still in the Diaspora" (p. 123).
These two geographical realms and communities should not be thus conflated.

Therefore, of the long list of fascinating questions scholars have raised in reference to the internal polemics of the sixth and the fifth centuries B.C.E., I am particularly interested in four:

1. On the historical-sociological level: Why did these harsh polemics initially evolve between the two divisions of the people, who had been split by *external* forced waves of deportation, and who had previously comprised one nation, one kingdom, worshipping Yahweh, the God of Israel in Jerusalem?
2. On the social-psychological level: How did each group redefine its identity to create the "we" and the "them" in these conflicts? On what did each of them base its arguments as to who was included and who excluded?
3. On the ideological level: What divided the two communities conceptually? What were the contents of these polemics? And what were the ideological transformations undergone by these polemics over time?
4. On both the sociological and the ideological levels: How are we to explain the triumph of the Repatriates over Those Who Remained? It seems that the roles of center and periphery had changed quite early, as the Babylonian Exiles, then Repatriates, gained superiority. But the claims of social superiority set already by the Jehoiachin Exiles,[19] and developed in Babylon and then back in Yehud, stand in clear contradiction to traditional conceptions of land and of exile (such as Deut 4:25–28; 28:36, 64). How did this conceptual/legal inferior status of the Exiles become switched into claims of superiority by both the Jehoiachin Exiles and the Repatriates?

1. *Literature, Ideology, and Identity:* *"Babylonian Exilic Ideologies"*

From the literary perspective, the ideological victory of the Babylonian Repatriates over Those Who Remained is apparent in biblical literature throughout both the Neo-Babylonian and the early Persian periods. Although arguments of Those Who Remained following the deportations are quoted occasionally in Ezekiel and extensively in Jeremiah, the Exiles' voices control prophetic literature as early as Ezekiel (and in the

---

19. On the Jehoiachin perspective of 2 Kgs 24–25, see Christopher R. Seitz, *Theology in Conflict: Reactions to the Exile in the Book of Jeremiah* (BZAW 176; Berlin: de Gruyter, 1989), 215–22.

Babylonian redactional layers of Jeremiah).[20] In addition, it is variations on this exilic perspective that are voiced by the prophetic and other literature produced from the beginning of the Restoration period. Thus, while it is likely that literary creativity continued in Neo-Babylonian Judah after 586 B.C.E., it is clear that the voices of Those Who Remained were silenced and gradually vanished, still within this period. This literary silencing is in itself evidence for the social-political situation, and provides an initial clue that this intensive polemic started well before the Restoration period.[21]

Consideration of this ca. 150-year time frame compels an introductory discussion of chronological terminology. Three chronological terms have been applied to biblical compositions of the sixth and fifth centuries B.C.E.: preexilic, exilic, and postexilic. The defining dates were the fall of Jerusalem in 586 B.C.E., the fall of Babylon and the Cyrus Edict of 539/8 B.C.E., down to the arrival of Ezra and Nehemiah by 458, 432 B.C.E. These three time definitions raise many unanswered questions of their adequacy;[22] but even more importantly, they share the clear scholarly tendency to put greater value on the Babylonian exile as the time of great crisis that led to even greater literary creativity, and thus has assumedly gained the greatest importance in Judaic/Jewish history and religion. In proposing to define 586–517 B.C.E. as "the templeless age," Jill Middlemas has aptly pointed out the faults of these "exilic" designations; yet even her attractive terminology seems inadequate for the present discussion.[23] Thus, in the course of this study I will designate this period simply as the sixth–fifth centuries B.C.E., and reserve "exilic" for other uses.

While "exilic" (literature, ideology, theology, etc) initially provides a chronological reference, it also serves as a *locative terminology*. From this locative angle, "exilic literature" specifies exile as the place of writing, compiling, and editing literary compositions. This designation thus identifies the large corpus of biblical literature authored or edited in Babylon during the sixth and the fifth centuries (and probably thereafter).[24]

---

20.   See the discussion in Chapters 6 and 7.

21.   See further below, n. 24.

22.   Questions that challenge the appropriateness of these categories may be found in Coggins, *Haggai, Zechariah, Malachi*, 9–11.

23.   Jill Middlemas, *The Templeless Age: An Introduction to the History, Literature, and Theology of the "Exile"* (Louisville: Westminster John Knox, 2007), 1–8.

24.   See David Winton Thomas, "The Sixth Century BC: A Creative Epoch in the History of Israel," *JSS* 6 (1961): 33–46. While there is a general agreement that the compositions of the Deuteronomistic School, like the editorial strata of Jeremiah and

But "exilic literature" is also used to designate a category of *author-ship*, that is, literature written by Exiles, such as the prophetic books of Ezekiel and Deutero-Isaiah.[25] To develop this definition even further, the term should also include literature written by Repatriates (former Babylonian Exiles) in Achaemenid Yehud.[26] Within this category of Repatriate authorship fall the late sixth-century prophetic books of Haggai and Zech 1–8; the "Jerusalem Chapters" in Deutero-Isaiah; and the fifth-century historiography of Ezra–Nehemiah.

Recognizing that the perspectives of Babylonian Exiles (or former Exiles) govern almost all sixth- and fifth-century compositions preserved in the biblical canon, the present study advances the phrase "Babylonian exilic ideology(/ies)" as an overarching term to cover the entire spectrum of ideological perceptions reflected in the literature written (and/or compiled) *both* by Exiles in Babylon *and* by Repatriates in Achaemenid Yehud.[27] This recognition of the exilic perspectives behind the diverse biblical witnesses has obvious consequences for any discussions of group identity issues raised by the biblical materials.

With that said, this definition of Babylonian exilic literature and ideology stands independently of the reasonable assumption that literary creativity had also continued during the exilic period among Judeans

the other prophetic collections, gained their final shape and diverse additions under the circumstances of the Babylonian exile, most of these writings are recognized as having earlier strata that originated in Judah (and to a lesser extent even earlier, in Israel). For the gradual growth of Kings (as but one example), see André Lemaire, "Toward a Redactional History of the Book of Kings," in *Reconsidering Israel and Judah: Recent Studies on the Deuteronomistic* History (ed. G. N. Knoppers and J. G. McConville; SBT 8; Winona Lake: Eisenbrauns, 2000), 446–60. David M. Carr (*The Formation of the Hebrew Bible: A New Reconstruction* [New York: Oxford University Press, 2011], 225–51) considered the exilic period to be the time the Bible was formatted as "the Bible for exiles" (p. 226). Scholarly treatments of this literature tend to ignore the option of ongoing literary activity in Judah. See n. 28, below.

25. For other compositions written in Babylon during the Persian period, see Albertz, *Israel in Exile*, 15–44.

26. Peter Ackroyd (*Exile and Restoration: A Study of Hebrew Thought of the Sixth Century B.C.* [OTL; Philadelphia: Westminster, 1975], 12–13) emphasized the extensiveness of this exilic period, in which he included "the time of Judah's collapse," and "the dark years of exile," as well as the restoration period. Compare to Albertz (*Israel in Exile*), who discussed the exilic literature down to Deutero-Isaiah, but did not include the Repatriate literature of the late sixth century in his thorough discussion.

27. Kessler ("Persia's Loyal Yahwists," 91) recognized the importance of what he simply terms "Golah"—that is, the "community of exiled and returned Judeans"— on the biblical literature, and indeed he briefly discussed a few passages in Ezek 11:1–21 and 33:23–29 and Jer 24 before he focuses his attention on Ezra–Nehemiah.

who remained in the land.[28] My assumption is that in late sixth-century Yehud, authors from (at least) two Judean communities (Repatriates and "Non-exiled" groups) were active, writing from independent, and even antagonistic, perspectives.[29] Thus, my study focuses on what has become the biblical (literary and ideological) mainstream voices, which are clearly governed by the communities of the Babylonian Exiles and Repatriates.

One of the best examples of this continuum of exilic authorship is the collection of oracles attributed to Deutero-Isaiah, which presumably first took shape in Babylon (Isa 40–48), but continued to develop in Yehud (Isa 49–66),[30] where it was clearly redirected to the community of Exiles-now-turned-Repatriates.[31]

Chronologically, the development of Babylonian exilic ideologies spans the years between the first wave of Judean Exiles to Babylon in the Neo-Babylonian era (i.e. the Jehoiachin Exile, 597 B.C.E.),[32] and

28. See Enno Jannssen, *Juda in der Exilszeit: Ein Beitrag zur Frage der Entstehung des Judentums* (Göttingen: Vandenhoeck & Ruprecht, 1956); and H. G. M. Williamson's discussion of the penitential prayer in Neh 9:6–37 ("Structure and Historiography in Nehemiah 9," in *Proceedings of the Ninth World Congress of Jewish Studies, Panel Sessions: Bible Studies and the Ancient Near East* [ed. M. Goshen-Gottstein; Jerusalem: World Union of Jewish Studies, 1988], 117–31; and idem, "Laments at the Destroyed Temple," *Bible Review* 6, no. 4 [1990]: 12–17, 44). See recently, Jill Middlemas (*Templeless Age*); although, apart from Lamentations and Isa 63:7–64:11, I am more skeptical as to our ability to discern that Judah was indeed the place of authorship for those communal laments that Middlemas so designated (pp. 28–51).

29. Thus, I would counter Ackroyd's insistence on general continuity throughout the period, see Ackroyd, *Exile and Restoration*, 232–56.

30. On this conception of the cause of the literary division of Deutero-Isaiah (chs. 40–48, 49–66), see Menahem Haran, *Between Ri'shonot (Former Prophecies) and Hadashot (New Prophecies): A Literary-Historical Study on the Group of Prophecies Isaiah 40–48* (Jerusalem: The Hebrew University/Magnes, 1963 [in Hebrew]), 81, 101–2; and Shalom M. Paul, *Isaiah 40–66* (Grand Rapids: Eerdmans, 2012), 1–12. However, I would challenge the arguments they each make for the unity of authorship of these two sections. See the detailed discussion in Chapter 5, pp. 99–104, 121–36.

31. In contrast to Albertz (*Israel in Exile*, 381, 399–404, 428–33) who found Isa 40–66 to be the product of two editorial groups both active in Yehud: DtIE[1] (521 B.C.E.; 381, 399–404) and DtIE[2] (after 515 and early in the fifth century B.C.E., 429–30). I disagree with Albertz's assumption that upon return to Judah the DtIE[1] group had changed its audience and was now addressing those who had stayed in Judah, in an attempt to enfold them into the Repatriate enclave (*Israel in Exile*, 403–4, 432).

32. Dan 1:1 (as also 2 Chr 36:6) opens with mention of an exile that took place during the reign of Jehoiakim, father of Jehoiachin, 606/5 B.C.E.; while there is no

concludes with the later waves of return, those of Ezra and Nehemiah (458–432 B.C.E.) deep in the Persian period. Accordingly, the geographical spectrum encompasses both literature produced in exile (Ezekiel, Isa 40–48, the Babylonian and redactional strands in Jeremiah) and Repatriate literature written in Persian Yehud (Isa 49–66 and the final edition of the book of Isaiah; Haggai; Zech 1–8; Ezra–Nehemiah).

From the thematic standpoint, the study of "Babylonian-exilic ideologies" over this long period requires beginning with the latest stage of ideological development. Ezra–Nehemiah's perceptions of group identity have long been a major target of scholarly criticism. The Repatriates' exclusion of other Yahwist groups from the new polity has been contrasted with valuable data primarily from extrabiblical, but also from biblical, sources that illustrate the continuation of Judean existence in Judah/Yehud, albeit in reduced measure, throughout the Neo-Babylonian and Persian periods.[33] This contrast between historical and archaeological evidence, on the one hand, and the Repatriates' exclusive ideology, on the other, has dictated the scholarly categorization of Ezra–Nehemiah's perspectives as deliberately biased, reflecting an intensive postexilic conflict, thought to have flared up in Yehud during the Restoration period.[34]

I would like to address further this ideological, indeed biased, internal polemic, but using a somewhat different approach: namely, by examining Ezra–Nehemiah's arguments within a wider context and over a longer time span. Within early Persian period literature, Ezra–Nehemiah illustrates only one opposition between "the people," that is, the Repatriates, and all "other" communities residing in Yehud. Another and different opposition is reflected in the prophecies of Zechariah (1–8), and as I suggest below, remains in the background of Haggai. I argue as well that these two oppositions should be examined diachronically, by looking back to the ideologies of the earlier Babylonian exilic literature. While several ideological shifts may be discerned during this transitional period, Babylonian exilic ideologies themselves show clear lines of continuity with Ezekiel.

Joseph Blenkinsopp has recently argued for a connection between the Ezekiel school and Ezra–Nehemiah, and pointed out similarities between

way to corroborate this historical event (see Albertz, *Israel in Exile*, 20), Louis F. Hartman (*The Book of Daniel* [AB 23; Garden City, N.Y.: Doubleday, 1978], 29–42) suggested that "the seer of the Book of Daniel is among the exiles in Babylon" (34).

33. Oded Lipschits, *The Fall and Rise of Jerusalem: Judah Under Babylonian Rule* (Winona Lake: Eisenbrauns, 2005), 258–71.

34. Blenkinsopp, *Ezra–Nehemiah*, 60–70.

Ezek 40–48 and Persian-period exclusivism.[35] I would go much further: In studying the entire book of Ezekiel (focusing on chs. 1–39), I find this prophet of the Jehoiachin Exiles to have laid the foundations for exilic identity ideologies that operate throughout the Neo-Babylonian and Persian periods, in both Babylon and Yehud—or from an internal biblical perspective, throughout the time span encompassed by the books of Ezekiel to Ezra–Nehemiah. Hence, I argue here that Ezra–Nehemiah does not mark the beginning of the internal polemic in Yehud, but rather carries forward and transforms a longer-lived polemic initiated in the early sixth century B.C.E. This study elucidates these polemics in their major points of transition and transformation.

2. *Methodology: Sociological and Psychological Paradigms*

The strength of the biblical evidence concerning these periods and the topics under investigation does not seem to be historical, but rather ideological. Hence, while research of the Neo-Babylonian and the Persian periods (the exilic and postexilic eras) has turned to various disciplines in addition to the philological study of the texts,[36] the present study observes the Judean identity conflicts through the lens of social psychology, using studies of ethnicity and group identity. Thus, this monograph joins fairly recent and intriguing studies that have looked at personal and/or national reactions to the disastrous events of the sixth and fifth centuries, from sociological, anthropological, and psychological perspectives.[37]

35. See Blenkinsopp, *Judaism, The First Phase*, 117–59.
36. Kessler ("Persia's Loyal Yahwists," 97–98) counted eight different fields of research, to which he added his own area of group identity studies.
37. This study takes also into account the earlier works of Otto Plöger, *Theocracy and Eschatology* (trans. S. Rudman; Oxford: Blackwell, 1968); and Paul Hanson, *The Dawn of Apocalyptic: The Historical and Sociological Roots of Jewish Apocalyptic Eschatology* (Philadelphia: Fortress, 1975; 2d ed. 1979). One crucial difference between Hanson's study and the current approach concerns the sociological point of departure. Hanson followed Karl Manheim, Max Weber, and Ernst Troeltsch in their studies of sociological relationships between diverse religious groups that struggle over cultic issues. The three (each in his own way) contributed important observations on the relationships between privileged ruling groups and alienated disprivileged "others." These relationships that were set mostly on the analogy to the Church and minor sects brought Hanson to his suggested dichotomy (*Dawn of Apocalyptic*, 211–20). While social struggles of power over cult might plausibly have occurred during the sixth and fifth centuries, the current study focuses on dislocation as the more general trigger that demanded all groups (in their different social strata) to react. Thus intergroup relationships and group-identity definitions

In *The Religion of the Landless: The Social Context of the Babylonian Exile*, Daniel L. Smith[-Christopher] described social and socio-psychological behavior patterns among deported and forced migratory groups of what he defined (following Nelson H. H. Graburn) as Fourth World peoples.[38] On the basis of four case studies drawn from the modern era, Smith[-Christopher] identified four behavioral patterns, which he referred to as "mechanisms for survival," within biblical reactions to the Babylonian exile: structural adaptation, the rise of new leadership, creation of "boundary rituals," and folklore innovations such as hero stories. His cautious points of analogy and his restrictions merit quotation:

> The point of this book is not to suggest a direct analogy between any of the cases that are considered and the Babylonian Exile (an overly simplistic generalization), but rather to use the collective sociological and anthropological data to suggest themes and questions to inform exegesis. We are interested in how groups respond, especially in religious patterns, to the specific kind of crisis that mass deportation represents… [F]amiliarity with cases of human behavior in forced removal and minority existence will allow a reader of a text to comprehend a text more fully when that text comes from similar social circumstances.[39]

The point of similarity that allows this analogy is, therefore, the understanding of the Babylonian exile as a profound national crisis, in which self-preservation becomes a major concern, and which brings about both continuity and change in faith and practice, as well as in definitions of national and group identity.

Smith[-Christopher] focused first on the social dynamics involved in the existence of Judean deportees among non-Judeans in Babylon, and subsequently on their partial return to Zion after two generations of minority existence in a land not their own. He paid attention to definitions of identity, to its preservation, and to the dynamics of social

---

seem to be of more relevance. For further and different criticism on Hanson, see for instance Coggins, *Haggai, Zechariah, Malachi*, 52–59. See further below, pp. 266–69.

38. Smith[-Christopher], *Religion of the Landless*, 8–11. For the concept of Fourth World peoples, see Nelson H. H. Graburn, *Ethnic and Tourist Arts: Cultural Expressions from the Fourth World* (Los Angeles: University of California Press, 1976), 1–2: "all aboriginal or native peoples whose lands fall within the national boundaries and techno-bureaucratic administrations of countries of the First, Second, and Third Worlds. As such, they are peoples without countries of their own, peoples who are usually in the minority and without power to direct the course of their collective lives."

39. Smith[-Christopher], *Religion of the Landless*, 11, 13.

boundaries and changes within the deportee community (such as, for instance, changes in its social organization and leadership), as well as to intergroup dynamics that may be reconstructed from the Babylonian Diaspora's experience as an exiled minority. Smith[-Christopher] high-lighted: the community's self-chosen isolation; their drive to create unity under conditions of threat and/or interaction with the conquering culture and with other minorities; their high investment in sacred categories of language, myths and the maintenance of "scriptures." All these add to the impact of discrimination and domination on the community's social formation as "a *conquered* minority, *under domination*" and "reveal the creativity of a minority group in fashioning a viable counter-culture for survival."[40] Moreover, Smith[-Christopher] addressed the group's "sociology of return," as based on the mechanisms of survival and resistance developed through its experience as a minority group in exile. Upon return, feelings of group solidarity are of central importance, as exile (or the specific crisis experience in general) becomes a "'separating' boundary" between the exiles and those who did not share that experience. Smith[-Christopher] thus considered the conflict between Exiles and Those Who Remained to be "the final sociological element in the crisis of the Exile." Yet, in this context, he stated that "[t]his conflict would not necessarily reflect the 'degeneration' of religious faithfulness of those left in Palestine, but only that the crisis led to different social configurations."[41] The following study proves this last observation to be an understatement.

In his discussion of the sociology of return,[42] Smith[-Christopher] considered the debates of the postexilic era as illustrations of the double "culture shock" resulting from the return in itself and from the new encounter between the two communities of Repatriates and Those Who Remained. Three major issues were at the core of the conflict: the economic position of the disadvantaged Repatriates; the issue of the "Samarians"; and the rebuilding of the Temple. Smith[-Christopher] thus found the conflicts among Judeans, both in exile and back in Yehud, to be essential products of the separatist boundaries established by those landless Exiles in Babylon. In a later book, *A Biblical Theology of Exile*, Smith-Christopher combined methodology from refugee studies and trauma studies to illuminate the biblical literature written in the exilic

40. Ibid., especially 58–63; note the bibliographical references there; and see the entire discussion on 49–92.
41. Ibid., 64–65.
42. Ibid., Chapter 8.

arena. In this conceptual framework, Ezekiel's prophecies, for instance, demonstrate the post-traumatic reactions of an exile, a refugee.[43]

A different sociological observation was made by Peter R. Bedford in his 2002 paper, "Diaspora: Homeland Relations in Ezra–Nehemiah."[44] Bedford examined relationships between the Babylonian Repatriates and their parent community of Exiles in Babylon using the construct of core–periphery.[45] He aptly showed how the Repatriates became a Babylonian colony in Yehud, never to gain independent status or leadership, or the freedom to rule their own life back in Yehud. The Babylonian community of Exiles continues to claim its legitimacy as leading the Yehud community throughout the Persian period, reactivating time and again separatist positions developed by the Babylonian Repatriates to guarantee their exclusivist identity.[46] Bedford tied these separatist notions in Ezra–Nehemiah to its evolution in the middle to the end of the fourth century B.C.E., the era of ongoing conflict with the Samarians and other "non-Repatriate" groups in Yehud.[47] According to Bedford, this extreme position differs significantly from that of the earlier Haggai and Zech 1–8. The latter represents the first generations of Repatriates, who had not yet developed separatist tendencies, just as, according to Bedford, the notion of the empty land had not yet occurred in Judean thought.[48] I will

43. Among other discussions of Ezekiel's personal trauma, cf. D. J. Halperin, *Seeking Ezekiel: Text and Psychology* (University Park: Pennsylvania State University Press, 1993); and see T. S. Kamionkowski, who has pointed out a psychological crisis over gender-related self-identity issues in Ezek 16 (*Gender Reversal and Cosmic Chaos: A Study on the Book of Ezekiel* [JSOTSup 358; Sheffield: Sheffield Academic, 2003]). Compare to C. L. Patton's emphasis on the function of the gender metaphors (in Ezek 23) on the rhetoric of defeat, arising from the prophet's experience as a member of the Exiles' community ("'Should Our Sister Be Treated Like a Whore?': A Response to Feminist Critiques of Ezekiel 23," in *The Book of Ezekiel: Theological and Anthropological Perspectives* [ed. M. S. Odell and J. T. Strong; SBLSymS 9; Atlanta: Society of Biblical Literature, 2000], 221–38).

44. In his earlier book, *Temple Restoration*, Bedford had employed the term "millenarian movement," used in sociology of religion to refer to groups under oppression who wish to regain political power, and who perceive that only divine intervention will lead to ultimate and "this-worldly collective salvation." Bedford argued that Haggai and Zechariah were "prophets of a millenarian movement" (299, and see the discussion on pp. 264–70). This label seems anachronistic and betraying a Christian bias.

45. For core and periphery as defining internal relationships among Judean groups, see below, pp. 82–98.

46. Bedford, "Diaspora: Homeland Relations in Ezra–Nehemiah," 158–59.

47. Ibid., 160–61.

48. Ibid., 161–63.

challenge Bedford's argument on reintegration and inclusivity in Haggai and Zech 1–8, and likewise his late dating of the conflict between the Babylon and Repatriate communities in Ezra–Nehemiah.[49] However, I find his observations on core–periphery issues valuable to understanding these tensions among the Babylonian Exiles and their Repatriate community.

The social relationships among the Babylonian Exiles and Repatriates have inspired yet a third paradigm, suggested by John Kessler. In his 2006 paper, "Persia's Loyal Yahwists: Power Identity and Ethnicity in Achaemenid Yehud,"[50] Kessler adapted the sociological model suggested by John Porter to describe Canadian intergroup relationships.[51] The notion of a "charter group" (Porter's term) representing the "sociology of power" as retained and employed by an elite immigrant community, served Kessler in several of his discussions of the status and the role of the Repatriate community in Yehud.[52] Kessler defined a charter group as follows:

> A Charter Group is an ethnically defined elite that moves into a new geographical region, establishes its power base (if necessary, displacing the indigenous power bases), and creates a sociopolitical structure distinct from the one that already exists. The Charter Group comes to dominate the key political, economic, and religious institutions of the region. The group consists of its own inner diversity and retains a loyalty to its own milieu of origin. It may understand its own mission, purpose, and destiny in terms of a Charter Myth. Certain outsiders may be allowed to participate in the society dominated by the Charter Group. Admissibility is often determined on the basis of a mythology of race, whereby certain groups are said to possess desirable (or undesirable) characteristic. If admitted, these groups are sometimes given an entrance status that may be susceptible to change over time.[53]

49. See below, pp. 53–55, 61–98.
50. See n. 12, above.
51. John Porter, *The Vertical Mosaic: A Study of Social Class and Power in Canada* (Toronto: University of Toronto Press, 1965); see Kessler, "Persia's Loyal Yahwists," 98–107.
52. Kessler utilized this paradigm both in his discussions of Ezra–Nehemiah, and in his studies of Haggai and Zechariah; see idem, "Diaspora and Homeland in the Early Achaemenid Period: Community, Geography and Demography in Zechariah 1–8," in *Approaching Yehud: New Approaches to the Study of the Persian Period* (ed. J. L. Berquist; Semeia 50; Leiden: Brill, 2008), 137–66; and see idem, "The Diaspora in Zechariah 1–8 and Ezra–Nehemiah."
53. Kessler, "Persia's Loyal Yahwists," 101.

The charter group is a fascinating model, and at face value it is very attractive for the situation in Yehud. Kessler found three aspects of the Babylonian Repatriates' attitudes upon their return to accord with the notion of a charter group:[54] (1) the Golah is indeed a community that left Babylon to settle in Yehud, claiming to be an elite in its renewed place; (2) the Repatriates gain control over key sociopolitical institutions; (3) the Golah is very much interested in developing its identity and continuing the struggle for self-identification in the "new" location, by employing ideological categories of inclusion and exclusion.

Yet, Kessler aptly noted three features of this model to be incompatible with the situation of the Golah Returnees: First, in distinction to the colonial phenomenon, where the Charter Group has no ethnic or religious relationship to the land to which they immigrate, the Golah do return to their own-previous land, thus they may be considered as *re*establishing themselves as a charter group. Second, the Repatriates held dual loyalty to the Persian crown and to their parent community of Exiles, and they continued to be under the influence of the parent group. Finally, according to the biblical sources at our disposal, and in contradistinction to charter groups, the Golah had but little interest in economic or demographic issues, while, on the other hand, according to the literary sources, it had deep ethnic, historical, and religious bonds to the land it returned to.

Nevertheless, Kessler validated his suggestion by examining issues of hegemony, empowerment, construction of identity, and socio-religious inclusion and exclusion, addressed from the Repatriates' perspective. Kessler pointed out transformations and divisions within the Golah, noting two oppositional tendencies among them: that of inclusion of native outsiders, as found in Haggai and Zech 1–8, and that of exclusion of such populations, as expressed in Ezra–Nehemiah. Such tendencies in the latter instance result from the community's feelings of threat to its social, political, and religious hegemony.[55]

These differences between the conception of a charter group and the Golah Repatriates in Yehud are significant enough to undermine Kessler's proposal. I would further add a fourth basic obstacle—the Golah-Repatriates and Those Who Remained seem to belong to the one and the same nation and sociological institutions, yet each of the two groups (at least in its early stages) creates its own unique identity characteristics by claiming to continue exclusively the earlier national heritage.

---

54. Ibid., 102–4.
55. Kessler further developed his discussion of these two antagonistic tendencies in his recent paper, "The Diaspora in Zechariah 1–8 and Ezra–Nehemiah."

These three paradigms have indeed tapped into social anthropology and social psychology, and specifically concepts of ethnicity, group identity, and intergroup relations developed in those fields, as valuable interdisciplinary perspectives for the study of Judahite communities during the Neo-Babylonian and Persian periods.[56] Yet, in addition to, and in distinction from, the emphases placed by these three paradigms on sociological intergroup relations of the Exiles, conceived as a minority among foreigners, on homeland/Diaspora core and periphery relationships, or on the Repatriates community's status as a charter group coming from the outside into Yehud, the present study focuses on the internal and ideological process of the establishment of group identity definitions following crucial events of dislocation (both exile and return). I aim to describe, (1) the ways in which each of the two principal Judean communities, the Babylonian Exiles/Repatriates and Those Who Remained, defined themselves and their "others" by establishing group boundaries and creating "otherness" relationships; and (2) the ways in which these boundaries and the rhetoric that supports them was transformed over time.[57]

3. *Definitions of Group Identity:*
Communal Beliefs and "Otherness"

Sociological and social psychological studies characterize an ethnic group as a group (or society) that defines its members by what they are (not by what they do). Being a collective of individuals, a nation (the group), is trans-generational, in that it contains a diversity of all ages (as

---

56. Smith[-Christopher], *Religion of the Landless*, 56–63; Rainer Albertz, *A History of Israelite Religion in the Old Testament Period* (trans. J. Bowden; OTL; 2 vols.; Louisville: Westminster John Knox, 1994), 1:231–42; 2:370–75; Kessler, "Persia's Loyal Yahwists," 98–107. Methodological comments on ethnic identity research in biblical texts were presented by Mark G. Brett, "Interpreting Ethnicity," in *Ethnicity and the Bible* (ed. M. G. Brett; Biblical Interpretation Series 19; Leiden: Brill, 1996), 3–22; and by Kenton L. Sparks, *Ethnicity and Identity in Ancient Israel: Prolegomena to the Study of Ethnic Sentiments and Their Expressions in the Hebrew Bible* (Winona Lake: Eisenbrauns, 1998), 1–22.

57. This same interest in the interrelationships between Jews and their Gentile neighbors drives David Biale's edited volume on Jewish culture(s) in diverse Diaspora communities in Jewish history; see Biale, ed., *Cultures of the Jews: A New History* (New York: Schocken, 2002), xvii–xxxiii. John J. Collins (*Between Athens and Jerusalem: Jewish Identity in the Hellenistic Diaspora* [2d ed.; Livonia, Mich.: Dove, 2000], 1–25) discussed the relationships of Gentiles to Hellenistic Jewish communities in Egypt, as well as in Judah itself.

well as both sexes), and the group shows solidarity that results out of its members' loyalty.[58] Solidarity and loyalty are based on principles of kinship (that is, communal memories of shared ancestors), along with shared language, culture (including religion), and, finally, territory (or, in the case of Diaspora communities, reflections on a homeland territory). Together these elements form the components of (national) group identity.[59]

The unifying threads that go through those identity characterizations of an ethnic group are shared group beliefs. In the book *Group Beliefs: A Conception for Analyzing Group Structure, Processes, and Behavior*, Daniel Bar-Tal suggested the following definition:

> Group beliefs are defined as convictions that group members (a) are aware that they share and (b) consider as defining their "groupness"... Group beliefs provide the cognitive basis that group members view as uniting them into one entity.[60]

According to Bar-Tal, group beliefs may be numerous and diverse in their contents.[61] They are by definition relative and subjective;[62] they are those shared beliefs that "foster the differentiation process" in the definition of in-group and out-group,[63] and thus they are foundational in

---

58. For the society as the collective unit of reference, see Daniel Bar-Tal, *Shared Beliefs in a Society: Social Psychological Analysis* (Thousand Oaks, Calif.: Sage, 2000), xvi–xvii. Social psychological studies have devoted great attention to the issue of personal and social identity over the second half of the twentieth century; see, for instance, Philip L. Hammack ("Narrative and the Cultural Psychology of Identity," *Personality and Social Psychology Review* 12, no. 3 [2008]: 222–47), who discussed three aspects of identity: its ideological content, its narrational structure, and the process of identity development in a social context. The current study focuses on the social and communal aspect: the prophets, as also Ezra and Nehemiah, are clearly representatives of their communities, illustrating individual and communal processes of reidentification.

59. Anthony D. Smith, *The Ethnic Origins of Nations* (Oxford: Blackwell, 1986), 23–46; idem, "Chosen Peoples," in *Ethnicity* (ed. J. Hutchinson and A. D. Smith; Oxford: Oxford University Press, 1996), 189–97. For these sociological characteristics in modern American sociological studies, see Talcott Parsons, "Some Theoretical Considerations on the Nature and Trends of Change of Ethnicity," in *Ethnicity: Theory and Experience* (ed. N. Glazer and D. P. Moynihan; Cambridge, Mass.: Harvard University Press, 1975), 53–83, especially 56–63.

60. Daniel Bar-Tal, *Group Beliefs: A Conception for Analyzing Group Structure, Processes, and Behavior* (New York: Springer, 1990), 36.

61. Ibid., 41–43.

62. Ibid., 42.

63. Ibid., 60.

defining the essence of the group: its strengths,[64] its behavior,[65] and the guarantees that maintain the group's existence.[66]

In his later monograph, *Shared Beliefs in a Society: Social Psychological Analysis* (2000), Bar-Tal discussed the societal and public nature of beliefs shared by group members. These shared beliefs are formed "through social processes in social situations,"[67] and communicated in interpersonal contexts (oral or written). Bar-Tal noted that the clear awareness of these beliefs "turns sharing into a powerful psychological mechanism that has crucial effects on a group, or a society."[68] Accordingly:

> these shared beliefs may influence the nature of social reality that group members construct, the sense of solidarity and unity they experience, the intensity and involvement of group members with these beliefs, the conformity expected from group members, the pressure exerted on leaders, and the direction of action taken by the group.[69]

Characterizing group beliefs, Bar-Tal mentioned three ways in which they are maintained:[70] (1) by the shared confidence in their being facts of truth; (2) by the shared recognition of the centrality of these beliefs in establishing the sense of "groupness"; and finally, (3) by their functionality for the group. Bar-Tal suggested that group beliefs perform two major functions. Through the "identification function," they "provide the basis for group membership"; even more, they "often provide a criterion for differentiation. Group beliefs draw the line between the in-group and out-groups."[71] A second function is the "informative function":

> group beliefs allow the organization of the social world with the categories about the group. They enable group members to *know* what makes them unique and different from the out-groups. Moreover, group beliefs may provide the structure with which group members can organize their knowledge about their own group. They provide the *raison d'etre* for the group and specify knowledge about various contents, such as group

64. Ibid., 107–8.
65. Ibid., 108–10.
66. Ibid., 105–6.
67. Bar-Tal, *Shared Beliefs*, 1.
68. Ibid., 4.
69. Ibid.
70. Bar-Tal, *Group Beliefs*, 57–61. Bar-Tal further developed these observations in his *Shared Beliefs* (pp. 6–14), but I find his earlier formulation easier to integrate into the current discussion.
71. Ibid., 59.

history and group goals. Thus, group beliefs allow an understanding of
the group's past and of its present bonds, and possibly predict the group's
future course of action.[72]

Bar-Tal considered the identification and information functions to be of
major importance for the group's process of identity-information self-
identification and for the shaping of the knowledge about the group
acquired by its members. The two functions are also crucial to the maintenance of the group beliefs over time.

Bar-Tal's attention to the formation of both the cognitive aspects and
the content of intergroup relationships (as these surface in both oral and
literary contexts) is of paramount importance for the present study of the
group beliefs held by the Babylonian Exiles/Repatriates; and only in
reference to the early period is it possible to trace the group beliefs of
Those Who Remained in Judah. See for instance, Bar-Tal's observation
that:

> The mapping of group beliefs is a necessary condition for understanding
> the dynamics of specific group. The contents indicate the group's goals,
> values, or norms.[73]

The dynamics of the relationship between these specific groups of
Judeans were of an internally competitive nature, suggesting that they
distinguished themselves from one another both by drawing on competing self-categorizations as the "in-group," and by utilizing counter-
categorizations of all others as "out-groups." These definitions establish
the group's identity, its distinctiveness, and its rules for exclusion.

In drawing border lines, group beliefs join with, or even facilitate, the
ideological components of intergroup (and likewise interpersonal)
psychological processes. These processes involve feelings of superiority
and hostility, along with strategies of discrimination and delegitimization, and testify to inter-group conflicts based on opposing claims and
arguments. As investigated by Henri Tajfel and John C. Turner, these
processes motivate each group to present itself as the more prestigious; a
group often develops its conceptions of self-esteem out of a struggle with
a discriminative counter-attitude on the part of the other group(s).[74]

---

72. Ibid., 60–61.
73. Bar-Tal, *Group Beliefs*, 111.
74. Henri Tajfel and John C. Turner, "The Social Identity Theory of Intergroup
Behavior," in *Psychology of Intergroup Relations* (ed. S. Worchel and W. G. Austin;
Chicago: Nelson–Hall, 1986), 7–24.

I suggest that it is illuminating to observe the conflicts between the Exiles, the Repatriates, and the People Who Remained in Judah throughout the sixth and the fifth centuries B.C.E., within the social psychological context of inter-group relationships, using the basic framework of the function of group beliefs for group identity. Each community constructed and reconstructed group beliefs in the process of self-definition, and developed counter-definitions to delegitimize the other(s).[75]

Additional concepts that serve in definitions of intergroup relations are helpful here, as well.

(1) Group beliefs concerning the ethnic identities of peoples or of groups within a people are well-rooted in that people's history and heritage (including their myths, shared memories and so on), but they tend to change under threat or distress.[76] The Neo-Babylonian waves of exile during the early decades of the sixth century, and the subsequent return to Zion during the late decades of the sixth and through the fifth century B.C.E., were the historical events that awakened the vital need for reidentification by now separated groups of Judeans who needed to reconstruct their "groupness" time and again as individual Judahite communities.[77]

Under these differentiating circumstances, the two Judean communities had to be ideologically creative. They had to supply new criteria for distinctions between in-group and out-group. In defining themselves as the in-group, they had to adapt long-established national beliefs to their own group's situation; this entailed reconfiguring some previously negative conceptions (as, for instance, the meaning of exile) to give these ideas new and positive values in the current context. Since the out-groups now included other Judean communities, each group had articulated the other groups' clear inferiority to their own.[78]

(2) Ethnic group identity is built by using relative categories of comparison and distinction, which establish boundaries of "otherness." Jonathan Z. Smith suggested the following definition of "otherness":

75. Robert A. Markus, "The Problem of Self-Definition: From Sect to Church," in *Jewish and Christian Self-Definition*. Vol. 1, *The Shaping of Christianity in the Second and Third Centuries* (ed. E. P. Sanders; London: SCM, 1980), 1–15.

76. Fredrick M. Barth, "Introduction," in *Ethnic Groups and Boundaries: The Social Organization of Culture Difference* (ed. F. Barth; Bergen: University of Bergen Press, 1969), 1–38, especially 32–37; Sparks, *Ethnicity and Identity*, 18; Bar-Tal, *Group Beliefs*, 71; idem, *Shared Beliefs*, 82–83.

77. Smith[-Christopher], *Religion of the Landless*, 49–68.

78. For these principles of social change, see Tajfel and Turner, "The Social Identity Theory," 19–20.

"Otherness"…is a matter of relative rather than absolute difference. Difference is not a matter of comparison between entities judged to be equivalent, rather difference most frequently entails a hierarchy of prestige and ranking. Such distinctions are found to be drawn most sharply between "near neighbors," with respect to what has been termed the "proximate other." This is the case because "otherness" is a relativistic category inasmuch as it is, necessarily, a term of interaction.[79]

According to social psychology, inter-group relations are constructed according to a certain group reference that may be built on geographical–physical contiguity.[80] As Tajfel and Turner define the out-group, it "must be perceived as a relevant comparison group. Similarity, proximity, and situational salience are among the variables that determine the out-group comparability, and pressures toward in-group distinctiveness should increase as a function of this comparability."[81]

Hence, in relation to the two Judahite communities, I call attention here to inner-ethnic group identity conflicts, to communal distinctions arising in the relations between homeland and exile/Diaspora within the people of Judah as of the early sixth century B.C.E. It is of interest that the web of self-reference that governs biblical sources of the sixth and fifth centuries B.C.E. is not built on physical/geographical proximity.[82] On the contrary, though physically divided, inter-group relationships are perceived between the two Judean communities, the Babylonian Exiles and Those Who Remained. These two recognize their common point of reference in their common ethnic and religious origin, as can be adduced

79. Jonathan Z. Smith, "What a Difference a Difference Makes," in *"To See Ourselves as Others See Us": Christians, Jews, "Others" in Late Antiquity* (ed. J. Neusner and E. S. Frerichs; Chico, Calif.: Scholars Press, 1985), 3–48, quotation on p. 15. The process of setting "ethnic boundaries" has been emphasized in social anthropology research, in the major contribution of Barth's studies, and in the collection he edited (*Ethnic Groups*); binary division has also been stressed by Brett (*Interpreting Ethnicity*, 10–15). Tajfel and Turner ("The Social Identity Theory," 16) suggest an equally interesting definition for "social identity" that is built on relative comparison: "Social groups…provide their members with an identification of themselves in social terms. These identifications are to a very large extent relational and comparative: they define the individual as similar to or different from, as 'better' or 'worse' than, members of other groups."

80. Tajfel and Turner, "The Social Identity Theory," 7–24.

81. Ibid., 16–17.

82. Exceptions appear only in Deutero-Isaiah's prophecies against idolatry (Isa 44:9–20; 45:20–25), which may reflect cultural negotiations with other non-Judean communities of exiles in Babylon, or with Babylonians themselves. However, they seem even more plausibly to address Judean Exiles.

from the ongoing contacts between them (Ezek 33:21; Jer 28; 29, etc.).[83] Throughout this period of over 150 years, each of the communities, separately and polemically, demonstrates the urgent need to redefine its national identity in counter-distinction to the other, even at a distance. Thus, despite their geographical distance, the relevance of the above definition of "otherness" still obtains.

(3) In reference to this comparative, differentiating quality of "otherness," William Scott Green says:

> A society does not simply discover its others, it fabricates them by selecting, isolating, and emphasizing an aspect of another people's life and making it symbolize their difference.[84]

In addition, Green pointed out the caricatured nature of definition by "otherness," which concentrates on the life of the collective. In fact, homogeneity, stigmatization, and stereotyping serve both sides of the process, in the formation of in-group and out-group definitions alike. Both communities characterize positively the in-group and accentuate negatively, by ascribing denigrating images and beliefs to the out-group.[85]

As investigated by Tajfel and Turner, social-psychological mechanisms that involve conflicts, opposing claims, and arguments govern intergroup relationships and contribute to the development of each group's identity. Positive conceptions of self-esteem arise in the struggle to counter the discriminative attitudes of the other group. Relationships of political (or cultural) dominance and subordination evolve between the two groups, and these may affect in-group self-conceptions in a negative way. Tajfel and Turner observed:

83. William Scott Green wrote: "The most critical feature of otherness thus presupposes familiarity and reciprocity, and perhaps resemblance, between and among groups" ("Otherness Within: Towards a Theory of Difference in Rabbinic Judaism," in Neusner and Frerich, eds., *"To See Ourselves as Others See Us,"* 49–69 (50).

84. Green, "Otherness Within," 50.

85. On stereotyping and homogeneity, see Rupert Brown, "Social Identity Theory: Past Achievements, Current Problems, and Future Challenges," *European Journal of Social Psychology* 30 (2000): 745–78, especially 750–51; on the effect on both in-group and out-group definitions, see Walter G. Stephan and Cookie W. Stephan, *Intergroup Relations* (Social Psychology Series; Boulder: Westview, 1996), 1–33, 89–114; Daniel Bar-Tal and Yona Teichman, *Stereotypes and Prejudice in Conflict: Representations of Arabs in Israeli Jewish Society* (Cambridge: Cambridge University Press, 2005), 4–8, 20–91.

> [T]he mere perception of belonging to two distinct groups—that is, social
> categorization per se—is sufficient to trigger intergroup discrimination
> favoring the in-group. In other words, the mere awareness of the presence
> of an out-group is sufficient to provoke intergroup competitive or discrimi-
> natory responses on the part of the in-group.[86]

Differentiating "us" from "them" is thus founded on the selection,
isolation, and emphasis of one major divisive difference. In the conflict
between the Exiles and Those Who Remained, geographic location—
residence in the land of Yahweh versus residence in foreign lands—
comes to "symbolize the difference." The theological consequences of
this division are examined in relation to the intertwined conceptions
of God–People–Land in times of partial dislocation following the
Destruction, as also in times of partial restoration following the change
of the imperial regime.

(4) "Otherness" as a relative category often involves the reidentification of all parties. Indeed, this redefinition of identity was not restricted
to the Exiles (later to be Repatriates), whose interestedness in this
process seems vital. The discussion below shows that in its early phases,
the group referred to here as Those Who Remained had just as much at
stake as the Exiles in building an exclusive identity.

(5) "Otherness" as a term of interaction leads groups to use diverse
strategies to reshape group beliefs and improvise new ones, in order to
effect the self-affirmation and boundary building of one community vis-
à-vis the other.

Donald L. Horowitz suggested that four patterns of identity changes
occur within groups. They are governed by two major contradictory
strategies: *assimilation* and *dissimilation*.[87] In choosing *assimilation*, the
group opts for either *amalgamation* with (meaning: A + B = C), or
incorporation of (A + B = A) the other group; the choice for *dissimilation* leads either to *division* (A yields B + C) or *proliferation* (A yields
A + B).

Division, indeed, seems to be the primary strategy adopted by both
Those Who Remained in Judah and by the Exiled communities from the
early sixth century through the fifth century B.C.E. In practical terms, a
sense of *division* resulted from the physical separation that was forced
upon the people of Judah; it is articulated in the biblical writings by

86. Tajfel and Turner, "The Social Identity Theory," 8–15 (13). Tajfel and
Turner were highly influenced by Muzafer Sherif's observations on intergroup
relations (*Group Conflict and Co-Operation: Their Social Psychology* [London:
Routledge & Kegan Paul, 1967], especially 1–20, 60–70).

87. Donald L. Horowitz, "Ethnic Identity," in Glazer and Moynihan, eds.,
Ethnicity: Theory and Experience, 111–40.

announcements of superiority from both groups, which crystallize a hierarchy of prestige and rank.[88] Consequently, a binary opposition between the communities develops, with each of them delegitimizing the "other" group's existence. These strategies of division, built on conceptions of "otherness," formulate the exclusive identity of each group.

This is the point at which the biblical texts not only allow us to illustrate ancient portrayals of group beliefs and of "otherness," but also call us to investigate the diverse ways in which this perception of "otherness" led each of the Judaic communities to construct perceptions of their own exclusivity. Hence, the following discussion focuses on the strategies and constructs of distinctiveness on which each of the communities drew in its quest to reidentify itself as "*the* (only) people of God." Self-legitimization, on the one hand, and delegitimization of the opposing group, on the other, constitute the main strategies of *division* used to establish the superiority and even exclusivity of one community over the other.[89]

4. *Exclusivity: The Consequence of "Otherness"*

Exclusivity is, therefore, the major consequence of setting boundaries between groups, of narrowing down the perception of shared characteristics by the process of *differentiation*.[90] Exclusivity is the result of employing a perception of the superiority of one group over any other, and of applying particular stereotyped characteristics that symbolize the differences between the antagonistic groups. Motivated by new circumstances, reidentification involves retrospective reflections, reevaluations of shared historical traditions so as to produce new narratives of that history for the now separated groups.[91]

Reading the biblical sources from the sixth and fifth centuries B.C.E., it occurred to me that these are to a large extent occupied with reshaping their shared group beliefs, in what Bar-Tal calls the "informative function."[92] From the methodological vantage point of looking at these

88.   Smith, "A Difference," 15; Green, "Otherness Within," 49.

89.   On delegitimization as a major strategy for differentiating between groups, see Daniel Bar-Tal, "Delegitimization: The Extreme Case of Stereotyping and Prejudice," in *Stereotyping and Prejudice: Changing Conceptions* (ed. Daniel Bar-Tal et al.; New York: Springer, 1989), 169–82; idem, *Shared Beliefs*, 121–36.

90.   On the process of identity formation in this period, see Jon L. Berquist, "Constructions of Identity in Postcolonial Yehud," in Lipschits and Oeming, eds., *Judah and the Judeans in the Persian Period*, 53–65, especially 63–64.

91.   Barth, "Introduction," 32–37; Sparks, *Ethnicity and Identity*, 18.

92.   Bar-Tal, *Group Beliefs*, 60–61.

"shared beliefs," I was able to isolate three types of arguments used by the various authors to establish exclusive claims to the shared heritage of Israel: *continuity*, *entirety*, and the *annexation* of national-religious traditions. These three strategies of exclusivity serve both sides of the process of group identity formation, shaping both the self-legitimizing claims of the in-group and the delegitimizing arguments directed at those designated as the out-group. On the axis of time, these exclusive argumentations redescribe the past, the present, and the future of each of the opposing communities.[93]

Continuity. Claims to *continuity* assert that the current in-group is the only successor to the past national-religious history, and therefore the only present people of God.[94] This exclusive strategy designates the other community, the out-group, as continuing non-Israelite groups from the community's past; that is, they are the "people of the land," they have never been "Israel."

Entirety. Claims of *entirety* insist that the in-group completely encompasses all heirs to the group's history. Counter-designations and arguments serve to denigrate and expel all "others" out of "*the* (entire) people."

Annexation. The *annexation* of national (historical) traditions and religious institutions marshals the group's claims to exclusive status as the one and only legitimate community of Judeans, Jews, people of Israel, people of God. Every community relies on past national traditions and on cherished conceptions, which through inner-biblical interpretation gain new relevance. Appropriating and transforming these traditions, conceptions, and practices for the group's new circumstances serves as an additional means to delegitimize the other community.

These arguments and counter-arguments serve furthermore in projecting the future fate of each of the opposing communities. Prophetic forecasts, manifest either in divine words of consolation and promise (and statements of the people that refer to such promises) or in prophecies of judgment, clearly differentiate between the communities and declare the priority of one community over the other.

Hence, looking to the past, struggling with the present, and hoping for the future, all motivate the rhetoric of *division*. The dynamics of

93. Bar-Tal (*Shared Beliefs*, 43–46) observed the relevance of societal beliefs on this axis of time, characterizing them as both descriptive by nature (touching on past experiences and present concerns) and prescriptive (looking at future desires).

94. The argument of continuity concurs with Bar-Tal's attention to the durability of societal beliefs; to quote his own observation, "Societal beliefs…are pillars of a society and allow its continuation. But their durability does not imply that societal beliefs are unchangeable" (ibid., 40; and see the entire discussion, pp. 39–43).

cohesion and exclusion operate by continually setting in opposition social designations and counter-designations, as well as arguments and counter-arguments advanced to legitimize one group and delegitimize the other(s). Finally, the opponents employ social strategies and counter-strategies designed to enact the changes advanced in their rhetorical statements of identity. Therefore, Horowitz's model of *dissimilation* through *division* (A yields B + C) requires a significant modification when applied to the biblical conflicts. In this case, each of the groups that emerge in the process of division (B, C) claims to continue exclusively the earlier A community—that is, A yields "true-A" + C—and claims that no other (C) community is in continuity with A.

I argue that this dynamic of exclusivity, as a construction of *division*, undergirds the biblical expressions of the internal Judean conflicts among Exiles (/Repatriates) and Those Who Remained in Judah. Since these internal conflicts of the sixth and the fifth centuries B.C.E. are built on those divisive arguments of *continuity*, *entirety*, and *annexation*, they by nature delegitimize those who are designated as out-groups, at the same time as they reinforce an inclusive sense of identity and belonging for those self-designated as the in-group. Thus, the dynamic of community building in the Persian-period documents is always "exclusive inclusivity."

5. *Plan of the Current Study*

In order to tease out the ideological shifts that took place in the postexilic Judean communities, this monograph proceeds from the latest evidence to the earliest. This reversed sequence is demanded by the nature of the evidence: early Persian (postexilic) biblical literature written by Repatriates advances two distinct perceptions of group exclusivity, a fact which calls for examination of the roots of each.

The first part of this study is dedicated to the Persian period (late sixth and fifth centuries B.C.E.). The second chapter opens, then, with exploring what seems to be a significant conceptual differences between the historiography of Ezra–Nehemiah, in Chapter 2, and the prophetic compositions of Zech 1–8, Haggai, and Deutero-Isaiah (Isa 40–66), in Chapters 3 to 5.[95] Yet, despite these differences in ideology, these compositions share a narrowed construction of the people of God that excludes Those Who Remained in Judah.

95. With this distinction I call for a more delicate differentiation within the larger body of Repatriate literature than suggested, for instance, by Robert P. Carroll, "The Myth of the Empty Land," *Semeia* 59 (1992): 79–93; and following him, Lester L. Grabbe, *Ezra–Nehemiah* (London: Routledge, 1998), 136–38.

The second part of this study brings us back to the Neo-Babylonian era, to the period of the waves of deportation from Judah. In Chapter 6, these early and constitutive phases of the intra-communal conflict are dominated by the prophet of the Jehoiachin Exiles, Ezekiel, in his central role as constructor of group beliefs for the Judeans in Babylon. However, the book of Ezekiel itself shows that the prophet's extreme rhetoric was moderated by his followers. Chapter 7 addresses the book of Jeremiah, which poses a special challenge as it reveals two different sets of identity claims—those voiced by the prophet on behalf of his *Non*-exiled Judean community and those counter-claims articulated by the book's Babylonian authors and redactors. The Judean voice in Jeremiah is of great interest, as it supplies our major source for perspectives obtaining among Those Who Remained.

Chapter 8 summarizes the transformations within these diverse Babylonian exilic ideologies. Traits of both continuity and change throughout sixth- and fifth-century literature are considered. The summary notes highlight the "land orientation" of the Babylonian exilic ideologies and Ezekiel's central contribution to these Babylonian ideologies that survived and transformed throughout these over 150 years in Babylon and in Persian Yehud.

Part I

PERSIAN-PERIOD IDEOLOGIES OF EXCLUSIVITY
(POST-538 TO FIFTH CENTURY B.C.E.)

Chapter 2

EZRA–NEHEMIAH

Ezra–Nehemiah has justifiably set the stage for the investigation of group identity issues in Babylonian and Persian Yehud.[1] In its present form, the book holds a wealth of data on definitions of the in-group and the out-group.[2]

1. Ezra–Nehemiah's exclusive ideology has been a central topic in the commentaries and in all studies of the Persian-period history and literature. Its prevalence is particularly noticed when scholars have projected these exclusive views backwards and related exclusive perspectives to that same era. See the discussions below on Hag 2:10–19, pp. 62–74, which may be considered chronologically close. It is even more surprising to notice such retrojections as far back as Jeremiah. See, for instance, Robert P. Carroll, *From Chaos to Covenant: Uses of Prophecy in the Book of Jeremiah* (London: SCM, 1981), 249–68, especially 259. The current study sets each composition in its distinct context.

2. The following discussion presumes the book's division into three major literary segments: Ezra 1–6; 7–10; Neh 1–13; where Nehemiah's Memoir is to be differentiated from the other materials. For a much more detailed, but less convincing, discussion of the book's evolution as a *creatio continua*, see Jacob L. Wright, *Rebuilding Identity: The Nehemiah-Memoir and Its Earliest Readers* (BZAW 348; Berlin: de Gruyter, 2004), 330–40. Wright's unpersuasive preliminary assumption is that the original Nehemiah account advanced an ideology of "religious, ethnic and sociopolitical reconsolidation of Judah" (p. 332); this assumption is based on his understanding of Neh 1:2, discussed earlier at pp. 62–65. He argued that through the book's growth, and only in reaction to opponents, did the text develop into a composition that retains contemporary identity polemics. Thus, Wright (ibid., 340) relegated most of the exclusivist arguments to the third, fifth, and sixth strata, but primarily to the seventh and final stratum (as, for instance, Neh 7:4–72; 8:1–12, 13–18; 9:1–3; and of course 13:1–3, among others). This categorization raises the suspicion of a circular argument; in any event, it substantiates evidence for exclusivist arguments in the book, even if Wright wanted to distance these from Nehemiah himself.

1. *In-group Self-Definition:*
Arguments for Inclusivity Between the Babylonian Exiles
and the Repatriates

With the return to Yehud, the Babylonian Diaspora community, the source of the Repatriate in-group, becomes for them the group left behind: וכל הנשאר מכל המקמות אשר הוא גר שם ("anyone who stays behind, wherever he may be living there," Ezra 1:4). Yet, as of the first waves of return and throughout Ezra's and Nehemiah's missions in Jerusalem, it becomes clear that functionally, the core community continues to be that in Babylon; the Repatriates are its periphery. Bedford has aptly shown the functioning of this core–periphery relationship between the Babylonian-Persian Diaspora and the Repatriates: (1) the local leadership consistently comes from the "home" community in Babylon; (2) the Repatriates appear as inactive and dependent upon the parent community in all respects, including aspects of identity and cultural traditions; (3) the parent community continues to set the terms for claims of legitimacy, based on the experience of exile, while the Repatriate community is portrayed as at risk for impurity, as a result of their connections with outsiders.[3] While these observations are very plausible, I would question Bedford's suggestion that this situation reflects fourth-century circumstances. Rather, I would concur with scholars who find these points valid for the late sixth and fifth centuries B.C.E.[4]

Throughout this period, and without minimizing internal tensions, the Repatriates consider themselves part of the community of Babylonian Exiles carried away from the land by Nebuchadrezzar II.[5] This is apparent both in reference to the return under Zerubbabel and Joshua (Ezra 2:1; 3:8; Neh 7:6), and again in reference to that under Shesh-bazzar (Ezra 5:11–16). Similarly, the later Returnees under Ezra (Ezra 7:6; 8:1) identify themselves as a פליטה ("remnant," 9:8) coming from Babylon; upon arrival in the land, they designate themselves as הבאים מהשבי בני הגולה ("The returning exiles who arrived from captivity," 8:35). To all these Returnees, in their different waves of return, belong these labels: הגולה (Ezra 9:4; 10:6), בני הגולה (4:1; 6:16, 19, 20; 8:35;

---

3. Bedford, "Diaspora: Homeland Relations," 158–59.

4. So, for instance, Kessler, "The Diaspora in Zechariah 1–8 and Ezra–Nehemiah," 129–37; Knoppers, "Ethnicity, Genealogy, Geography, and Change."

5. Knoppers ("Ethnicity, Genealogy, Geography, and Change," 168) wrote: "The returnees living back in their ancestral territory derive their primary identity neither from their homeland nor from their eponymous ancestor but from their ancestral links to the Diaspora."

בני ישראל השבים מהגולה (10:8), and קהל הגולה (6:21), בני גלותא (10:7), (6:21).[6] Finally, Nehemiah's Memoir also appears to contain allusions to the Repatriates as those "from the captivity." Those Returnees who preceded Nehemiah are described as היהודים הפליטה אשר נשארו מן השבי (Neh 1:1–3; 7:5–6).

This phrase has garnered three different primary interpretations, based on its three key terms: הפליטה ("the survivors"); נשארו ("those who remained/were left"); and שבי ("captivity"). Each of the suggestions has clear implications for the way scholars evaluate Nehemiah's own group membership and his position on these group identity issues. The three readings are as follows:

First, היהודים הפליטה אשר נשארו מן השבי, a unique phrase using "heavily charged language," as Joseph Blenkinsopp noted, must denote those who had escaped Babylonian captivity in the first place, and thus should be identified with the remnant left in Judah, that is, Those Who Remained. Accordingly, Nehemiah's care for this group demonstrates a clearly inclusive attitude, which differs significantly from that of Ezra.[7]

Second, in this formulation Nehemiah groups together the earlier Repatriates with Those Who Remained. H. G. M. Williamson articulated: "The context is sufficient to make clear that the remnant terminology is applied loosely by Nehemiah to all surviving Jews in Judah."[8]

These two interpretive routes, however, are scarcely consistent with the data presented above concerning Nehemiah's (and definitely Ezra–Nehemiah's) clearly exclusive conception of the Babylonian Repatriate community.[9]

---

6. Ezra 4:12, די יהודיא די סלקו מן לותך עלינא אתו לירושלם ("the Jews who came up from you to us have reached Jerusalem"), is considered by Blenkinsopp (*Ezra–Nehemiah*, 113) to refer to an "aliyah" during the reign of Artaxerxes I (465–424 B.C.E.), rather than one following the Edict of Cyrus.

7. This is the view of Blenkinsopp, *Ezra–Nehemiah*, 207; and see Wright, *Rebuilding Identity*, 298–301. F. Charles Fensham (*Ezra and Nehemiah* [NICOT; Grand Rapids: Eerdmans, 1982], 151) rightly criticized this option, which depends on the association of both שבי and פליטה with the Repatriates; cf. Ezra 8:35; 9:8.

8. Williamson, *Ezra–Nehemiah*, 171.

9. Compare to Wright (*Rebuilding Identity*, 62–65), who argued that Nehemiah himself (based on Neh 1:1b–4) is interested in "all those remaining in the province and thus escaped deportation" (p. 64); while only "the authors of the texts" (i.e. of Neh 1, and 8–9, along with the final editors of Ezra–Nehemiah) are responsible for the separatist terminology that defines the exclusivist Repatriate community (p. 65). This distinction is hard to sustain: Wright's schema of seven stages of evolution of the text of Nehemiah (pp. 330–39 and the chart on p. 340) shows that the language of separation begins to operate as of stage 3, and becomes more prominent through stages 5–7. Hence, Wright would have to admit that *most* of the phases of the literary

The most plausible reading, in my view, understands all three terms to apply to the Repatriates alone. Nehemiah might certainly be interested in the situation of those earlier Repatriates, who indeed were his kinsmen (the Hanani mentioned in ch. 1 might well be Nehemiah's biological brother, mentioned in 7:2);[10] at the point where Nehemiah's narrative begins, these earlier groups had been resettled in Yehud for over seventy years. Thus, *they* were those who had survived Babylonian captivity (or more plausibly, descendants of the actual Repatriates).[11] Several other linguistic features support this reading: (1) Ezra 1:4 uses וכל הנשאר to designate "everyone of those who remained" in Babylon, in the Diaspora; (2) שבי and פליטה clearly refer to the Repatriates in Ezra 8:35; 9:8, 13, 15; and (3) Nehemiah itself refers further on to the Repatriate community as כל הקהל השבים מן השבי (Neh 8:17). Thus, even after they had already been long resettled in Yehud (for three or four generations), this group continues to identify themselves (and to be identified by their parent community in Babylon) as those who had returned from exile. All these designations clearly refer exclusively to the Babylonian Repatriates, and do not encompass any of the People Who had Remained in Judah following the Babylonian destruction.

The exclusiveness of these designations is reinforced by the three argumentative strategies that I identified in Chapter 1 as *continuity*, *entirety*, and *annexation*.[12] These strategies are frequently employed in Ezra–Nehemiah to delimit the boundaries of the (new) Judean in-group to those repatriated from Babylon, and they are further utilized to delegitmize any other Judean community as the out-group.

Claims of *continuity* assert that the in-group is the successor to the past history of the group.[13] The Repatriates designate themselves as: אנשי עם ישראל ("the men of the people of Israel," Ezra 2:2; Neh 7:7); וכל ישראל (Ezra 10:5); בני ישראל (in Neh 1:6 [×2]; 2:10; 8:14, 17; 9:1); זרע ישראל (Neh 9:2); they are said to have returned, each to his own city (איש לעירו, Ezra 2:1, 70).[14] The Repatriates' spokespeople further

evolution of Nehemiah are separatist and exclusivist in nature; and this is clearly and uniformly the position of the materials in Ezra.

10.   See Blenkinsopp, *Ezra–Nehemiah*, 207; Fensham, *Ezra and Nehemiah*, 151.

11.   So Wilhelm Rudolph, *Esra und Nehemia* (HAT 1/20; Tübingen: Mohr, 1949), 104; Fensham, *Ezra and Nehemiah*, 151.

12.   See the discussion above on pp. 27–29.

13.   Williamson (*Ezra–Nehemiah*, 20, 39, 51, and passim) emphasized continuity as a major theme in Ezra 1–3 and throughout; the following discussion focuses only on continuity within group identity definitions.

14.   For a wide-ranging discussion of the usage of ישראל in Ezra–Nehemiah, in comparison with earlier and later sources, see Williamson, "The Concept of Israel in

re-embrace the terms עם יהודה (Ezra 4:4) and ישבי יהודה וירושלים ("the residents of Judah and Jerusalem," 4:6; 5:1). Nehemiah uses the group self-designation היהודים (translated "the Jews," Neh 1:2; 3:33, 34; 4:6; 5:1, 8, 17; 6:6), or בית יהודה (in 4:10), as he emphasizes that his contemporaries descend from העולים בראשונה ("those who were the first to come up," Neh 7:4–5). Note also the Aramaic designation, שבי יהודיא ("the elders of the Jews," Ezra 5:5; 6:7, 8, 14).

Continuity is further illustrated through the Ezra–Nehemiah's use of genealogy, which functions to demonstrate kinship relationships for the purpose of establishing religious claims and/or political legitimacy.[15] In fact, genealogy serves both in-group and out-group argumentations in these group conflicts, though in different ways. In terms of conflicts within the in-group, genealogy is used to establish the authority of Ezra: to show that his Priestly roots go all the way back to Aaron (Ezra 7:1–5), and to demonstrate that his present role as religious leader of the Repatriate community is rooted in a family tradition of priestly leadership that goes back in unbroken succession to the Jerusalem Temple of old (through Seraiah the priest).[16] Gary Knoppers highlighted the important role Ezra's lineage plays in the internal conflict over exogamy between the Diaspora of Ezra's time and the long-resettled Repatriates.[17]

In relation to conflicts between the in-group and its out-groups, genealogy, as the process of designating birthright, establishes the basic opposition between זרע הקדש and עמי הארצות (Ezra 9:2), or between זרע ישראל and בני נכר (in Neh 9:1–3). Bob Becking accurately argued that זרע הקדש "shows a radical self-interpretation of the Ezra-group," combining the Deuteronomic concept of election (עם קדוש, Deut 7:6), with

---

Transition." Williamson has aptly treated the usage of ישראל as a strategic tool ("slogan," in his words) to claim legitimacy for each of the different fractions in the Judean communities (150). The data presented above shows that ישראל was but one designation (though clearly major) upon which the Repatriates relied.

15. For studies on genealogy and its implicit function of legitimizing claims to religious and political authority, see Robert R. Wilson, *Genealogy and History in the Biblical World* (New Haven: Yale University Press, 1977); idem, "Genealogy, Genealogies," *ABD* 2:929–32; Marshall D. Johnson, *The Purpose of the Biblical Genealogies* (SNTSMS 8; Cambridge: Cambridge University Press, 1988), 42–44, 77–82.

16. The interest in and importance given to genealogy may be seen in the lists naming the Temple servants and the priests, in Ezra 2:59–63 and Neh 7:61–65.

17. Knoppers, "Ethnicity, Genealogy, Geography, and Change," especially 150–58. See also other studies that designated genealogy as a device to express claims of continuity in exilic literature; e.g. Albertz, *Israel in Exile*, 106–7; Kessler, "Persia's Loyal Yahwists," 107–8.

the "biological category" of the origins of Israel, זרע אברהם ישחק ויעקב ("seed of Abraham, Isaac, and Jacob," as in Jer 33:26; Isa 41:8, etc.).[18] Ezra and Nehemiah's independent demands for separatism are thus aimed at defining "the Diaspora Repatriates" as "the true Israel."[19]

Claims of *entirety* insist that the in-group completely encompasses all heirs to that history. The Repatriates claim to be the entire people of Israel, כל העם ("all the people," Neh 10:9, 13); or simply העם ("the people," Ezra 3:1, 11, 12, 13 [×3]).[20]

Another and even more powerful device for establishing *entirety* is the frequent use of lists in Ezra–Nehemiah. The Repatriates are socially categorized within specific subgroups, the totality of which builds a complete community. Twenty-one times in Ezra–Nehemiah is the community listed according to its components. Seventeen of these lists follow the pattern: Israel (בני ישראל, or "the chiefs of the clans of Judah and Benjamin"), priests, and Levites (ראשי האבות ליהודה ובנימן והכהנים והלוים; Ezra 1:5; 3:8, 12; 6:16, 20; 7:7, 13, 24; 8:29; 9:1; 10:5; Neh 8:13). At times these three categories are complemented by the mention of other Temple personnel: singers, gatekeepers, and servants, for example, הכהנים והלוים ומן העם והמשררים והשוערים והנתינים ... וכל ישראל (Ezra 2:70; Neh 7:72; 10:29, 35–40; 11:3).[21] This division into the subgroups of Israel, priests, and Levites, which dominates Ezra, occurs in Nehemiah as well, though with some variations (e.g. Neh 7:6–72; 9–12).[22]

---

18. Bob Becking, "Continuity and Community: The Belief System of the Book of Ezra," in *The Crisis of Israelite Religion: Transformation of Religious Tradition in Exilic and Post-Exilic Times* (ed. B. Becking and M. C. A. Korpel; OTS 42; Leiden: Brill, 1999), 256–75, especially 270–72, quotation from p. 271.

19. On the definition of out-groups, see pp. 41–45, below. Gary Knoppers ("Intermarriage, Social Complexity, and Ethnic Diversity in the Genealogy of Judah," *JBL* 120 [2001]: 15–30) perceived Ezra's and Nehemiah's demands at one and the same time as "religious, political, and social in nature" (28).

20. העם / כל העם, "(all) the people": Neh 4:7, 8, 13, 16; 5:1, 15, 19; 7:4; 8:1; and in parallelism with Israel: 8:3, 5 (×3), 6, 7 (×2), 9 (×3), 11, 12, 13, 16; 10:35; 11:1 (×2), 2; 12:30, 38; 13:1.

21. Williamson (*Ezra–Nehemiah*, 15) described this tripartite division as "the regular sociological division of the people in the Persian Period," understanding the tribes of Judah, Benjamin, and Levi "as the only true community" (p. 15).

22. See for instance the list of leaders in Neh 10:1: שרינו לוינו כהנינו ("our officials, Levites, and priests"), mentioned by name and followed by an additional list of names under the title ראשי העם, v. 15; or הלוים mentioned together with Israel, בני ישראל, זרע ישראל (in Neh 9:1–5; and also 10:2–34, 35–40; 11:3–36; 12:1–30, 31–47).

A second pattern governs four lists in Nehemiah, where the people
are labeled as Jews, priests, nobles, prefects, and other officials (וליהודים
ולכהנים ולחרים ולסגנים וליתר עשה המלאכה, Neh 2:16; 4:8, 13; 7:5; and in
Nehemiah's adversarial relationship with the Jerusalemite leadership,
5:7–8; 13:4–14).[23] This same pattern designates the entire population as
well: היהודים stands for "the population at large"; followed by the priests;
and closing with the leaders of the community: סגנים ("officials") and
חרים ("nobles").[24]

For the sake of the present discussion it is not necessary to delve
deeper into the differences behind these two list patterns. While they
may indeed reflect different levels of literary evolution, both patterns
designate the community as a whole, throughout Ezra–Nehemiah.[25]
These listings seem to indicate more than simple sociological divisions,
and seem to serve not merely as a stylistic feature in the historiography
of Ezra–Nehemiah. Their ideological significance is substantiated by
their occurrences in highly important contexts, concerning the arrival of
the Repatriates back in Yehud, the reinstitution of the Temple and its
cultic worship, and the communities' re-commitment to the covenant
with God. In reference to the Raptriates' arrival, lists introduce the
Repatriates coming with Zerubbabel and Jeshua in Ezra 2 and Neh 7;
Ezra's arrival in 7:7 (and the people that accompanied him in 8:29); lists
of these social groups are mentioned as part of Artaxerxes' royal decree
in 7:13; and they detail the priests and Levites that arrived with Zerubbabel and Jeshua in 12:1–26. Concerning the Temple, lists are recorded
on the occasion of the laying of the foundations for the Temple in Ezra
3:8–13 (where three lists occur; vv. 8, 10–11, 12); the dedication of the
Temple in 6:13–22; celebration of Passover in 6:19–20; the reading of
the *torah* in Neh 8:13 (reflected also in v. 9); the dedication of the
Jerusalem wall in 12:27–30; the granting of donations to the Temple
personnel in 12:47. On the community-national arena, lists open the
intermarriage problem in 9:1 (this is also reflected in the subgroups that

---

23. Neh 13:4–14 refers to the general population by the term וכל יהודה (v. 12),
and see vv. 16–17; v. 3 mentions groups of Temple personnel, closer to the first
pattern.

24. So Williamson (*Ezra–Nehemiah*, 191), who thus rejected the option that
these terms are restricted to administrative groups. For that other approach, see
Wright (*Rebuilding Identity*, 106–9), who held that these terms refer to "an independent administrative class" (107), and thus translated סגנים as "rulers," and חרים
as "officials." Wright further addressed the duplication of סגנים in 2:16 and reconstructed its redactional evolution (107–9).

25. For a detailed discussion of the literary levels and layers of redaction in
Nehemiah, see Wright, *Rebuilding Identity*, and his concluding chart on p. 340.

are mentioned in 10:16, 18, 23, 25); the *amana*-covenant in Neh 10:1, 15, 29, 35; and the naming of the residents in Jerusalem and Judah in Neh 11:3, 10, 15, 20.[26] Although they mention different subgroups, these lists express the self-reliant status of the Repatriates—clearly reinforcing a sense of community cohesiveness that embraces all the people, embraces "all Israel." Yet, this inclusiveness is actually a rhetorical strategy which functions to restrict the community to the Repatriates group only, הגולה, and to exclude all others. In sociological terms, *entirety* is the most appropriate conceptual framework by which to recognize the establishment of in-group/out-group categories which designate who is considered part of the community and who is not.

Finally, *annexation* marshals religious institutions and historical traditions in the service of the group's claims. The Repatriates reconstruct the city and appropriate its religious institutions: the sanctuary; the Temple with its vessels and personnel (Ezra 1–6); the city walls (Neh 3–4). Each wave of Repatriates reinstitutes festivals and daily cultic customs. Zerubbabel and Jeshua are responsible for the reinstitution of the Passover (Ezra 6:19–21); Ezra reinstitutes the Sukkoth festival (Neh 8:13–18; 9:1–5) and the practice of reading from the Torah on the initial days of the seventh month, along with its daily interpretation during Sukkoth (Neh 8). Nehemiah reports on the reestablishment of the covenant with God (Neh 10). He also reorganizes the reinstituted ritual institutions of the Jerusalem Temple (Neh 12:44–47; 13:1–13, 28–31); and he emphasizes the Sabbath (Neh 13:15–22) and advances social aspects of moral obedience to God (Neh 5). Legal obligations are specifically determined by adherence to ספר (תורת) משה ("the scroll of the teaching of Moses," Neh 8:1; 13:1).[27] The Repatriates appropriate to themselves the notions of peoplehood and nation, calling themselves "all Israel." Furthermore, they depict their own recent history by taking over national historical traditions, such as the Exodus and the settlement of

---

26. For the central roles these lists play, see Shemaryahu Talmon, "Ezra and Nehemiah," *IDBSup* 317–29; Tamara Cohn Eskenazi, *In An Age of Prose: A Literary Approach to Ezra–Nehemiah* (SBLMS 36; Atlanta: Society of Biblical Literature, 1988), 48–53. While these scholars have called attention to this phenomenon and its ideological importance in emphasizing the full participation of the entire people in those crucial events, they did not look at the function of this *entirety* as an exclusivist strategy.

27. Sara Japhet, "Law and 'The Law' in Ezra–Nehemiah," in Goshen-Gottstein, ed., *Proceedings of the Ninth World Congress of Jewish Studies, Panel Sessions*, 99–115. Note also "the book of their God" (Neh 9:3) and "and You ordained for them laws, commandments and Teaching, through Moses Your servant" (9:14).

the land under Joshua.[28] Casting themselves as the heirs to and guardians of the historical heritage of Israel, the Repatriates from Babylon build a powerful argument advocating their exclusive status as the one and only legitimate community of Judeans, Jews—people of Israel, people of God.

2. *Defining the Out-group:*
The Strategy of Amalgamation

Counter-designations and counter-arguments play equally important roles in Ezra–Nehemiah. Throughout the three waves of return, the Repatriates never identify the "others" who they encounter in the land as Judean Yahwists, or even as Yahwistic Israelites.[29] They are constantly delegitimized, categorized as foreigners, "the people(s) of the land(s)" (עם הארץ, עמי הארץ, עמי הארצות).[30] Since this topic has been extensively discussed, it suffices merely to call attention to the fact that Ezra–Nehemiah applies three major yet different "non-Judahite" identifications for those "people(s) of the land(s)."

First, in referring to the return of Zerubbabel and Jeshua (Ezra 1–6), the actual identities of the commingled groups designated as עמי הארצות, "the peoples of the land," or the singular עם הארץ, is obscured. The only characteristics they do explicitly possess (and possess *in common*) is their being "of the land," and their portrayal as adversaries of העם ("the people," Ezra 3:3), or "the people of Judah," that is, the Repatriates (4:4).

Labeled צרי יהודה ובנימין ("the adversaries of Judah and Benjamin") by the author of Ezra (Ezra 4:1–4, and vv. 9–10, 17), these peoples are

---

28.   For the theological significance of the list of Returnees (Ezra 2) and its similarities to the occupation traditions under Joshua, see Blenkinsopp, *Ezra–Nehemiah*, 83–84. Additional similarities to Joshua appear in Ezra's role in the reading of the Torah (Neh 8), which evokes Deut 31:9–13 and Josh 8:30–35.

29.   Exception to this categorical dichotomy may only occur in Neh 5:8, 17, but see Williamson, *Ezra–Nehemiah*, 239–40, 244–45. This opposition suggested in Ezra–Nehemiah does not recognize any of the other Yahwistic communities that were in existence as of the early sixth century; for instance, the community of Judeans in Egypt. See Albertz, *Israel in Exile*, 134–35. Compare to Kessler's repeated references to "other Yahwists" ("The Diaspora in Zechariah 1–8 and Ezra–Nehemiah," 132, 134).

30.   On the possible meanings of these designations, see Ernest W. Nicholson, "The Meaning of the Expression עם הארץ in the Old Testament," *JSS* 10 (1965): 59–66; Blenkinsopp, *Ezra–Nehemiah*, 108; and recently, but less persuasively, Lisbeth S. Fried, "The ʿam haʾares in Ezra 4:4 and Persian Administration," in Lipschits and Oeming, eds., *Judah and the Judeans in the Persian Period*, 123–45.

made to describe themselves as the descendants of multi-ethnic deportees brought from afar to the Assyrian province of Samaria; they do not
even belong to a single national group.[31] The author uses the argument
of *continuity* against these peoples, via an assertion of *discontinuity* with
the land and the people of Israel, put into their own mouths. They cannot
even claim to be the ancient (autochthonic) residents of the land. They
define themselves as deportees of foreign nationalities who had no
previous connection to God, to the land, or to the people of Israel.
Moreover, they themselves recognize the continuing relationship of
YHWH to the Repatriates (כי ככם נדרוש לאלהיכם)—God is *their* (the
Repatriates') God, while צרי יהודה ובנימין only "offer sacrifices to Him"
(אנחנו זבחים [*Qere*: ולו] ולא, v. 2).[32]

Second, in the chapters dedicated to Ezra's return to Jerusalem (Ezra
7–10), outside groups are mentioned only in the context of the issue of
intermarriage (chs. 9–10). Here we are told that "the people of Israel" or
"the holy seed" (9:1–2) have not separated themselves from "the peoples
of the lands" (9:2, 11), who are characterized as acting in continuity with
the behavior of a detailed list of former foreign adversaries: the
Canaanites, the Hittites, the Perizzites, the Jebusites, the Ammonites, the
Moabites, the Egyptians (v. 2).[33] As much as the typological nature of

31. Although the exact historical reference in this passage to Esarhaddon as the
Assyrian king who brought foreign peoples to Samaria does not accord with 2 Kgs
17:24–41, it is quite enough rhetorically (in terms of the present discussion) to
substantiate the foreign origin of the "other" peoples currently living in the land. For
the possible historical background, see Blenkinsopp, *Ezra–Nehemiah*, 105–7.
Richard J. Coggins (*Samaritans and Jews: The Origins of Samaritanism Reconsidered* [Oxford: Blackwell, 1975], 28–74) emphasized the fact that while we posses
only scant evidence concerning Northern Israel from within sixth-century prophecy,
both Jeremiah and Ezekiel treat that population as Israelite (Jer 41:5; see also Jer
3:11; and more elaborately, Ezek 23; and similarly within their prophecies of consolation, e.g., Jer 30–31; Ezek 37 and within chs. 28–36). Coggins further showed
that "these two groups [the northerners and those who had remained in Judah] came
to be identified with one another, and both would be dismissed [by the Returnees] as
no part of the true people of God" (p. 37).
32. The *Qere/Ketib* tradition (*Ketib*: ולא, *Qere*: ולו) tells of the theological and
ideological difficulties the Masoretes faced in reading this phrase. See Williamson,
Ezra–Nehemiah, 42; and compare to his reconstruction of the tension between the
"native" Judahites and the Returnees as political, based on 4:3 (pp. 49–50). In
support of Williamson's contention is the fact that Zerubbabel interprets King Cyrus'
decree to the Returnees as restricting the personnel authorized to join the project.
33. Other general references to the foreign women characterize them as from
"the peoples of these abominations" (Ezra 9:14); and "the peoples of the land" (10:3,
11, 17, 44). Ezra 9:1 (and 12) alludes to legal materials and creates an "exegetical

this list of ancient peoples gives it no historical credibility, and can hardly shed light on the contemporary identity of these peoples of the land, these very characteristics are extremely valuable for their implicit ideological statement. These peoples of the land are certainly foreign—as foreign as they could possibly be. They are peoples with whom interrelationships have been and still are legally forbidden: the Canaanites, the Transjordanian peoples, and the people of Egypt.[34]

Third, Neh 1–13 suggest two distinct counter-designations for the other residents of Yehud that reinforces this distinction. Chapters 9–10 utilize the obscure and general terms and set up an opposition between זרע ישראל ("the stock of Israel") and בני נכר ("all foreigners," lit. "the children of foreigners"), from whom they are to separate (Neh 9:2), and the oath the Repatriates take to follow "the Teaching of God," his commandments, rules and laws, opens with the demand to cut themselves off from "the peoples of the land" (עמי הארץ, Neh 10:31, 32).

In Nehemiah's Memoir, however, Nehemiah's opponents are very clearly marked and defined by personal name and national identity: Sanballat the Horonite, Tobiah the Ammonite, and Geshem the Arab (Neh 2:10, 19; 6:1–9, 11–19; 13:1–13). The conspiracy against the people in Jerusalem headed by Sanballat and Tobiah is joined by the Arabs, the Ammonites, and the Ashdodites (4:1–2).[35] Similarly, Nehemiah's list of "foreign women," unlike Ezra's (Ezra 9:2), includes only Ashdodites, Ammonites, and Moabites (Neh 13:23).[36]

---

blend" out of Deut 7:1–4; 23:4–9 (thus Blenkinsopp, *Ezra–Nehemiah*, 175–76). See also Exod 23:23–24; 34:11–16; as well as Lev 18:1–5, which adds the abhorrent deeds of Egypt to those of Canaan (as Williamson pointed out, *Ezra–Nehemiah*, 129–31). See Sara Japhet, "The Expulsion of the Foreign Women (Ezra 9–10): The Legal Basis, Precedents, and Consequences for the Definition of Jewish Identity," in *Teshurah Le-ʿAmos: Collected Studies in Biblical Exegesis Presented to ʿAmos Hakham* (ed. M. Bar-Asher, N. Hacham, and Y. Ofer; Alon Shevut: Tevunot, 2007), 379–401 (in Hebrew).

34. Robert P. Carroll ("The Myth of the Empty Land," especially p. 85) pointed out this analogy, and referred to both to Ezra 4:1–5; 10:1–5 as reflecting one and the same perspective.

35. On the geographic orientation of this list of adversaries, see Blenkinsopp, *Ezra–Nehemiah*, 247; Williamson, *Ezra–Nehemiah*, 225.

36. While the Ashdodite women are the focus of this incident (Neh 13:24), the mention of Ammonite and Moabite women seems to follow Deut 23:4–8. Together with the reference to Solomon's sins (1 Kgs 3:12–13; 11:1–6), both texts supply an appropriate basis from which to exhort Nehemiah's community. On the application of these authoritative texts, see Blenkinsopp, *Ezra–Nehemiah*, 363–64.

The overarching opposition in Ezra–Nehemiah is posed between the Repatriates and the peoples of the land(s), which the sources introduce as an amorphous group of different nationalities. The absence of any reference to Judeans or Israelite–Yahwistic communities in the land is noteworthy in a context that intentionally obscures other national identities; the three major characterizations of "the peoples" are marked by inconsistencies and deviations, and feature the anachronistic mention of the ancient peoples of Canaan and its surroundings. Hence, Lester L. Grabbe observed correctly that "the text simply refuses to admit that there were Jewish inhabitants of the land after the deportations under Nebuchadnezzar… One can only conclude that many, if not all, these 'people of the land' were the Jewish descendants of those who were not deported."[37]

Accepting what seems to indeed be an inevitable conclusion, I want to call attention to the argumentation strategies which advance this ideological stance. As we have just seen, the strategy designated by Donald Horowitz as *amalgamation* (A + B = C) functions in Ezra–Nehemiah as an overall strategy to distance and denigrate outsiders by dissolving the distinctions between them.[38] In contradistinction, the Repatriates distance themselves from this amalgamated mongrel "other" population by advocating their own genuine and distinctive (vs. "amalgamated") status; in

37.   Grabbe, *Ezra–Nehemiah*, 138; see also Williamson, *Ezra–Nehemiah*, 46: "The possibility of true Jews being among them is simply not envisaged in these books." Efforts to uncover the historical-sociological situation behind the rhetoric has borne out the assumption that any existing Yahwistic communities of either Judean or Israelite descent were ignored. Yonina Dor (*Have the "Foreign Women" Really Been Expelled? Separation and Exclusion in the Restoration Period* [Jerusalem: The Hebrew University/Magnes, 2006 (in Hebrew)], 94–98, 245–52) arrived at this same conclusion by employing literary and anthropological methodologies, arguing that six different ceremonies of separation are described in Ezra–Nehemiah.

38.   Horowitz, "Ethnic Identity," 115–16, 124–26, 139. See above, pp. 26–27. Becking addressed this issue in two studies. In "Continuity and Community" he made this observation: "What is at hand in the narratives of the Book of Ezra is a mystification of the 'others' by being unspecific about them" (273; see, more fully, pp. 272–75). My understanding follows quite the same lines, with the additional step of framing this process of mystification as part of an overall process of group identity formation directed against outsiders. In his recent study, "On the Identity of the 'Foreign' Women in Ezra 9–10" (in *Exile and Restoration Revisited: Essays on the Babylonian and Persian Periods in Memory of Peter R. Ackroyd* [ed. G. N. Knoppers and L. L. Grabbe, with D. N. Fulton; LSTS 73; New York: T&T Clark International, 2009], 31–49), Becking spoke of stereotypification and demonization of the women as "others." The present discussion extends this insight to the general situation described in Ezra–Nehemiah.

all of the following areas—genealogy, religion, culture, national history, law, and politics—the Repatriates are "*the* Judeans (Jews)"—or should we say "the [true] Judeans (Jews)."

Driving Ezra–Nehemiah's calumnious strategy of amalgamation are the same three arguments of exclusivity—*continuity, entirety,* and *annexation*—this time turned *against* the out-group, as counter-arguments.

As noted above, the argument of *continuity* is used against these resident peoples. These assertions are put into their own mouths (Ezra 4:2) or stated by Ezra (as in Ezra 9:10–14), Nehemiah (Neh 13:24–27), and the narrator (Neh 13:1–2). The "people(s) of the land(s)" are said to be the descendants of either the Canaanite peoples long ago expelled from the land, or of those foreign exiles brought into the land by the Assyrians. They are clearly not Israel or Judah.

The concept of *entirety* also operates within this presentation of the resident groups as "people(s) of the land(s)," insofar as this blanket designation enfolds all groups apart from the Repatriates and does not allow for any other "not-foreign" resident community. This, of course, reinforces the argument of entirety as used by the in-group Repatriates, who consider themselves to constitute the entire people of Israel.

A counter-*annexation* argument may also be recognized. The different designations of continuity use inner-biblical allusions to create analogies between the resident communities and those foreign Canaanite (or Assyrian peoples), characterized as adversaries in pentateuchal legal traditions and historiography. Ezra 9:1–15 brings together Deut 7:1–5; 12:28; 23:4–9, and echoes Lev 18:24–30; Neh 13:1–3 alludes to Deut 23:4–5; Neh 13:23–27 evokes Deut 7:3 and 1 Kgs 11:1–6 as it echoes 1 Kgs 3:12–13.[39] Furthermore, the overall assertion that comes out of this separatist rejection of exogamy is that these foreign "people(s) of the land(s)" threaten the Repatriate community just as their ancient predecessors endangered Israel upon entering the land: by seeking to share in the restoration of the cult and intermarry with the Repatriates, they threaten their (exclusive) covenant relationship with God.

These observations demonstrate the dual direction of these three arguments of exclusivity to both validate in-group superiority, and to invalidate the out-group.

---

39. This abundant list of allusions to pentateuchal and historiographical passages concerning the necessity of cutting off any relations with the peoples of the land render unnecessary the scholarly effort to pinpoint the social-historical identities of the peoples mentioned. Cf. Knoppers, "Intermarriage, Social Complexity, and Ethnic Diversity," 29–30.

3. *Ezra 6:19–21:*
Incorporation—An Implicit Exclusionary Strategy

The reinstitution of Passover in Jerusalem (Ezra 6:19–21) uses, at least at face value, a different approach. This passage describes the celebration of the Passover by the Returnees (בני הגולה, v. 19; or בני ישראל השבים מהגולה, "the children of Israel who had returned from exile," v. 21), led by the priests and the Levites (vv. 19–20), and joined by all who had separated themselves from the uncleanliness of the nations of the lands וכל הנבדל מטמאת גוי הארץ "to worship the LORD of Israel" (v. 21). Several questions need to be addressed here: (1) Who might those "separating themselves" be?[40] Could this be somewhat loose evidence for the existence of a community of Non-exiled Judeans?[41] If so, (2) Does this celebration mark a change in the exclusionary tendencies of the Repatriates?

While the answer to the first question may only be guessed, that to the second is much clearer. Evaluating this celebration according to Horowitz's model of identity change, we may definitely consider the inclusion of those "separating themselves" to be a form of *incorporation* (A + B = A), one of the two modes of boundary changes that allow for the *assimilation* of disparate groups.[42] In this case, it appears that the Repatriates (the A group) had initiated the invitation to incorporate some individuals from those anonymous "foreign" resident groups, whether they were proselytes or former Judeans. The vague language of וכל הנבדל מעמי הארצות (in both Ezra 6:19 and Neh 10:29) reveals the A group's perspective. These "separating" individuals stand for the B component, but do not seem to represent an entire (homogeneous) group. It is as if the A group "swallows up" and basically obliterates the former (group)

40.   So Jacob M. Myers (*Ezra–Nehemiah* [AB 14; New York: Doubleday, 1965], 54), who cited Num 9:14 as a reference for the inclusion of foreigners in the Passover celebration. Williamson (*Ezra–Nehemiah*, 85) understood Ezra 6 to be referring to proselytes, and added: "in the outlook of this writer's circle, the recognition of legitimate Jews who nevertheless stood in a different tradition from their own was generally denied." Blenkinsopp (*Ezra–Nehemiah*, 132–33) considered these participants to be drawn from the "local population, including no doubt some from the region of Samaria" (133). Blenkinsopp found Ezra 6 and Ezra 4:2 to be parallel to 2 Chr 30:18–19, the story of Hezekiah's Passover—which itself included many of the "remnant" left in the North following the Assyrian exile, even though they had not properly purified themselves.

41.   We might make such a deduction based on the absence of the well-known term גר in this context (in contrast to Num 9:14).

42.   Horowitz, "Ethnic Identity," 115; and see above, pp. 26–27.

identifications of those who assimilate into this dominant community.[43] From their distinctly superior vantage point, the A group allows individuals to join them, but does not recognize the new members as having a former community identity.[44] Thus, exclusivity, rather than heterogeneity, remains the determining characteristic of בני הגולה, while denigration and delegitimization of the earlier population(s) of the land continues, even in the process of their assimilation.[45]

While Ezra–Nehemiah's extreme exclusionary orientation is often recognized, scholars debate the relationship between Ezra–Nehemiah and the Persian-period prophets Haggai and Zechariah, in terms of this issue of exclusion and inclusion. As we now go on to consider a wider context within the sixth–fifth centuries B.C.E., I want to suggest that the exclusionary tendencies we have noted in Ezra–Nehemiah illustrate but one type of exclusive opposition shaping group identities in Yehud. Another, and quite different, opposition is established in the prophecies of Zechariah (1–8).

43. Horowitz (ibid., 124) mentioned that "To be 'eligible' for incorporation, the group to be merged (group B…) will probably be required to demonstrate its acceptability by modifying its behavior in advance so as increasingly to assume the modal attributes of members of the incorporating group… At least some acculturation, therefore, may be a precondition of incorporation."

44. Sara Japhet ("People and Land," 117) considered Ezra 6:19 and Neh 10:29 as examples of early religious conversion, although she recognized the fact that the terminology is unique, and that there are no formal procedures accompanying this incorporation of new members.

45. I therefore disagree with those who find in Ezra 6:19–21 an example of inclusive tendencies in Ezra–Nehemiah. Compare to Blenkinsopp (*Ezra–Nehemiah*, 133), who praised this passage, saying: "their inclusion illustrates the openness of the postexilic Jewish community to outsiders who wished to become insiders"; and see Kessler, "Persia's Loyal Yahwists," 109–10.

Chapter 3

ZECHARIAH (1–8) AND HAGGAI:
THE RESTORATION PROPHETS

Haggai and Zechariah son of Berechyahu son of Iddo are the two prophets that are genuinely connected with the period of the Restoration in
Yehud. This is established by their own accounts and because they are
mentioned in Ezra 5:1; 6:14. However, scholars have noted differences
between the historiography of Ezra–Nehemiah and the prophecies of
Haggai and Zechariah, differences which go beyond the distinctions of
genre. One of the major points of difference is indeed the conceptions of
group identity employed in the two sets of writings; scholars have found
Haggai's and Zechariah's perspectives to differ from Ezra–Nehemiah's
extreme exclusivity and in fact to differ from one another as well.

The current discussion addresses each of the prophetic books separately, establishing the data and challenging the scholarly perspective
that argues for inclusive positions in one or both. I argue that the fact that
they each deal only to a limited extent with conflicts between Those Who
Remained in Yehud and the Babylonian Exiles does not imply a vision
of renewed community inclusive of both. On the contrary, Zechariah and
Haggai (separately and differently) do take exclusivist stands on group
identity issues; yet they express the relationship between the Babylonian
Repatriates and Those Who Remained using different metaphors than
those employed by Ezra–Nehemiah. This rhetorical divergence thus
constitutes the major difference between the two Persian-period sources,
the historiography of Ezra–Nehemiah and the prophetic literature of
Haggai and Zechariah.

My discussion begins with Zech 1–8, where views on identity issues
are explicit, whereas in Haggai's they are only implicit. For each prophet,
I present the data that tell of his orientation on group identity issues,
followed by a discussion of the three arguments for exclusivity that he
uses. The present chapter leads to a discussion (in Chapter 4) of the
common denominators shared by the two prophets: the terms they use to
designate the community and distinguish between groups—העם הנשאר]
or שארית העם, and כל עם הארץ.

1. *Zechariah Son of Berechyahu Son of Iddo*
(Zechariah 1–8)

Zechariah's prophecies fall within a short time span of prophetic activity (522–520 B.C.E.), and the prophet is said to belong to a priestly Repatriate family.[1] These are the two facts that scholars agree upon, even as they debate, for instance, the identity of Zechariah's audience.

Zechariah's hearers are said to be either the community of Babylonian Repatriates in Jerusalem,[2] or the Non-exiled population of Judah and Jerusalem.[3] A middle path argues for a combined audience, indifferent to its origins, consisting of both Repatriates and People Who Remained.[4]

---

1. This assumption is based on the genealogical information regarding Iddo found in Neh 12:4, 10, 16. See David L. Petersen, *Haggai and Zechariah 1–8* (OTL; Philadelphia: Westminster, 1984), 109. Mark Boda (*Haggai, Zechariah* [NIV Application Commentary; Grand Rapids: Zondervan, 2004], 33) learnt from this information that Zechariah was still a young man in 520 B.C.E., as his grandfather was the one who returned to Yehud with Zerubbabel. But there is no compelling need to adopt a linear chronology here. For a more skeptical position concerning these genealogical ties, see Coggins, *Haggai, Zechariah, Malachi*, 44. For a discussion of Zechariah's patronymic, see Ralph L. Smith, *Micah–Malachi* (WBC 32; Waco, Tex.: Word), 167–68.

2. Ackroyd (*Exile and Restoration*, 148–49, 171–217) noted indications of Zechariah's activity in Babylon prior to his return (197), and he understood both Haggai and Zechariah to be among the Repatriates (149, 195). See also Kessler, "The Diaspora in Zechariah 1–8 and Ezra–Nehemiah," 121–27. The possibility of Babylon as the birthplace of the three prophets, Haggai, Zechariah, and Malachi, was already suggested in *b. Zebaḥim* 20a.

3. So Japhet ("People and Land," 111) who argued that Zechariah's "main address is to the people of Judah and Jerusalem, who are called 'the remnant of this people' (8:6, 11, 12)… But the purview of his prophecies is actually much broader." While Japhet admitted that Zechariah does refer to the exile and to the return, she nevertheless suggested that, "Those to whom he refers as 'coming from Babylon' are probably individuals whose names are given; nowhere in his prophecies is there any mention, or even a hint, of a community of 'returned exiles' in Judah" (111). Bedford (*Temple Restoration*, 264–92) distinguished the two prophets: Haggai was part of the Non-exiled population, whereas Zechariah was a Repatriate, who was "prompted by Haggai" (272–73). Collaborating, sharing a unified ideology (277), the two "millenarian" prophets initiated the reconstruction of the Temple as a project that included both communities.

4. Boda, *Haggai, Zechariah*, 35–36. This also seems to be Ackroyd's presupposition (*Exile and Restoration*, 200–217); he referred to Zechariah's message to the people in general, and emphasizes the prophet's inclusive approach regarding repatriates from east and west, as also his general universalistic stance (2:10–17; 8:20–23). See below, pp. 59–60.

The first proposition, that this collection addresses Repatriates (and possibly also the Babylonian Diaspora),[5] is most plausibly substantiated by the following data: Ezra–Nehemiah mentions the two prophets, Haggai and Zechariah, together, as encouraging the Jews in Jerusalem to complete the reconstruction of the Temple (Ezra 5:1; 6:14; in terms of that work's chronology, this had taken place by the third year of Darius, Ezra 4:24); the Repatriate community's leaders, Zerubbabel and Joshua, are major addressees of Zechariah's prophecies (Zech 3–4; as also in Haggai, see below); and, other persons mentioned in Zechariah include Heldai, Tobijah, Jedaiah, and Josiah son of Zephaniah, who are designated (via an *inclusio*) as part of הגולה: "from the Exiled community," people "who have come from Babylon" (Zech 6:9–14). To these may be added the personal names that retain Babylonian bureaucratic or governmental titles, בית אל שר אצר and רגם מלך (Zech 7:2).[6]

Furthermore, thematic arguments may also be taken into consideration. Zechariah's prophecies focus on the return following the exile (as in Zech 2:1–4), which he designates, first and foremost, as the return of God after a long period of anger and absence (Zech 1:7–17; 8:1–3; and see 2:9, 14–16). Having returned to Zion, His city, God brings the

5. Paul L. Redditt (*Haggai, Zechariah, and Malachi* [NCB Commentary; Grand Rapids: Eerdmans, 1995), made an interesting suggestion concerning Zechariah's night visions (Zech 1:7–17, 18–21; 2:1–5; 4:1–6a, 10b–11, 13–14; 5:1–4, 5–11; 6:1–8). He proposed (41–42) that Zechariah experienced the visions after his return to Yehud, but that his addressees were the Exiles in Babylon. These visions formed the original core of the collection, which was subsequently enlarged, possibly even by Zechariah himself, to include the passages focusing on Zerubbabel and Joshua (3:1–10; 4:6b–10a; 6:11b–13); the expanded collection was aimed at "the Jerusalem community" (42), by which I assume Redditt meant the Repatriates.

6. J. Philip Hyatt ("A Neo-Babylonian Parallel to *BETHEL SAR-ESER*, Zech 7:2," *JBL* 56 [1937]: 387–94) has already discussed Wellhausen's proposal (of 1898) to identify ביתאל-שראצר as a compound theophoric name, by analogy with the personal name *Bit-ili-šar-uṣur* in Neo-Babylonian tablets from Uruk, just as רגם מלך was understood to have evolved from the title רב מג המלך. See David Winton Thomas, "Zechariah," *IB* 6:1082. These possibilities led Karl Elliger (*Das Buch der zwölf kleinen Propheten* [ATD 25; Göttingen: Vandenhoeck & Ruprecht, 1982], 2:133) to suggest that the term denotes a Babylonian delegation; and see Redditt, *Haggai, Zechariah, and Malachi*, 80. The possibility of connections between Repatriates and their families in Babylon was already suggested by Rashi (who, nevertheless, treated Beit El as locative): "Righteous people they were, and they sent to their relatives who were in Beit El to come and seek help from God in Jerusalem for their sake, and to inquire of the priests to notify them whether they should cry in the month of Av, since the construction of the House was continuing" (translations of Medieval exegetes are my own, unless otherwise specified).

people, Judah, and resettles them in the land, in their previous territorial allocation (1:16–17; 2:10–17; 8:4–8).[7] The Repatriates are now to fill the towns of Judah once again (1:17; 8:11–13), specifically Jerusalem (1:17; 2:5–9, 16; 8:6–8).[8] The restoration of the Temple and the city of Jerusalem were the major missions of the time articulated by both Zechariah and Haggai (Zech 4:9; 6:9–14; 7:1–7; 8:9, 18–19; Hag 1:2–14; 2:1–9, 10–19).[9] Restoration includes as a major component the reinstitution of the covenant between God and "the Remnant of this people," a phrase that clearly denotes those brought back from exile by God (Zech 2:5–9, 10–17; 8:6–8).[10] In a reversal of their previous fate of distress and displacement among the nations, the people are now to be permanently resettled in their land (8:11–13).[11]

The setting of the book of Zechariah within the Repatriate community goes hand in hand with the way Zechariah conceptualizes the state of the land of Judah during the exile. The prophet describes a single destruction, leading to a total deportation (1:15; 2:12; 7:14), that left Judah in complete desolation; note, for instance, the retrospect reflection offered by Zechariah on the exile: ואסערם על כל הגוים אשר לא ידעום והארץ נשמה אחריהם מעבר ומשב וישימו ארץ חמדה לשמה ("I dispersed them among all those nations which they had not known, and the land was left behind them desolate, without any who came and went. They caused a delightful land to be turned into a desolation," Zech 7:14; and see 1:7–17; 8:11–13).

---

7. Zech 2:16, ונחל יהוה את יהודה חלקו על אדמת הקדש, is usually translated as "The Lord will take Judah to Himself as His portion in the Holy Land" (NJPS); this translation construes "His portion" to be in apposition to Judah—the people, not the territory (see also Carol L. Meyers and Eric M. Meyers, *Haggai and Zechariah 1–8* [AB 25B; Garden City, N.Y.: Doubleday, 1987], 162, 169; Petersen, *Haggai and Zechariah 1–8*, 183–84). The Meyers aptly suggested the use of נחל in Exod 34:9 and Ps 82:8 as parallels. I would not exclude another option, which would suggest a double meaning here: "The Lord will bestow upon Judah his portion in the Holy Land." This suggestion adopts the more common meaning of נחל, which normally requires the causative (Hiphil) with two objects: "YHWH/PN *hinḥil ʾet*-(Nation/PN) ʾet-(Land)" (as in Deut 3:28; 21:16; Josh 1:6; Prov 8:21). Hence, Zech 2:16 may add to God's return to Zion, His city, a mention of Judah's resettlement in its land. This possibility fits the hints suggested also in Zech 1:16–17 and 8:1–3, 4–8.

8. For further data on the geographical designations and literary pericope of Zech 1–8 as focusing on Judah/Jerusalem and the return from exile, see Kessler, "The Diaspora in Zechariah 1–8 and Ezra–Nehemiah," 124–27.

9. Contra Bedford, *Temple Restoration*, 264–92.

10. See Redditt's discussion of Zech 2:5–9, 10–17 (*Haggai, Zechariah, and Malachi*, 58–62).

11. The term שארית העם הזה is discussed below, pp. 82–92.

Accordingly, Zech 1–8 makes no mention of any population resident in Yehud prior to the Return. The only "others" thus named, whom Zechariah sets rhetorically in opposition to the Returnees, are their enemies from the past—those peoples who had functioned as God's agents to afflict Judah at the time of the Destruction, but had carried their mission too far and thus were doomed to God's judgment (1:15; 2:12).

Another implicit opposition is established between the land of Judah/God's people (i.e. the Repatriates) and Babylon, the symbol of evil (5:5–11). Interpretations of the vision in Zech 5:6–11 vary substantially. Redditt suggests that this vision presents Babylon as the symbol of wickedness, which resides at its core in its temple; the vision thus implicitly demonstrates the great divide between Babylon and Jerusalem, God's chosen place of residence.[12] The vision, according to Redditt, had two groups of readers/addressees: (1) the Exiles, who were called to leave Babylon and return to Jerusalem; and (2) the Repatriates, who were encouraged to complete the restoration of the Temple. Compare this interpretation with the theological antagonism between Jerusalem and Babylon suggested by Meyers and Meyers, who identified wickedness with idolatry ("non-Yahwistic worship and loyalty"); taken away from the land, Yehud, this wickedness is resituated in a temple in Babylon. Thus, the vision balances God's return with the departure of idolatry.[13] A third interpretation was advanced by Petersen, who suggested that the wickedness is understood to be residing among the Repatriates. But that will be solved by a two-way transfer of "Judahites from Babylon to Israel and evil person(s) from Israel to Babylon." This transfer is meant to achieve "a demographic equilibrium": to distance evil from and to guarantee purity within the land.[14] All these interpreters have agreed that Babylon, as the past conqueror of Jerusalem, is stereotyped as the locus of evil.

It is therefore apparent that in this vision, Zechariah is not expressing opposition to some contemporary, Persian-period group of Gentile enemies; similarly, he ignores the existence of any other contemporary residents (Judean or Gentile) in the holy land of God, the land of Judah.[15] According to Peter R. Ackroyd, Zechariah's major message is built on

12. Redditt, *Haggai, Zechariah, and Malachi*, 73–74.
13. Meyers and Meyers, *Haggai and Zechariah 1–8*, 313–14.
14. Petersen, *Haggai and Zechariah 1–8*, 261–63 (quotations from p. 261).
15. Contra Winton Thomas, "Zechariah," *IB* 6: 1054–55, who found Zechariah as well as Haggai to be hostile to the Samarians, that is, to the people of the former Northern Kingdom, and thus to blaze the trail taken later by "postexilic Judaism" (1055). I do not find this opposition in Zechariah (see further concerning Haggai, pp. 62–74, below).

this genuine reversal of fortune directed at the contemporary "ideal generation," which he identified as "the generation of the return."[16] Yet, Ackroyd did not consider Zechariah to participate in internal Judean conflicts like those attested so fiercely in Ezra–Nehemiah.[17]

I want to emphasize a different contrast to Ezra–Nehemiah, one that concerns the opposition articulated by Zechariah between the Repatriates and the notion of an empty city and land.[18] This conception of the land as a "vacuum" (commonly called "the empty land")—from the time of the exile to the return—conveniently ignores the ongoing presence of Non-exiled Judeans as well as any other peoples.[19] This metaphorical construction, which turns invisible all other occupants of the land, indeed distinguishes Zechariah from Ezra–Nehemiah; as we have seen, the "peoples of the land" are insistently present in the rhetoric of that book. This distinction further validates the suggestion that the empty land metaphor is an ideological construction, not based on historical circumstances.[20] In contrast to Ackroyd (and others), I find this omission of references to other Judeans in the land a sign that Zechariah does in fact share the exclusivist perspective of other early Persian-period Repatriates. His utilization of the three argumentative strategies for exclusivity confirms this impression.

a. *Zechariah's Three Arguments Towards Exclusivity*
The primary contrast in Zechariah is that between the presence of the Repatriates and the formerly empty land; therefore, the book lacks counter-arguments pertaining to various contemporary resident outgroups. Zechariah uses the three argumentation strategies for exclusivity

16. Ackroyd (*Exile and Restoration*, 203) wrote this in reference to Zech 1:6b, which he suggested brings messages of both warning and encouragement to the contemporary generation (see his n. 107).

17. Ibid., 208–9.

18. Compare to the scholarly perspective that has argued for the opposition of the Repatriates to the metaphor of the empty land in Ezra–Nehemiah. See, for instance, Blenkinsopp (*Judaism*, 79), who suggested that the Empty Land and the notion of the land populated by foreigners are two coexisting ideas in Ezra–Nehemiah. I think these two conceptions of the land should be kept apart, and I argue that the empty land metaphor does not occur in Ezra–Nehemiah at all.

19. Compare to Bedford, "Diaspora: Homeland Relations," 149–50 n. 8.

20. Another difference between Zechariah and Ezra–Nehemiah concerns Zechariah's relationship to the parent Diaspora community. Kessler ("The Diaspora in Zechariah 1–8 and Ezra–Nehemiah," 121–27) emphasized that in shifting his interest to Yehud and the concerns of the Repatriates, and in predicting their complete return, Zechariah never again refers to the Diaspora community left behind. Zech 2:10–17 and 5:5–11 seem to contradict this observation, however.

to build in-group identity definitions, in a way that further confirms the polemic nature of the prophet's words.

The prophet invokes the notion of *continuity* with the past by identifying present-day Zion as the Judeans living in Babylon: הוי ציון המלטי יושבת בת בבל ("Away, escape, O Zion, you who dwell in fair Babylon," 2:11).[21] "Zion" functions as a metonym for the community of Exiles in Babylon, in what seems to be a functional similarity to the Babylonian designation of their place of residence as *āl-Yāhūdu*, that is, "the town of the Judeans."[22] Zechariah, then, has diverse utilizations of the name Zion. He uses it as equivalent to Jerusalem (1:14; 8:2–3), the city that justly suffered destruction, desertion by its God, and the exile of its inhabitants. Yet, of even more interest is Zechariah's metonymic usage of Zion. Present-day Zion, to a large extent, is still located away; that is, the term designates the people, those still in exile, who are now being called to return to their homeland. It seems to me necessary to distinguish clearly this personification in 2:11 (Zion as the people; i.e., the Babylonian Exiles) from the metaphorical usage of 2:14, where *bat-Zion* is the empty city. The prophet emphasizes the transformation which will bring Zion, the deported people, back to God, back to Jerusalem (*bat-Zion*, v. 14), and will reinstitute the covenant relationship. *Bat-Zion* will regain its status as the chosen city and the people will reclaim their position as God's people (2:8–9, 11–13); the days of atonement will turn into days of joy for "the house of Judah" (8:18–19). Zechariah 2:11 is thus a remarkable indication of Zechariah's role in transforming the conception of core–periphery relationships in regard to the Babylonian Exiles, as he shifts Jerusalem into the core position for the Babylonian Exiles and the Repatriates.[23]

21. Compare to Petersen (*Haggai and Zechariah 1–8*, 176–77), who considered two possibilities for the identity of personified Zion—"Israel, or a special part of Israel"—that in any case is commanded to flee. While Rex A. Mason (*The Books of Haggai, Zechariah and Malachi* [CBC; Cambridge: Cambridge University Press, 1977], 43) and Redditt (*Haggai, Zechariah, Malachi*, 59–61) identified Zion in v. 11 as the community of Exiles in Babylon, they agreed with Petersen (*Haggai and Zechariah 1–8*, 179) considering the personification of *bat-Zion* (2:14).

22. On this Babylonian deportation policy of settling Exiles within national communities, see Vanderhooft, *The Neo-Babylonian Empire and Babylon*, 110–12. In recent years, texts from *āl-Yāhūdu* have been slowly published, and they clearly specify the location as *ālu šā lū ia-a-hu-du-a-a*, "the town of the Judeans"—or *(ša)Yāhūdu*. See Laurie E. Pearce, "'Judeans': A Special Status in Neo-Babylonian and Achaemenid Babylonia?," in Lipschits, Knoppers, and Oeming, eds., *Judah and the Judeans in the Achaemenid Period*, 267–78 (and see specifically 270 n. 2).

23. On the complicated core–periphery relationships between the Babylonian Diaspora and the Repatriates in Ezra–Nehemiah, see Bedford, "Diaspora," *VT* 52

This equation of Zion with the Exiles in Babylon (/the Repatriates) is of paramount importance also in regard to the second argument for exclusivity, that is, *entirety*. By appropriating the label Zion solely to the Exiles, Zechariah eliminates the possibility of using it for those who had stayed behind in Zion (the Non-exiled Judeans). I will argue, in fact, that nowhere in either the prophecies (1:1–6, and chs. 7–8) or the visions (1:7–6:8) does Zechariah allude to contemporary populations, either Judean or non-Judean, resident in the land, apart from the Repatriates themselves.

Zechariah uses three main phrases to designate the people: (1) עמי, ("my people," 8:7); (2) שארית העם הזה ("the Remnant of this people," 8:6, 8); and (3) כל עם הארץ ("all the people of the land," 7:5). These designations, which also occur in Haggai (1:12–14; 2:1–4), raise two major questions: Are these designations inclusive of all Yahwists in Yehud (that is, the Non-exiled Judeans as well as the Repatriates)?[24] Should they be connected with and analyzed through the lens of the phrases עם הארץ or עמי הארצות in Ezra–Nehemiah? I will consider these two questions in Chapter 4 below.[25]

The rubric of *entirety* is also utilized in Zechariah's reflections on the reconstruction of the Temple, Zerubbabel's main project (Zech 4:8–10; 6:12–13). In this context, we learn that הגולה, "the Exiled community" (6:9–15), executes this initiative. Zechariah mentions by name four individuals of the *golah* community (v. 10), for whom we have no other clues to identity than their Yahwistic theophoric names and their place of origin.[26] Yet, their participation in the project, even if only through the symbolic act of crowning Joshua son of Yehozadaq as high priest, is

(2002): 147–66, see 162 n. 19. This indeed is another point of difference between Zechariah and Ezra–Nehemiah. Zechariah seems to be calling for/expecting a complete return (which Bedford aptly observed, pp. 159, 162; though I cannot accept his other perspectives on Zechariah).

24. So Petersen, *Haggai and Zechariah 1–8*, 284–85.

25. See the discussion below, pp. 82–98.

26. For the many questions raised by this list of names, see Smith, *Micah–Malachi*, 217–19. Petersen (*Haggai and Zechariah 1–8*, 273–74) found these minimal details to emphasize "the 'orthodox' character of those returning from exile and to legitimate whatever wealth they contribute to the rebuilding efforts" (274). He nevertheless suggested two different possibilities for the men's identities: (1) all four were from the Babylonian Repatriate community; or (2) Heldai, Tobiah, and Yedaiah were Repatriates who brought the metals to Josiah, one of the group that had remained in Judah. Their joint endeavor thus represents a clear "act of integration" (274). The *inclusio* in v. 10, works against this latter possibility, however; as observed by Smith (*Micah–Malachi*, 218).

functionally similar to Ezra's account of the Repatriates' exclusive preparation of precious metals for the Temple (Ezra 1:4).[27] Though in Zechariah it is an argument *ex silentio* (nothing explicit is said to *ban* the participation of anyone outside of the Repatriate group), it appears that participation in the rebuilding is indeed restricted to the רחוקים, "Men from far away," who have come expressly for the purpose (Zech 6:15).[28]

The *annexation* of national historical traditions shows itself repeatedly in Zech 1–8 in references to the re-institution of the covenant relationship. Zechariah's opening prophecy (Zech 1:1–6) alludes to two corpora. It refers explicitly to prophetic traditions, to the "former prophets" and their admonitions, in which context it shows a variety of allusive connections primarily to the book of Jeremiah.[29] Furthermore, The prophecy implicitly evokes Deuteronomic conceptions of covenant, as these appear in the covenant blessings and curses.[30] By adapting prophetic (Jeremianic) perspectives on the people's breach of the covenant, reinforced by Deuteronomic conceptions of the God–people relationship, the prophet not only legitimizes his own prophetic status,[31] but also locates the struggles

27. See also the Persian king's decree and financial assistance in Ezra 7:12–20, given to Ezra to be brought back from Babylon and from the provinces on their way to Jerusalem (vv. 21–23).

28. Redditt (*Haggai, Zechariah, Malachi*, 76–78) counted this assurance to the Exiles as the main purpose of this passage. Carroll Stuhlmueller, *Rebuilding with Hope: A Commentary on the Books of Haggai and Zechariah* (Grand Rapids: Eerdmans; Edinburgh: Handsel, 1988), 98, wrote: "By silently overlooking the people of the land…Zechariah sees the new people of Israel to consist exclusively of those who have come back from exile. They are the true remnant; the others are contaminated by their pagan neighbors and have not been properly in the laws of Moses through the new editing of the Priestly and Deuteronomic traditions of the Torah during the Exile."

29. Compare Zech 1:4 and Jer 25:5–7; 35:15; as also Jer 6:17–19; 7:25–26; 11:6–8. Michael R. Stead (*The Intertextuality of Zechariah 1–8* [LHBOTS 506; New York: T&T Clark International, 2009], 74–86) mentioned in addition allusions to Ezekiel, Isaiah (52, 54), Lamentations (see below), and Deuteronomy.

30. For instance, Zech 1:6, אך דברי וחקי אשר צויתי את עבדי הנביאים הלוא השיגו אבתיכם ("But the warnings and the decrees with which I charged My servants the prophets did they not overtake your fathers?"), may be compared with Deut 28:15, 45, ובאו עליך כל הקללות האלה [ורדפוך] והשיגוך ("all these curses shall [pursue and] overtake you"). Zech 1:6b utilizes Lam 2:17 with a significant twist in which the prophet adds כדרכינו וכמעללינו as words of confession and justification to the harsh protest of Lam 2.

31. Zechariah's evocation of the former prophets, and particularly Jeremiah, to establish his own legitimacy has long been pointed out, as for instance in Petersen, *Haggai and Zechariah 1–8*, 135; Smith, *Micah–Malachi*, 184–85. This, however,

of the present generation of Returnees within the historical narrative of the relationships between God and His people (Zech 1:14–17).[32]

Likewise, the closing oracles in ch. 8 bring conceptions of covenant to the fore, by utilizing the covenant formula: והיו לי לעם ואני אהיה להם לאלהים באמת ובצדקה ("They shall be My people, and I will be their God—in truth and sincerity," 8:8).[33] This renewed covenant, like the covenant of old, guarantees agriculture prosperity and military protection (8:11–13; and cf. 2:8–9), just as it demands obedience to specific commandments (6:15b; 8:16–17).[34]

These connections with the long tradition of covenant relationships between God and His people are apparent in Zech 8:11–13 as well. In contrast to God's earlier judgment enforced on the people, these times of hope promise the transformation of curse into hope (vv. 11, 13).[35] Indeed, v. 12 illustrates this opposition referring to the repossession of the land:

---

seems to be only one aspect, and not the crucial one, of the prophet's message. On the emphasis given to the covenant relationship, see Stead, *The Intertextuality of Zechariah 1–8*, 75–86.

32. Petersen (*Haggai and Zechariah 1–8*, 134) found this prophecy to rely on "lamentable history," yet it develops into hopeful prospects for Zechariah's generation. See Ackroyd (*Exile and Restoration*, 200–209) for the emphasis on the reversal of destruction and desolation.

33. The covenant formula in its dual format occurs in Lev 26:12; Deut 29:12 (and see Deut 26:17), but is most typical of Jeremiah, where it appears twice in reference to the Sinai covenant (7:23; 11:4) and five times as part of the future covenant (24:7; 30:22; 31:1, 33; 32:38). In Ezekiel, the covenant formula occurs only in the context of the future renewal of the covenant (11:20; 14:11; 36:28; 37:23, 27). Zech 8:8 is unique in adding the phrase באמת ובצדקה; see Petersen, *Haggai and Zechariah 1–8*, 303.

34. Besides invoking Deuteronomic conceptions of covenant via allusions to Jeremiah (e.g. Zech 1:1–6; 7:7–14, which evokes Jer 11:1–14), Zechariah also alludes to Ezekiel and to Priestly sources. See, for instance, Zech 2:14–15, which evokes Ezek 37:24–27; 43:7–9; and the Priestly conception of the divine presence.

35. The opposition between כאשר הייתם קללה בגויים and והייתם ברכה echoes the Deuteronomic opposition between curses and blessings (as in Deut 11:26–29) that characterizes the covenant commitment and even its renewal ceremonies (Deut 27:9–26; Josh 8:30–34). The book of Jeremiah uses the phrase היה לקללה בגוים a number of times (Jer 44:8; in a string of curses at 24:9; 25:18; 42:18; 44:12; compare this to the designation of a land as לשמה ולקללה in 2 Kgs 22:19; cf. Jer 49:13). But Zechariah seems to carry this phraseology further and draw independently of Jeremiah on its Deuteronomic thematic context. On this literary tradition, see Janet E. Tollington, *Tradition and Innovation in Haggai and Zechariah* (JSOTSup 150; Sheffield: Sheffield Academic, 1993), 182–216, especially 205–15.

כי זרע השלום <u>הגפן</u> תתן פריה והארץ תתן את יבולה <u>והשמים יתנו טלם</u>
והנחלתי את שארית העם הזה את כל אלה

for [I will give them] the seed of **peace;**[36] The vine **shall produce its
fruit, the ground shall produce its yield,** and the skies shall provide
their moisture. I will bestow all these things on the Remnant of this
people.

This blessing alludes to that of the Holiness Code (Lev 26:4–6):

ונתתי גשמיכם בעתם ונתנה הארץ יבולה <u>ועץ השדה</u> יתן פריו ... וישבתם לבטח
בארצכם. ונתתי שלום בארץ

I will grant your rains in their season, **so that the earth shall yield its
produce** and the trees of the field **their fruit**...and you will dwell
securely in your land. I will grant peace in the land.

Zechariah's blessing brings together the four major components of Lev
26 in reverse order, repeatedly using the verb נתן to tie them together,
as in Leviticus. While these same elements, again governed by the verb
נתן, also appear in Ezekiel's covenant of peace (Ezek 34:25–30), it seems
that each prophet evokes Lev 26 independently.[37] Zechariah concludes
his vision of renewal by using נחל in the causative.[38] God bestows
optimal conditions for peaceful agricultural life upon this specific community which occupies the position of the sole Remnant of this people in
Zion, and is now starting afresh its settlement within the land.

Zechariah employs the strategy of *annexation* in other ways, as well.
For instance, he evokes the Exodus tradition and adapts it to the new
reality of the Exiles in Babylon (Zech 2:11). He draws on the conception
of Jerusalem as the divinely elected city (Zech 1:17; see 1 Kgs 11:13).
The institution of Zerubbabel as the anointed leader who directs the
rebuilding of the Temple (Zech 4) is modeled on the role of the Davidic

36. The difficult phrase כי זרע השלום has been translated and completed in
different ways, as for instance by NJPS, "but what it sows shall prosper"; Petersen
(*Haggai and Zechariah 1–8*, 304), "Indeed, there shall be a sowing of peace"; Smith
(*Micah–Malachi*, 234), "for they shall sow in peace." My own translation is based
on the similarities to Lev 26:4–6 and Ezek 34:25–30, and reflects a possible ellipsis
of the verb נתן.

37. Compare to Hinckley G. Mitchell (*Haggai, Zechariah, Malachi and Jonah*
[ICC; Edinburgh: T. & T. Clark, 1912], 210–11), who accentuated the points of
contact between Zechariah and Hag 1:10; 2:9.

38. Hiphil נחל, הנחיל, "to give possession of [something] to [someone]," is used
to describe God's granting possession of the land to His people, in Deut 12:10; 19:3;
and Jer 3:18. Compare this usage to הנחיל in reference to the military leadership of
Joshua (Deut 1:38; 3:28; 31:7; Josh 1:6). See Edward Lipiński, "נחל," *TDOT* 9:330–
33; see p. 51 n. 7, above.

king; the covenant with Joshua the high priest adapts Priestly traditions and symbols (Zech 3, evoking Lev 8:1–9; Exod 28:9, 17–21).[39] The Zion tradition with its divine promise of protection is adapted to the new circumstances (Zech 2:9), as is the conception of the divine presence within the people (Zech 2:15). This long list of familiar traditions plays its own role in the prophet's message to the Repatriates, helping them to reconstruct their community on the foundation of a historical past in this crucial time of restoration.

b. *Zechariah 8:20–23: Universalism and Exclusivity*

Of additional interest is that Zech 1–8 concludes with a passage that forecasts a multinational pilgrimage to Jerusalem to worship Yahweh. The expression עמים רבים וגוים עצומים ("many peoples and the multitude of nations," Zech 8:20–22) denotes those who will express their wish to join every Judean in the worship of God (v. 23). This phrase is often explained as part of Zechariah's inclusivist position, reflecting a supposed universalistic tendency towards conversion to Judaism in the postexilic period (as also in Zech 2:14–16; and see Isa 56:6–7).[40]

At face value, Zech 8:20–22, 23 illustrate an inclusive tendency. Yet two comments are in place. First, these two passages suggest an altogether different conception of group identity. In Zech 8:20–23 identity is described by the religious-cultic definition of seeking Yahweh (לבקש את יהוה צבאות), the God of the Judeans (see איש יהודי). The frame of reference for group identity thus differs, resting not on the internal Judean opposition between Diaspora and homeland, but on the religious-national definitions of Israel vs. foreigners. Therefore, when it comes to group beliefs, the distinction between the two sides belongs to the religious-cultic sphere. It illustrates an assimilatory tendency to recognize God and join in His worship, in the religious pilgrimage (vv. 21, 23; as in Isa 2:2–4; Mic 4:1–4).[41]

---

39. See Redditt, *Haggai, Zechariah, and Malachi*, 62–66.

40. So Redditt (ibid., 87), who wrote: "It would not be for Judeans only, but for 'the inhabitants of many cities' (v. 20)," which he nevertheless counted as suitable to the context of Zechariah addressing the Exiles; on this track, see also Stuhlmueller, *Building with Hope*, 111. Petersen (*Haggai and Zechariah 1–8*, 316–19) considered the phrasing of v. 20 to indicate the reversal of the earlier judgment upon the city (318). See also Petersen's detailed comparison of v. 23 to the previous verses (319–20).

41. Zech 8:21–22, 23 are either implicit or genuinely different from Isa 60:1–3 and 66:18–24, which bring the two contexts together—the international approach to Jerusalem (60:1–3) and the return of sons and daughters (v. 4)—in co-operative reconstruction of the city (vv. 5–22).

Zechariah demonstrates that what has been treated as a "universalistic" outlook does not necessarily conflict with the "localization" of the deity and the people in a specific national arena. It seems that inclusivity within Judean groups may differ from inclusivity without, that is, inclusivity that is open to including non-Judahites. Zechariah demonstrates that a prophet with an exclusivist view of internal Judean relationships may prophesy an inclusive eschatological future of universal recognition of God and His powers.[42]

Second, the strategy of change in group identity here remains that of *incorporation* (A + B = A); that is, these multitudes are expected to assimilate to "the people," to this Judean community in Jerusalem which insists on their own exclusivity and superiority. Hence, whether this eschatological vision indeed stems from Zechariah son of Iddo or from his followers, this inclusive (incorporative) perspective does not rule out the possibility that the prophet holds a more exclusive view when it comes to the formation of group identity within his own contemporary present.

To summarize Zechariah's argumentation on group identity issues: it is important to recognize that Zechariah knows the very simple dichotomy of Babylonian Exiles/Repatriates vs. Judah as an empty land, and that through this dichotomy he sets out very clear exclusionary arguments. He considers the Judean community of Repatriates to be "the (only) Remnant of this people," and completely ignores the possibility that any others might have existed in the land. Hence, there is no reason to conclude that the absence of explicit references to the internal Judean conflicts (in Yehud) should be understood as a counter-argument to the polemically charged stance of Ezra–Nehemiah. Evidence shows the contrary: Zechariah is yet another voice of the Repatriate community, which was united in its exclusive tendencies, even if divided in terms of specific strategies of argumentation.[43]

---

42. See the discussion on Deutero-Isaiah, pp. 121–25, below. In his reading of Zechariah in its final form, Edgar W. Conrad (*Zechariah* [Sheffield: Sheffield Academic, 1997], 20–22), argued that Zechariah's oracles are increasingly localized in the surrounding areas of Jerusalem and Judah. This tendency gradually increases from Zech 1–8 to chs. 9–11, and 12–14. He furthermore pointed out the localized-spatial perspectives in Zechariah and the emphasis on the "return" of God and the scattered people to dwell in Jerusalem (p. 21).

43. Contra Bedford, *Temple Restoration*, 264–68. 2 Chr 36:20–21 utilized a similar strategy, explicitly drawing on Jeremiah's prophecies of judgment, which projected total annihilation within the Land for seventy years (see, for instance, Jer 25:11).

Moreover, while at face value these differences in strategy reveal a major distinction between the historiographical perspective of Ezra–Nehemiah and the prophetic perspective of Zechariah, it is important to notice that both these Repatriate ideologies, rooted in and shaped by the experience of the Babylonian exile, share the same basic exclusionary tendency. The Repatriate community of the Persian period styles itself as the one and only people of Judah, the people of God, confronting upon return either an empty land or foreign peoples. Independently of each other, these two perspectives convey a complete disregard for any other Judean/Israelite-Yahwistic communities, in Yehud or elsewhere.

These observations concerning Zechariah's use of the "empty land" metaphor as the clearly exclusivist argumentative strategy of a Repatriate prophet raises even more forcefully the need to address the book of Haggai, to which we now turn.

2. *Haggai*

Haggai the prophet—who lacks patronymic or other biographical information, whose prophecies are reported on the third person, and cover but four months within 520 B.C.E. (Hag 1:1; 1:15–2:1, 10, 20)—intrigues scholars as to both his personal background and his orientation on issues of group identity.[44] As with Zechariah, three possibilities have been proposed: (1) Haggai was from the Repatriate community; (2) he represents the voice of Those Who Remained; and/or (3) the prophet is said to have an inclusivist perspective on group-identity, as he welcomes those from both Yahwistic groups to a reconsolidation of Judeans in Yehud.

These possibilities, which are still controversial among scholars of Haggai, seem to have arisen in reaction to Johann W. Rothstein's short but influential monograph of 1908: *Juden und Samaritaner*.[45] Rothstein

---

44. Haggai's biographical background is unknown, due to the lack of any genealogical information in the postscript to the book. Petersen (*Haggai and Zechariah 1–8*, 18–19) aptly pointed out that this exceptional gap in knowledge, in an era that is considered highly interested in genealogy, has brought scholars to question the prophet's identity. David Winton Thomas ("Haggai," *IB* 6:1037–39) concluded: "The fact is that nothing at all is known about the prophet's personality" and about the editor(s) of what seems to be a report on Haggai's prophecy. Coggins (*Haggai, Zechariah, Malachi*, 44) simply said that there is not enough information to determine whether or not Haggai was one of the Exiles.

45. Johann W. Rothstein, *Juden und Samaritaner. Die grundlegende Scheidung von Judentum und Heidentum: Eine kritische Studie zum Buche Haggai und zur jüdischen Geschichte im ersten nachexilischen Jahrhundert* (BZAW 3; Leipzig:

placed Hag 2:10–19 at the heart of his argument; he read it as reflecting upon (and contemporary with) the conflict of Ezra 4:1–5, the so-called struggle between the Repatriates and the Samaritans. In such a framework, Haggai and Zechariah (according to Ezra 5:1–2) fit well into the historical reconstruction of the events which are otherwise recorded only in Ezra–Nehemiah. Haggai's admonition and denigration of העם הזה הגוי הזה ("this people, this nation," Hag 2:14) as טמא הוא ("defiled") identifies the prophet as an authoritative advocate of the extreme exclusivist position otherwise known from Ezra 1–6.[46] Haggai is therefore said to have played an important role in rejecting the Samarians' request to join the Repatriates in rebuilding the House of God. The two prophets, and particularly Haggai, take a very clear stand in the struggle with the Samarians, themselves identified as an amalgam of Exiles of various nationalities, settled by the Assyrians upon the ruins of Northern Israel (2 Kgs 17:24–41).[47] Basing himself on Rothstein, Ernst Sellin considered Haggai's arguments to represent "the actual [original] birthday of postexilic Judaism" ("die eigentliche Geburtsstunde des nachexilischen Judentums").[48] Being at the heart of the debate, Hag 2:10–19 deserves special attention.

a. *"This People" (Haggai 2:10–19): Between Exclusive and Inclusive Perspectives*
Haggai 2:10–19 offers several challenges; the leading ones are the identity of העם הזה הגוי הזה in v. 14 and the relationship between vv. 10–14 and 15–19, which have led scholars to distinguish between them.[49]

Hinrichs, 1908). For Rothstein's important influence on Haggai studies and for a criticism of his views, see Rüdiger Pfeil, "When Is a *Goy* a 'Goy'? The Interpretation of Haggai 2:10–19," in *A Tribute to Gleason Archer* (ed. W. C. Kaiser and R. F. Youngblood; Chicago: Moody, 1986), 261–78.

46. Rothstein (*Juden und Samaritaner*, 5–40) had suggested a historical reconstruction of the circumstances the Judean/Jewish–Samarian conflict, in which Haggai fits well, validating the break in rebuilding the Temple due to the pressures of the people of the land (Ezra 4:1, 4, 24). Following Haggai and Zechariah's encouragement, the worship activity resumes, even in the face of new opponents (Ezra 5:3, 12).

47. See the discussion on the amalgamated references to the "others" above, pp. 41–45.

48. Ernst Sellin, *Zwölfprophetenbuch* (KAT 12; Leipzig: Deichert, 1922), 462–65, quotation from p. 463; and see Rothstein, *Juden und Samaritaner*, 76, 82.

49. Rothstein (*Juden und Samaritaner*, 5–40 and 53–73) discussed each passage separately, and suggested that 2:15–19 should follow the date superscription in 1:15a; see Sellin, *Zwölfprophetenbuch*, 454–59. But note Redditt's criticism of this proposal (*Haggai, Zechariah, Malachi*, 25–26).

The first subunit, vv. 10–14, is crafted as a dialogue with the priests, which focuses on issues of holiness and defilement within the cultic arena. Haggai evokes Priestly conceptions of sancta contiguity (which presumably transfers holiness; see Lev 5:1–4; 6:7–11, 17–20; 7:20–21) and corpse contamination (which clearly transfers defilement; Num 19:11–22).[50] He thus frames the two rhetorical questions, היקדש and היטמא, with respect to these widely accepted concepts (Hag 2:12, 13).[51] These two ritual/legal questions then serve the prophet as a platform for his prophetic proclamation concerning the people in v. 14:

> ויען חגי ויאמר כן העם הזה וכן הגוי הזה לפני נאם יהוה
> וכן כל מעשה ידיהם ואשר יקריבו שם טמא הוא

> Thereupon Haggai said: That is how this people and that is how this nation looks to Me—declares the LORD—and so, too, the work of their hands: Whatever they offer there is defiled.

Verse 14 is built in two pairs: this people and this nation, followed by their works, specified as their sacrifices.[52] Stylistically, this verse continues the Priestly phraseology in stating the final verdict: טמא הוא.[53] Setting these four components in a list, however, allows two different

---

50. טמא נפש (Hag 2:13; or טמא לנפש, Lev 21:1–5; 22:4–7; Num 5:2; 6:6–13; 9:6, 7, 10; see Redditt, *Haggai, Zechariah, and Malachi*, 27) is the most severe defilement caused by the human body. The allusion to Num 19:11–22 is particularly interesting, since Haggai employs this severe category of defilement related by the Priestly law to the defilement of YHWH's Temple (see Num 19:13, 20). See Jacob Milgrom (*Leviticus 1–16* [AB 3; New York: Doubleday, 2004], 449–55) for Haggai's limitation of the Priestly conception of holiness referred to as "sancta contagion."

51. While the principles are certainly clear, Hag 2:12 does suggest an otherwise unknown case in Priestly sources, as the sacred meat is held by a "man" (not specifically a priest) and the wrapping cloth touches other foods that seem not to belong in a sacred place (see הנזיד, which besides this occurrence does not appear in cultic context). See Petersen, *Haggai and Zechariah 1–8*, 76–78; Kessler (*Haggai*, 204) argued that the priests answer according to Lev 6:20.

52. This balanced structure may serve as an additional indication of the secondary nature of the addition in the LXX version of v. 14. See Tzipora Talshir, *Zechariah 1–8* (Olam HaTanakh; Tel Aviv: Davidson–Iti, 1994 [in Hebrew]), 162.

53. טמא הוא is a well-documented Priestly formula. It occurs in reference to pure and defiled animals (in the singular: Lev 11:4, 5, 7, 38; in the plural: Lev 11:8, 26, 27, 28, 41); this is the only context where this formula appears in Deuteronomy (Deut 14:8, 10, 19, and v. 7 in the plural). It is also used in the context of human defilements of scaly afflictions (leprosy, Lev 13:11, 15, etc.; and note the use of the opposite formula, טהור הוא, in 13:11 and 13); the defilement of a house (14:44); the male discharge (Lev 15:2); and defilement by contact with the dead (Num 19:20). Hag 2:14 is the only other occurrence of this formula in the Hebrew Bible.

understandings of who is to be considered defiled. According to the first, the four components are equivalent elements in a list, that is, the people and their products are perceived as equally defiled.[54] According to the second, the verse is built in the form of the elevated triad pattern of 3+1, and טמא הוא thus relates only to the last component, that is, their sacrifices.[55] Allowing these two ways of reading may be intentional. Haggai gives extra force to his analogy drawn from defilement caused by transferring contamination from their sacrifices backwards, to the entire deeds of their hands, and even more so to that denigrated people. And furthermore, to whom does the prophet refer—Judeans or non-Judeans, that is, Samarians?

As has long been noted, scholars are divided on this question. Rothstein suggested that a foreign people, the Samarians, were the denigrated subject of this speech. He found it inadmissible that Haggai would have referred to his Judean contemporaries as a defiled people—especially given the context of his other prophecies, in which he constantly encourages them to reconstruct the Temple (1:1–11; 2:4–5), repeats the message of אני אתכם ("I am with you," 1:12–14; 2:4–5), and promises blessing (2:19). Moreover, Rothstein could not accept Haggai's harsh admonition, seemingly delivered after the people had followed the prophet's call and indeed participated in the reconstruction project (2:1–5).[56] He thus interpreted העם הזה—the addressees of the admonition in 2:14—as the עם הארץ of Ezra 4:4.[57]

The Samarian option has gained support, and has even been elaborated.[58] Pursuing this interpretation of העם הזה / הגוי הזה as non-Judeans, but rejecting the Samarian option, Smith-Christopher focused on the

---

54. So Kessler, *Haggai*, 206.

55. This last possibility is adopted by Petersen, *Haggai and Zechariah 1–8*, 83–85. Redditt (*Haggai, Zechariah, Malachi*, 27) found it difficult to accept either possibility; he suggested that Haggai considered the Temple defiled (not the altar and the sacrifices that were already in practice by then, according to Ezra 3:1–5). Redditt, in addition, aptly refuted Ackroyd's suggestion (*Exile and Restoration*, 168–69) that the people are considered defiled for moral or social sins.

56. Rothstein, *Juden und Samaritaner*, 8.

57. See Sellin, *Zwölfprophetenbuch*, 464.

58. Winton Thomas ("Haggai," *IB* 6:1039) placed Haggai at "the beginning of that rigid exclusiveness which was to become so essential a characteristic of the postexilic community in Judah"; and see his discussion of Hag 2:10–14 (pp. 1046, 1047). He suggested that political conflict is the impetus to the earlier phases of this struggle towards exclusivity, as expressed in Haggai (p. 1039); this should be distinguished from the religious background of the later struggle depicted in Ezra–Nehemiah.

prophet's emphasis on impurity, and argued that Haggai utilizes notions of purity and pollution to set the boundaries of group identity (integrity). Accordingly, Hag 2:14 revives the controversy over defilement caused by contact with the impure peoples of the land (evoking Lev 18:24–30; 20:22–24).[59] Smith-Christopher added that even if "this people/this nation" in Hag 2:10–14 does refer to "the community of Jews," Haggai still deals here with the problem of (illegitimate) contact with the "impure people in the land." Thus, Smith-Christopher accepted the notion of a connection between the language of Haggai and Ezra 4, as he also mentioned references to Ezekiel and Jeremiah.[60]

Another scholarly path considers Haggai's exhortation to be addressed to his Judean audience. Klaus Koch's major criticism of Rothstein was of the latter's atomistic reading of vv. 10–14 as distinct from vv. 15–19.[61] This reading, indeed, leaves the proclamation of טמא הוא as a final verdict hanging without any discernible context, which intensifies the contradiction between the messages of denigration in vv. 10–14 and the positive and hopeful connotations of vv. 15–19. In contrast, Koch recognized a unifying genre of salvation prophecies that undergirds the structure of the book of Haggai. This takes the form of a tripartite pattern that repeats in 1:2–8; 2:1–7, and 2:10–19. In each case, the prophet first describes the current problematic situation, then suggests an impetus for change, and concludes with a prediction of salvation.[62] Hence, vv. 10–14, with their harsh admonition against the people, may be seen as well-integrated into Haggai's message. The first part of the prophecy (vv. 10–14) describes the current situation, using the metaphorical framework of cultic purity and impurity; the second suggests a turning point between past and future (ועתה, vv. 15–17); the third predicts the improvement of the situation (vv. 18–19). Koch considered Haggai's entire audience as "impure, returnees as well as remainees, because they have no undamaged holy place where purification is possible."[63] But this will change: impurity will come to an end when the foundation stone for the Temple is laid. Koch closed his study by concluding that Haggai advocates an integrative approach that includes all the inhabitants of the land.

---

59. Smith-Christopher, *Religion of the Landless*, 183–88, and see his references there to Coggins, *Samaritans and Jews*, 46–54.

60. Smith-Christopher (ibid., 187, and the discussion on pp. 186–88), where he said explicitly that Haggai "refers to *some* kind of group conflict" (188).

61. Klaus Koch, "Haggais unreines Volk," *ZAW* 79 (1967): 52–66.

62. Koch (ibid., 56–60) suggested this three-part structure, although he considered the authentic oral prophecies to be restricted to 1:2–8; 2:1–7, 10–19.

63. Ibid., 63.

Herbert W. May questioned Rothstein's basic understanding of the relationship between Haggai and his audience, the people. According to May it is no problem to understand that "the community needed strong prodding several times."[64] May distinguished Haggai and Zechariah from Ezra–Nehemiah, and pointed out the fact that in his first prophecy (Hag 1:1–11), Haggai does *not* hold the Samarians responsible for the delay in reconstructing the Temple. The opposite is true, "this people" of the earlier prophecy (1:2) is the same as addressed in 2:14, it is the Judean community.[65] Furthermore, May emphasized that each of the two phrases, העם הזה and הגוי הזה, "may carry overtones of reproach" within the same prophetic voice; he gave several pertinent examples from Jeremiah (see, for instance, העם הזה in Jer 6:19–21; 14:10, 11; and הגוי הזה in Jer 5:29; 7:28; and Judg 2:20).[66] גוי and עם also occur as a pair in reference to the people of Israel (e.g. 2 Sam 7:23; Isa 1:4; 10:6; Ps 33:12; and note עמך הגוי הזה, Exod 33:13). May followed this lexical discussion by placing the concept of holiness in Hag 2:10–14 on a trajectory in relation to the rest of the biblical writings. He understood the prophetic passage as contemporary with the Holiness Code (Lev 19:2; 20:7, 26) and Deutero-Isaiah (63:17; 64:5); the latter, like Haggai, draws an analogy from the ritual sphere to the people. May discerned a significant distinction, however, between Haggai and Deutero-Isaiah. He argued that Haggai's fury at the people was not inflamed by any specific ritual activity, but by the condition of the ruined Temple, which for Haggai symbolizes the people's neglect of God and their dishonor of Him.

May thus located the admonition of vv. 10–14 in the context of vv. 10–19 as one element in Haggai's general conception of the Temple and its acute need for reconstruction (1:1–11; 2:1–9), and within the framework of the prophet's eschatological hope for the people under the

---

64.   Herbert G. May, "'This People' and 'This Nation' in Haggai," *VT* 18 (1968): 190–97 (190).

65.   Ibid., 192. In his earlier study ("Studies in the Book of Haggai," *JJS* 3 [1952]: 1–13, especially 5–6), Ackroyd suggested that the rejection of the Samarians may be traced to the compiler of the book of Haggai, and not to the prophet himself. Nevertheless, he commented that "this people" in Hag 1 and 2, as well as the designation עם הארץ in 2:4, refer to the same community; all, in Ackroyd's understanding, denote "the local community, with no clear division indicated between the returned exiles and the survivors in Judah of the exilic period." Yet Ackroyd went on to suggest that by the time of the compiler of the book of Haggai, הגוי הזה had become a term used to refer to the Samarians, and that this text thus had later relevance in the Chronicler's controversy with the Samarians (ibid., 6).

66.   May, "'This People,'" 193.

leadership of Zerubbabel.[67] May understood the people's defilement as a consequence of "their failure to honor Yahweh with proper attention to his house; they had become, as it were, unclean."[68]

As we proceed to the second sub-unit, vv. 15–19, its differences from vv. 10–14 in nature, style, rhetoric structure, and concepts are readily apparent. I find persuasive, however, the exegetical line that sees Hag 2:10–19 as a single prophetic unit, addressed to the prophet's Judean (Repatriate) audience.[69] This second component addresses the people in the second person and lacks Priestly vocabulary and concepts; it is closer to Hag 1:1–11 in its evocation of the connections between agricultural productivity and the reconstruction of the Temple.[70] In syntactical structure, vv. 15–19 form two parallel compound sentences (vv. 15–17 and 18–19); each sentence opens with three time clauses preceding the indicative clause:

ועתה שימו נא לבבכם
מן היום הזה ומעלה
מטרם שום אבן אל אבן בהיכל יהוה
מהיותם בא אל ערמת עשרים והיתה עשרה בא אל היקב לחשף חמשים פורה
והיתה עשרים
<u>הכיתי אתכם</u> בשדפון ובירקון ובברד את כל מעשה ידיכם ואין אתכם אלי
נאם יהוה

And now take thought,
from this day forward:
as long as no stone had been laid on another in the House of the LORD,
if one came to a heap of twenty measures, it would yield only ten; and if one came to a wine vat to skim off fifty measures, the press would yield only twenty.
<u>I struck you</u>—all the works of your hands—with blight and mildew and hail, but you did not return to Me—declares the LORD. (vv. 15–17)

---

67. Ibid., 194–95.

68. May (ibid., 195–97, especially 196) referred also to Haggai's nationalistic perspectives, which he found to be embedded in the prophet's eschatology and thus to show a universalistic position. This line of offending God's honor is brought already by Qimhi to Hag 2:14.

69. This view is gaining increasing support in the commentaries; see Kessler, *Haggai*, 205, 211–18, especially 213–15, and references there.

70. Wilhelm Rudolph (*Haggai, Sacharja 1–8, Sacharja 9–14, Maleachi* [KAT, 13/4; Gütersloh: Mohn, 1976], 46–47) argued for a middle path, when he summarized the message of these verses as: "keine fremde Hilfe! Jahwes segen ist da" (46). Rudolph considered vv. 10–14 to refer to the Samarians, although vv. 15–19 belong to the same prophetic unit. In these two sub-units, Haggai declines outside assistance in the reconstruction, favoring divine help and blessings.

שימו נא לבבכם
מן היום הזה ומעלה
מיום עשרים וארבעה לתשיעי
למן היום אשר יסד היכל יהוה
שימו לבבכם
העוד הזרע במגורה ועד הגפן והתאנה והרמון ועץ הזית
לא נשא
מן היום הזה אַבָרֵךְ

Take note, **from this day** forward—
from the twenty-fourth day of the ninth month,
from the day when the foundation was laid for the LORD's Temple—
take note
while the seed is still in the granary, and the vine, fig tree, pomegranate,
and olive tree have not yet borne fruit.
for from this day on I will send blessings. (vv. 18–19)

This well-structured subunit focuses attention on previous lack of agriculture productivity, and promises a transformation to blessing as of the very day that the foundation of the Temple is laid. This theme is emphasized by two components that appear in the two indicative sentences: מעשה ידיכם (v. 17) and אברך (v. 19). When brought together, מעשה ידים and ברך evoke a well-known Deuteronomic construction (see Deut 2:7; 14:19; 16:15).

This reliance on Deuteronomic phraseology and thus on the Deuteronomic conception of the land is indeed of major importance to the message of Haggai. The mention of agricultural distress serves in Hag 1:1–11 as a clear testimony that the "cursed era" of destruction and annihilation has not yet ended (cf. Deut 29:22–30:1).[71] Working with the combined "curse-lists" of the Deuteronomic and Holiness Codes, Haggai constructs a new connection between the land's productivity and the Temple. The pentateuchal traditions emphasize the God–people covenant relationship as that which determines the fate of the people in the land allocated to them by God; Haggai transforms this understanding by setting the Temple at the heart of the covenant relationship. Rebuilding the Temple becomes the clear sign of the people's renewed commitment to obedience to God; thus it initiates the divine blessing for the people's agricultural products.

---

71. This proclamation is constructed via the following allusions: Hag 1:6, זרעתם הרבה והבא מעט, evokes Deut 28:38–40; אכול ואין לשבעה seems to rely on Lev 26:5, 26; Hag 1:10–11 evokes/echoes Deut 28:23 and Lev 26:19. יגיע כפים in Hag 1:11 is of interest. Contra Kessler (*Haggai*, 154) who referred to Deut 28:20 (בכל משלח ידך), I would prefer the references to יגיעך in Deut 28:33; and see Ps 128:2; Isa 55:2.

Haggai 2:10–19 works along these same lines, adding a significant new element to the conceptual complex of God–people–Temple (and land). The transition from vv. 10–14 to 15–19 has been recognized as abrupt, and indeed seems to rely on the thin connecting bridge of the repeated phrase, מעשה ידים (vv. 14, 17).

Ibn Ezra early considered vv. 10–14 as a parable for the following verses (vv. 15–19),[72] and critical scholars have suggested that this dialogue is "a prophetic symbolic action" (thus Kessler, among others).[73] Formally, Haggai opens his prophecies in 1:1–11; 2:1–9; 2:10–19 with an introductory unit that catches the audience's attention. The first prophecy begins with a provocative quotation and refutation (1:2–4); the second with a description of the people's dismayed reaction to the new Temple (2:2–3); and similarly the third, in 2:10–19, with this dialogue between the prophet and the priests over questions of purity and defilement.[74] In all three, ועתה marks the turning point from this opening to the proclamation of the prophecy, which promises imminent deliverance, or at least improvement (1:5; 2:4, 15).[75]

Another formal device that connects vv. 10–14 and 15–19 is the repetition of the phrase מעשה ידיהם/כם. But it is remarkable that this very phrase functions differently in the two subunits. In the first, it connects to concepts of defilement and to Priestly traditions, whereas in the second, it connects to blessings and curses (i.e. restoration and annihilation), activating Deuteronomic traditions.[76] It seems that the overall message of Hag 2:10–19 bridges these two arenas. Haggai had already advanced the idea, in 1:1–11, that transformation in the people's economic situation is possible only when their covenant relationship with

---

72. See Ibn Ezra's comment on the phrase ואשר יקריבו in Hag 2:14: וזה היה דרך משל דרך נתן אל דוד שתפסו בדבריו ואמר לו אתה האיש ויען גם נכון הוא להיות המשל בעבור שהם בונים בתים לשבתם ובית השם חרב על כן אחריו ("and this was a parable, parallel to the way Nathan spoke to David and caught him with his words and then said to him 'you are the man,' and he responded; and this parable is also true since they are building houses for themselves to settle in, while the house of God is still ruined").

73. Kessler (*Haggai*, 213, 217, 273) added that in context, vv. 10–14 may have formed part of a ceremony, and that vv. 15–19 might serve as the divine declaration of the Temple's purification that is to lead to the period of blessing.

74. Koch, "Haggais unreines Volk," 56–60; and see above, p. 65 n. 62.

75. Ibid., 57–60; Talshir, *Haggai*, 162; Kessler, *Haggai*, 206.

76. Compare to Rex Mason ("Prophets of the Restoration," in *Israel's Prophetic Tradition: Essays in Honour of Peter R. Ackroyd* [ed. R. J. Coggins, A. Phillips, and M. A. Knibb; Cambridge: Cambridge University Press, 1982], 137–54, see especially 144) who considered מעשה ידיהם to refer to the Temple. For criticism of that view, see Petersen, *Haggai and Zechariah 1–8*, 82–83, and Kessler, *Haggai*, 212–13.

God is reestablished; that is, when real action is taken to rebuild God's residence. The innovative component added in 2:10–19 concerns the reference to the impurity of מעשה ידיהם. The things they have already brought in sacrifice are considered defiled, and this sacrificial impurity affects the status of the people themselves.[77] Furthermore, by alluding to Priestly ideas of defilement in vv. 10–14, Haggai not only focuses attention on the status of the people and their products, but also evokes the conception that impurity threatens the very presence of God in the land, in the Temple.[78] This thematic dimension concerning impurity and the presence of God, which functions only in the background, seems to be the conceptual bridge between the two very different segments of this prophetic unit.[79]

While this literary analysis largely refutes Rothstein's reading of Hag 2:10–19, his perspective, nevertheless, has had a great influence on Sellin, and through him on many other Haggai (and Persian period) scholars over the twentieth and early twenty-first centuries.[80] This line of exegesis considers Haggai to be a Repatriate with extreme views.[81]

---

77.   Thus Kessler (*Haggai*, 215) accentuated the broad conception of the people's impurity; see his thorough discussion of this unit on pp. 197–218 (especially 204–6, 210–16), where he suggested several options for understanding this passage as part of the ceremonies around laying the cornerstone of the new Temple (217–18).

78.   While Kessler rightly pointed out the mutual interest in defilement that connects Haggai to Ezekiel, and to what Kessler termed "the *golah* during the exile" (*Haggai*, 215–16), he nevertheless seemed *not* to connect that shared interest to a shared (Babylonian and Repatriate) social context.

79.   Compare to Kessler (ibid., 212), who rejected the idea that Hag 2:10–19 raises the issue of reconstruction of the Temple a second time (following 1:12–14). I concur with Kessler (211–12) that the scholarly path that understood ritual purity to be only a metaphor for ethical integrity is not at stake. I would, however, distinguish this from the question of the covenant relationship, which I do think is constantly at the background. Here in the present passage, the stakes are raised by the issue of impurity and the divine presence.

80.   See Pfeil's very helpful discussion, "When Is a *Goy* a 'Goy'?," 269–71.

81.   Sellin, *Haggai*, 464. Haggai's evocation of Priestly concerns has also caused some scholars to count Haggai and Zechariah with Ezekiel among hierocratic circles, see Plöger, *Theocracy and Eschatology*, 106–17; Odil H. Steck, "Das Problem theologischer Stroemungen in nachexilischer Zeit," *EvT* 28 (1968): 445–58; Hanson, *The Dawn of Apocalyptic*, 209–79. This perception of distinct agendas has led Tim Unger ("Noch einmal: Haggais unreines Volk," *ZAW* 103 [1991]: 210–25) to maintain the division between vv. 10–14 and 15–19, taking the former to be a non-Haggaian prophecy. He argued that in its "theocratic" and separatist notions, vv. 10–14 belong with the presumed Chronistic redaction of Haggai (following Wim A. M. Beuken, *Haggai–Sacharja 1–8* [SSN 10; Assen: Van Gorcum, 1967], 64–77), whereas Haggai remains the "eschatological"-preaching prophet who refers

But, just as fierce has been the counter-reaction to Rothstein, a reaction that has caused scholars not only to distance Haggai from this struggle altogether, but has even opened the way to the opposite perspective, namely, that Haggai was an advocate of an inclusive community, and came from among the Non-exiled Judeans.

This position, more appealing to so many scholars, may be found already in Adam C. Welch's discussion in his *Post-Exilic Judaism*. Welch suggested that Haggai was active among the peasant community of Non-exiled Judeans (they are העם הזה, "the remnant Judeans"),[82] and that he addresses the returned Exiles under Zerubbabel and Joshua with new hope, since these recent Returnees came fired with the zeal of restoration.[83] Koch raised this integrative option in his own criticism of Rothstein;[84] and while Petersen said that "Haggai's own life history remains enigmatic," he, nevertheless, concurred that Haggai addressed both Repatriates and Non-exiled Judeans.[85]

Along these same lines, in an influential study of "People and Land in the Restoration Period," Sara Japhet opened her discussion of Haggai and Zechariah by saying that the two prophets "do not discuss the problem of identity… Yet their positions on several aspects of the issue can be learned from their prophecies."[86] Adducing what may be learned from the two short collections, Japhet differentiated Haggai from Zechariah, pointing out that the former makes no mention of any ethnic labels (no Israel; and Judah occurs only in Zerubbabel's title, Hag 1:1, 14; 2:2, 21); no mention of the geographic arena (no Jerusalem, Zion, Babylon, etc.); and when the prophet does refer to the people, he designates them by very general titles: העם (as in Hag 1:2) or שארית העם (in 1:12, 13; 2:2). This combination of factors caused Japhet to question whether the prophet is addressing the Repatriates or Those Who Remained.[87] This question is sharpened, on the one hand, by the bringing

---

to the people's future salvation in the most inclusivistic way. This entire direction seems to be entangled with Christian presuppositions that clearly move beyond the Hebrew Bible text.

82. Adam C. Welch, *Post-Exilic Judaism* (Edinburgh: Blackwood, 1935), 111.

83. Ibid., 108–13. Welch perceived Zechariah as in a similar position, and further thought (pp. 113–25) that Malachi was active in that same early Persian period (prior to the restoration of the Temple), though in the northern region of Israel, addressing the Non-exiled population in their relations with the Samarians.

84. Koch, "Haggais unreines Volk," 61–66.

85. Petersen, *Haggai and Zechariah 1–8*, 18–19, and see pp. 55–60.

86. Japhet, "People and Land," 109.

87. Ibid., 109. In n. 33 (p. 121) Japhet explained her presumption that the העם הנשאר were those who remained. Yet her apt reference to Ezra 3:12 proves the

together of הנשאר העם, the leaders Zerubbabel and Joshua, and עם הארץ, in one prophetic context, Hag 2:3–4, and on the other hand, by the lack of any explicit mention of exile, the Repatriates as a community, or the ingathering of the dispersed back into the land. Japhet, therefore, concluded:[88]

> Haggai's prophecies focus on Judah, where he is speaking to the "people of the land" regarding two issues: the rebuilding of the Temple and the approach of the eschatological events connected with it... We may conclude that Haggai does not exclude the returned exiles, nor does he discriminate against them in any way; he is focused on the people of Judah and the returned exiles are for him an integral part of the community, "the people of the land" who are in Judah. Is this relation true also for the people of the north? To this question we are left without an answer.

Scholars have subsequently built on Japhet's argument, noting in addition Haggai's focus on the rural agricultural aspects of Restoration. In conjunction with his designation of the people as כל עם הארץ (in 2:4), these factors appeared to strengthen the argument that Haggai came from the community of Those Who Remained, the Judeans who had never experienced exile.[89] It is hard to judge from Haggai's exhortation in 1:1–11, however, that rural life is his primary social context. Attention to agricultural matters may easily be noted, for instance, in the prophecies of Isaiah son of Amoz (Isa 5; 8, etc.), who is considered to be a resident of the city of Jerusalem; it may also be seen in Ezekiel's prophecies, spoken on Babylonian soil (e.g. Ezek 34 and 36). This imagery, therefore, cannot serve as a valid argument for Haggai's social background.

Furthermore, Japhet's valuable observations lent support to the scholarly perspective that took Haggai to propound a view of the newly restored community in Yehud that included both Non-exiled Judeans and Repatriates.[90] Kessler noted a clear ideological split among the *golah*

opposite. See the discussion of the identity of the Remnant, pp. 82–92, below. Compare to Kessler ("Persia's Loyal Yahwists," 108), who considered the Remnant to consist of the *golah*-returnees.

88. Japhet, "People and Land," 110.

89. Beuken, *Haggai–Sacharja 1–8*, 216–22; as also Hans W. Wolff, *Haggai: A Commentary* (trans. M. Kohl; Minneapolis: Augsburg, 1988), 16–17.

90. See Bedford (*Temple Restoration*, 37, 270–99) who argued that both Haggai and Zechariah (chs. 1–8) treated the reconstruction of the Temple as "a means of social integration...temple rebuilding afforded a way of reintegrating the two communities by means of a return to a state of normality under the sovereign rule of Yahweh and his chosen leaders" (37). Bedford (pp. 279–83) discussed Hag 2:10–14, focusing on v. 14, only to reject the various suggestions conflict; he did not pay attention to these verses' place in their context.

returnees' "Charter Group" community(/ies). He pointed out that already in the early Persian period this powerful Charter Group was divided over "boundaries of membership." This division is represented in its literary production: the historiography championed exclusion, whereas the prophetic literature, and Haggai in particular, demonstrated inclusive tendencies.[91] Thus observed Kessler:[92]

> [T]he *absence of conflict* evidenced in Haggai is highly striking. Simply put, the book contains *no "other"*—that is to say, *no denigrated population distinct from "true Israel"*… The book deliberately obscures whatever divisions may have existed and presents a stylized and schematic portrait of the community as *acting in concert* in obedience to the word of Yahweh through the prophet Haggai.

The claim that the book of Haggai presents *"no 'other'"* led Kessler to the conclusion that Haggai was a non-Repatriate, that is, that he was from Those Who Remained, or at the very least did not return with Zerubbabel.[93] In addition, he stated that Haggai had an inclusive view of "all Israel":[94]

> In the early period, the book of Haggai is inclusivistic in orientation, calling all without distinction to participate in the rebuilding project (2:1–5). The entire community, described as a remnant, is presented as acting in concert, in obedience to the prophet's words (1:12–15).

I would like to challenge this view of Haggai. Indeed, there is scant but sufficient evidence to validate the assumption that Haggai, like Zechariah, was of Repatriate stock (whether they returned with Zerubbabel and Joshua, the group whose story is related in Ezra 5:1; 6:14, or with different groups), and that they both addressed the community of the Repatriates from the Babylonian captivity in Yehud—and only this group (Hag 1:1, 12–15; 2:2).[95]

---

91. Kessler, "Persia's Loyal Yahwists," 109–10.

92. Kessler, *Haggai*, 263–64; and see the thorough presentation of the scholarly viewpoints on Haggai, pp. 1–30.

93. For a similar suggestion, see also Bedford, *Temple Restoration*, 273.

94. Kessler, "Persia's Loyal Yahwists," 109; similarly, idem, *Haggai*, 275–79. See also Byron G. Curtis (*Up the Steep and Stony Road: The Book of Zechariah in Social Location Trajectory Analysis* [SBL Academia Biblica 25; Leiden: Brill, 2006], 87): "Both *golah* and non-*golah* Jews are included by it, and there is yet no indication of community disruption between the two groups at this time. Haggai addresses all."

95. I thus follow Ackroyd (*Exile and Restoration*, 148–49), who counted both prophets among the Repatriates. See also Rex Mason, "The Purpose of the 'Editorial Framework' of the Book of Haggai," *VT* 27 (1977): 413–21, and idem, "Prophets of

Like Zechariah, Haggai's purported ignorance of, or his failure to mention, any "others," should not be taken as an indication of inclusivity. Rather, it seems to point to the same conception of "invisibility" utilized by the notion of the empty land. Haggai uses a consciously (or perhaps even unconsciously) exclusionary strategy—subtle in comparison to Zechariah, but still there.

b. *Haggai's Implicit Arguments of Exclusivity*
While on the surface Haggai remains an enigma in terms of the question of group-identity, at a deeper level the three arguments of exclusivity— *continuity*, *entirety*, and *annexation* of diverse religious and national traditions—shape the rhetorical message of this short prophetic collection.[96]

(1) *Arguments of continuity and entirety.* Three arenas for rhetorical strategies of continuity may be observed in Haggai: communal designations; the attitude towards Zerubbabel (Hag 2:20–23), which opens the door to Haggai's clear stance of discontinuity vis-à-vis Jeremiah; and Haggai's conception of his prophetic role.

As pointed out, the lack of national designations for Israel (with Judah occurring only in Zerubbabel's title as "the *pehah* of Judah," 1:1, 14; 2:2, 21) constitutes an obvious difference from Zechariah, and is indeed puzzling. But, when it comes to other types of self-designations, Haggai does use titles that draw lines of continuity to the national recollection of the people and even refer to the prophet's audience as an entire people: הגוי הזה ("these people," Hag 2:14), העם הזה ("this people," 1:2; 2:14), וכל שארית העם ("all the rest/Remnant of the people," 1:12, 14; 2:2); similarly, the phrase מי בכם הנשאר ("who is there left among you," 2:3) is glossed as כל עם הארץ ("all you the people of the land," 2:4). Before delving into the significance of these designations, I would list one by one the prophet's other strategies of *continuity*, *entirety*, and *annexation*.

---

the Restoration," 142. Mason argued that Haggai addresses "the community of returned exiles," and thus he found that the editorial framework in Haggai further accentuates the identification of the returned community and its leadership as the remnant. For other scholars who considered Haggai to be a Babylonian Repatriate, see Stuhlmueller, *Rebuilding with Hope*, 11–14; Elie Assis, "A Disputed Temple (Haggai 2,1–9)," *ZAW* 120 (2008): 582–96, especially n. 6.

96. Kessler (*Haggai*, 247–51) had articulately shown that the internal structure of Haggai is built of four episodes in an alternating order A/B/A/B. The A units (1:2–11; 2:10–19) set out conflicts over the relationship between God and his people, the B units (2:1–9; 2:20–23) suggest overt and covert conflicts brought on by the people's disappointment in facing the realities of the early Achaemenid period, specifically in matters concerning the Temple and the leadership, i.e., Zerubbabel.

(a) *Portrait of Zerubbabel*. Given the lack of a clear identification of Haggai's social context, his references to the leadership of Zerubbabel and Joshua become important markers of his Repatriate orientation (Hag 1:1, 12–14; 2:2). But, as has been emphasized time and again, those references are generally attributed to what has been accepted as the (later) framework of the book, thus to the compiler (or, according to Kessler, "the framers of the book of Haggai"[97]). More difficult to reject as a non-Haggai passage is the eschatological prophecy to Zerubbabel (Hag 2:20–23).

Haggai's condensed utilization of "theologically loaded terms" (Kessler) in 2:23—בחר ,שם כחותם ,ושם ... לקח ,עבדי—clearly alludes to Jeremiah's judgment prophecy against Jehoiachin in Jer 22:24–30. These terms, used to portray Zerubbabel's status, construct his position in direct continuity to the chosen Davidic kings,[98] and thus function as a corrective to Jeremiah's prophecy: כתבו את האיש הזה ערירי ... כי לא יצלח איש ישב על כסא דוד ומשל עוד ביהודה ("Record this man as without succession…for no man of his offspring shall be accepted to sit on the throne of David and to rule again in Judah," Jer 22:30). According to 1 Chr 3:17–19, Jehoiachin indeed was Zerubbabel's ancestor.[99] In place of the cumulative verbal phrases of rejection (נתן ,הטיל את ,הטיל ,השליך ,נתק ביד), Haggai draws his verbs from the semantic field of chosenness: לקח ,שם (כחותם) ,בחר. It is certainly possible that this opposition between Haggai and Jeremiah reflects sociological divisions of different sorts between the Judean communities. But Haggai's predisposition for Zerubbabel may more likely be a further indication of the prophet's Repatriate origin, representing a later phase of Ezekiel's preference for the Exiled king (see Ezek 17:21–24).[100] As we will see in Chapters 6 and 7 below, the relationship with Jehoiachin has been a debatable issue by the early sixth century, and the two prophets, Jeremiah and Ezekiel, were extremely divided on this issue. In contradistinction to Jer 22, Ezekiel articulated a position that considered the Exiles, with Jehoiachin, the Davidic heir, at their head, as bearing a special status of chosenness

---

97. Kessler, *Haggai*, 277–78, and passim; see Mason, "Editorial Framework."

98. To mention but some pertinent examples: עבדי refers to David in 2 Sam 7:5, 8; 1 Kgs 11:13; 14:8; 2 Kgs 19:34; לקח denotes choosing a person for leadership, e.g., 2 Sam 7:8; שים means to appoint a person over others with special authority (by God in Num 11:17; Deut 1:13; by the people, 2 Kgs 10:3).

99. Thus Kessler, *Haggai*, 231.

100. On Ezek 17:21–24 as the closing passage of the prophecy in ch. 17, and a genuine pronouncement of Ezekiel, see Moshe Greenberg, *Ezekiel 1–20* (AB 22; New York: Doubleday, 1983), 319–24.

by God.[101] If that is the case, Haggai indeed presents a genuinely Babylonian stance towards the Davidic kingship, left undeveloped since Ezekiel.

(b) *Other Discontinuities between Haggai and Jeremiah.* (1) While Jeremiah is remembered as a prophet whose audience refused to obey God's words, whether given through him or through previous prophets (e.g. שמעו בקולי...ולא שמעו, Jer 11:4, 7–8), Haggai's prophecies are assumed to have indeed caused a change ("Zerubbabel son of Shealtiel and the high priest Joshua son of Jehozadak and all the rest of the people gave heed to the summons of the LORD their God and to the words of the prophet Haggai, when the LORD their God sent him; the people feared the LORD," Hag 1:12, and see v. 14). (2) While Jeremiah fiercely opposes prophecies of peace, Haggai authors such a prophecy: ובמקום הזה אתן שלום נאם יהוה צבאות ("and in this place I will grant prosperity—declares the LORD of Hosts," Hag 2:9; compare to Jer 14:13: כי שלום אמת אתן לכם במקום הזה, "but I will give you unfailing security in this place"). (3) While the Temple has become for Jeremiah a target for criticism (Jer 7:1–15), Haggai situates the Temple as central to the reinstitution of the God–people relationship (1:1–11; 2:1–9), and for receiving God's blessing (1:8; 2:19). These differences are intriguing, as Haggai clearly differs from Zechariah in his relationship to Jeremiah (see, for instance, Zech 1:1–6).[102]

It is quite remarkable that Kessler indeed enumerated all these deviations from Jeremianic traditions and yet concluded that those same "interactions," crafted by "the framers of Haggai," were purposely done

> to demonstrate to those who revered the Jeremianic traditions that they too stood within the same prophetic tradition… Thus the followers of Jeremiah are being invited to see themselves as participants in *the era of restoration as prophesied by Jeremiah himself.*[103]

Kessler found these major differences to result from changed circumstances, and thus to be a clear indication of continuity between the prophets.

I myself find the opposite view to be much more persuasive. Those differences indeed show that Haggai is prophesying in opposition to Jeremiah, the former prophet of the People Who Remained.[104] Haggai

101.   The only later mention of Jehoiachin is in Mordechai's genealogy, Esth 2:5–6. See below, pp. 140–85.

102.   For the close relationships of Zech 1–8 to Jeremiah, see Stead, *The Intertextuality of Zechariah 1–8*, 55–60, and passim.

103.   Kessler, *Haggai*, 277–78.

104.   See the discussion of Jeremiah in Chapter 7.

sets himself not only against Jeremiah's attitude toward the exiled Davidic line, but also against his prophetic experience and judgmental message; most of all, he opposes Jeremiah's conception of the Temple. It seems most plausible to think of Haggai, as a Repatriate, investing his efforts in adapting Jeremiah's prophecies for the sake of the Repatriated community.[105]

From this perspective, it is interesting to see that Haggai advances the concept of *continuity* with Moses in portraying his own prophetic role. As a second Moses, Haggai calls the people and their leaders to rebuild the Temple, so that God will again reside among them (Hag 1:8; 2:1–9).[106] The connection between the two distinct events is drawn through an implicit thematic reference. Haggai 1:8 is built as two-sided command:

עלו ההר והבאתם עץ ובנו הבית
וארצה בו ואכבד (ק: ואכבדה) אמר יהוה

> Go up to the hills and get timber, and rebuild the House;
> then I will look on it with favor and I will be glorified—said the LORD.

The prophet first gives the people instructions to collect the wood (עלו...והבאתם), and to build the house (ובנו); this leads to a statement of God's pleasure with the Temple (וארצה בו), and his promise to cause His glory to dwell in it (ואכבדה).[107] This unique usage of כבד may be deduced from the parallel structure of Exod 25:2–8:

ויקחו לי תרומה ... ועשו לי מקדש ושכנתי בתוכם

> Tell the Israelite people to bring Me gifts... And let them make Me a sanctuary that I may dwell among them. (Exod 25:2, 8)

Hence, although there is no verbal similarity between the two texts, there seems to be implicit thematic influence from the Tabernacle traditions and the portrayal of Moses' role in relation to the Tabernacle on this

---

105.   Adapting Jeremian prophecies during the Persian period seems to be recorded in the book of Jeremiah itself; see Rom-Shiloni, "Group-Identities in Jeremiah," 11–46; and below, pp. 244–52.

106.   See Mason, "Editorial Framework," 145.

107.   The root כבד occurs in the Niphal, in a reflexive sense (God Himself expresses His presence); it is a denominative from כבוד יהוה, genuinely connected to the divine Tabernacle and Temple, as in Exod 40:34–38; 1 Kgs 8:10–11; and see Hag 2:7, ומלאתי את הבית הזה כבוד, which utilizes the common meaning of כבוד as "honor" (compare to an altogether different sense, where God lays His heavy (כבד) hand upon Pharaoh: Exod 14:4, 17, 18; Isa 26:15; 66:5; Ezek 28:22; 39:13).

portrayal of Haggai and his contemporaries in the reconstruction of the Second Temple. This line of continuity with Moses stands in contrast to Haggai's accentuation of his distinction from Jeremiah.

Arguments of *continuity* and e*ntirety* may also be gathered obliquely from the comparison of two passages, Ezra 3:8–13 and Hag 2:1–9.[108] The passages seem to refer similarly to reinstitution of cultic worship in the rebuilt Temple (Ezra 3:10, 13). The two descriptions nevertheless differ on the date and the specific chronology of this reinstitution. The reconstructed altar was prepared during the seventh month and dedicated during Sukkoth (Ezra 3:1–7); according to Haggai, this took place in 520 B.C.E. This cultic reinstitution occurred prior to the actual establishment of the Temple (Ezra 3:1, 6: והיכל יהוה לא יסד); although preparations for the building of the Temple, including laying its foundation, are mentioned subsequently (Ezra 3:8–10; Hag 2:1).[109] Another clear contact between the passages is the description of the loud, desperate cry of the elderly people, as they recognize the great difference between the First Temple and that which they now see before their eyes (Ezra 3:12–13; Hag 2:3). This last scene merits further comment.

H. G. M. Williamson considered Ezra 3 to be "a theological interpretation" of juxtaposed events from the reigns of both Cyrus and Darius, meant to suggest a narrative alternative to the accounts in Ezra 5–6 and Hag 2.[110] Williamson's conclusion is important: "Since, with one, or perhaps two, exceptions the narrative is constructed out of other biblical material, it is both a mistake of method, and a misunderstanding of the writer's intention, to use this section primarily for the purpose of historical reconstruction."[111] Indeed, while historical reconstruction is to be avoided here, a sociological perception of the groups involved may still be gathered from the comparison of these passages. While this comparison highlights the different terminologies used by each of the compositions, the literary similarities and the interpretive motivation may shed light on the perceptions of this event in the eyes of the audience mentioned in Haggai and referred to by Ezra.

---

108.   Myers (*Ezra–Nehemiah*, 29) argued that Ezra 3:12–13 "appear to be based on Hag ii 3." Scholars of Haggai have mentioned the shared circumstances behind these passages; see Boda, *Haggai, Zechariah*, 86, 118; Coggins, *Haggai, Zechariah, Malachi*, 12–13; Assis, "A Disputed Temple," 583, and see the discussion below.

109.   Ezra 3:1 does not specify the year; 1 Esd 56 refers the laying of the foundations to Zerubbabel's first year; see Myers, *Ezra–Nehemiah*, 26–27. On the chronological difficulty of Ezra 3 and its agreement with Hag 2, see Williamson, *Ezra–Nehemiah*, 43–45.

110.   Williamson, *Ezra–Nehemiah*, 43–45.

111.   Ibid., 45.

Ezra 3:8–13 refers to the entire people, that is, the entire community of Repatriates who participate in the celebration. The elders of all sub-groups are listed—priest, Levites, and chiefs of the clans:

ורבים מהכהנים והלוים וראשי האבות הזקנים אשר ראו את הבית הראשון
ביסדו זה הבית בעיניהם בכים בקול גדול ורבים בתרועה בשמחה להרים קול:
ואין העם מכירים קול תרועת השמחה לקול בכי העם כי העם מריעים תרועה
גדולה והקול נשמע עד למרחוק:

Many of the priests and Levites and chiefs of the clans, the old men who had seen the first house, wept loudly at the sight of the founding of this house. Many others shouted joyously at the top of their voices. The people could not distinguish the shouts of joy from the people's weeping, for the people raised a great shout, the sound of which could be heard from afar. (Ezra 3:12–13)

There is no reason to doubt that these labels refer exclusively to the Repatriates in Ezra; based on the usage of this list genre, it is even possible to suggest that the entire people is mentioned as present on the occasion.[112] It is thus surprising that Hag 2:1–5 has brought scholars to consider מי בכם הנשאר, שארית העם, like עם הארץ (v. 3), as referring to the Non-exiled Judeans:[113]

בשביעי בעשרים ואחד לחדש היה דבר יהוה ביד חגי הנביא לאמר: אמר נא אל
זרבבל בן שאלתיאל פחת יהודה ואל יהושע בן יהוצדק הכהן הגדול ואל **שארית**
העם לאמר: **מי בכם הנשאר** אשר ראה את הבית הזה בכבודו הראשון ומה
אתם ראים אתו עתה הלוא כמהו כאין בעיניכם: ועתה חזק זרבבל נאם יהוה
וחזק יהושע בן יהוצדק הכהן הגדול וחזק **כל עם הארץ** נאם יהוה ועשו כי אני
אתכם נאם יהוה צבאות: את הדבר אשר כרתי אתכם בצאתכם ממצרים ורוחי
עמדת בתוככם אל תיראו:

---

112.   Williamson (ibid., 46–49) pointed out the many echoes in Ezra 3:1–7, 8–13 of the dedication of the First Temple by Solomon (1 Kgs 8), understanding them all as part of the author's interest in continuity between the First and the Second Temples. This list that mentions the entire community in Ezra 3 thus stands in parallel to the repeated mention of כל קהל ישראל in 1 Kgs 8:2, 14, 22, 55, 62, 65. On the lists in Ezra–Nehemiah as illustrating the entire people, see above, pp. 38–41.

113.   Compare to Redditt (*Haggai, Zechariah, Malachi*, 24), who concurred that those elders were of the Remainees, based on the calculation of life spans—that is, presumably they could not have gone to exile and made the trip back. Thus, he interpreted their cries as objections to the new Temple. Boda (*Haggai, Zechariah*, 120–21) said, on the one hand, that Haggai addresses the remnant as "those truly purified through the Exile and still among the community"; but then in n. 11, he argued that "Haggai's question does not offer us a clue to whether he was an exile or remained in Palestine during the Babylonian period." I would agree with the first observation, and count Haggai and his audience as Repatriates.

> Speak to Zerubbabel son of Shealtiel, the governor of Judah, and to the high priest Joshua the son of Jehozadak, and to **the remnant of the people**:[114] **Who is there left** among you who saw this House in its former splendor? How does it look to you now? It must seem like nothing to you. But be strong, O Zerubbabel—says the LORD; be strong, O high priest Joshua son of Jehozadak; be strong, **all you people of the land**—says the LORD—and act! For I am with you—says the LORD of Hosts. So I promised you when you came out of Egypt, and My spirit is still in your midst. Fear not. (Ezra 2:2–5)

Based on these above-mentioned similarities between Ezra 3:8–13 and Hag 2:1–9, I see no reason to assume that Haggai addresses the Non-exiled population in Yehud. On the contrary, the comparison to Ezra 3:8–13 reinforces the assumption that Haggai's audience is precisely those people led by Zerubbabel and Joshua, the audience that considers itself to be the Remnant of the people.[115]

(2) *Arguments towards annexation.* By means of implicit allusions, Haggai makes analogies, harmonizes, systematizes, generalizes, adapts, expands, and ties together pentateuchal concepts from both the Priestly and Deuteronomic traditions concerning the Land, covenant traditions, and elements of covenant blessings and curses (particularly in 1:1–11; 2:10–19). He adapts Exodus and Sinai covenant traditions (2:5), Zion theology (2:6–9), Temple conceptions concerning God's presence and כבוד (Hag 1:8; 2:1–5), and the Davidic covenant (2:23).[116] He thus employs historical, legal, prophetic, and psalmodic traditions to serve his message to his current audience.[117] John Kessler rightly summarized Haggai's prophetic undertaking in reference to Hag 2:1–9:

> In an innovative and unique fashion, the prophet configures a variety of traditional elements in order to assure his audience that the postexilic community stands in continuity with the Yahwistic community of the past, and that of the postexilic community was the legitimate heir of the institutions (covenant, temple) and beneficial acts (deliverance, presence of Yahweh) of the past.[118]

114. NJPS translates here "the rest of the people."
115. In this I would thus differ from Wolff (*Haggai*, 51–52, 73, 96), who, while accepting כל שארית העם as clearly referring to the Repatriates, still argued that כל עם הארץ also includes those Judeans that had remained.
116. Kessler (*Haggai*) has done a remarkable job of presenting the wealth of evocative language and older traditions utilized by Haggai in a variety of ways to establish these lines of continuity. See his discussions of each individual passage, along with his summary (pp. 271–75), where he pointed out the different exegetical strategies Haggai uses in his prophecies.
117. Mason, "Prophets of the Restoration," 142–45.
118. Kessler, *Haggai*, 184.

The only point on which I part ways with Kessler is concerning his con-ception of the motivation for this impetus to *continuity*. I find Haggai's emphasis on past traditions to be a manipulative strategy of *annexation*, by which Haggai participates in building up the Repatriates' self-con-ception as the sole people of God.

The discussion of Zechariah (chs. 1–8) and Haggai has brought us to realize that both prophets address the same community of Babylonian Repatriates, whom they accept as the entire people of God. Another common denominator the two prophets share is their designations of this group as "the people that remained," as the Remnant; and this leads us to the next chapter.

Chapter 4

העם הנשאר, כל שארית העם, עם הארץ:
RELATIVE DESIGNATIONS OF EXCLUSIVITY—
CORE AND PERIPHERY

The most intriguing phrases in Haggai and in Zech 1–8 are those they use for group designations, employing the root שאר and the phrase עם הארץ (Hag 1:12, 14; 2:2–4; Zech 7:4; 8:8, 11, 12). These expressions interest scholars by virtue of the range of their possible meanings in the context of the two prophetic books, and they raise even more challenging questions when considered together with similar phrases in Ezra–Nehemiah. In what way does the singular עם הארץ of Haggai and Zechariah relate to the single occurrence of עם הארץ in Ezra (4:4)? Do references to the Remnant point to one specific community, or are the connotations of this terminology constantly changing? and how do these constructions relate, if at all, to the plural constructions otherwise found in Ezra–Nehemiah, עמי הארצות (Ezra 9:2, 11) and עמי הארץ (Neh 10:31, 32)? This is certainly an appropriate point in the study to pose these questions, and address distinctions between the historiography and the prophetic literature of the Persian period.

The focus of this chapter is this terminology in relation to the people, shared by Haggai and Zechariah: עם הארץ and שארית העם. An investigation of these designations, both in terms of their distinction from the vocabulary of Ezra–Nehemiah, and their place in a historical trajectory of postexilic conceptions of people and Remnant, provides an important window onto the self-perceptions of the Repatriate community in the days of the Restoration. Furthermore, this discussion enables us also to retroject on these designations and their occurrences in earlier sixth-century sources, in Jeremiah and Ezekiel, and thus to suggest functional distinctions and transformations over time. The discussion, therefore, leads us to consider the entire spectrum of the literature portrayed in this study.

1. *Conceptions of a Remnant:*
Relative Perspectives of Core and Periphery

The conception of the Remnant (שארית העם) has been widely discussed in biblical scholarship. Addressing the semantic value of the term, Eric W. Heaton defined שאר as "to remain or be left over from a larger number or quantity which has in some way been disposed of." The most frequent "disposals" are the consequence of "violence involving death, or removal into captivity" (see for instance, Gen 32:9; Deut 4:27), and thus שאר designates "'the rest'—the second of two classes."[1] Heaton pointed out the hierarchal difference between the two classes, arguing that the group left behind illustrates the part, the "antecedent loss" from the point of view of the whole.[2] This, however, seems to be a matter of perspective, and Heaton was very much aware of the diverse references to the Remnant, emphasizing that there is no one doctrinal conception of the "Remnant" in the prophetic books.[3]

Given the semantic value of the term, in conjunction with its contextual usages, the root שאר, in the two phrases הנשאר (as in Hag 2:3) and שארית העם (in Hag 1:12, 14; Zech 8:6, 11, 12), has been understood in two different ways: as a fixed and anchored terminology; or as a term with relative and transitory meaning.

An exemplary discussion of the conception of the Remnant as a fixed term was offered by Sara Japhet in reference to Restoration-period literature.[4] Japhet characterized this conception as "one form of Israel's response to situations of severe crisis that threatened its national existence,"[5] and as an "eloquent testimony to the centrality of the questions of identity, community, and self-definition, which occupied the community of Israel in the Restoration Period."[6]

---

1. Eric W. Heaton, "The Root שאר and the Doctrine of the Remnant," *JTS* 3 (1952): 27–39 (28).

2. Ibid., 28–29, and n. 1.

3. This indeed seems to be one of the greatest contributions of Heaton's study, as he pointed out the distinctions between the Hebrew Bible and the Christian doctrinal positions on this matter; see particularly ibid., 27, 38–39.

4. Sara Japhet, "The Concept of the 'Remnant' in the Restoration Period: On the Vocabulary of Self-Definition," in *From the Rivers of Babylon to the Highlands of Judah: Collected Studies on the Restoration Period* (Winona Lake: Eisenbrauns, 2006), 432–49, first published in *Das Manna fällt auch heute noch: Beiträge zur Geschichte und Theologie des Alten, Ersten Testaments, Festschrift für Erich Zenger* (ed. F.-L. Hossfeld and L. Schwienhorst-Schönberger; HBS 44; Freiburg: Herder, 2004), 340–57.

5. Ibid., 449.

6. Ibid., 432.

In her reconstruction of the transformations of the notion of the Remnant within the Restoration period, Japhet argued for a general tendency toward inclusivity in both Haggai and Zechariah, in Chronicles, and even in Neh 1:2–3—which leaves Ezra 9–10 as the only passage reflecting an extremely exclusive outlook. Accordingly, she argued that Haggai exemplifies an adaptation and actualization of Jeremiah's conception of the Remnant; he concurs that the Remnant designates "'those who remained' in the land."[7] It is interesting that Japhet did recognize that references to the Remnant of the people occur side by side with the mention of Zerubbabel and Joshua, the Repatriates' leaders (Hag 1:12, 14; 2:2); and yet, because of the lack of any concrete evidence pointing to either the exile or the return in Haggai, she found this conjunction to demonstrate the self-understanding of the community in Yehud, dominated by "those who remained." The latter presumably had accepted the Babylonian Repatriates within their ranks, without changing their own self-identification. The proximity of כל שארית העם and עם הארץ in both Haggai and Zechariah further strengthens Japhet in observing a similar and even stronger claim introduced by Zechariah. Though indeed attentive to the persistence of the Diasporan community in Babylon (and even to the presence of non-Judeans in the land; Zech 2:20–23), Zechariah still retains the definition of the "Remnant" as "those who survived and live in the land"; Japhet even went further, suggesting that "whether they remained in the land all along or went into captivity and returned is of no consequence."[8]

Japhet saw this same dynamic at work even in the book of Nehemiah. In connection with the Judeans (היהודים) in Jerusalem, Nehemiah and then Hanani put together three designations: היהודים הפליטה אשר נשארו מן השבי ("the Jews/Judeans, the survivors, who remained from the captivity," Neh 1:2, 3).[9] Japhet cited Exod 10:5 as a parallel syntactic construction, הפליטה הנשארת לכם מן הברד, to show that those left were the survivors who had remained *in situ*, concluding: "Accordingly, 'the remnant' referred to in Neh 1:2, those 'who remained from the captivity,'

---

7. Ibid., 435–36.

8. Ibid., 437.

9. Japhet (ibid., 438) recognized aptly the accumulation of three titles in these verses. This inclusivist perspective on Nehemiah has also led Williamson (*Ezra, Nehemiah*, 165, 171), who, while suggesting the translation "about the Jews—those who, having escaped, were left of the captivity—and about Jerusalem" (165), raised some concerns about the identity of this remnant, and finally gathered that "the remnant terminology is applied loosely by Nehemiah to all surviving Jews in Judah" (171).

would be the people who survived after all the others were taken captive—that is, those who did not go into Exile."[10]

But, at the same time, I want to suggest an opposing interpretation for this phrase. The parallel passage, Exod 10:5, can be brought to bear in a very different way, pointing to the experience, rather than to the stability of place. The group referred to as היהודים הפליטה אשר נשארו מן השבי may be understood as those who indeed have suffered captivity and survived it—that is, those who were deported and returned. Similar to the vegetation that survived the hailstones, so have the Exiles held on through the experience of deportation and the return. Thus, Nehemiah is here asking Hanani, one of his brothers—that is, one of the Repatriates—about the fortune of those Repatriates who have already been struggling in the land for nearly one hundred years.[11]

Ezra 9 (particularly vv. 7–8) is the only passage where Japhet found an understanding of this concept of the "Remnant" as an exclusionary term (exclusively referring to the Repatriates[12]). She argued: "The transition from Neh 1:2–3 to Ezra 9–10 could not be greater: 'Remnant' has been transformed to refer to returned exiles. They are 'the Rest of Israel' by definition; the root of Israel's future existence and hopes."[13]

Japhet also pointed out that this same exclusionary viewpoint is found in specific passages in Jeremiah (she mentioned Jer 23:3; 31:6, 24) and Ezekiel, but she emphasized that neither prophetic books applies the root שאר to the community of deportees, whom they find to be the future hope of Israel. Thus, the terminology of remnant is kept throughout the earlier tradition for the people who remained in the land.[14] Ezra 9–10 represents a combination of the Judean position that designates the community of Non-exiled Judeans as "Remnant" with the view of Jer 24 and Ezekiel that it is the Exiles (and then Repatriates) who will continue the future existence of Israel (and see also Japhet's discussion of Ezra 1:4).[15]

10. Japhet, "The Concept of the 'Remnant'," 438–39.

11. The two interpretations reside on a long exegetical Jewish tradition. Rashi interpreted this phrase in Neh 1:2 as referring to those who were never exiled, an explanation carried on by Japhet, Williamson, and many others; Myers (*Ezra–Nehemiah*, 93), for instance, preferred this option, though only as a probable explanation without giving his arguments. In contradistinction, Metsudat David said: "נשארו. For most of the Exiles continued to sit in Babylon, in captivity, and only few ascended, therefore, he called them שארית." I would concur with this latter option.

12. Japhet, "The Concept of the 'Remnant'," 439–41.

13. Ibid., 441.

14. Ibid., 442.

15. Ibid., 443, 445.

From the point of view of the social psychology on group identity relationships, two major points render improbable this entire inclusivist scenario. First, this reconstruction implicitly assumes that those who remained have utilized an *incorporation* strategy (A + B = A), by which they enfolded the Repatriates within their community. To state but the most serious obstacle to such an assumption: *incorporation* is a strategy employed by a dominant group, which embodies all others within its own social structure; the price of such inclusion, of course, is that those "others" give up their own unique identifications.[16] Such a strategy does not concur with the biblical evidence of both prophetic books and Ezra–Nehemiah, which agree upon the dominance of the Returnees; it is this group that employs and adapts conceptions of exile and of return in the rhetoric of Restoration Yehud. Second, this reconstruction considers the conception of the "Remnant" to be a static, one-dimensional term, referring only to the community that remained in the land of Judah throughout the exilic period.

I will take an opposing perspective and offer three observations:

(1) The concept of the Remnant plays a crucial role in constructing exclusivist ideologies; each group uses it differently in arguments to re-build its status as the one and only legitimate continuing community of the people of God.[17] This signification is embedded in the semantics of שאר (as also יתר and שרד) and its utilization shows a very sectarian usage. In Jeremiah and Ezekiel, the שארית certainly designates the community remaining in the land. On the one hand, this community may be valued positively; it is seen as having a prestigious position, set apart from all other groups. The Remnant (i.e. the group that is left) claims to be the only remaining vestige of the original community, and thus the sole bearer of the original group's beliefs and heritage (as, for instance, Jer 40:7–12).[18] But on the other hand, the Remnant may be seen by those

16. For *incorporation* as a strategy of assimilation and thus inclusivity, see above, pp. 26–27.

17. Contra Jutta Hausmann (*Israels Rest: Studien zum Selbsverständis der nachexilischen Gemeinde* [Stuttgart: Kohlhammer, 1987], 253, 256), who found the conception of Remnant to be a unifying conception inclusive of all Israel, and a construct that was open for expansion and for the acceptance of new members.

18. Heaton ("The Root שאר," 33) indeed recognized such a positive attitude toward the שארית in Zeph 3:12–13, where he found a clear example of what he designated as "the doctrine of the Remnant," characterized by the following elements: "Yahweh is speaking, the *hiphʿil* perfect is used, the natural meaning of the root is retained in the words 'afflicted and poor,' and the preserved residue is described as a faithful community." I will discuss below other examples of the positive connotations given to this term when it is used as a self-designation.

who belong to the counter-community, as doomed to total annihilation (as in Ezek 11:1–13).

These mutually exclusive usages may be traced in accordance with the social orientation of their bearers. For instance, the Judean Deuteronomistic historiographer defines Judah as the Remnant in 2 Kgs 17:18, excluding the Northern Kingdom; but later historiographers treat the small Remnant in Judah following the Jehoiachin exile as doomed to total elimination, following 586 and the general flight to Egypt (2 Kgs 24:14; 25:11, 22, 25). This latter rhetorical use of the term in relation to Those Who Remained in the land following 597 B.C.E. is but one of the indications that have led scholars to recognize the pro-Jehoiachin–Exiles perspective of the author(s) of 2 Kgs 24–25; these two chapters implicitly project a conception of the Jehoiachin–Exiles community in Babylon as the (true) Remnant, portraying the land of Judah as empty of inhabitants.[19] This pattern forecasts the annihilation of the Remnant, that is, the Yahwists remaining in Judah following 597, and thus leaves the land empty for "my people," that is, the Exiles, to return. This is the pattern that governs Ezekiel's prophecies against Jerusalem and in favor of the Jehoiachin Exiles (see Ezek 1–24, especially 5:10; 9:8; 11:1–13; 36:1–15); it is also the perspective of Deutero-Isaiah governing his two uses of שאר (Isa 46:3; 49:21).[20]

Jeremiah 40–44 represents a clashing of these two understandings of the Remnant. The story of the Remnant of Judah under the leadership of Gedaliah, with its note of hope for the future, is reworked by the Babylonian-exilic editors according to the Babylonian pattern—so that with the descent into Egypt of any remaining survivors, the land is left empty (43:1–7; 44).[21] Such contradictory perspectives may also be perceived among the minor prophets. The conception of the Exiles as the Remnant occurs in consolation prophecies, such as Mic 2:12–13; 4:6–7; 5:6–8, which promise deliverance and restoration in the land. Zephaniah, however, refers to the Remnant as situated in the land (Zeph 2:7–9; 3:12–13).

(2) Three transformations may be discerned in the definitions of the Remnant during the sixth and the fifth centuries. Even more significant is the fact that these transformations follow the shift in perception of Jerusalem/Judah and Babylon, even then, in terms of which was seen as the core community and which was seen as the periphery.

---

19. Seitz, *Theology in Conflict*, 164–203.
20. Rom-Shiloni, "Ezekiel as the Voice of the Exiles"; and see the discussion below, pp. 140–85.
21. See the discussion below, pp. 228–41.

At the beginning of the Exile, Jerusalem was perceived as the center of the community and Babylon as the periphery, the place of deportation. This is, indeed, the background to the agreement between Jeremiah and Ezekiel in designating Jerusalem/Judah as the Remnant.[22] Thus, Jeremiah designates the Jerusalem community of post-586 as העם הנשארים בארץ and שארית העם (Jer 40:6), שארית יהודה (as in 40:15; 42:15), as opposed to כל גלות ירושלים ויהודה המגלים בבלה (in 40:1).[23] This same point of departure leads Ezekiel to treat Jerusalem as the שארית but with extremely negative connotations, as he constantly prophesies its total annihilation (as in Ezek 5:10; 6:12; 11:1–13).[24] Furthermore, Ezekiel adds another important element in the transition: probably in the very early years of the Jehoiachin exile, he might have been the first to articulate the idea of Jerusalem's total destruction (Ezek 9:8; 11:13), and thus to pave the way for denoting the Jehoiachin Exiles as the alternative (and only) Remnant (Ezek 11:14–21).[25] By denying the status of Remnant from the Jerusalemites that remained in the land following the Jehoiachin exile, the prophet releases the term שארית from its descriptive and locative meaning and transforms it to be serving as an argument of exclusiveness.

Ezekiel thus represents the ideological transformation to the second stage, the highly important shift that turned the Judean community in Babylon into the core community and relegated Jerusalem to its periphery. This line continues in Deutero-Isaiah, who addresses the House of Jacob on one occasion as כל שארית בית ישראל (Isa 46:3). While the prophet rarely uses these terms, he does perceive Jerusalem as left alone, surprised at the thought that abundant people would return and resettle it

22. Japhet, "The Concept of the 'Remnant'," 442; and see Hausmann (*Israels Rest*, 112–13), who noted the distinction between the positive attitude towards the Judean Remnant in Jer 40:7–12; 40:13–41:10; 41:16–18; 43:5; 44:28a; and the critical Deuteronomistic position against it and in favor of the *golah* in Jer 42:7–8; 44:7–14, 24–30. The complicated picture in Jeremiah will be discussed at length below, pp. 220–52.

23. Jer 24, a non-Jeremian passage, establishes an opposition between גלות יהודה, that is, the Jehoiachin Exiles (vv. 3–7) and שארית ירושלים הנשארים בארץ הזאת והישבים בארץ מצרים, together with King Zedekiah and his officials (vv. 8–10). See the discussion below, pp. 233–37.

24. On the negative attitude to the (Jerusalem) Remnant in Ezekiel, see Hausmann, *Israels Rest*, 82–95.

25. See the full discussion, pp. 144–53. Scholars tend to relate to Ezek 11:14–21 as a late, secondary, corrective passage following 11:1–13 (see, for instance, Walther Eichrodt, *Ezekiel* [OTL; trans. C. Quin; Philadelphia: Westminster, 1970], 142–43). I do not find the arguments for its secondary character persuasive. The two segments seem to be two disputation speeches focused on one and the same theme (so Greenberg, *Ezekiel 1–20*, 203–4).

(הן אני נשארתי לבדי אלה איפה הם, Isa 49:21). It is thus clear that the notion of the empty land (and empty city) plays an important role in presenting the Remnant as the community of Exiles in Babylon, while the homeland and home-city was left completely desolated.[26]

By the late sixth century, we see a third stage in the transformation of the concept of Remnant, in which two different perceptions of the core–periphery relationship may be discerned. The prophetic literature shows the first signs of transition to the new stage. Zechariah refers to כל שארית העם (Zech 8:6, 11, 12) as part of God's return to His city and the restoration of His people from east and west (v. 7); thus he follows the same Babylonian-exilic ideological line that was constructed by Ezekiel and Deutero-Isaiah. He knows the Remnant as the community of Repatriates that has returned to the empty land of Yehud.[27] The Babylonian core is now acquiring a new definition as it sends branches back to the homeland, which for several decades has been counted a neglected periphery. In speaking of the return of God to His city, Zechariah shifts Zion into core position once again; in fact, he almost totally avoids explicit reference to the Babylonian Diaspora.[28] This is the framework in which Zechariah indeed expects a general return (Zech 2:10–17).

At this final stage, a different path is taken by the historiography of Ezra–Nehemiah. While the Repatriates resettle Yehud, Ezra–Nehemiah tells of the ongoing dominance of the Babylonian Diaspora as the core community, with the Yehud community as their subordinate group of בני הגולה. Nevertheless, by the late sixth century, in both prophetic literature and the historiography, the Repatriates have definitely claimed for themselves the label of the Remnant.[29]

(3) Where does this reconstruction leave Haggai? Ackroyd has argued that the references to the people as the Remnant belong to the compiler of Haggai, that is, the editorial framework and the narrative material (Hag 1:12, 14; 2:2).[30] In the actual words of the prophet, however, the community is referred to as "the people" (1:2; 2:14) and "all the people of the land" (2:4), which, according to Ackroyd, is simply a synonym for "people."[31] Hence, the conception of Remnant belongs only to the

26. The concept of the empty city and land in Isa 40–66 is treated below, pp. 106–21.

27. On the notion of the empty land in Zechariah, see pp. 51–61.

28. For Zechariah's almost total neglect of the Babylonian Diaspora (except for Zech 2:10–17), see pp. 49–53 above.

29. See Bedford, "Diaspora: Homeland Relations."

30. Ackroyd, "Studies," 1–13.

31. Ackroyd, *Exile and Restoration*, 162; and see his full discussion of עם הארץ on p. 150 n. 50.

"compiler," whom Ackroyd characterized as follows: "This compiler stands…very closely in the tradition of the prophet and has simply made explicit what in Haggai is implicit."[32] Ackroyd assumed that Haggai's compiler was influenced by Zechariah's more explicit observations on this issue.[33] The status of Remnant is based on this community's exclusive involvement in rebuilding the Temple, being "the divinely chosen survivors of disaster" and "men who have returned from exile" (Zech 4:10–11).[34]

Hence, is it possible to absolve Haggai of the charge of exclusivity, settling it squarely on the compiler's shoulders? Beuken indeed argued that there was a great difference between the prophet and the compiler, whom he connected to the Chronicler, and thus to Ezra–Nehemiah.[35] While criticizing Beuken's sharp distinctions between the two layers, Rex Mason also considered שארית העם הזה to be part of the editorial level in Haggai (occurring in Hag 1:12, 14; 2:2).[36] Added to its accentuation on the returned community's leadership, Mason argued that this phrase refers to the entire community, and suggested that Haggai's usage represents an early prophetic exegesis of this concept of the Remnant in the prophetic literature. The concept of the Remnant that appears in two antagonistic contexts, as "both threat of judgment or promise of deliverance,"[37] is presented in Haggai referring to the "community of returned exiles" and identifying them as "heirs to the old prophetic promise of salvation."[38]

Following Ackroyd, Kessler suggested four meanings for שאר and שארית in Haggai,[39] but concluded that Haggai's phrase מי בכם הנשאר

32. Ibid., 162.

33. Ibid., 163, 175.

34. Ibid., 162–63.

35. Beuken (*Haggai-Sacharja 1–8*, 31–48) thought the compiler was the Chronicler, the exclusivist author of Ezra–Nehemiah; see below, pp. 92–93.

36. Mason, "Editorial Framework," 413–21. See also Mark Boda ("Haggai: Master Rhetorician," *TynBul* 51 [2000]: 295–304), who called attention to Haggai's rhetorical strategies; his observation should lead to a reconsideration of too strict a division between the layers.

37. Mason, "Editorial Framework," 417–18.

38. Ibid., 418.

39. Kessler suggested four meanings for שאר and שארית in Haggai, based on usages elsewhere in the biblical literature: (1) In a "more theological sense" he found שארית to refer to "those who turn to Yahweh after a time of purificatory suffering"; he noted as examples, 2 Kgs 19:30; Isa 37:31; Isa 4:3; Ezek 17:21. (2) "Survivors of military actions directed against Israel, often as divine chastenings"—under this rubric, Kessler recognized the utilization of שאר to refer both to those deported

(Hag 2:3) is "simply designating a portion of the community, individuals more than seventy years of age..."[40] He proposed that the prophet here calls to mind those individuals (from the Repatriates) who survived to see the Second Temple under construction; for the sake of rhetoric, he views the situation "through their eyes." Hence, Kessler did not recognize any additional significance in the utilization of שאר, and he said nothing of its possible meaning in terms of issues of group identity.

However, the above discussion of core-periphery relationships and the Remnant does not seem to leave many open questions concerning Haggai. As Winton Thomas said briefly: "The phrase 'the remnant of the people' as used in Haggai (cf. v. 14; 2:2) and Zechariah (8:6, 11, 12) always means the returned exiles."[41]

To my mind, it is unlikely that Haggai (and Zechariah) would utilize this overloaded terminology in a neutral or inclusive way. Although, indeed, the prophet does not refer to either the exile or to the return, I find his references to the (Repatriate) leaders Zerubbabel and Joshua, together with his insistence on addressing the people as the Remnant, a telling indication of his orientation on questions of group identity. Haggai seems to follow Ezekiel, and Deutero-Isaiah, and be in line with Zechariah—all great advocates of the Babylonian Diasporan community and, upon return, of the Repatriate community back in Yehud.

It appears that both Judean communities utilized this terminology of "Remnant," transforming it over the course of the sixth and fifth centuries B.C.E. in accordance with the grand shifts of perceptions of core and periphery among Judean social communal relationships. Furthermore,

---

(2 Kgs 25:11; Jer 8:3; 52:15; Ezra 1:4), and to those who remained in the land (Jer 24:8; 40:6; 41:10). Kessler's list of examples (*Haggai*, 165) is very problematic: Ezra 1:4 refers to those who remained in the Babylonian diaspora, and the rest refer to the community who remained in Jerusalem under Zedekiah, who suffered additional deaths, before some of them were taken to exile (2 Kgs 25:11; Jer 52:15); Jer 8:3 seems to combine two different perspectives, and thus Kessler's division between those deported and remained cannot be sustained. (3) Kessler defined the Niphal participle (נשאר) as "a quasi-technical term" that refers to "those who survived the ravages of war, especially wars sent as divine judgments" in Lev 26:36, 39; Deut 7:20; 19:20. The fourth meaning seems to be very general: (4) נשאר would stand for "those who remain or are left over" from a group that suffered diminution (Gen 14:10; 1 Sam 11:11; 2 Kgs 10:21).

40. Kessler, *Haggai*, 165.

41. Winton Thomas, *Haggai*, 1042. Stuhlmueller (*Building with Hope*, 112) explained this phrase as referring to those who had returned from exile (and see her clear explanation on p. 89).

these transformations and the utilization of the conception of the Remnant serve to explain the differences between the historiography and the prophetic literature of the early Persian period. These differences also govern the occurrences of עם הארץ and עמי הארצות.

2. עמי הארצות *vs.* עם הארץ: *Further Differences Between the Prophetic Literature and the Historiography*

Among the group designations in Hag 2:1–5, כל עם הארץ is paired with the two leaders, Zerubbabel and Joshua (v. 4), and with the reference to this community as שארית העם or כל הנשאר (vv. 2–3). This pairing parallels the proximity of כל שארית העם in Hag 1:12, 14 to those same leaders. In Zech 7:5, כל עם הארץ, together with the priests and prophets (v. 3), are Zechariah's addressees in Jerusalem; they are approached by a delegation, headed by two persons who seem to bear Babylonian names: בית אל שר אצר ורגם מלך.[42] What might be the relationship between עם הארץ and כל שארית העם in Haggai and Zechariah? Are these designations synonymous with Ezra–Nehemiah's עמי הארץ (Ezra 10:2, 11) and עמי הארצות (Ezra 9:1, 2, 11; Neh 9:30; 10:29; see also 2 Chr 32:13)? Or should they be distinguished from them? How do these Persian-period phrases relate to other occurrences of עם הארץ in the Hebrew Bible? These questions underlie the rich scholarly treatments of this topic. The following comments address these questions from the perspective of group identity issues.

Wim Beuken differentiated between כל שארית העם and כל עם הארץ in Haggai and Zechariah. He considered כל עם הארץ of Hag 2:4 to denote the never-deported "agrarian" Judean community to which Haggai belonged, in distinction from שארית העם, which Beuken considered a designation for the Babylonian Repatriates. Beuken drew his sociological conclusions concerning Haggai's milieu from his literary distinction between the prophet and the compiler.[43] This strata of land-owners who had never been deported, and thus had never returned, had maintained their preexilic monarchic social organization and networks. Beuken explained Hag 1:3–4 as the Chronicler's intrusion: by adding the Repatriate leaders' names, he established them as the initiators of the restoration of the Temple.[44]

---

42. See the discussion and the references to these names, above, p. 50 n. 6.

43. Beuken, *Haggai–Sacharja 1–8*, 220–22, and see his discussion of שארית העם in Hag 1:12–14, on p. 30, along with the discussion of עם הארץ in 2:4, on pp. 54–56.

44. Ibid., 56.

Following a similar line, and accepting Beuken's observations about the Chronicler as editor, Richard J. Coggins proposed that עם הארץ in Haggai and Zechariah was yet a transformation of earlier nationalistic Judean elitist circle, which had previously objected to the interference of the nations in Judean affairs mentioned (2 Kgs 23:30, 35). According to Coggins, this circle had redirected its resentment at the Persian Empire. It was Haggai and Zechariah who encouraged this (native) group to join in the rebuilding of the Temple.[45]

But as scholars have noticed, there is no syntactic divergence between Hag 2:2 and 4, in terms of their addressees; in fact, as mentioned above, the Babylonian leaders are paired with כל עם הארץ as well as כל שארית העם.[46] Thus, the usage of these two terms by the prophet had also facilitated an inclusive perspective on Haggai (and Zechariah). Kessler, for instance, adopted Ackroyd's position, holding that Haggai uses both terms to refer to the entire Judean population, indifferent to whether these constituents were Repatriates or Non-exiled. These alternative phrases have become a major piece of evidence for the scholarly picture of Haggai's presumed inclusivity.[47] The two phrases are taken as appositions, so that this "Remnant" is recognized as כל עם הארץ, "the entire people of the land." Yet, who might this Remnant be? Sara Japhet indeed concluded that "the remnant of the people" are "the people of the land," that is, those who were never exiled.[48]

Keeping in mind these perspectives on Haggai, it seems necessary now to mention two major studies of the expression עם הארץ, studies that have paved the way for many papers thereafter. Ernst Würthwein has explored the significance of עם הארץ as a social designation, basing his observations mostly on the occurrences of this term in 2 Kings. According to Würthwein, עם הארץ denotes the fully entitled citizens of a country, who held political, economic, and military powerful roles in the country's affairs.[49] This definition worked perfectly for Würthwein in 2 Kings, and thus was the prism through which he considered all other occurrences of the phrase in the Hebrew Bible.[50]

---

45. Coggins, *Samaritans and Jews*, 48–50.

46. Japhet ("The Concept of the 'Remnant'," 434–35) pointed out the parallel construction of Hag 2:2 and 2:4, as the phrases indeed interchange.

47. Ackroyd, *Exile and Restoration*, 150 n. 50; Kessler, *Haggai*, 168–69.

48. Japhet, "The Concept of the 'Remnant'," 434–37.

49. Ernst Würthwein, *Der ʿamm haʾarez im Alten Testament* (BWANT 4/17; Stuttgart: Kohlhammer, 1936), 18, and the entire discussion on pp. 12–18.

50. See, for example, Würthwein's explanation of Ezek 12:13 and other occurrences in Ezekiel (ibid., 47–50).

Ernest W. Nicholson aptly challenged the scholarly treatments that treated עם הארץ as a *terminus technicus*, as a "fixed and specific social or political class or group."[51] Commenting on the various occurrences of the term one by one, Nicholson emphasized the general meaning of עם הארץ, as designating the population as a whole: the entire, ordinary, varied members of a community, any community.[52]

From the perspective of this investigation of group identity, I would like to articulate a clear distinction between two different utilizations of עם הארץ in the Hebrew Bible, both of which occur in sixth- and fifth-century sources. The first use comprises part of the Judean in-group's positive self-definition, designating a component within the people of Israel/Judah; the second use negatively characterizes outsiders, "others," as belonging to the authochtonic populations of the land. Both meanings rely on pentateuchal (Priestly) conceptions, first mobilized by Ezekiel, in the early years of exile, and continuously used by both prophets and historiographers throughout the sixth and fifth centuries.

As used by an in-group to distinguish an out-group, עם הארץ refers to the foreign population of a given territory (Gen 23:12, 13; 42:6; and see עם ארצו in Neh 9:10); more specifically in pentateuchal sources, עמי הארץ are the native peoples of the land of Canaan.[53] Leviticus 18 and 20 seem to draw an important distinction between בני ישראל and אנשי הארץ אשר לפניכם (Lev 18:27); they are also called הגוים אשר אני משלח מפניכם (v. 24); and הגוי אשר לפניכם (v. 28; and see 20:23a). The common denominator in all these designations is that the definition of the "other"

---

51. Nicholson, "The Meaning of the Expression עם הארץ," 59–66 (60).

52. Seitz (*Theology in Conflict*, 42–51, 55–64 [47]) suggested quite a similar broad meaning of עם הארץ (similar to עם יהודה), being the "wider population of Judah, distinct from Jerusalem," yet those who took residence and were active within the capital as of 701 or even 721 B.C.E. Seitz nevertheless restricted his observations to the occurrences in 2 Kings, Jeremiah, and Ezekiel. On this limitation of the sources, Seitz followed Shemaryahu Talmon ("The Judaean ʿam haʾares in Historical Perspective," in *The Fourth Congress of Jewish Studies, Papers* [Jerusalem: Hebrew University, 1967], 1:71–76), who had taken a kind of a middle way when he argued that עם הארץ were the people of the land, though residents of Jerusalem and loyal to the Davidic dynasty.

53. As foreign peoples, see Josh 4:24; 1 Kgs 8:43, 53, 60 (2 Chr 6:27, 33); Ezek 31:12; 39:13; Zeph 3:20; Esth 8:17; Neh 10:32; 2 Chr 32:19; Neh 9:24 (עממי הארץ). Exceptional is only Exod 5:4, where עם הארץ refers to the Israelites in Egypt (so William C. Propp, *Exodus 1–18* [AB 2; New York: Doubleday, 1998], 245, 253–54); see the Samaritan version reading מעם הארץ, thus alluding to the Egyptians. See John I. Durham, *Exodus* (WBC 3; Waco: Word, 1987), 64–65, who preferred MT, and understood עם הארץ to mean "land-people" or simply "peasants."

population as עם הארץ reflects the perspective of those who come to the land from the outside. The allochthonic element is accented in Abraham's negotiations with Ephron (Gen 23) and in the descriptions of the Israelite entry into Canaan, which emphasize the essential need for the Israelites to separate themselves from the peoples of the land (Lev 18; 20; and in different terms in Deut 7, etc.). That is, the identification of foreign peoples as being "of the land" is emphasized precisely in narratives of possession or conquest of the land by the divinely designated new possessors, coming from outside. This opposition is already brought into play by Ezekiel (see Chapter 6), and then by Ezra–Nehemiah (as presented in Chapter 2).

In the realm of in-group (or self-) definition, עם הארץ in 2 Kings seems indeed to designate persons involved in the royal court and the political arena.[54] But, as Nicholson showed, the term could very well be referring to the entire population; that is, anyone who is not the king and does not belong to the other marked circles of officials, priests, and so on. This general usage of עם הארץ to signify the entire population of Israel hearkens back to the Priestly usage of עם הארץ to designate the entire people (Lev 4:27).[55] It may function as a synonym for the Priestly terms עדה and קהל (as in Num 10:1–10; and see Num 16:33–34, with its use of קהל and ישראל);[56] and it may also relate to the occurrence of עם and קהל as referring to the entire in-group community (as in Joel 2:16; Pss 35:18; 107:32; Neh 5:13).

It is telling that Ezekiel uses the phrase עם הארץ in both these internal and external contexts, and he even utilizes its most general meaning, that is, to designate the population of any land, of unspecified origin (Ezek 33:2). The internal sociopolitical nuance occurs in two of his

54. עם הארץ designates a Judean social stratum, in 2 Kgs 11:14, 18, 19, 20; 15:5; 16:15; 21:24; 23:30, 35, and maybe even 24:14; 25:3, 19 (and see the parallel passages in 2 Chr 23:13, 20, 21; 26:21; 33:25; 36:1). See Shemaryahu Talmon, "The Judean ʿAm Haʾaretz in Historical Perspective," in *Proceedings of the Fourth World Congress of Jewish Studies* (Jerusalem: World Union of Jewish Studies, 1967), 71–76; Hayyim Tadmor, "'The People' and the Kingship in Ancient Israel," *Journal of World History* 11 (1968): 3–23; Antonius H. J. Gunneweg, "עם הארץ—A Semantic Revolution," *ZAW* 95 (1983): 437–40.

55. Milgrom (*Leviticus 1–16*, 251–52) started his interpretation of the phrase with this general interpretation: "commoners…who are neither the ruler nor the priests (Ezek 45:22; cf. 7:27; 45:16) and those who are neither king, nor officials, nor priests (Jer 1:18; Hag 2:4)." But then Milgrom added that עם הארץ does have its technical meaning in Kings.

56. See קהל העם in Jer 26:17; it signifies a different group from the officials, the priests, the prophets and זקני הארץ, and stands for the people in general.

prophecies.[57] In Ezek 7:27, the prophet mentions the king, the *nasi*ᵏ, and the עם הארץ in his description of the agony following the Destruction;[58] similarly, in Ezek 22:23–31, the עם הארץ are the last to be mentioned among leading, aristocratic, ruling circles in Jerusalem. Following a list specifying prophets, priests, officials, and closing again with prophets (vv. 25–28), עם הארץ are named as jointly responsible for the general all-embracing social and ethical sins committed within the city.[59]

Ezekiel's great innovation, however, seems to be in his transformation of עם הארץ as a designation for outsiders. In his polemical struggle against Jerusalem, the prophet creates an analogy between Jerusalem and the אנשי הארץ of Lev 18:27. Ezekiel portrays Jerusalem as descended from the Canaanites, the foreign peoples of the land (Ezek 16:3). In opposition to the Jerusalemites-as-peoples-of-the-land, the prophet draws another analogy between the Jehoiachin Exiles and the people of Israel (called mainly בית ישראל), in Ezek 20:1–38. The two prophecies and Ezekiel's positions are dealt at length in Chapter 6, below.

Ezra–Nehemiah proceeds along this same line of separation, posing the opposition between the Repatriates and Those Who Remained as an opposition between the allochthonous Israelites and the עמי הארצות, the autochthonous peoples of the land.

---

57. Jeremiah uses עם הארץ in a fairly similar way, as a general term for the people, see Jer 1:18; 37:2; 44:21; 52:25. Thus Jack R. Lundbom, *Jeremiah 1–20* (AB 21A; New Haven: Yale University Press, 1999), 245–46; and while Yair Hoffman (*Jeremiah 1–24* [Mikra LeIsrael; Jerusalem: The Hebrew University/Magnes Press; Tel Aviv: Am Oved, 2001 (in Hebrew)], 121) considered both options for the meaning of the phrase—the more general one and the presumably elite meaning—he preferred the former option, on the basis of the other occurrences in Jeremiah.

58. This may also be the meaning in Ezek 45:16, 22; 46:6, 9, which uses the phrase in proximity to the נשיא, who stands as the highest leader; so also Dan 9:6; Job 12:24, which mention the heads of the community. Yet, Ezek 7:27 divides leadership between the king and the נשיא (translated therefore as "chief, prince" following Ezekiel's distinction between the two functions in 32:29), see Greenberg (*Ezekiel 1–20*, 156), who also proposed that these two terms may be synonyms; thus the dichotomy between the leader and the general population is maintained.

59. Moshe Greenberg (*Ezekiel 21–37* [AB 22A; New York: Doubleday, 1997], 465, 569) pointed out aptly that עם הארץ closes this list of ruling classes by referring back to ארץ, the anonymous land, of v. 24, and thus helps to construct a picture of the "total corruption" of Jerusalem. Another quite obscure reference is Isa 24:4, where the phrase עם הארץ closes the parallel phrases הארץ and תבל, in a context that refers to settlers of the land in vv. 5–6 as ישביה or ישבי הארץ. Yet, commentators prefer reading it ʿim haʾareṣ, "with the earth," in this passage (so, for instance, Joseph Blenkinsopp, *Isaiah 1–39* [AB 19; New York: Doubleday, 2000], 350–51).

Of great interest is Ezekiel's unique usage of עם הארץ, in Ezek 12:17–20. Used as a positive term, it serves to designate Ezekiel's own community, his immediate audience consisting of the Jehoiachin Exiles; here they are the עם הארץ, listening to the prophecy of doom forecast for יושבי ירושלים אל אדמת ישראל (v. 19).[60] The sign action the prophet is commanded to do (v. 18) is explained as predicting the total annihilation of this community and its entire ecological surroundings (למען תשם ארצה ממלאה, "because their land will be desolate of its multitudes," v. 19b).[61] This prophecy illustrates the polemical tone between the Jehoiachin Exiles and the residents of Jerusalem even prior to its destruction.[62] The extraordinary designation of the community of Exiles as עם הארץ seems to be Ezekiel's purposeful usage of this term applied intentionally to the Jehoiachin Exiles in Babylon, whom the prophet, nevertheless, counts as the true genuine community.[63]

---

60. Medieval and modern commentators debate over the question of this prophecy's audience and its addressees. See Moshe Greenberg (*Ezekiel 1–20*, 222–25) who, among others, accepted the identification of עם הארץ with the Exiles. Greenberg followed Qimhi and Eliezer of Baugeuncy who distinguished between עם הארץ as the Exiles (whom Qimhi called בני הגולה) that were the prophets' immediate audience, and the inhabitants of Jerusalem who were the addressees of this judgment prophecy. Walther Zimmerli (*Ezekiel* [trans. R. E. Clements; Hermeneia; Philadelphia: Fortress, 1979], 1:276–77) understood עם הארץ to refer to the Jehoiachin Exiles, whom the prophet calls by their previous designation, since they were from the upper classes of Jerusalem (following Würthwein).

61. Compare to Ezek 4:9–17, which focuses on the suffering of exile; see Block, *Ezekiel 1–24*, 381. Kelvin G. Friebel (*Jeremiah's and Ezekiel's Sign-Acts* [JSOTSup 283; Sheffield: Sheffield Academic, 1999], 281–89) argued that this sign-act polemicizes against the conception of the inviolability of Jerusalem, still held by the Exiles (pp. 288–89).

62. While the prophecy is not dated, the designation of the Jerusalemites and ישבי ירושלים stands in parallel to Ezek 11:14; compare to Ezek 33:24, where after the Destruction the survivors are referred to as ישבי החרבות האלה; so Greenberg, *Ezekiel 1–20*, 225.

63. Compare the reading of Block (*Ezekiel 1–24*, 382), who found this usage "remarkable, and perhaps ironic," in that Ezekiel's fellow exiles "by definition are a people without a land," with that espoused already by Eichrodt (*Ezekiel*, 154), who attributed to Ezekiel "extreme irony in…addressing them in a title they are no longer qualified to bear"; I, for one, do not think it works with the prophet's group-identity. Hence Block pointed out the importance of this phrasing: "it reminds the prophet at least that God recognizes the exiles' claims." I would indeed accept this understanding as the prophet's message to his fellow Exiles. See also Joyce, *Ezekiel*, 119. The suggestion that this is said ironically had already been suggested by Eichrodt (*Ezekiel*, 154–55), though he did not mention an internal polemic between the Judean groups.

Understanding Ezekiel's contrasting usages of this term opens the way to a reevaluation of the occurrences of עם הארץ and עמי הארצות in Persian-period sources. עם הארץ in both Haggai and Zechariah follows Ezek 12:19, and refers positively to the in-group community of the Exiles, now Repatriates (and truly again in the land). On the contrary, Ezra–Nehemiah follows the lead of Ezekiel's equation of the residents of Judah as the עמי הארץ (Ezra 10:2, 11) and עמי הארצות (Ezra 9:1, 2, 11; Neh 9:30; 10:29; as also 2 Chr 32:13), and even elaborates on the equivalence to the Canaanite foreign peoples drawn from the analogy to pentateuchal traditions in Leviticus and Deuteronomy.

We can thus see that the prophetic literature differs significantly from the historiography of Ezra–Nehemiah in outlook and terminology, and should not be conflated. Haggai's terms should not be taken as parallel to those in Ezra–Nehemiah; and this distinction is most important in reference to עם הארץ in Hag 2:4. Indeed, the parallel between, or the interchange of כל שארית העם and כל עם הארץ, suggests that Haggai uses the two phrases as alternative (positive) designations of the Repatriate community, considered to be the "Remnant of this people" (2:2–3).

This difference of terminology reflects a distinct observation of the oppositions between the Judean communities. Haggai does not use (and probably does not know of) Ezra–Nehemiah's opposition of "otherness." According to that latter opposition, the denigrating analogy between Israel and the Canaanite peoples was re-adapted to their current conflict between Repatriates and Those (Judeans) Who Remained in the land. Haggai seems to be closer to Zechariah's positioning of Repatriates as the settlers of an empty land, a conception that simply does not see *any* "others"; they are as if transparent, as if invisible.

Hence, even without designating the out-group in any way, merely by utilizing the arguments of *entirety* (by way of the terms שארית העם, הנשאר) and of *continuity* from past to present (by calling on the elders to "Remember!" the First Temple, and by evoking the first covenant, following the Exodus as a model for the present, 2:4–5), Haggai articulates his own exclusive view: the Repatriates are עם הארץ (as in Ezek 12:19); they are the "Remnant of this people"—and no others share in this community.

Chapter 5

DEUTERO-ISAIAH:
FROM BABYLON TO JERUSALEM
(ISAIAH 40–48, 49–66)

With Deutero-Isaiah (Isa 40–66), we move further back in time and broaden our geographical spectrum.[1] In its earlier part, Isa 40–48 are assumed here to have been written in Babylon in an era that reflects the transition between empires, namely, the early years of Persian control over Babylon. Thus these chapters attest to the closing years of the second phase of confrontation within exilic literature prior to the return. The second part, the "Jerusalem chapters" (Isa 49–66), contains miscellaneous materials, assumed here to have been collected and written in Yehud after the return, and may primarily be dated to the "first century of Persian rule."[2] Thus, these "Jerusalem chapters" at the earliest parallel the time of Haggai and Zechariah, in the closing decades of the sixth century B.C.E., and they may be as late as the period of Ezra and Nehemiah's activity, that is, the mid-fifth century.

In a recent and very helpful study, Lena-Sofia Tiemeyer has presented the rich, diverse, and challenging scholarly discussions of Isa 40–66.[3] Focusing on the composition history of the book, which has been reconstructed on the basis of literary themes and theological conceptions, Tiemeyer pointed out that the contradicting poles of continuity and discontinuity in Isa 40–66 have governed the diverse scholarly approaches.

1. In addition to this prophetic compilation, the editorial levels of the books of Jeremiah and Ezekiel may have been shaped in this period as well; see Chapters 6 and 7 below.
2. Joseph Blenkinsopp (*Isaiah 56–66* [AB 19B; New York: Doubleday, 2003], 43, and see the entire discussion, 42–54) mentioned this time frame for Isa 56–66.
3. Lena-Sofia Tiemeyer, "Continuity and Discontinuity in Isaiah 40–66: History of Research," in *Continuity and Discontinuity: Chronological and Thematic Development in Isaiah 40–66* (ed. L. S. Tiemeyer; FRLANT; Göttingen: Vandenhoeck & Ruprecht, forthcoming). I thank Dr. Tiemeyer for allowing me to read her paper prior to its publication. See her *For the Comfort of Zion: The Geographical and Theological Location of Isaiah 40–55* (VTSup 139; Leiden: Brill, 2011), 13–51.

Lines of *thematic continuity/discontinuity* entangled with portrayals of *geographic continuity/discontinuity* have led scholars to quite dissimilar reconstructions of the prophetic voice (or rather voices); of the time(s) and place(s) of his (/their) activity; and thus of his (/their) audience(s).

Concerning issues of *continuity* and *discontinuity*, I follow Menahem Haran and Shalom M. Paul; indeed, I find myself only generally following the Jewish and Israeli scholarly line that presumes basically (and though quite simplistically) one prophet prophesying first in Babylon prior to the Restoration, and then in Jerusalem following his return.[4] Menahem Haran considered Isa 40–48 to be the product of a relatively short period of prophetic activity, 539–529 B.C.E.; that is, following the Persian subjugation of Babylon, during the presumed period of the first returns and prior to 529 B.C.E., the end of Cyrus's regime. In fact, Haran even narrowed the time of composition to a year or two within the earliest part of this period, prior to the first return.[5] Chapters 49–66 present the prophecies of this same individual upon his return, differing only in geographical location and circumstances. Haran further argued (on the basis of Isa 63:7–64:10; 66:1–2) that the time frame of these later chapters reflects a period prior to the reestablishment of the Temple; therefore, the mention of the city walls is only part of the prophetic visions (56:5; 62:6; and its gates, 54:12; 60:11).[6]

Hence, according to Haran and Paul, the literary division of chs. 40–48 and 49–66 accords *geographical discontinuity* illustrated by the transition from Babylon to Jerusalem, and it further accords a chronological distinction between prophecies that were said prior to the return and post-return prophecies.[7] Nevertheless, out of this discontinuity, both scholars argued for a *thematic continuity* in Isa 40–66.

---

4. Tiemeyer, "Continuity," 1. While Yehezkel Kauffman (*History of Israelite Religion* [Jerusalem: Bialik, 1976 [in Hebrew], 4:55–63) was the influential advocate of continuity within Deutero-Isaiah, I cannot accept his position regarding geographical continuity: he restricted the composition of both units to the Babylonian arena and to the beginning of the reign of Cyrus (539–530 B.C.E.).

5. Haran, *Between Ri'shonot*, 29–32.

6. Ibid., 89–102. See Paul (*Isaiah 40–66*, 5–22) for additional arguments for the unity of Isa 40–66 and a dating of the entire book within the sixth century. This argument is dependent upon the assumption that segments like Isa 63:7–64:11 are the prophet's (Haran, *Between Ri'shonot*, 93; Paul, *Isaiah 40–66*, 560). I would, however, question this assumption; I prefer the possibility that Isa 49–66 includes additional miscellaneous materials of different hands, and see below.

7. Haran, *Between Ri'shonot*, 81, 101–2; Paul, *Isaiah 40–66*, 1–12. This view is of course but one of the various perspectives on Isa 40–66. Most scholars continue to hold to Duhm's designation of Deutero-Isaiah as chs. 40–55 and Trito-Isaiah as

An opposite perspective on the Judahite provenance of Deutero-Isaiah was carried on and developed by Hans M. Barstad in several papers and monographs published between 1982 and 2003.[8] In his monograph, *The Babylonian Captivity of the Book of Isaiah: "Exilic" Judah and the Provenance of Isaiah 40–55*, Barstad surveyed the scholarly discussions that had already perceived the composition of Second Isaiah as taking place outside Babylonia,[9] criticized the nineteenth- and twentieth-century traditions of Deutero-Isaian scholarship that adhered to the Babylonian context;[10] and put forth his own opinion that this prophet might well have been active among the Judeans who had remained in the land and never been exiled.[11] But Barstad did limit his conclusions, saying that "none of the 19th-century arguments in favour of a Babylonian setting of Isa 40–55 can any longer be regarded as valid."[12] Rather, Barstad assumed that "the text in question originated on Palestinian soil."[13] In the following discussion I argue that Barstad did not take into consideration socio-psychological arguments concerning intergroup relations, and that therefore he missed the rhetorical strategies and themes in the book that clearly suggest its Babylonian origin and its continuous thematic Babylonian orientation upon return.

Delving more into the question of authorship and audience addressed in Isa 40–66, I would like to point out a surprising agreement between two opposite scholarly perspectives. As to the prophet's audience, Haran offered two distinct possibilities. On the one hand, he repeatedly flagged particular prophecies as addressing the Repatriates (referring to 56:8; 66:20; calling them "mourners" in 57:18; 66:10, and see אבלי ציון in

chs. 56–66. See Bernhard Duhm, *Das Buch Jesaja übersetzt und erklärt* (HKAT 3/1; Göttingen: Vandenhoeck & Ruprecht, 1892; 4th ed. 1922); and see Tiemeyer, "Continuity," 3.

8. Hans M. Barstad, *The Babylonian Captivity of the Book of Isaiah: "Exilic" Judah and the Provenance of Isaiah 40–55* (Oslo: Novus, 1997); idem, "On the So-called Babylonian Literary Influence in Second Isaiah," *SJOT* 2 (1987): 90–110. Tiemeyer (*For the Comfort of Zion*, 363) followed Barstad and located the composition of the entire book of Deutero-Isaiah in Yehud, and argued for its long period of evolution in Templeless Judah as part of the "continuous Judahite Isaianic prophetic tradition." Yet her observation accentuates the need to address the sociological questions concerning the prophet, his audience(s), and his opponents (mostly indicated in Isa 65–66).

9. Barstad, *Babylonian Captivity*, 23–24.

10. Ibid., 58–75.

11. Ibid., 84–87, 93.

12. Ibid., 87.

13. Ibid., 93.

61:2–3). On the other hand, however, based on the prophet's reference to Abraham (Isa 51:2, and its presumed connections with Ezek 33:24), he argued that in his Jerusalem prophecies, the prophet addresses Those Who Remained.[14]

Adducing a very different scholarly perspective, Rainer Albertz discussed the evolution of Isa 40–66, and assumed that these chapters are the product of two editorial groups, both active in Yehud: DtIE[1] (521 B.C.E.); and DtIE[2] (from after 515 through the fifth century B.C.E.).[15]

While Haran and Albertz suggested clearly distinct pictures of the literary evolution, authorship, and date of this prophetic collection, they agreed on the issue of the prophet's audience in Yehud. They separately argued that upon return the prophet, or the DtIE[1] group, changed, or at least enlarged, his (/its) audience and now addressed those who had stayed in Judah, in an attempt to enfold them into the Repatriate enclave.

Confronting what may seem quite a chaotic literary mix, I find that the concept of *geographical discontinuity* that, however, retains a *thematic continuity* serves as a valuable tool for sorting the materials in Isa 40–66, for accepting its division to Babylonian chs. 40–48, and to Jerusalem ones in chs. 49–66. Moreover, I believe this is exactly the point at which the socio-psychological framework for making sense of intergroup relations may be usefully utilized, in order to explore the relationships between the *thematic continuity* and the *geographic discontinuity* in these chapters. In contrast to the foregoing scholars, I argue that *geographic discontinuity*, that is, the new setting in Yehud, does not mark a change of authorship and audience(s). Isaiah 40–66 hold mainly the prophecies of one Babylonian prophet who first prophesied in Babylon prior to the Restoration, and then experienced the return and continued his mission in Jerusalem following his return. But, as regularly in the prophetic litera-ture, this collection holds much more than the words of that anonymous prophet.[16] Chapters 56–59 and 63–66 contain miscellaneous materials

14. On Haran's understanding of the change only as a change of place, see *Between Ri'shonot*, 102 (and passim). On the notion that the prophet also addresses Those Who Remained, see p. 84 and n. 25.

15. Albertz, *Israel in Exile*, 381, 399–404, 428–33.

16. Hanson (*Dawn of Apocalyptic*, 32–46) pointed out the need to distinguish between literary or thematic similarities and the question of authorship. While recognizing multiple authorship in Isa 56–66, he argued (p. 37) that similarities result from the common tradition that unites the entire Isaianic school, and that Isa 56–66 clearly "develops out of the message of Second Isaiah"; yet the two units show evidence of distinct sociological backgrounds (p. 42). The miscellaneous character of chs. 49–66 may be illustrated by the diversity of literary materials within these chapters, which lend themselves to the portrayal of a diversity of conflicts and

that bring together both earlier and later passages.[17] Group identity perspectives that surface in these prophecies (and will be thoroughly presented below) show that Isa 49–66 (in its miscellaneous character) follow Isa 40–48, and treat only the community of the Repatriated Exiles as the in-group of God's people.

The following discussion shows that from the thematic point of view, Isa 40–66 indeed demonstrate *thematic continuity* of Babylonian exilic ideologies that remain constant in Babylon and subsequently in Yehud. In fact, while the present study distinguishes two major eras (the Persian and Neo-Babylonian periods) and two geographical arenas (Babylon and Judah/Yehud), discussing Isa 40–66 from the point of view of the exploration of group identity demonstrates clear thematic congruence between the Babylonian and the Jerusalem chapters.[18] This *thematic*

antagonistic groups (see below). See Jan L. Koole, *Isaiah III*. Vol. 1, *Isaiah 40–48* (HCOT; Kampen: Kok Pharos, 1997), 19–30. The possibility of diverse prophetic voices/authors within the earlier part of the book only increases the likelihood of an even more diverse array of voices by the last chapters of Isaiah; see Tiemeyer, *For the Comfort of Zion*, 13–51.

17. The scholarship on Isa 40–66 is very diverse and highly interesting. I will only mention two studies which I found to be particularly thought-provoking. Norman H. Snaith ("Isaiah 40–66: A Study of the Teaching of the Second Isaiah and Its Consequences," in *Studies on the Second Part of the Book of Isaiah* [ed. H. M. Orlinsky and N. H. Snaith; VTSup 14; Leiden: Brill, 1967], 135–264) wrote of "a common authorship and origin" (p. 141). That is, Isa 40–66 forms one editorial whole, in three original units. Chapters 40–48, 49–55, and 60–62 are assigned to different periods of the life and activity of a single anonymous prophet, Second Isaiah, the prophet of the Babylonian Exiles and the Repatriates; whereas chs. 56–59, and 63–66 are of different origin (pp. 139–46). For a detailed and more complex description of the authors' identity(/ies) in Isa 40–55, 56–66, and for a view of the evolution of these chapters, consult Koole, *Isaiah III*, 1:1–43. Koole challenged the accepted internal chronological order within Isa 40–66, and considered chs. 56–66, usually treated as Trito-Isaiah, to be the product of several authors (p. 21); he proposed that those materials were based on an early exilic nucleus closely connected to Lamentations, and that they thus reflect the first decades after the 587/6 catastrophe (pp. 27–28, 31–33). This earlier nucleus was elaborated through several redactional revisions, before it was incorporated in the book of Isaiah. Yet Koole entertained the possibility that the author of chs. 56–66 was an exilic prophet who had "personally experienced the return...and finally continued his work in Jerusalem" (p. 19).

18. Snaith (*Isaiah 40–66*, 147–53) argued that the Return and the Restoration were the climax of this prophet's message, and emphasized his unambiguous nationalistic perspective, tuned to the salvation of the Exiles as "the new people of God" (154–65, quotation from p. 158). Snaith has convincingly set aside the notions of univeralism and humanism that are supposed (by traditional scholarship) to have governed these chapters as secondary in occurrence and importance (147–48).

continuity, therefore, supports the case for an exilic-Repatriate authorship and audience throughout. Yet, within the Jerusalem chapters (and specifically in 56:9–57 and chs. 65–66), there are indications of inter-group polemics that deepen our perspective on the postexilic communities in Yehud during the period of the Restoration.[19]

The major question posed in this study concerns the group orientation(s) that appear(s) in Isa 40–66; of paramount importance, then, is determining the geographical and social location of the prophet and his addressees. I have already stated my assumption that the prophet (and the subsequent tradents) was/were part of the Babylonian exilic community—but of which group? The Jehoiachin Exiles, or Exiles of the subsequent waves of deportees? Does the change of setting involve a change of audience? Did the prophet continue to address only his fellow Repatriates? Did he turn to Those Who Remained? Were the prophet and his school inclusivist (speaking to both groups) or exclusivist (addressing only the Repatriates)? The following discussion enters the lively scholarly debate on Deutero-Isaiah from this very focused angle, to articulate the parameters of group identities that shape these complicated prophetic texts of the exilic and Restoration periods.

1. *"My city and My exiled people" (Isaiah 45:13): Arguments of Exclusivity in Isaiah 40–66*

a. *In-group Designations: Arguments of Continuity and Entirety*
Thematic continuity shows itself in Isa 40–66 as a whole, in the focus given prominently to the bond between God and His people, or rather, His Exiled- and then Repatriated-people. The prophet uses the idiom of personal relationships in both units, chs. 40–48 and 49–66: the people are God's (chosen) people, and the proximity between them is accentuated repeatedly by the use of the first (or third) person possessive pronoun עמי / עמו (Isa 40:1; 43:20; in chs. 49–66: 49:13; 56:3; 57:13; 63:8; and עמי ולאומי, "My people, My Nation," 51:4). The prophet uses parallelism to invoke God's relationship with the forefathers: "My people" parallels "My servant," "Jacob / Israel" (note "His servant Jacob," 48:20; "Remember these things, O Jacob, for you, O Israel, are My servant," 44:21; 49:3). Commonly the people is designated by the paired names "Jacob / Israel" (40:27; 42:24; 43:1–7, 22, 28; 44:5, 21, 23; 48:12; 49:5,

---

19. Hanson (*The Dawn of Apocalyptic*, 42) designated the topic of God's relationship to the community and its fortunes as one of "two dominant characteristics" in Isa 56–66 that "stand in full harmony with the theology of Second Isaiah"; the other is the "pervasive polemical element" that governs these chapters as well.

6, 7); variations on this equation with "the fathers" include: "My people / the house of Jacob" (58:1);[20] "Israel / Jacob / the seed of Abraham" (41:8); "the house of Jacob / Israel / Judah" (48:1); "Abraham / Israel" (63:16); "Jacob / Judah / My chosen and My servant / My people" (65:9–10).[21]

These designations illustrate implicitly the exclusive arguments of *continuity* and *entirety*. Throughout Isa 40–66, the Exiles and the Repatriates are the direct descendants of Jacob, the house of Jacob, seed of Jacob, and the seed of Abraham, as they are also designated by the national names, mostly as Israel, and twice as Judah (48:1; 65:9).

This line of *continuity* appears also in reference to God; it is seen in the designations of His roles and epithets with regard His people. By the epithet בורא ישראל ("the Creator of Israel," 43:15; and elaborated in 64:7), God is repeatedly characterized as the Creator of His people, with whom He initiated His covenant, ואצרך ואתנך לברית עם ("I created you, and appointed you a covenant people," 42:1, 6; 49:8; and see 43:7, 21). The purpose of this creation of the people was to form Israel as God's obedient servant, who was never to forget his Creator (44:21). Yet, in a cosmological context, this creation of the people guarantees also the divine promises of salvation (44:24–28). Other epithets within Deutero-Isaiah designate God as the God of Israel (41:17; 45:3, 15; 48:1, 2; 52:12); as the King of Jacob (41:21) and of Israel (44:6); as "the Mighty One of Jacob" (אביר יעקב, 49:26); and as Father (63:16; 64:7); but frequently as גואל, "Redeemer" ("your Redeemer"), accompanied with the epithet קדוש ישראל ("I your Redeemer, the Holy One of Israel," 41:14, 16, 20; 43:3, 14). Note also the accumulation of formulae: אני יהוה קדושכם בורא ישראל מלככם, "I am your Holy One, the LORD, your King, the Creator of Israel" (43:15; and 48:17; 49:7; 54:5, 8; 55:5).

Applying these epithets of God and the national names to the Babylonian Exiles (then, Repatriates) in such an accentuated way seems to signal a new step towards re-identifying this community as Israel. Williamson aptly argued that **Isa 49:1–6** and specifically v. 3 (ויאמר לי עבדי אתה ישראל אשר בך אתפאר, "And He said to me, 'You are My servant, Israel in whom I glory'") *designate* (rather than simply describe)

---

20. Each of the patronymic names also occurs separately: "Israel" (Isa 45:17; 46:13; 49:3; and "the seed of Israel," 45:25); "Jacob" (48:20; and "the seed of Jacob," 45:19); "Jacob/Jeshurun" (42:2).

21. While these designations run through chs. 40–66, Williamson ("The Concept of Israel in Transition") paid attention to their more frequent use in Isa 40–48, and the decrease in the use of the national patronymic names in Isa 49–55, and particularly in chs. 56–66 (pp. 145–47).

the servant as Israel.[22] Williamson suggested that the servant, whom he
called the "new Israel," is identified with "a righteous remnant amongst
the people,"[23] which he nevertheless found to be no different than
Jacob/Israel. Yet, Williamson reconstructed an additional step in "the
concept of Israel in transition" whereby the prophet, in the face of the
lack of a response from the people, presumably restricted his definitions
of Israel to merely "a faithful individual or group within the community."[24] While I would consider this last suggestion to be beyond the
evidence of our material, it seems that Williamson perceived what I
also recognize as Deutero-Isaiah's reidentification of the (entire) community of Babylonian Exiles as the exclusive new Israel. Thus, indeed,
the concept of Israel has gone through a transition in Deutero-Isaiah, a
transition that has reconceived the (entire) community of Babylonian
Exiles (and Repatriates) as the "true Israel."[25] This observation of an
exclusive reidentification of Israel gains further support from the subtle
opposition mounted in Isa 40–66.

b. *Erasing the Out-group Opposition: Zion as an Empty City and Land*
Isaiah 40–66's address to the prophet's compatriots in the Babylonian
Exile, and then back in Yehud, relies on the narrative flow that these
chapters enfold: exiled by God from Jerusalem as a divine punishment
for various misdeeds (40:1–2; 52:3–6),[26] this exilic community is now
promised redemption (40:9–11; 43:6; 49:9–12; 51:9–11);[27] it will be led
out of its present location in exile: כי הלך לפניכם יהוה ומאספכם אלהי
ישראל ("The LORD is marching before you, the God of Israel is your rear

22. Ibid., 146–47.
23. Ibid., 147.
24. Ibid.
25. Contra Williamson, and in distinction from Snaith (*Isaiah 40–66*, 166–76),
who considered Second Isaiah to have been produced for the Jehoiachin Exiles in
Babylon, I would describe differently the relationships between Deutero-Isaiah and
Ezekiel and their books, see pp. 265–76.
26. The following passages reflect on sin and punishment brought against
Jerusalem as the reason for the present distress in exile: Isa 42:23–25; 43:22–28;
47:6; 48:1–8, 18; 50:1–3; 51:17–23; similarly in chs. 56–66: 56:9–57:13; 57:16–19;
58:1–12; 59:1–8, 9–15; 63:7–64:11.
27. References to the places of exile, thus departure points for the redemption,
are few (43:14; 48:20), although the general geographic direction of north to east
seems indicative (41:2, 25). Compare this with the general reference to "the ends of
earth" (41:5; 42:1–9, especially, v. 10), the four cosmological directions (East, West,
North, and South: 43:5–7; 49:12), or the furthest areas across desert and waters
(42:13–17; 43:1–7, 16–21). See below, pp. 108–11.

guard," 52:11–12).[28] Their redemption will conclude in their return to Zion. The prophecies emphasize that the city awaits, "bereaved and barren," for their return (49:14–21; 51:9–11; 52:7–10, 11–12; as also in chs. 56–66: 61:1–9), and the land is empty and desolate (51:3; 61:10–11). Thus, restoration includes the rebuilding of Jerusalem, the cities of Judah, and the Temple itself (44:26–28; 65:21–23). Moreover, redemption and return are intertwined with God's return to Zion, and His reappearance on its hills (40:9–11; 52:1–2, 7–10; 54:1–10; 62:10–12).

These prophecies of redemption and return articulate distinction between Zion and the prospected Repatriated Exiles, led by the returning God (Isa 40:9; 41:27; 51:3). Counter to Williamson, who maintained that Deutero-Isaiah's references to Zion and Jerusalem refer proleptically to the people (Jacob/Israel, or Israel alone), I argue that Isa 40:9–10; 44:26; 49:14–21; 52:7–10, all treat Zion (and the rest of the cities of Judah, 44:26) as separate entities from the people, waiting empty for the Babylonian Repatriates to return (along these lines see also 46:13; and explicitly, 48:1–2).[29]

The rhetorical opposition between Diaspora and Homeland in Isa 40–66 is thus between the Babylonian exilic community and Zion, or to put it more precisely, between the Repatriates and the empty, desolate city, indicated by the succession of metaphors in the feminine: ותאמר ציון עזבני יהוה ואדני שכחני ("The LORD has forsaken me, My Lord has forgotten me," 49:14); ואני שכולה וגלמודה גלה וסורה ("I was bereaved and barren, exiled and disdained," 49:21), עקרה לא ילדה ... שוממה ("barren…who bore no child…a wife forlorn," 54:1–10),[30] עזובה ושנואה ("forsaken and rejected," 60:15). The delight of its restoration is the incredible transformation Zion will go through from her barren and desolate state to having her children brought back from afar, reborn and multiplied (49:21; 54:1–4), and regaining her majesty and glory

---

28. Isa 52:11–12 alludes to the Exodus Traditions (and note the allusion to the deliverance at the Sea, 43:16–19). This has been broadly recognized by interpreters; see, for instance, Claus Westermann, *Isaiah 40–66* (trans. D. M. G. Stalker; OTL; London: SCM, 1969), 127, 253; John D. W. Watts, *Isaiah 34–66* (WBC 25; Waco, Tex.: Word, 1987), 134–35. Paul (*Isaiah 40–66*, 393–96) called attention to the similarity to Lam 4:15, and to Jer 51:45, before noting the reversal of the Exodus tradition in v. 20; the similarities heighten the splendor of the deliverance from Babylon.

29. Williamson, "The Concept of Israel," 145; compare to Snaith (*Isaiah 40–66*, 173–76) who held that Isa 48:1–11 polemicizes against Those Who Remained in the land.

30. See further Isa 62:4, לא יאמר לך עוד עזובה ולארצך לא יאמר עוד שממה, where 4QIsaᵃ reads שוממה, a reading which is also reflected in other Versions.

(52:1–2)—both in the eyes of the Repatriates, and in the sight of all nations (45:1–8; as also 60:1–15).

62:1–9 and 10–12 convey the distinction between the city (the land) and the Repatriates. The passage begins by addressing the restoration of Zion, including transformations of the designations for both the city and the land (vv. 1–9, specifically vv. 2–4). Verses 10–12 demonstrate the clear distinction and yet the close connections between בת ציון (v. 11) and the Repatriated Exiles, whom God has led back to her.[31] As in Isa 40:3; 57:14, the people have been led on the road from afar (62:10). Their arrival in *bat*-Zion has completed the transformation in status of both people and city. They are to be termed עם הקדש גאולי יהוה ("The Holy People, The Redeemed of the LORD," v. 12; and note also עם קדשך in 63:18); the city is now to be known as דרושה עיר לא נעזבה ("Sought Out, A City Not Forsaken," 62:12) for she has ceased to be neglected (compare also 62:2).[32]

In these two intertwined passages, Isa 62 adds to the earlier examples a further illustration of the same tendency to reidentify, redesignate, the people (the Repatriates), the city, and their interrelationships. In mobilizing this opposition between the Repatriates and the empty city and land, Deutero-Isaiah precedes (or is contemporary with) Zechariah son of Iddo, the prophet of the Repatriates.[33]

c. *Inclusivity among Repatriates Arriving from Afar*

The tendency to identify the Repatriated Exiles as the people is further emphasized in those prophecies of consolation that describe the gathering of the dispersed from afar (43:6; 60:4; 65:9–10; 66:7–9):[34] they cross mountains, walk through deserts, and pass flowing waters (42:13–17;

31.   Isa 62:10–12 differs from 62:1–5 in its restricted focus on the city and complete disregard of the land (compare to v. 4). For the secondary character of these verses that close chs. 60–62, and the proposal that they comment on Deutero-Isaiah (alluding particularly to 40:3, 10; 52:11), see Westermann, *Isaiah 40–66*, 378–79. Watts (*Isaiah 34–66*, 321) considered this prophecy to be the fulfillment of Isa 54.

32.   Hanson (*The Dawn of Apocalyptic*, 60–61) noted the thematic similarities between Isa 60–62 and Second Isaiah.

33.   Similarities are indeed apparent when Isa 49:15–21 is compared with Zech 8:1–15.

34.   Westermann (*Isaiah 40–66*, 405) argued that Isa 65:9–10 is an intrusion into the later Judean context of "a prophecy spoken during the exile," conveying a promise of return to and repossession of the land addressed to the Exiles, as is typical of Deutero-Isaiah. He further noted comparable similarities between Isa 66:7–9 and 49:20–23, and considered 66:6 a response to skeptic doubts concerning the return and its possible cessation (p. 419).

43:16–21). The Repatriates' distant point of departure is specified as east and north (46:11; see also 41:2, 25; it is implied in 49:12). Thus the target of return is clearly the Land of Israel, and the directions are oriented with it as core. Yet, it is just as clear that the text points to the area of Babylon as the Diasporic center. These chapters contain three calls to leave Babylon (Isa 48:20–22; 52:11–12; and 55:12), and they perceive it to be the place of deliverance with or even without actually mentioning it (compare to 43:14).[35]

In contradistinction to this focus on the Babylonian Exiles as the sole remnant, two prophetic passages describe the ingathering of Exiles from the four corners of the world, and from מקצה הארץ, the utmost "end of the earth" (43:5–6; 49:12).

The four directions are mentioned in **Isa 43:5–6**:

אל תירא כי אתך אני ממזרח אביא זרעך וממערב אקבצך:
אמר לצפון תני ולתימן אל תכלאי הביאי בני מרחוק ובנותי מקצה הארץ

Fear not, for I am with you: I will bring your folk from **the east**, I will gather you out of **the west**; I will say to **the north**, "Give back!" and to **the south**, "Do not withhold! Bring My sons from afar, and My daughters from the end of the earth.

The general references to "the end(s) of earth" (see also 41:5; 42:1–10, especially v. 10), to the four cosmological directions (east, west, north, and south, 43:5–7; 49:12); or to the furthest areas across desert and water (42:13–17; 43:1–7, 16–21)—all serve to embellish the description of deliverance. According to Westermann, this is part of the portrayal of God as Lord of History, a description that intentionally avoids referring to any specific geographical or political context.[36] Indeed, I concur with Westermann that these glorifying verses should not be used as the basis for the historical reconstruction of other presumed Yahwistic communities worldwide; and I would not derive from such proclamations an inclusive promise for a universal deliverance.[37]

---

35. See Paul, *Isaiah 40–66*, 331–32.

36. Westermann, *Isaiah 40–66*, 119. For east and west as testifying to God's universal sovereignty, see Isa 45:5–6; note also קצה הארץ in 42:10.

37. Compare to Paul, *Isaiah 40–66*, 208–9; Koole, *Isaiah III*, 1:297. Scholars have relied on these passages to construct a universalistic outlook for Isa 40–66. See, for instance, Watts (*Isaiah 34–66*, 133), who argued that the vision (Isa 43:5–6) follows the pattern of Isa 2:1–4 and 66:18–21; and while it does not promise the regaining of political power, it does project a general return. John N. Oswalt (*Isaiah 40–66* [NICOT; Grand Rapids: Eerdmans, 1998], 141) cited Isa 11:11–12; 27:13; 49:12; and 60:4 as concurring in their universalistic perspective. He suggested three different interpretations from (1) the particular limited prophecy to restore the actual

The figure of the four corners of the world appears again in **Isa 49:12**, in a more challenging context, since it presents a unique oppositional order, different from the common pairing of east–west, north–south:

הנה אלה מרחוק יבאו והנה אלה מצפון ומים ואלה מארץ סינים

Look! These are coming **from afar**, these from **the north** and **the west**, and these from **the land of Sinim**.

This verse suggests the order: east—north—west—south. In Isa 46:11 (קרא ממזרח עיט מארץ מרחק איש עצתו), "I summoned that swooping bird from the East; from a distant land, the man for My purpose"), מרחק stands in apposition to "the east," and is even specified as a territory, a distant land, that is, east of Babylon; thus מרחוק in 49:12 may refer here as well to that east direction.[38] The sequence of 49:12 closes with מארץ סינים, which should be read סונים (see 4QIsaᵃ: סוניים), pointing to southern Egypt (סונה ,סון, Ezek 29:10; 30:6).[39] This special description is of crucial importance, since it reveals that the prophet maintains a Babylonian exilic orientation. He places Zion/Yehud at the center, as the target for the return; from that center point the prophet names the different directions from which the returnees will journey, beginning with Babylon, and then moving to the north, west, and south.[40]

While these global descriptions of deliverance are exceptional, they are of significance, since through them the prophet expresses an inclusive definition of the ingathered people as in-group. Divine salvation is targeted at *all* those who are away from the empty land (this conception may follow the Deuteronomic perspective of Deut 30:3–4).

This rhetoric in Isa 40–66 adopts a broader viewpoint than the spokespersons of either former Exiles or later Repatriates. On the one hand, the rhetoric of these Isaianic chapters differs from the exclusive Babylonian

dispersions of 721 B.C.E. from Israel, or of 586 B.C.E. from Judah; to (2) the wider diasporic existence following the Second Temple destruction of 70 C.E. or even 135 C.E.; and to (3) a universal sense (and even modern one). The two latter options are, to my mind, far-fetched. This entire scholarly approach was already challenged by Snaith (among others) in the 1950s and 1960s, though Christian dogmatics and modern universalism have continued to maintain this unsound line of interpretation. See Snaith, *Isaiah 40–66*, 154–65 (and the bibliography there).

38. See Paul, *Isaiah 40–66*, 331–32.

39. This is the view of Paul (ibid.); on the possibility that v. 12 is a secondary addition, see Westermann, *Isaiah 40–66*, 216.

40. It is hard to say, though, whether the prophet's own point of departure is Babylon or Yehud. See Koole (*Isaiah III*, 1:13–14) who aptly observed that for the Babylonian Exiles "Babylon remained foreign territory and Jerusalem the spiritual center" (p. 13).

focus of Ezra–Nehemiah and Zech 1–8; on the other hand, these chapters deviate from Ezekiel's more restricted view of the superior status of the Jehoiachin Exiles (Ezek 11:14–21; 14:12–23).[41] Isaiah 40–66, thus, does express inclusive views of a Yahwistic in-group. These two passages (43:5–6; 49:12) are clearly aimed at including all Exiles, with no mention of specific Diasporan communities. However, this inclusive view restricts salvation only to the Exiles; thus, Deutero-Isaiah's perspectives are clearly nationalistic, and are even narrowed down to those Exiled (or Repatriates) from among them.[42]

d. *Reidentification of the In-Group: Zion as the Repatriated Exiles*
Notwithstanding the clear distinction between the returning Exiles and the empty, desolate city of Jerusalem (subsection b, pp. 106–8, above), once they have returned, we find a second, opposing tendency to build very close connections between the Repatriates and Zion/Jerusalem (e.g. ופדויי יהוה ישובון ובאו ציון ברנה, Isa 51:11). Four passages from both units of Isa 40–66 are dealt with below (Isa 45:13; 51:12–16; 52:1–11; 61:1–9).

Isaiah 45:1–13 is a prophecy presenting Cyrus as the divinely elected agent of salvation for the exiled community (משיחו, vv. 1–7, 8, 9–13). The emphasis on the role of Cyrus (who is addressed in the second person in vv. 2–5), in addition to repeated phrases and themes that emphasize divine sovereignty, shape the polemical tone of these verses; and indeed, the internal polemic between the prophet and his assumed Babylonian audience has been recognized by commentators.[43] The final verse of the passage makes a clear connection between the exilic community and "the city": אנכי העירתהו בצדק וכל דרכיו אישר הוא יבנה עירי וגלותי ישלח ("It was I who roused him for victory and who level all roads for him. He shall rebuild My city and let My exiled people go"). In addition, this passage contributes an implicit but highly important element in terms of its perspective on group-identity, which I believe deserves a further look.

The noun גלות serves here as to designate the community of Exiles (as in Jer 28:4; and see also Isa 20:4). The Babylonian Exiles retain their in-group tagging (as more common with הגולה, see Ezek 11:25; שבי הגולה, Ezra 2:1, etc.). The possessive pronouns reveal the divine care extended

41. Ezekiel's orientation is dealt on pp. 140–85.
42. So already Snaith, *Isaiah 40–66*, 154–65.
43. See Watts, *Isaiah 34–66*, 154–58; Paul, *Isaiah 40–66*, 215, 259–64. Compare to Westermann (*Isaiah 40–66*, 164–65), who at first suggested that the polemic was between God and the foreign nations and their gods (44:24–28; 45:1–7), but then argued that vv. 9–13 refute perceptions within Israel.

to both עירי וגלותי, "My city and My exiled people." The city's reconstruction is connected with, equated to, and mentioned "in one breath"
with its anticipated repopulation by the Babylonian Exiles.[44]

Isaiah 51:12–16 opens with אנכי אנכי הוא מנחמכם ("I, I am He who
comforts you!," v. 12); as noted by Shalom Paul, this opening evokes the
opening consolation call of the whole prophetic collection, directed to
the people still in exile: נחמו נחמו עמי (Isa 40:1).[45] The section closes
with ולאמר לציון עמי אתה ("I have said to Zion: *You* are My people!,"
v. 16). The apposition between Zion and "My people" is of crucial
importance in this passage, functioning within the poetic context to identify implicitly the exiled people of Isa 40 with Zion itself.[46] Thus, the
prophecy reinstitutes the covenant relationship between God and His
people in a particular and delimited form: that is, between God and His
comforted and Repatriated people, who reside in His city.

Isaiah 52 shows both the prophet and his audience to be members of
the group of Repatriated Exiles who are already in Zion/Jerusalem. The
prophecy falls into three sections: vv. 1–6, 7–10, 11–12. The first calls
Jerusalem to regain its previous glorious status (v. 1), and to release itself
from the bondage of captivity (vv. 2–3). While vv. 4–6 refers back to the
people's past, the prophecy's major focus is the proclamation of God's
return to Jerusalem as King (vv. 7–10). This leads to a call addressed to
His people who are still "there" to return to Zion from among the nations
(vv. 11–12).[47]

Verses 1–2 refer to Jerusalem and (*bat-*)Zion as captives:

עורי עורי לבשי עזך **ציון**
לבשי בגדי תפארתך **ירושלים** עיר הקדש
כי לא יוסיף יבא בך עוד ערל וטמא:
התנערי מעפר קומי **שבי ירושלים**
התפתחי מוסרי צוארך **שביה בת ציון**

---

44. The same proximity of city and people also characterizes Isa 44:24–28,
where God's four proclamations refer to the restoration of Jerusalem and the
desolated cities of Judah (v. 26, of which God is said to be acting, אקומם), to God's
forces of creation (v. 27), and, finally, to Cyrus as responsible for executing God's
desires, including the restoration of Jerusalem and its Temple (v. 28). There is one
significant difference between the passages, however: the Repatriated residents of
Jerusalem are not mentioned in 44:28, as they are in the phrase עירי וגלותי of 45:13.

45. Paul, *Isaiah 40–66*, 372.

46. Westermann, *Isaiah 40–66*, 244.

47. This is the second call to go out, to leave Babylon; see Isa 48:20–22 and
55:12. See Paul, *Isaiah 40–66*, 393–94; Watts, *Isaiah 34–66*, 217. Koole (*Isaiah III*,
1:13–14) mentioned these verses as arguments for possible authorship in Judah
(together with 43:14; 48:20; 52:11), but he still argued that the place of authorship
"cannot be determined with certainty" (14).

> Awake, awake, clothe yourself in splendor, **O Zion**!
> Put on your robes of majesty, **Jerusalem**, holy city!
> For the uncircumcised and the unclean shall never enter you again.
> Shake off the dust; arise, **O captive Jerusalem!**
> Loose the bonds from your neck, **O captive *bat*-Zion!**

The two opening verses utilize an A B B′ A′ structure to create a tight parallelism between Jerusalem and (*bat*-)Zion. In the first part Zion and then Jerusalem are called to garb themselves in garments of victory and glory; in the second, to put off the dust and the garb of captivity. The grammatically anomalous שבי and the *hapax* שְׁבִיָּה (usually שְׁבִיָה, as in Deut 21:13; and Jer 48:46) figure as synonymous characterizations of Jerusalem and *bat*-Zion, contrasting to the awakened and revived Jerusalem and Zion of v. 1.[48] This usage of שבי and שְׁבִיָה, however, is exceptional on semantic as well as linguistic grounds. שבי and שְׁבִיָה designate the captured human beings and beasts taken away from a conquered territory into exile (Deut 32:42; 2 Chr 28:11, 14, 15). הלך בשבי is the common biblical phrase utilized for deportations following defeat and destruction (e.g. Deut 28:41; Ezek 12:11; Lam 1:20, etc.; and in reference to the enemies' fate, Jer 30:16; or specifically to that of the Babylonians, Isa 46:2). As presented above, שבי became the marked designation of the Babylonian Exiles (see Ezra 3:8; Neh 8:17). שְׁבִיָה בת ציון and שבי ירושלים seem to be in line with the constructs

---

48. Following Qimhi and Luzzatto, who understood שבי to be a noun (as in Num 31:12, 26; and in Isa 46:2; 49:24, 25, where it parallels מלקוח), and based on the parallelism of שבי and שְׁבִיָה, as in Jer 48:46. The grammatical problem, though, remains, namely, the non-correlation between the masculine noun שבי and the preceding feminine verbs in v. 2a. The feminine forms are probably governed by the *nomen rectum*, Jerusalem. Compare this with the common reading of קומי שבי ירושלים as two verbs, reflected already by 4QIsaᵃ, וקומי ושבי, as well as by the Peshitta, ܐܘܪܫܠܡ ܗܩܘܡܝ ܘܬܒܝ. The LXX, καὶ ἀνάστηθι κάθισον Ιερουσαλημ, adds the conjunction καὶ before קומי but keeps the asyndesis of שבי. This reading is reflected also in the Masoretic pointing, and thus is followed by medieval Jewish interpreters, such as Saadyah Gaon, Rashi, and Ibn Ezra; it continues to be reflected in modern critical commentaries, such as Westermann's translation (*Isaiah 40–66*, 247): "Arise, sit up, Jerusalem." Paul (*Isaiah 40–66*, 386) suggested that both meanings play their roles in a Janus parallelism: looking backwards, שבי appears as the verb, as in the construction קום / ישבת in Gen 27:19; looking forwards, שבי functions as a noun, suggesting the parallelism שבי and שְׁבִיָה. On the traditional Jewish exegesis of this passage, see Simcha Kogut, *Correlations Between Biblical Accentation and Traditional Jewish Exegesis* (Jerusalem: The Hebrew University/Magnes, 1994 [in Hebrew]), 233–35. I thank Dr. Noam Mizrahi for checking the Qumran readings.

שבי מצרים and גלות כוש of Isa 20:4,[49] phrases that designate these deported communities by their national origins.[50] Yet Deutero-Isaiah uses these two phrases for his Jerusalem audience, thus emphasizing their particular origin as those who had returned from the Babylonian captivity. Claus Westermann recognized that "the people whom the prophet has chiefly in mind are the [E]xiles—he often gives them the name Zion."[51] But it seems we can even go a step further—שבי ירושלים and שְׁבִיָּה בת ציון completely equate the city with its population, designated as שבי/שְׁבִיָּה, thus identifying this people as the Repatriated Exiles from Babylon. The rhetorical strategy of *entirety* seems to be working here; that is, the city and the "captives" are entirely identified with each other, in a way that excludes any other communities from being part of *bat*-Zion.

Verse 3 expresses divine recognition of, even regret over, the people's condition in exile, and sets forth a prospect of deliverance: "You were sold for no price, but not with money shall you be redeemed."[52] This extraordinary reference to exile implicitly makes God responsible for selling His people for no price (חנם).[53] This reading of the first part of the

---

49. 4QIsaᵃ at Isa 20:4 reads גולת כוש (yet גולה never occurs in MT in the construct; compare to the construct גלות in 2 Kgs 25:27; Obad 20, etc.). This pair, exceptional in Isa 1–39, adds to the other unique features of Isa 20:1–6; see Blenkinsopp, *Isaiah 1–39*, 320–23.

50. This construction may also stand behind what seems otherwise to be a redundant phrase, שבי הגולה (Ezra 2:1; Neh 7:6); perhaps we should understand this to mean "the captives that come from 'the exile,'" where "the exile" is a geographical designation, the place where they are living; and see my suggestion for Neh 1:3: אשר נשארו מן השבי, pp. 84–86, above.

51. Westermann, *Isaiah 40–66*, 247. Westermann considered 52:1–3 to be the closing passage of Isa 51:9–52:3, and even suggested that 51:11 be moved to follow 52:3, as the hopeful conclusion to this poem. This suggestion, however, is not relevant for the current discussion of identity.

52. See Watts, *Isaiah 34–66*, 214; and compare to John L. McKenzie's translation: "You were sold for nothing, and it was not for money that you were redeemed" (*Second Isaiah* [AB 20; New York: Doubleday, 1968], 121); compare to the NJPS translation, "You were sold for no price, and shall be redeemed without money"; this denigrating perspective of fierce rejection seems to be behind Watts' interpretation (*Isaiah 34–66*, 216), but I find hard to accept the admonishing tone related to these verses.

53. See Isa 50:1: מי מנושי אשר מכרתי אתכם לו הן בעונתיכם נמכרתם ("And to which of My creditors was it that I sold you off? You were only sold off for your sins"). מכר appears in contexts of defeat and subjugation in the repeated phrase in וימכרם ביד (Judg 2:14; 3:8; 4:7; 10:7; 1 Sam 12:9); in Ezek 30:12 it expresses a divine action in a prophecy against Egypt; and see Joel 4:4–8.

verse gains support from its closing phrase: ולא בכסף תגאלו. While both verbs (נמכרתם, תגאלו) are presented in the passive, refraining from presenting explicitly their agent, Isa 40–66 (and, in fact, throughout the Hebrew Bible) is consistent in using verbs of redemption only with God as the subject.[54] Thus, v. 3 seems to draw on the equation, just as God is the implied agent of redemption in this transaction (גאל), so is He the implied initiator of the captivity (מכר).

This portrayal of salvation, as the reversal of a divine act of rejection, correlates well with another unique passage in Isa 40–66. In Isa 54:7–8 the prophet admits that God had deserted His people; but he deals with this desertion by limiting its time span and enlarging the time available for consolation and salvation. Isaiah 52:3 seems to treat this same rhetorical concern. Here, the prophet does accept the idea that God is the author of the people's distress. The prophet might have entertained this idea himself (Isa 50:1); or he might have heard it from his contemporaries (see Ps 44:13: תמכר עמך בלא הון ולא רבית במחיריהם, "You sell Your people for no fortune, You set no high price on them").[55] Isaiah 52:3 seems to be refuting such protests. First, the prophet describes the action utilizing the passive voice (rather than, for example, making God the expressed subject of the verb), thus leaving vague the agent of this sale. Second, the prophet mitigates the divine responsibility for the people's distress by minimizing its duration and suggesting a great transformation in its wake (as he does in Isa 54:7–8).

This line is further developed in the elevated prose of Isa 52:4–6, which refer to the people's past, and indeed elaborate further on this notion of חנם נמכרתם:

כי כה אמר אדני יהוה מצרים ירד עמי בראשנה לגור שם ואשור באפס עשקו:
ועתה מי (ק: מה) לי פה נאם יהוה כי לקח עמי חנם משלו (ק: משליו) יהילילו
נאם יהוה ותמיד כל היום שמי מנאץ: לכן ידע עמי שמי לכן ביום ההוא כי אני
הוא המדבר הנני:

For thus said the LORD GOD: Of old, My people went down to Egypt to sojourn there; but Assyria has robbed them, giving nothing in return. Who (*Qere:* What) therefore do I gain here?—declares the LORD—for My people has been carried off for nothing, their mockers (*Qere:* leaders)

54. For God as the sole agent of redemption, see the occurrences of גאל, פדה, ישע, etc. This usage seems to be behind the exceptional designation of Cyrus as God's agent in Isa 45:12–13: הוא יבנה עירי וגלותי ישלח לא במחיר ולא בשחד ("He shall rebuild My city And let My exiled people go without price and without payment"), with Cyrus gaining divine authority to save.

55. Other nonprophetic statements of protest against God for His desertion may be found at Pss 74:1–2, 18–23; 89:47.

> howl—declares the LORD—and constantly, unceasingly, My name is
> reviled. Assuredly [they shall learn] on that day that I, the One who
> promised, am now at hand. (Isa 52:4–6)

Although different because of their prose style, and interpretive in their
theme, these verses are of essential importance in this context, and thus
should not be taken as a secondary gloss.[56] Rather, the prophet focuses
on the restoration of those who were earlier sold/deported and now are
promised a grand redemption, not with money, but through a divine
salvation that will bring the people to acknowledge God (v. 6), on the
model of the original redemption from Egypt. These verses draw lines of
continuity to the people's history.

The historical overview goes as far back as Jacob's descent to Egypt
(see Gen 47:4), and draws a direct analogy from that earliest sojourn and
redemption to the current (Assyrian/) Babylonian exile(s).[57] The common
denominator in these events is the people's residence *outside* the land of
Israel.

The theme of the people's sojourn outside the land, where God
initiates (and reinitiates) covenant relationships with them constitutes a
central element in Ezekiel's retrospective on the God–people covenant
relationship and the status of God as King of His (deported) people
(Ezek 20:1–38).[58] Isaiah 52:4–6 appears to draw on the same thematic
issues that occupied Ezekiel, the Judean existence in exile and the
God–people relationship. Verse 6 reads לכן ידע עמי שמי ... כי אני הוא
המדבר הנני ("Assuredly, My people shall learn My name, ... that I, the
One who promised, am now at hand"), thereby verifying this general
thematic context as it couches the present redemption in terms that allude
to the first stage of God's acquaintance with His people in Egypt, when
He had revealed His name to them (see Exod 3:13–14; 6:2–8).[59]

56. Westermann (*Isaiah 40–66*, 248) considered vv. 4–6 as a secondary gloss
interpreting the word חנם of v. 3; and see McKenzie, *Second Isaiah*, 127; Oswalt,
Isaiah 40–66, 362.

57. Paul (*Isaiah 40–66*, 387–88) referred to the pairing of Egypt/Assyria and
followed medieval exegetes who suggested that the latter implicitly includes or
refers to Babylon (Qimhi, Luzzatto). Watts (*Isaiah 34–66*, 216) mentioned the difference between the voluntary descent to Egypt and the divine judgment at work in
the Assyrian invasions and deportations. However, this distinction does not seem to
have been made by the prophet at all in vv. 4–5. Rather, both events are said to be
human, political actions against God's people.

58. See Rom-Shiloni, "Ezekiel as the Voice of the Exile," 20–31; and below,
pp. 156–69.

59. Compare to Paul (*Isaiah 40–66*, 389–90) who drew connections to other passages within the prophetic and psalmodic literature, where the words of God approve
his deeds (see, e.g., Isa 48:15; Ezek 5:13).

The passage also makes clear that God is *currently* present with the Exiles, outside of the land: "What therefore do I gain here?—declares the LORD—for My people has been carried off for nothing" (v. 5a).[60]

An additional phrase within this prophecy also demonstrates close connections with Ezekiel, and thus underscores its Babylonian-exilic ideological orientation. The notion that the people's circumstances of exile have caused God's name to be reviled (מנאץ, v. 5) is similar to Ezekiel's concern for the profanation of God's name among the nations (מחלל בגוים, in Ezek 36:16–32; and in Ezek 20:9, 14, 22).[61] Like Ezekiel, the prophet links the restoration of God's name (through the people's knowledge thereof) with the reinstitution of God's relationship with His people; that is, with the deportees (v. 5). Isaiah 52:1–10 thus plays an important role in identifying "captive Zion" (v. 2) as the deported people of God (עמי, vv. 5, 6; עמו, v. 10), who were at last redeemed and brought back to the ruins of Jerusalem (vv. 8–10). The prophecy thus identifies the Repatriated Exiles as the exclusive inhabitants of Jerusalem.

In **61:1–11** those previously in captivity (captives and prisoners, v. 1b), are set free (לקרא לשבוים דרור, v. 1).[62] These released captives are further called אבלי ציון ("the mourners of Zion," v. 3); they are the ones who will rebuild the devastated cities (v. 4).[63] They are the community with whom God will reestablish eternal covenant (v. 8), and who will be recognized worldwide as זרע ברך יהוה ("a stock the LORD has blessed," v. 9). While

60. On the dynamic divine presence among the Exiles, see Ezek 11:16; and the discussion below, pp. 150–53.

61. For concern about the divine name in situations of subjugation, see Ps 74:10, 18. מנאץ is a *hapax*, morphologically combining the Hithpael (Hithpoal) and the Pual; see Paul, *Isaiah 40–66*, 389.

62. Commentators disagree over the question of whether v. 2, לקרא לשבוים דרור ולאסורים פקח קוח, refers to the people, that is the Exiles (see, for instance, Paul, *Isaiah 40–66*, 538–40), or to prisoners in general. On the national level, Koole (*Isaiah III*, 1:265, 272–73) drew attention to the Jubilee laws, which refer to the release of human beings and the return of lands to their previous owners (Lev 25, as echoed also in Isa 61:4, 7); Koole argued that "the theology of liberation makes way for a theology of Israel" (273). But on the individual level, Westermann (*Isaiah 40–66*, 366) mentioned Isa 58:6 as another instance where Trito-Isaiah refers to "prisoners of debts and the like."

63. לשום לאבלי ציון is difficult, as the verb לשום requires an object, which is lacking in the current context. Samuel Kraus (*Isaiah* [1905] in Abraham Kahana's *Torah, Nevi'im, Kethubim with Critical Interpretation* [Jerusalem: Makor, 1969 (in Hebrew)], 62) preferred the emendation to לשלם, following Isa 57:18, whereas Arnold B. Ehrlich (*Jesaia, Jeremia* [Randglossen zur Hebräischen Bibel 4; Leipzig: Hinrichs, 1912], 217) suggested emending לשום to לשוב. Others would rather treat this phrase as an addition, and thus ignore it (as, for instance, Westermann, *Isaiah 40–66*, 367). See Koole, *Isaiah III*, 3:275–76.

there is no clear reference to relocation in this passage, I consider it to refer to the Repatriated Exiles due to its national perspective;[64] the references to releasing captives, who go through personal and national transformation (v. 3); the prospect of rebuilding and restoring the desolated cities (v. 4);[65] and the prospect of possessing a double portion of their land, as part of the restoration (לכן בארצם משנה יירשו, v. 7b).[66] In thus transforming the land and transforming themselves, this community gains ultimate (and exclusive) national status as the people desired by God (v. 3: משרתי אלהינו;[67] כהני יהוה and אילי הצדק מטע יהוה להתפאר;[6] v. 9: זרע ברך יהוה), who thus are brought in eternal covenant (v. 8). This prophecy designates and reidentifies the Repatriated Exiles as *the* people of God, who are to reinhabit the city and the land, as its exclusive ruling residents.

These four passages demonstrate group identity definitions that may be found throughout Isa 40–66. In these passages, the people are those about to be repatriated or already returned from Babylon, from among the Exiles, resettled in empty and desolate Zion. Their identification with empty Zion is so complete that they are labeled with its name. They are considered the released captives, the people of God, who had returned to their own lands; no other Judean community is thus recalled.

e. *Annexation of Religious-Historical Traditions—The Third Argument of Exclusivity in Isaiah 40–66*
Several prophecies within Isa 40–66 employ the third argumentative strategy of exclusivity, the *annexation* of religious-historical traditions. Major traditions are appropriated in these chapters: the fathers traditions (Abraham and Sarah, 51:2; Abraham and Israel as forefathers, 63:16); the Exodus traditions (as in 48:20; 52:4–6, 11–12; 55:12); the Covenant

64. The national perspective is revealed in the following features: (1) other references to אבלים in Isa 57:18; 66:10, which appear in a clearly national context; (2) the mission to rebuild the ruined cities (v. 4); (3) the presentation of the opponents as זרים and גוים, בני נכר and עמים (vv. 5–6, 9); (4) the reference to an eternal covenant (v. 8), as in Isa 55:3; and (5) the people's universal fame as זרע ברך יהוה (v. 9).

65. Westermann (*Isaiah 40–66*, 370) found בנה, "to build," a characteristic marker of Trito-Isaiah (cf. 58:12; 60:10; 61:4; 65:21, 23; 66:1), in distinction from Deutero-Isaiah's emphasis on the return.

66. For לכן בארצם משנה יירשו, see Koole, *Isaiah III*, 1:286–88, and his apt discussion of the echoes to Lev 25 and the Jubilee laws, pp. 265, 272–73.

67. The opposition between כהני יהוה and משרתי אלהינו and the nations (גוים, בני נכר and זרים in v. 5) follows the designations of Israel as ממלכת כהנים וגוי קדוש in Exod 19:5, as part of defining the community by clear cut categories. See Paul, *Isaiah 40–66*, 543–44.

traditions (51:2); and the Settlement (54:2–3; 65:21–23).[68] These traditions create an exclusive identification of the Repatriated Exiles as the
sole legitimate heirs to the historical past of Israel and Judah.

Isaiah 51:2 presents Abraham and Sarah as the ancestors of this
people: הביטו אל אברהם אביכם ואל שרה תחוללכם כי אחד קראתיו ואברכהו
ואַרבהו ("Look back to Abraham your father and to Sarah who brought
you forth. For he was only one when I called him, but I blessed him and
made him many").[69] The allusion to the call and the blessing recalls God's
summons, לך לך, in Gen 12:2–3. Its fulfillment in the "multiplication" of
Abraham evokes the theme of progeny in the Abraham tradition, and
even suggests a *Qal VaHomer* argument ("from the minor to the major"),
naming the Exiles as Abraham's multiplied descendants.[70] It is of interest
that this verse in Isaiah does not refer explicitly to the promise of the
land or to its actual possession by Abraham (compare to Ezek 33:24).[71]

A prominent topic that recurs in several prophecies is God's reinstitution of the covenant relationship with His people; that is, first with the
Exiles in Babylon, then with the Repatriates in Yehud. Major passages
that draw on this theme have already been dealt with in subsection d
(pp. 111–18, above; Isa 61:1–9; and implicitly 52:4–6); thus, I will
discuss here two additional passages, from Isa 65–66.[72] The concept of
blessing in **Isa 65:8–16** (כי ברכה בו, v. 8), in line with the closing phrase
of Isa 61:9, serves to create a dichotomy between those designated as

68. Referring to Isa 54:2–3, Snaith (*Isaiah 40–66*, 162) pointed out the use of
ירש, which refers to no less than "the Joshua invasion all over again, for much of
Deuteronomy and virtually all of the Second Isaiah is a second occupation of
Canaan." I note also the allusion in these verses to the promise to Jacob (Gen 28:14).

69. Following קראתיו, the reading of ואברכהו ואַרבהו should be a *wayyiqtol* form,
and this is indeed reflected in the different Versions (see McKenzie, *Second Isaiah*,
123). 4QIsa[a] has ואפרהו, which reflects the pair פרה ורבה; however, in this context,
this pair focuses only on the progeny theme, and does not retain the allusion to the
Abraham tradition.

70. See ibid., 123, 125; Michael A. Fishbane, *Biblical Interpretation in Ancient
Israel* (Oxford: Clarendon, 1988), 375.

71. See the discussion on Ezek 33:24, pp. 153–56, below. Compare Haran,
Between Ri'shonot, 84 and n. 25; and see John Van Seters, *Abraham in History and
Tradition* (New Haven: Yale University Press, 1975), 269–78; idem, *Prologue to
History: The Yahwist as Historian in Genesis* (Louisville, Ky.: Westminster John
Knox, 1992), 238–42; and Sparks' criticism of Van Seters, *Ethnicity and Identity*,
288–91.

72. Isa 65–66 have been recognized as a miscellaneous collection that might
be responding to the communal lament of 63:7–64:11; see Oswalt, *Isaiah 40–66*,
634–36. Westermann (*Isaiah 40–66*, 399–429) set out the different polemics within
Isa 65–66. My discussion is limited to the utilization of covenant conceptions. For
the possible identities of the groups in conflict, see pp. 127–34.

"My servants" (65:9) and עזבי יהוה ("those who forsake the LORD,"
v. 11). These verses tie together the Repatriated Exiles, considered עבדי
("my servants," v. 8; and note the plural designations in vv. 9, 13–15), to
their possession and to their settlement in the land,[73] presented as the
fortune of but a meager remnant (v. 8); they are designated as those
among the people who enquire of God (לעמי אשר דרשוני, "For My people
who seek Me," v. 10). On the other extreme, there are those who are said
to desert God and forget His holy mountain: עזבי יהוה השכחים את הר
קדשי ("But as for you who forsake the LORD, who ignore My holy
mountain," v. 11).

Verses 9–10 play a central role in this prophecy, as they forecast or
describe the actual possession of the land of Judah: והוצאתי מיעקב זרע
ומיהודה יורש הרי וירשהו בחירי ועבדי ישכנו שמה ("I will bring forth offspring from Jacob, from Judah, heirs to My mountains; My chosen ones
shall take possession, My servants shall dwell thereon"). Westermann
argued that vv. 9–10 are "a prophecy spoken during the exile, promising
the descendents of those then living in foreign countries that they will
eventually re-possess the land."[74] This intriguing suggestion allows us to
see that the covenant traditions operate in the background of this entire
passage, and that these traditions were constantly adapted to suit ever-
transforming circumstances. The promise of blessing, entangled with the
promise of land, gets here not only an actualization, but also a further
limitation, because it is now restricted to לעמי אשר דרשוני ("to My people
who had inquired of Me").

The accentuation of the blessing and its projected fulfillment occurs
again in **Isa 65:17–25**, which reflects the interests of the Repatriated
Exiles. The Repatriates are promised full restoration in the land (vv. 21b,
22a, 23a), a promise that reverses known curses of the covenant (compare v. 21 to Deut 28:28; and see 6:10–12; Jer 29:4–6), as well as the
judgment prophecies of Jeremiah (compare vv. 18–19 to Jer 7:34; 16:9;
25:10), and accords with Jeremiah's prophecies of consolation (compare
Jer 33:10–11).[75] These evoked texts serve to designate the Repatriated

73. Otherwise in Isa 40–66 עבדי appears in the singular, as in Isa 42:1; 44:1, 2,
21; 45:4; 49:3.

74. Westermann, *Isaiah 40–66*, 405.

75. For the reversal of literary allusions and for the beautiful wordplay on גולה,
transformed to גלתי and גילה, see Benjamin D. Sommer, *A Prophet Reads Scripture:
Allusion in Isaiah 40–66* (Stanford: Stanford University Press, 1998), 41–43; Paul,
Isaiah 40–66, 603. While גלתי is exceptional in its reference to God as agent, שוש
does occur in 65:18 and in 62:5 as a divine action. Beyond the connections to
Jeremiah that Sommer pointed out, I want to highlight here the direct connections to
Deuteronomy.

Babylonian community as the one that enjoys blessing rather than curse: כי זרע ברוכי יהוה המה וצאצאיהם אתם ("But they shall be a people blessed by the LORD, and their offspring shall remain with them," 65:23; and see 61:9).[76]

Hence, the argument of *continuity* of the Repatriate group with the history of Israel and Judah is reinforced by the strategy of *annexation of national traditions*, as employed by the author of Deutero-Isaiah to apply solely to his own community; together, these two strategies shape the notion of *entirety* in relation to the prophet's people—that is, the idea that his group alone is the legitimate heir to and continuation of Israel/ Judah of the past.

Besides using these rhetorical strategies to describe and establish his own group, the prophet also alludes to other claimants to *continuity* with Israel's past, and employs some specific strategies to defuse these claims. It is to this aspect of Deutero-Isaiah's rhetoric that we now turn.

2. *Other Groups in Deutero-Isaiah's Jerusalem Chapters: Out-group Designations*

When we come to examine the designation of out-groups in Isa 40–66, it is clearly necessary to distinguish the Babylonian chapters (40–48) from the Jerusalem ones (49–66). This distinction allows us to differentiate between two major rhetorical oppositions over Deutero-Isaiah as a whole.

In the Babylonian prophecies and in many of the Jerusalem chapters as well, the prophet completely ignores any other Judean communities within the land of Yehud or in Egypt. It is significant that while these prophetic compilations evidence plenty of self-designations for the Exiles in Babylon, counter-designations for other communities are absent. Similar to Zech 1–8, this lack of designations for other groups goes well with the rhetorical figure common to Isa 40–66 and Zechariah: the opposition between "My exiled people" and "My [empty] city." Hence, the people of God are those Exiles who are to resettle it following a new Exodus back to the land, and no one else.

Over against this ruling opposition in Isa 40–66, and occurring only within the Jerusalem prophecies of Isa 49–66, there are additional references to internal confrontations between the Repatriates and "others"

---

76. Isa 65:17–25 starts with Jerusalem and its people, God's people (vv. 17–19), but then describes the new orders within the entire creation with special attention to those who are said to be blessed by God. See Koole, *Isaiah III*, 3:447–48.

in the land, which are actually presented in two different conceptual frameworks.[77]

The first suggests an inclusive perspective, presenting these others as בני הנכר הנלוים על יהוה ("the *foreigners* who attach themselves to the LORD," 56:6).[78] הנלוים על יהוה grants membership in the community only to those foreigners who have "joined themselves to YHWH," and not generally to any foreigners.[79] Although the identity of this group is vague, בני הנכר may refer to foreigners who had joined the Exiles in Babylon before the return, as might be understood from the prophet's promise והביאותים אל הר קדשי ("I will bring them to My sacred mount," 56:7).[80] Or, the term might also encompass foreign sojourners in the land (גרים), depending on the understanding of Isa 54:11–17: הן גור יגור אפס מאותי מי גר אתך (Rofé translates v. 15 as "If a sojourner should dwell in the land, it is only by My will that he lives with you").[81] Dwelling among the

77. Hanson (*The Dawn of Apocalyptic*, 61) enumerated three significant differences between Isaiah 56–66 (Third Isaiah) and Second Isaiah: (1) divine salvation is accentuated in Second Isaiah, in comparison to statements that explain the delay of salvation in 58:1–5, 6–9a; 59:1–4; 63:7–64:11, etc.; (2) judgment in Third Isaiah is still a future prospect (as in 65:11–12; 66:3–4, 15–17); (3) restoration is restricted to but one segment of the people—to God's servants, the chosen ones (as in 65:8–16; 66:5–6), the others are doomed to annihilation (as in 65:11–12). Hanson's observations are apt, though I would take them as reflecting a variety of intergroup struggles, in keeping with the miscellaneous character of the Jerusalem chapters, Isa 56–59, 63–66; see also below.

78. Isa 56:1–8 is to be distinguished from the references to בני נכר ומלכיהם ("foreigners [NJPS: aliens]…and their kings") in 60:10 and 61:5. The latter are portrayed as foreign nations subordinated to Jerusalem as national entities ruled by their native kings. See Blenkinsopp, *Isaiah 56–66*, 137. These two passages clearly counter the common scholarly assessment of a supposedly universalistic message in Isa 40–66. See Snaith, *Isaiah 40–66*, 154–65.

79. See Brooks Schramm, *The Opponents of Third Isaiah: Reconstructing the Cultic History of the Restoration* (JSOTSup 193; Sheffield: Sheffield Academic, 1995), 122. Koole (*Isaiah III*, 3:11–14) pointed out the difference between גר and נכרי; he assumed that בן הנכר in Isa 56 goes with Ezekiel's attitude in Ezek 44:4–14, but see below.

80. Isa 66:18–21 does not mention בני נכר, but refers to "the nations," which accompany Israel on its return and might even serve in the Temple (v. 21), see p. 123 n. 85, below.

81. Note the LXX, ιδου προσήλυτοι προσελεύσονταί σοι δι εμου και επι σε καταφεύξονται, which reflects the reading of גור יגור as גר יגור; see Oswalt, *Isaiah 40–66*, 425; and see Alexander Rofé, "Isaiah 66:1–4: Judean Sects in the Persian Period as Viewed by Trito-Isaiah," in *Biblical and Related Studies Presented to Samuel Iwry* (ed. A. Kort and S. Morschauser; Winona Lake: Eisenbrauns, 1985), 205–17, esp. 214 n. 46. Westermann (*Isaiah 40–66*, 277–79) and Paul (*Isaiah 40–66*, 431)

Repatriates in Yehud, these people, too, enjoy divine approval, and thus are to be accepted within Israel (56:6).[82]

According to the prophet, these בני הנכר who join themselves to God participate in five types of loyal service, presented via the infinitive or the participle:[83] לשרתו ("to serve Him"); ולאהבה את שם יהוה ("and to love the name of the LORD"); להיות לו לעבדים ("to be His servants"); כל שמר שבת מחללו ("all who keep the Sabbath and do not profane it"); ומחזיקים בבריתי ("and who hold fast to My covenant"). These five categories of loyal service are required of any lay member of Israel.[84] Thus, by the merit of this active loyalty to God these foreigners are accepted into the community. Through the use of the phrase הבדיל מעל עמו ("Let not the foreigner say, who has attached himself to the LORD, 'The LORD will keep me apart from His people'," 56:3), these verses oppose the point of view expressed in Ezra–Nehemiah's demand for separation from בני הנכר (Ezra 9:1; Neh 10:29), and for the exclusion of בני הנכר from serving with the Temple personnel in Ezekiel (Ezek 44:4–14).[85]

suggested the meaning of "to be hostile" as in והתגר בו מלחמה ("engage him in battle," Deut 2:24) and the Akkadian *geru* 2, "to be hostile, to make war" (*CAD* G, 61–63). Medieval exegetes have suggested three different meanings for גור in this context; see Rashi ad loc.

82. Shemaryahu Talmon ("Return to Zion—Consequences for Our Future," *Cathedra* 4 [1977]: 26–31, esp. 29 [in Hebrew]) suggested yet another possibility: that בני הנכר are Judeans who had remained in exile, and that the prophecy encourages them to return and join the Repatriates in Yehud. The combination of בני נכר and סריס ("eunuch") in Isa 56:4 evokes Deut 23:1–9, which places sexual and national restrictions on the participation in the communal cultic life. See Koole, *Isaiah III*, 3:13.

83. For the semantic value of אל יהוה (הנלוה)ים, see Diether Kellermann, "לוה I," *TDOT* 7:475–76. לוה על/אל Niphal designates close connection to a human being (Gen 29:34; Esth 9:27; Ps 83:9; Dan 11:34; as also in reference to the Levites, Num 18:2, 4; and see Isa 15:1 with the parallel phrase נספח על). But of more relevance for the present context are instances where the verb denotes a person or a nation joining to God; this may be used of Israel (Jer 50:5), or of the nations (Zech 2:15; for individuals from among the nations, see Isa 56:3, 6).

84. See, for instance, Deut 10:12; 11:13; Exod 31:16; all these passages refer to loyalty to God, His covenant and the Sabbath, and address the entire people of Israel. See Paul, *Isaiah 40–66*, 453, 455–56.

85. Fishbane (*Biblical Interpretation*, 138–43) wrote aptly on these contrasting perspectives: "we have here hit upon a live post-exilic issue" (138; and see his final comment on pp. 142–43). But it seems that there is a crucial point of distinction between Ezek 44 and Isa 56 on the matter of the status of these foreigners— depending on whether they are lay persons or cultic personnel. Oswalt (*Isaiah 40– 66*, 456–57) argued against what he called a "false dichotomy" between Ezekiel and

In this context of controversy, the decision to designate a group of foreigners as הנלוים על יהוה ("those who attach themselves to the LORD," Isa 56:6, and in the singular in v. 3), who are allowed to serve Him (לשרתו), is a polemical interpretive allusion. As noted by Fishbane, it participates in an ideological struggle, "via Scriptural exegesis,"[86] over the issue of who may and may not be included in the new religious-political entity of Yehud. Taking an inclusive stance, Isa 56:1–8 makes an analogy between these foreigners and the Levites, who are defined in Num 18:1–7 as follows:

אחיך מטה לוי שבט אחיך הקרב אתך וילוו עליך וישרתוך

> You shall also associate with yourself your kinsmen the tribe of Levi, your ancestral tribe, to be attached to you and to minister to you. (Num 18:2)

Although in relation to the Levites, this terminology suggests their cultic function, Isa 56:1–8 uses this terminology to suggest the incorporation of these foreigners into the religious lay community (הנלוים על יהוה לשרתו, v. 6a).[87] The loyalty requirements in vv. 6b–7 do not imply any cultic, "Levitical" function for those foreigners (in contrast to Isa 66:21).[88] These verses simply welcome foreigners into the general pious community of Yahwist worshipers, the community of Israel (v. 8).[89]

Ezra on the one hand and "Trito-Isaiah" on the other. According to Oswalt, Isa 56:1–8 does not counteract the exclusivity that typifies Isa 57:1–13; 65:1–7.

86. Fishbane (*Biblical Interpretation*, 143). Fishbane (138–39) further defined Ezek 44:9–16 as "an *exegetical oracle*" because of its reference to Num 18:1–7, 22–23; on pp. 142–43 he referred briefly to an allusion to Num 18 in Isa 56:1–7 as well. I suggest that this passage can similarly be considered an "exegetical oracle." Note also Blenkinsopp's suggestion (*Isaiah 56–66*, 138) that Isa 56:1–8 debates Deut 23:2–9.

87. The connection of the root שרת to the cultic service of God, and specifically to the function of the Levites, is often specified in Priestly sources, as well as in Deuteronomistic passages: Deut 10:8; 18:5, 7; 21:5; 1 Sam 2:18, etc. But see Ps 101:6 for the use of the term in a noncultic context of pious loyalty. Isa 56:6 may be expanding this cultic context, in line with 61:6. For this broad perspective, see Oswalt, *Isaiah 49–66*, 459–60.

88. Compare to Blenkinsopp (*Isaiah 56–66*, 140), who concluded that these verses allow foreigners to hold priestly offices; and see also his list of similarities between Isa 56:1–8 and 66:15–24, which I do not find persuasive (p. 132). The reading of Isa 56:6–7 that I have suggested here leaves Isa 66:21 as the only exception that allows foreigners to serve as priests and Levites. Compare Paul, *Isaiah 40–66*, 629–30.

89. This innovative strategy of incorporation may be compared to the exclusion of foreigners from the cult, as in Lev 22:25; see Blenkinsopp, *Isaiah 56–66*, 138.

A second rhetorical strategy, however, that at face value seems to be fiercely exclusive, operates within **Isa 57–59** and **65–66**. In both contexts the out-group, the "others," are accused of participating in syncretistic cults in Jerusalem and perpetrating societal misdeeds. But notwithstanding these common points of departure each of the two units deserves a separate discussion.

Chapters 57–59 designate the out-group with the following denigrating phrases: בני עננה זרע מנאף ("You sons of a sorceress, you offspring of an adulterer and a harlot," 57:3); ילדי פשע זרע שקר ("you children of iniquity, offspring of treachery," 57:4); הרשעים ("the wicked," 57:20, 21). Their behavior is characterized in both religious-cultic terms (57:5–7; 58:1–5, 5–13; 59:1–4, 13) and in social terms. They do not act with justice and piety (59:4), and they are accused of various social sins (59:1–4, 5–8, 9–15). Most crucial of all is their neglect of God and His demands (57:8, 11; 59:1–4). Therefore, they are doomed to continuous suffering—without peace (57:20), without salvation (59:9–11).

In-group designations in Isa 57–59 consist of descriptions of the people as (at least potentially) righteous and pious (הצדיק and אנשי חסד, 57:1); they are called עמי ("My people," 57:14; 58:1) or בית יעקב ("the House of Jacob," 58:1). They are said (or admonished) to be looking for God's presence and to show trust in Him (57:14; 58:2). Accordingly, their fate is portrayed with hope. God is to respond favorably to the people's transformation and repentance (58:6–14; 59:16–21). Divine guidance and restoration in the land are promised (58:11, 12, 14) to those who trust in God: והחוסה בי ינחל ארץ ויירש הר קדשי ("But those who trust in Me shall inherit the land and possess My sacred mount," 57:13).[90] Yet, the structure of each of these three chapters, their miscellaneous literary character and mix of genres, stand against a view of chs. 57–59 as a single polemical unit directed by one particular group in Yehud against another group or groups.[91]

---

90. The promise of life endurance and inheritance of land for those who trust God in Isa 57:13b (as also the portrayal of the wicked, as in 57:20–21) resemble the traditional wisdom conception, as presented in Ps 37, see vv. 3, 11, 22, 29, 34. I thank Dr. Ruth Clements for pointing this out.

91. Space does not allow a full discussion of each passage. I would particularly highlight the opposition between the righteous and the wicked in ch. 57. Consult the commentaries for a range of interpretations of this chapter. See, e.g., Blenkinsopp's discussion of 57:1–2 as a "lament over the dead prophet and his disciples" (*Isaiah 56–66*, 148–52); compare to Paul (*Isaiah 40–66*, 461–63), who described the passage in more general terms as "the death of the righteous." This opening closes aptly with reference to the fortune of the wicked (57:20–21).

The exhortation in **Isa 58:1–14**, for instance, seems less a directive against an out-group than a response to the people's (i.e. the in-group's) complaints regarding their perception of ongoing divine desertion, of the lack of God's presence and salvation (vv. 9–11, 14).[92] As suggested by Brooks Schramm, the prophecy addresses "the restoration community" itself, a community that struggles with feelings of disappointment stemming from the unfulfilled promises of Deutero-Isaiah.[93] Schramm mentioned Isa 59:1–21 as another passage that continues this exhortation by suggesting that the community's moral misconduct explains the lack (or delay) of divine salvation.[94] The communal lament in **59:9–15** shows that this distress is shared by the in-group; when the group confesses its sins it is answered by a prophetic promise of hope, divine salvation, and reassurance that the eternal covenant is established with that entire community (vv. 15b–21).[95] Hence, both the exhortation and the promise of salvation target the same group, namely, the in-group of those pious ones that are defined as שבי פשע יעקב ("those in Jacob who turn back from sin," 59:20).[96]

These passages, then, while they clearly designate an internal polemic between an "approved," righteous group that is distinguished from a "condemned" wicked group, may be completely detached from the polemical context of group identity issues. It seems that chs. 57–59 focus on altogether different topics that occupied the Repatriates within their own in-group upon their return, similar to the local concerns of Haggai

92. Hanson (*The Dawn of Apocalyptic*, 106–8) argued for a transformation of the genre of the judgment prophecy in 58:1–12.

93. Schramm, *The Opponents*, 133–37. Compare to Hanson (*The Dawn of Apocalyptic*, 108), who in his discussion of 58:1–12 pointed out that the division of "My people" into righteous and wicked is set through the juxtaposition of vv. 2–5 and 6–12. But he, nevertheless, thought that salvation was promised to all (in clear contradistinction to 65:13, for instance). This, of course, stands in opposition to Hanson's further observation (p. 109) that the passage does present an "unmistakable" polemic over control of the cult, and the righteous resemble the religious elite, the visionary party that ridicules the hierocratic adherence to cultic specifities (pp. 110–13). I would concur indeed that the polemic sets a hierarchy of piety between the antagonists, but I understand the polemic to be internally directed, i.e., at the Repatriate in-group itself.

94. Schramm, *The Opponents*, 138–43.

95. Hanson (*The Dawn of Apocalyptic*, 113–34, especially 118–20) argued for the unity of ch. 59 in its three segments.

96. Compare Hanson (ibid., 120–22), who pointed out parallels between 58:1–12 and 59 to validate his assumption that the controversy between Levitical visionaries and hierocrats governs this chapter as well.

and Zechariah (as in Hag 1:1–11; 2:15–19; Zech 1; 7).[97] The animosity within this in-group contest are nevertheless quite amazing.

Chapters 65–66 present new challenges.[98] The "other" in these chapters is clearly a different group, an out-group designated as an "other" people: גוי לא קרא בשמי ("a nation that did not invoke My name," 65:1). This is a community that does not inquire after or seek God; and a chain of no fewer than seven active participles indicates their religious-cultic misbehavior. They are:[99] עם סורר ("a disloyal people," 65:2); ההלכים הדרך לא טוב (those "who walk the way that is not good," v. 2); העם זבחים בגנות המכעיסים אותי ("the people who provoke My anger," v. 3a); ומקטרים על הלבנים (those "who sacrifice in gardens and burn incense on tiles," v. 3b);[100] הישבים בקברים ובנצורים ילינו (those "who sit inside tombs and pass the night in secret places," v. 4a); האכלים בשר החזיר ופרק פגלים כליהם (those "who eat the flesh of swine, with broth of unclean things in their bowls," v. 4b); האמרים קרב אליך אל תגש בי כי קדשתיך ("Who say, "Keep your distance! Don't come closer! for I would render you consecrated," v. 5). Isaiah 65:11–12 makes additional accusations against עזבי יהוה ("you who forsake the LORD," v. 11), השכחים את הר קדשי ("who ignore My holy mountain," v. 11). These denigrating descriptions are accompanied by a further list of cultic misdeeds in which they rather prefer the cult of Gad and Meni (v. 11b). They are, therefore, destined to die as a result of disloyalty (v. 12), over against the fate of "My servants" (vv. 13–15). Isaiah 66:3 adds specific practices of illegitimate sacrifices that are defined as idolatrous (66:3c). This roster of practices points to two different cultic contexts. Isaiah 65:3–7 refers

---

97. This thematic similarity to Haggai, together with the focus on fasting (58:3–9) and the promise of restoration of the ruins (58:12) has caused scholars to date Isa 57–59 to the late sixth century, in parallel to Zech 7. See Hanson, *The Dawn of Apocalyptic*, 104–13. Hanson thus perceived this segment to take a middle position within the materials of Third Isaiah, clearly distinguishable from chs. 65–66 (pp. 44–45).

98. For the structure, ideas, and the position of chs. 65–66 at the close of the book of Isaiah, see Marvin A. Sweeney, "Prophetic Exegesis in Isaiah 65–66," in *Writing and Reading the Scroll of Isaiah: Studies of an Interpretive Tradition* (ed. C. C. Broyles and C. A. Evans; VTSup 71; Leiden: Brill, 1997), 455–74. Schramm (*The Opponents*, 154–55, and references on p. 155 n. 1) accepted the scholarly observation that 65:1–25 is a reply to the communal lament of 63:7–64:11.

99. Blenkinsopp, *Isaiah 56–66*, 270. See Paul (*Isaiah 40–66*, 613), who follows Luzzatto.

100. 4QIsaᵃ reads: וינקו ידים על האבנים ("they suck hands on the stones"); see Blenkinsopp (*Isaiah 56–66*, 271) for the suggested reading of הלבונה ("frankincense") instead of הלבנים.

to the "people" as conducting various cultic sins in public places, but clearly not in the Temple.[101] The misconduct attacked in 65:11 and 66:3, however, takes place during public worship in the Temple; and yet there is no explicit mention of priests or Levites conducting these ceremonies. Nevertheless, scholars claim that this criticism (of 65:11; 66:3) is addressed against the priests of Jerusalem, who thus stand accused of "idolatry, apostasy, and participation in idolatrous mysteries."[102] While the precise accusations may apply only to these priestly practices (65:5, 11; 66:3), the denigration of those holding to these practices seems to be of even wider scope, certainly not restricted to religious functionaries.[103] This group, however constituted, stands over against the party that is designated "My servants," "Jacob," "Judah," "My chosen," the "heirs to My mountains," "My people who seek Me" (65:8–10), and those "who tremble at [God's] word" (66:2, 5).[104] The distinction between the two groups has fatal consequences for those who desert Yahweh (vv. 6–7, 12, 15), and in sharp distinction from בני הנכר, they are clearly excluded from the divine re-creation of new heavens and earth, including the new Jerusalem that is to be built "as a joy, and her people as a delight" (v. 18).

These chapters of Isaiah have attracted significant scholarly attention; several suggestions have been made to explain the social and religious tensions of Isa 57–59 and 65–66. But is it possible to pinpoint the exact conflict(s)? Do these chapters reflect the Ezra–Nehemiah conflict between the Repatriates and the People Who Remained, or an internal struggle within the Repatriate community itself?

101.   This general and popular cultic behavior is further established by the many allusions to Deuteronomy and Jeremiah, see Paul, *Isaiah 40–66*, 595–97; it seems that the prophet makes his rhetorical case against these people through those allusions.

102.   See Rofé, "Isaiah 66:1–4," 207–12 (212). Hanson (*The Dawn of Apocalyptic*, 145–52) tied these cultic denigrations to 57:5–8; 59:5–6, and found them all to illustrate polemical accusations against the Zadokite priesthood, as conducting Canaanite cultic practices within the central cult. He wrote that these chapters address "the religiously elite leaders of the normative cult" (p. 147), that is, the ruling priestly party.

103.   Blenkinsopp (*Isaiah 56–66*, 51–54, 270–73) argued that the religious practices reflect "both the popular and state level, during the last century of the Judean kingdom" (272); Paul (*Isaiah 40–66*, 599–600) treated 65:11 as an addition to the list of practices in 65:3–7, attributed to the lay group of עזבי יהוה; yet he did suggest that 66:3–4 admonishes the priests (pp. 613–15).

104.   So Blenkinsopp, *Isaiah 56–66*, 51; NJPS: "You who are concerned about His word!" The same title החרדים אל דברו occurs with minor differences in Ezra (כל חרד בדברי אלהי ישראל, Ezra 9:4; החרדים במצות אלהינו, Ezra 10:3), where it designates a prestigious title for the pious Repatriate elite.

Westermann has concluded that these chapters indeed show an internal cleavage among brothers: אחיכם שנאיכם מנדיכם למען שמי ("your kinsmen who hate you, who spurn you because of Me," 66:5). Yet he nevertheless argued that this contest does not reflect the conflict between the two groups indicated in later Persian sources.[105] Westermann understood the exhortations in Isa 65–66 to be aimed at individual transgressors practicing cultic offenses that are still not considered apostasy (65:3–5, 11; 66:3–4). He gathered that these prophecies testify to a revival of cultic customs that had been earlier condemned by Ezekiel (Ezek 8:7–17).[106] These transgressions do not affect the entire nation; punishment will be meted out only to those who have sinned (65:6–7; 66:4, 5, 16–17), just as salvation is restricted to those who have been chosen (65:22–34; 66:5, 6).[107] Westermann thus found these passages to represent a significant change in Trito-Isaiah's message of judgment, presumably a consequence of the collapse of nationhood after the 587 destruction and following. Westermann considered 65:11–12 (as also vv. 9–10; and 66:3–4, 17) to be intrusions of "stock-terms used in the announcements of judgment of older days."[108] Accordingly, these passages represent "polemic in worship against cultic abuses dressed up as the old announcements of doom."[109] Westermann showed the repeated reliance on earlier prophetic announcements and dated these chapters as earlier than Isa 60–62; that is, still within Trito-Isaiah's salvation framework, yet prior to "the parting of the ways between the two groups within the nation."[110]

Looking at these passages of cultic polemic from a sociological perspective, Paul Hanson, in his influential discussion of Third Isaiah in *The Dawn of Apocalyptic*, suggested a tentative, relative chronology of the Judean conflict as represented within Isa 56–66.[111] He considered chs. 65–66 to stem from the final stages in the religious-cultic and social contest between two parties in Persian Yehud: the powerful Zadokite-priestly hierocratic party that was initiated by Ezekiel and supported

---

105.   Westermann, *Isaiah 40–66*, 399–402, 411–17, especially, p. 417.

106.   Ibid., 422. In reference to 66:14, Westermann (p. 421) identified איביו, as in v. 6 and explicitly in vv. 18–21, to be the nations. Paul (*Isaiah 40–66*, 599–600) observed this same internal distinction in worship and cultic obedience to God.

107.   Westermann, *Isaiah 40–66*, 409–10, 415–17, 422. This individualistic approach was also taken by Koole, *Isaiah III*, 3:431–45.

108.   Ibid., 405, and see p. 414.

109.   Ibid., 417.

110.   Ibid.

111.   Hanson, *The Dawn of Apocalyptic*, 32–45.

by his school (including Haggai and Zechariah); and the minority Levitical-visionary-prophetic party, insignificant in numbers and in power, to which Second (and Third) Isaiah belonged.[112] Controversy had arisen over the distinct conceptions of restoration held by these two groups,[113] as well as their respective interests in control of the cult; this stands behind Isa 65–66. These last chapters of Trito-Isaiah represent the final stage in the transformation of eschatological prophecy into apocalyptic eschatology.[114] The entire last segment of the book, chs. 56–66, relies on and further develops the Isaianic tradition,[115] and the final phases of its composition were contemporary with Ezra–Nehemiah. In reference to Isa 60–62, Hanson was cautious in ascribing an exclusivist perspective to these chapters:

> Thus in these two programs we have the seeds of the two currents which run parallel throughout subsequent Jewish history, currents, which, to be sure, were not exclusive of one another. For both are essential elements of one faith, but were often tragically polarized into two imbalanced extremes, resulting in tension and even conflict as visionary parted company with realist, and realist disassociated himself from visionary.[116]

This is one point (of many) where Hanson's assumptions and conclusions about the two antagonistic groups seem to me less than adequate, and his basic division between visionaries and hierocrats seems unacceptable.[117]

The path scholars have commonly taken is to read the conflicts of Isa 57–59, 65–66 through the social lens of Ezra–Nehemiah. A few examples will suffice here. Alexander Rofé tied Trito-Isaiah to Nehemiah (or to the period immediately before him)—that is, to the early fifth century; he suggested that these chapters reflect a conflict between the prophet and the Jerusalem priests of his time. According to Rofé, the conflict has social, religious, and political elements, yet the characteristic phrases are too general and vague to allow a clear identification of the antagonistic

---

112.   In reference to Isa 66:1–2, Hanson (ibid., 173–79) elaborated on the place of Haggai (and Zechariah) within the hierocratic party; he suggested that this passage represents "a powerful propaganda piece for the official restoration program" (176), but that it is also tied to the visionary followers of Second Isaiah.

113.   Ibid., 74–76.

114.   Ibid., 44–45.

115.   Ibid., 37, 42, and passim.

116.   Ibid., 76–77. Hanson (159–61) discerned a harsher perspective, even hostility (to cultic deviants) in Isa 65–66; he related this perspective to the growth of apocalyptic eschatology, beginning as early as the end of the sixth century. Hanson (172) dated 66:1–2 to ca. 520.

117.   See pp. 266–69, below.

groups.[118] Based on similarities between Trito-Isaiah and Nehemiah, Rofé reconstructed a struggle among priestly circles over legitimacy in the Jerusalem Temple.[119] These Priestly circles comprised of Repatriate priests and Levites, confronted Jerusalemites who had already served in the Temple. Relying on Isa 66:20–22, Rofé observed that God was to appoint priests and Levites from those that had been brought from afar, so as to break "the monopoly of the Jerusalemite priests."[120] Trito-Isaiah thus is in line with Nehemiah, who indeed belonged to the Repatriated community in Yehud, and had contributed his share in helping to form "Judaism in the land of Israel in the image of the Eastern Jewish Diaspora."[121]

Joseph Blenkinsopp considered the phrases חרד/ים על/אל דברי of Isa 66:2, 5 and החרדים במצות אלהינו / חרד בדברי אלהי ישראל of Ezra 9:4; 10:3 to be referring to the same group; the use of these labels designates a move toward sectarianism in both Trito-Isaiah and Ezra.[122] In his commentary on Isa 56–66, Blenkinsopp suggested that the controversy represented in both is religious in nature, and that the historical and social circumstances are the same in both writings, although the two works present this conflict from different points of view and reflect distinct historical junctures.[123] He located Isa 65–66 as earlier than Ezra 9–10, since in the former the חרדים אל דברו are but a "shunned minority," while in the latter they are the dominant group. Thus, he suggested that the timeframe Isa 65–66 is before the activity of Ezra, that is, any time between the dedication of the Second Temple (516/515) and Ezra's

---

118.   Rofé, "Isaiah 66:1–4," 205–17.

119.   According to Rofé (ibid., 211–12), this is apparent also in Jer 33:14–26; Mal 3:3.

120.   Ibid., 212.

121.   Ibid., 217. Yair Hoffman (*Isaiah* [Olam HaTanakh; Tel-Aviv: Revivim, 1986 (in Hebrew)], 258, 274–75) claimed that the prophet's exhortation is aimed at the Repatriates, based on similarities to Ezra 9–10, the struggle against intermarriage with the peoples of the land. But due to the scarce evidence, Hoffman does not determine the identity of the antagonistic groups beyond this general statement. Compare Paul (*Isaiah 40–66*, 480–81, 497–98, 567–68, 589–91; and in the Paul's, pp. 19–21), who did not run to this paradigm of comparison with Ezra–Nehemiah, and did not see differences in those who are denounced in chs. 57–58 from those who are accused of moral iniquities in ch. 59:1–8; just as he found chs. 65–66 to be a response to the communal lament of Isa 63:7–64:11.

122.   Joseph Blenkinsopp, "The 'Servants of the Lord' in Third Isaiah: Profile of a Pietistic Group in the Persian Epoch," *Proceedings of the Irish Biblical Association* 7 (1983): 1–23.

123.   Blenkinsopp, *Isaiah 56–66*, 52–54.

arrival (458 B.C.E.).[124] Furthermore, the polemic differs from that of Ezra–Nehemiah, and is similar to Mal 2:10–12 in its focus on cultic abominations done within Jerusalem.[125]

Brooks Schramm, while accepting Rofé's and Blenkinsopp's observations on the agreements between Trito-Isaiah and Ezra–Nehemiah, understood these connections to reflect only a religious conflict within the restoration community itself.[126] He suggested that, without specifying the names of his opponents, the prophet attacks the leaders of the restoration community (56:9–57:13), and details their detestable cultic practices (57:3–13; 65:1–7; 66:3–4).[127] Schramm considered Trito-Isaiah "a true forerunner of Ezra,"[128] whose battle is with "the traditional, syncretistic cult of YHWH, a battle in which the Priestly, Pentateuchal tradition and the prophetic tradition fought on the same side!"[129] This viewpoint brought Schramm to consider Trito-Isaiah as a "representative of the interests and the theology of the Babylonian גולה," whose theological perspectives had been molded in the Babylonian Diaspora.[130] Throughout his study, Schramm elaborately and consistently refuted Paul Hanson's theory of a prophetic–priestly dichotomy, that is, Trito-Isaiah vs. Zadokite–Ezekelian cultic religion. It seems that in his apt refutation of Hanson's positions, Schramm was nevertheless reluctant to place the struggle only within the religious sphere—that is, as the struggle over the nature of Second Temple period Judaism and its cult.[131]

In spite of the above-noted similarities with Ezra–Nehemiah on the one hand, and to an even greater extent, the internal antagonism focused on cult and worship within the land on the other, I do not think we have enough data to identify fully the two opposing Judean groups. Nevertheless, the polemic erects clearly exclusive barriers between the two groups.

---

124. Ibid., 54.

125. Ibid., 300. Without using the terminology, it seems that Blenkinsopp pointed to an internal in-group contention, similar to the one I would pinpoint in Isa 57–59.

126. Schramm, *The Opponents*, 168–69.

127. Ibid., 112–14. Toward closing his detailed discussion of chs. 56–66, and particularly referring to Isa 66:3–4; 65:1–7, 11; and 57:3–13, Schramm (171) pointed out that these iniquities are all condemned in the Pentateuch.

128. Ibid., 114.

129. Ibid., 177.

130. Ibid., 179–81.

131. Ibid., 158.

Beyond the general denigration of the out-group in Isa 65–66, these chapters adduce positive identifications only for the in-group. This feature has been recognized as a device used exclusively throughout Second Isaiah. These chapters portray the chosen community as those who have come from afar to Zion; those who have returned to a barren land, which all of a sudden has given birth to multiple descendants, to a nation (see Isa 66:7–9, 12–14; in accordance with 49:21; 60:4, 9; 62:4–5).[132] This identification is the paramount literary link between this entire polemic and the major opposition between Repatriates and empty Zion in the earlier chapters of Isa 40–66 (see sections 1.a–e, pp. 104–21, above). But, in distinction from the previous chapters, Isa 65–66 add the recognition that the land has never, in fact, been completely empty. These chapters implicitly reveal that the land had been settled by those non-legitimate "Yahwistic pretenders," that is, Those Who Remained; the same group earlier treated by the Babylonian Repatriates as their fierce opponents. This opposition is similar to and was even further developed in Ezra–Nehemiah.

I suggest that we follow the insight of Norman H. Snaith, who has argued that chs. 65–66 illustrate the struggle between the Babylonian Repatriates and Those Who Remained.[133] Yet, while Snaith accumulated a complete list of evidence for the struggle between the Babylonian Repatriates and the Judeans left in the land, I suggest that we need to refine these observations and distinguish between two different expressions of this controversy within Isa 40–66. The struggle in the bulk of Second Isaiah (40–55, 60–62) is mostly implicit, focused on constructing in-group claims and ignoring the out-groups altogether; thus, the city is repeatedly portrayed as empty of any other inhabitants. From this standpoint, chs. 65–66 seem exceptional in their portrayal of an actual struggle over group identity issues, as they bring to the fore denigrating designations of an out-group. Utilizing arguments of *continuity* and *entirety*, these chapters construct the legitimacy of the one group as closely connected to God (עמי, בחירי, עבדי, etc., 65:8, 9, 19); as chosen and blessed by Him (65:8, 9, 23), genuinely obedient to His words (66:5). These chapters, furthermore, denigrate and delegitimize the status of those who malpractice Yahweh's cult (as in 65:3–5, 11–12; 66:3–4, 17).

---

132. Compare Paul (*Isaiah 40–66*, 617–19), who referred this imagery to the description of God as Warrior, intertwined with imagery of a woman in labor (Isa 42:13–14); or to the multiplicity of descendants (44:4). I would concur with Blenkinsopp (*Isaiah 56–66*, 304–7), who argued that vv. 7–14 serve as a conclusion to the entire unit of chs. 56–66, thus shows abundant of literary dependency on chs. 60–62, as also on chs. 40–54.

133. Snaith, *Isaiah 40–66*, 239–43.

These religious and cultic differences serve as distinctive characteristics of those otherwise anonymous Judean communities. Restoration is restricted to this chosen group (65:8–9, 13, 16–25; 66:5, 7–9, 10–14), whereas those who are denigrated for their cultic behavior are doomed to annihilation (65:6–7, 14–15; 66:5b, 17).[134]

3. *Conclusions*

Isaiah 40–66 includes no fewer than three different proclamations concerning the state of the land of Israel and the exclusivistic nature of the Repatriated community. First, and governing this entire section of Isaiah, is the opposition between the Repatriates and empty Zion, which, as mentioned in reference to Zech 1–8, shows a complete disregard of any other community, besides the one identified to be the true people of God.

Second, in contradistinction to this repeated line that runs throughout Isa 40–66 (and matches the prophetic opposition in Zech 1–8), the "Jerusalem chapters" do give clear indications of the existence of other Judean and foreign groups in Yehud. Chapters 65–66 focus on the struggle with other Judeans, probably coming from among Those Who Remained, and they thus come close to the other presentation that characterizes the Persian-period historiography of Ezra–Nehemiah. This late strand in Isa 40–66, which distinctively portrays one group over against the other is, therefore, either earlier than or contemporaneous with Ezra–Nehemiah's exclusive perspective.

The third rhetorical strategy further illustrates this exclusive tendency, as it reveals the attitude towards specific individuals (or groups) who are designated as בני הנכר הנלוים על יהוה ("the foreigners who attach themselves to the LORD," 56:3, 6). They are allowed into the in-group despite or because of their foreign origin, under the condition that they have accepted the obligation of complete loyalty to God. Thus *incorporation* is employed as an inclusive strategy to assimilate fully these "foreigners" into the Babylonian Repatriate community.

These strategies create one clear picture that reserves hope only to the Repatriates (including incorporated foreigners), and excludes all others.[135] Both by considering the internal arguments of Isa 40–66, and by observing the larger context of the book within biblical literature, we

---

134. For an earlier similar distinction, see Ezek 11:14–21, and see the discussion on pp. 144–56, below.

135. Compare with and see Paul (*Isaiah 40–66*, 447–50), who, like many other exegetes, found in this incorporation an indication of the universalistic inclusivity of Deutero-Isaiah. I would keep incorporation strategies completely apart from universalism tendencies.

can see that an exclusivist outlook is certainly implicit and even out-spoken in Deutero-Isaiah, as in other sixth- and fifth-century biblical literature. The collection demonstrates that one religious outlook was indeed shared by communities of the same nation, and yet these communities were polarized over group identity issues (not over religious issues *per se*). The prophetic voices recorded in Isa 40–66 present the dominant voice of the Babylonian Repatriate community, which delegitimated all others.

These prophecies further illustrate the boundaries of inclusivity, or the exclusive inclusivity of Deutero-Isaiah. Foreigners are welcomed only if they express the intention to be incorporated into Israel; but this openness to non-Israelites has no effect on the exclusivist perspectives directed against other Judean communities besides the Repatriates.

The presence of Babylonian exilic (and Repatriate) perspectives on the definitions of in-group and out-group in Isa 40–66 validates the possibility that the prophet was originally with the Exiles in Babylon and then himself experienced the return, continuing to serve as a prophet of the Repatriates. This prophet and his circle were responsible for the crystallization of the entire book of Isaiah; and under these circumstances, in the late sixth and fifth centuries, miscellaneous materials were added.

Among the unsolved challenges, the question of whether the prophet was a descendant of the Jehoiachin Exiles or the 586 Exiles from Jerusalem remains vague. It seems clear to me that Isa 40–66 shows an exclusive preference for the Babylonian Exiles and Repatriates. Yet, in distinction from Ezekiel, these prophecies cast a net of inclusivity that encompasses all Babylonian Exiles as a single in-group.[136]

The early Persian period opened a new era in the internal relationship between Judean communities, when after at least seven decades they found themselves in close geographic proximity. Repatriates and Those Who Remained shared the territory of Yehud.

---

136.   Snaith (*Isaiah 40–66*, 170) identified the Servant as "the first batch of exiles, those who went into captivity with the young king Jehoiachin in 597 B.C., together with a tendency to include also the 586 B.C. Exiles. Ultimately, all the exiles in Babylon are the true People of God, and it is they who are to return to Jerusalem and restore the situation, but with increased prestige and in the end with world-wide success." I accept these observations of Snaith, but contest those that follow. Notably Snaith (170–72) referred to Jer 24 as a Jeremian prophecy (see below, pp. 233–37); he portrayed Ezekiel as prophesying first in Judah but as being deported to Babylon by 586; he connected this polemic with the Jewish–Samarian conflict; and he proposed an accord between Jeremiah and Ezekiel on this preference for the Exiles in Babylon. All these are, to my mind, unsound arguments.

My discussions of Deutero-Isaiah, Haggai and Zechariah, and Ezra–Nehemiah have brought two distinct strategies to the fore. Both strategies serve in these sources of the Persian period, and they are both clear markers of the exclusivistic outlook of the Babylonian Repatriated Exiles.

The diversity among these exclusive outlooks leads me to suggest that exclusivity was not an innovation of the Restoration period, nor an invention introduced for the first time in Yehud upon the Repatriates' return.[137] To discover the origins of this exclusive ideology, which intentionally ignores the existence of other Judean communities, we must make a diachronic survey, and pursue our investigation of Babylonian exilic ideologies backwards to its earliest phase.

Deutero-Isaiah serves as an earlier Diasporic and then Repatriate link to the exclusive ideologies presented by the later prophetic voices of the Repatriates of the early Persian period: Zechariah and, implicitly, Haggai. Deutero-Isaiah's inclusive designations of the Exiles as the present entire people becomes particularly significant when one realizes that Deutero-Isaiah does not use any of the restricted terms (as, for instance, שארית ירושלים, גלות יהודה) known from the earlier exilic prophet, Ezekiel, from the Judean prophet, Jeremiah, and from the early Persian-period prophets, Haggai and Zechariah.

Hence, the next step would be to observe the Neo-Babylonian period, and to see how the opposition between the Judean and Babylonian communities is established when Ezekiel and Jeremiah (and their books) are drawn also into this picture.

---

137. Contra Blenkinsopp, *Ezra–Nehemiah*, 60; and Smith[-Christopher], *The Religion of the Landless*, 179–200, who considered the return as the point of clash and reformulation. Bedford (*Temple Restoration*, 20) noted that the foundations of the social conflicts known in the Persian period were laid already within the Neo-Babylonian era, but he did not discuss the actual relationship between these two periods. Bedford (147–66) rejected the possibility of an actual internal conflict during the Neo-Babylonian and early Persian periods, and argued that it came into existence only at the time of Ezra and Nehemiah in the fifth century (150–51).

Part II

NEO-BABYLONIAN EXCLUSIONARY STRATEGIES
(EARLY SIXTH CENTURY TO CA. 520 B.C.E.)

Chapter 6

EZEKIEL AND HIS BOOK:
HOMOGENEITY OF EXILIC PERSPECTIVES

The books of Ezekiel and Jeremiah bring us to the early formative phase of these conflicts—that is, to the early sixth century, following the deportations from Judah to Babylon and on. This part of my study explores the exciting and dramatic period when Judah and its residents were under Babylonian subjugation, prior to Jerusalem's destruction and in its aftermath—a period during which two antagonistic Yahwistic communities were initiated, one in Jerusalem and its vicinity and one in Babylon, each recreating itself as the legitimate successor to preexilic Judah. These chapters address each of the two prophetic books in turn, taking into consideration stages of evolution within them, and locating redactional layers and expansions added to each of them over the course of the sixth century B.C.E. I will argue that the social and geographical distance between Babylon and Judah/Yehud is the major cause of the differences in perspective between the two prophets, as well as those between each of them and their respective "followers," "disciples," or redactors.

This chapter addresses Ezekiel, the prophet I take to be the originator of the Babylonian exilic ideology(/ies), from as early as the beginning of his prophetic career (592 B.C.E.). The discussion of Ezekiel delineates the prophet's orientation and focuses on the ways he constructs his separatist ideology, as he struggles with traditional conceptions of land and exile. His clear preference for the Jehoiachin Exiles as the elect segment of the exilic community is accompanied by a profound delegitimization of Those Who Remained in Jerusalem. The discussion also touches on prophetic passages in the book of Ezekiel that do not cohere with this narrow focus on the Jehoiachin Exiles. These passages, which manifest a more generally inclusive attitude toward the larger group of Exiles in Babylon, are considered here to be non-Ezekielian elements within the book, assumed to originate with the prophet's successors, and thus to demonstrate early exilic transformations within Ezekiel's Babylonian exilic ideology.

This chapter is also the place to begin to discover the Judean voices of Those Who Remained after the Jehoiachin Exile (597 B.C.E.). They may be heard only in short quotations in Ezekiel; as we will see, they receive a greater level of exposure in the major prophetic pronouncements of Jeremiah.

1. *Ezekiel's Restricted Exclusivity: The Jehoiachin Exiles*

a. *Ezekiel as the Prophet of the Jehoiachin Exiles*

Although the book of Ezekiel includes only scanty biographical details about the prophet, the outstanding fact is that Ezekiel was a member of the Jehoiachin Exiles. The priest Ezekiel son of Buzi was called to his mission while "in the community of exiles" (בתוך הגולה, Ezek 1:1–3) by the Chebar Canal in Babylon, in the fifth year (592 B.C.E.) of the exile of King Jehoiachin, his court, and the Jerusalem elite to Babylon (597 B.C.E., 2 Kgs 24:8–17). The Exiles (הגולה) are the prophet's own people: "Go to your people, the exile community" (בא אל הגולה אל בני עמך, Ezek 3:11; as also 11:24, 25); and Ezekiel's concept of time is shaped by that event, as he counts the years לגלותנו ("of our exile," 33:21; 40:1).[1] The first person plural pronoun clarifies that he is part and parcel of that community.[2]

The prophet's ideological orientation clearly favors his community over against Those Who Remain under Zedekiah in Jerusalem. This observation will be validated throughout this chapter, thus two examples may suffice here as initial illustrations.[3]

---

1. The year of the Jehoiachin Exile stands behind all of the chronological superscriptions in Ezekiel as the determinative date (even without a specific mention of לגלותנו); see Ezek 8:1; 20:1; 24:1; 26:1; 28:17; 30:20; 31:1; 32:1, 17.

2. This observation sets apart the current study from the scholarly trend that had located Ezekiel himself (or the beginning of his prophetic career) in Judah, in the land of Israel; see, e.g., Charles C. Torrey, *Pseudo-Ezekiel and the Original Prophecy, and Critical Articles* (New York: KTAV, 1930; 2d ed. 1970). See the commentary of Zimmerli for solid refutations of these arguments (*Ezekiel 1 and 2*, 1:16–17, 2:564, and passim. Andrew Mein (*Ezekiel and the Ethics of Exile* [OTM; Oxford: Oxford University Press, 2001], 40–75, 257–63) established further the notion of Ezekiel's Babylonian context based on his sociological and ideological outlook that Mein found to represent "strategies for survival" in exile. William H. Brownlee unconvincingly tried to set Ezekiel in Gilgal (*Ezekiel 1–19* [WBC 28; Waco, Tex.: Word, 1986], xxiii–xxxii). He therefore considered the disputations in Ezek 11:14–21 and 33:23–29 to refer to "the controversy over property rights which broke out among those left behind" ("The Aftermath of the Fall of Judah according to Ezekiel," *JBL* 89 [1970]: 393–404, quotation from 394–95).

3. The present study also differs greatly from Karl F. Pohlmann's more recent approach to Ezekiel and to the polemic under discussion (*Ezechielstudien: Zur*

(1) *Disputation speeches in Ezekiel.* The prophetic genre of the disputation speech is counted among the primary sources for studying ideological debates in biblical literature of the sixth century B.C.E.[4] With its two-part pattern—the citation of the opponents' position and the prophet's counter-speech—this prophetic *genre* reflects some of the internal controversies between prophets and their contemporaries.[5]

Throughout the nine disputations in Ezekiel, the prophet differentiates between statements made by ישבי ירושלים ("the inhabitants of Jerusalem," 11:15), or על אדמת ישראל ("upon the soil of Israel," 12:21; 18:2),[6] and the assertions of his fellow Exiles, designated as בני עמך ("your

Redaktionsgeschichte des Buches und zur Frage nach den ältesten Texten [BZAW 202; Berlin: de Gruyter, 1992]; idem, *Das Buch des Propheten Hesekiel: Kapitel 1–19* [ATD 22/1; Göttingen: Vandenhoeck & Ruprecht, 1996]). From a redaction-critical point of view, Pohlmann argued for multiple layers in Ezekiel; but he connected none of them to the prophet or to the early period of the sixth century B.C.E. (see *Hesekiel*, 40–41). In fact, Pohlmann suggested that the "golaorientierte Redaktion" is a second, Babylonian layer in the book that reworks an original layer of Judahite, pro-Zedekiah, laments over the 587 destruction (Ezek 19:1–9, 10–14; 23; 31). By promoting the exclusive status of the earliest group of exiles, this redaction denigrates the population that remained in Jerusalem as doomed to annihilation (Ezek 14:21–23; 15:4b–8; 17:19–21, 22–23; 24:2, 21b, 25b–26; 33:21–29). A third layer in the literary evolution of the book gives precedence to several other Diasporic voices, which do *not* evidence antagonism against the population that remained in Judah after 597 (Ezek 20; 36:15–28; 38–39). Pohlmann thus understood this whole book as a collection of late exilic or postexilic reflections on early Jerusalemite laments. In contrast, the present study follows Greenberg's historical reading, and largely accepts his holistic approach to Ezekiel (*Ezekiel 1–20*, 12–27). I argue that the book of Ezekiel as a whole reflects the social division between the two communities that existed from 597 B.C.E. on, division also found in Jer 24. Furthermore, I claim that a pro-597-Exiles perspective governs Ezekiel's general attitude against Jerusalem and for the Jehoiachin Exiles throughout, not only in the few passages suggested by Pohlmann. For further criticism of Pohlmann, see Albertz, *Israel in Exile*, 349–50, especially in reference to Ezek 11:14–21 and 33:21–33, which will be discussed below.

4. Herman Gunkel, "Einleitungen," in D. H. Schmidt, *Die grossen Propheten* (Göttingen: Vandenhoeck & Ruprecht, 1923), xi–lxxii; Claus Westermann, *Sprache und Struktur der Prophetie Deuterojesajas*, mit einer Literaturübersicht "Hauptlinien der Deuterojesaja-Forschung von 1964–1979," zusammengestellt und kommentiert von A. Richter (Calwer Theologische Monographien 11; Stuttgart: Calwer, 1981), 41–51, see especially 42–43; Adrian Graffy, *A Prophet Confronts His People: The Disputation Speech in the Prophets* (AnBib 104; Rome: Biblical Institute, 1984); Donald F. Murray, "The Rhetoric of Disputation: Re-examination of a Prophetic Genre," *JSOT* 38 (1987): 95–121.

5. Graffy, *A Prophet*, 105–29.

6. For discussion of the phrase על אדמת ישראל, see ibid., 53.

fellow countrymen," 33:30), or בית ישראל ("the House of Israel," 33:10; 37:11).[7] Categorized according to the speakers of the quotations, the disputation speeches in Ezekiel fall into two groups: refutations of Jerusalemite assertions (11:1–13, 14–21; 12:21–25; 18:1–20; 33:23–29) and refutations of Exiles' pronouncements (12:26–28; 20:1–38; 33:10–20; 37:1–14).[8] Ezekiel presents the quotations said על אדמת ישראל either as sinful speeches (11:3, 15; 12:22; 33:24), or as bitter protest (18:2), whereas he quotes the Exiles as speaking from a place of embarrassment and desperation (12:27; 18:19, 25, 29; 20:32; 33:10, 17, 20; 37:11).[9] The paramount importance of this difference in treatment is further shown in the prophetic refutations. Ezekiel answers sinful pronouncements with prophecies of judgment, which fall mainly upon the people remaining in Judah (as, e.g., Ezek 11:1–13); but he speaks with consolation to the Exiles, who are in a desperate mood (37:1–11, and also in 11:14–21).

This distinction reveals, first of all, Ezekiel's preference for the Exiles and antipathy against the People Who Remained. Secondly, by observing Ezekiel's general tendencies in argumentation, we can establish the existence of a lively and vital conflict between the Judahite communities in Jerusalem and Babylon already by the early years of the sixth century B.C.E.[10] Finally, these disputation speeches cast Ezekiel in an important role, as he supplies ideological support to the community of the Jehoiachin Exiles.

7.   The use of בית ישראל to address the Exiles' community is in itself a marker of exclusion; see Paul M. Joyce, "Dislocation and Adaptation in the Exilic Age and After," in *After the Exile: Essays in Honor of Rex Mason* (ed. J. Barton and D. J. Reimer; Macon, Ga.: Mercer University Press, 1996), 45–58, especially 51; and compare to Zimmerli, *Ezekiel 2*, 563–65.

8.   This socio-geographic categorization differentiates Ezekiel from the other prophets who use the disputation speech to refute their audiences. Graffy (*A Prophet*, 123–24, etc.) pointed out Ezekiel's exilic orientation, but did not distinguish Ezekiel as making special ideological use of this genre.

9.   The status of the quotation in 12:26–28 attributed to "the House of Israel" is uncertain. Graffy (ibid., 57–58) suggested that, in contrast to the previous passage, which refers to words spoken "in the land of Israel" (12:21–25), the quotation in 12:26 was presented in "a less aggressive tone," and thus refuted in an encouraging way. Following Zimmerli (*Ezekiel 1*, 414), I understand Ezek 20:32 as a desperate saying and not as a rebuke; see below, pp. 157–59, and Dalit Rom-Shiloni, "Facing Destruction and Exile: Inner-Biblical Exegesis in Jeremiah and Ezekiel," *ZAW* 117 (2005): 189–205. In addition, Ezekiel refutes other "sinful" quotations pronounced in Jerusalem (8:12; 9:9), but they are not cast in the disputation pattern. Sinful sayings attributed to the Exiles are rare in Ezekiel, and appear as the words of false prophets (13:6, 7).

10.   The chronological headings of some of the prophecies specify the time period as extending from the sixth year after Jehoiachin's exile (592/1 B.C.E., see 8:1) to the

(2) *Leadership.* References to the current leadership provide another angle through which Ezekiel's pro-Exile orientation is apparent. The allegory of the two eagles, the (lofty) top of the cedar, and the vine (Ezek 17) conveys an obvious distinction between Jehoiachin, the exiled king, who is symbolized by the cedar and thus has royal legitimacy and respect (vv. 3b–4, 12–13), and Zedekiah, who is symbolized as the low vine. Although the latter could have had great political success, he failed because of his rebellion against the Babylonian king and against God (vv. 5–8, 9–10, 15–21). In contrast to the total condemnation projected for Zedekiah and the Jerusalemites (vv. 16–21), hope rests with "the lofty top of the cedar"; who, it is promised, will be brought back to the land of Israel, be replanted, and prosper as "a noble cedar" (vv. 22–24). The "topmost bough" of the cedar refers clearly to Jehoiachin in 17:3–4 as the object taken away and replanted afar (ויקח את צמרת הארץ את ראש יניקותיו קטף ויביאהו), but the future leader's identity remains vague, in the phrase ולקחתי אני מצמרת הארז הרמה ונתתי מראש ינקותיו רך אקטף ושתלתי אני in v. 22. Hence, the phrase might refer to other, later scions of the Davidic line (as was indeed suggested by Greenberg). In any case, and in contrast to Jeremiah (22:24–30), the future belongs to an exilic leader, a descendent of Jehoiachin.[11]

This allegory and the allegory of the lioness and her two cubs (referring to Jehoahaz and Zedekiah; Ezek 19:1–14), as well as other straightforward prophecies against Zedekiah (12:8–16; 21:23–32), show Ezekiel's support for Jehoiachin in Exile, and his blunt condemnation of Zedekiah of Jerusalem.[12]

Ezekiel's membership in the community of the Jehoiachin Exiles is, then, not just a biographical datum that reflects his geographical setting. The prophet's empathy with the Exiles has brought him to more than a mere interest in their "mental and spiritual transformation."[13] In what follows, I illustrate the proposition that, as a member of the community

fall of Jerusalem (586 B.C.E., see 33:21, 23–29), and probably to the following years as well (33:10–20; 37:1–14). See Christopher R. Seitz, "The Crisis of Interpretation Over the Meaning and Purpose of the Exile," *VT* 35 (1985): 78–97; idem, *Theology in Conflict*, 201–2.

11. Greenberg, *Ezekiel 1–20*, 317–24.

12. Ezekiel's attitude towards the two leaders has been interpreted as the prophet's political point of view by Bernard Lang, *Kein Aufstand in Jerusalem: Die Politik des Propheten Ezechiel* (Stuttgart: Katolisches Bibelwerk, 1978), 135–86. I suggest looking at the broader ideological context of Ezekiel's attitude towards the two communities.

13. So Daniel I. Block, *Ezekiel 1–24* (NICOT; Grand Rapids: Eerdmans, 1997), 15–17, 222.

of Jehoiachin Exiles, the prophet was motivated to reevaluate the status of both his own community and Those Who Remained behind in Judah as the people of God, and to supply divisive ideological arguments to distinguish between the two and to establish the legitimacy of the one over against the other. Hence, although Ezekiel was ordained to speak for Yahweh alone, and never occupied any official appointment as speaker for the Exiles,[14] through his ideology of exile, he established the community of the Jehoiachin Exiles as the exclusive people of God. Thus in retrospect, Ezekiel should indeed be considered both as the voice of the Jehoiachin Exiles and as the constructor of a new Babylonian exilic ideology.

b. *Ezekiel as Constructor of the Babylonian Exilic Ideologies*
Tracing Ezekiel's ideology concerning the group identity of the Jehoiachin Exiles may be best accomplished by proceeding from explicit cases to implicit ones. The discussion below is built, therefore, in three steps. First, I present the two disputation speeches, Ezek 11:14–21 and 33:23–29, which explicitly articulate the ideological opposition between the two groups, that of Those Who Remained vs. the Jehoiachin Exiles, and I draw attention to their divisive arguments. Second, I argue that in 16:1–43 and 20:1–38, Ezekiel implicitly supplies different retrospective histories for each of the two communities and in that way differentiates their futures, contrasting calamity with continuity. The prophet constructs his arguments for the one community and against the other by utilizing both Priestly and Deuteronomic legal traditions to authorize his message. Third, I illustrate how Ezekiel's attitude towards the homeland community throughout chs. 1–24 is consistently characterized by the denigration of Jerusalem, which implicitly strengthens the binary distinction he makes between these communities. In these prophecies of judgment, the prophet (and at times his disciples) struggle(s) with the linear sequence of iniquity–destruction–exile–restoration, adapting it to the exilic perception of the new reality of two geographically separate Judahite communities.

(1) *Explicit Disputations between Exiles and Those Who Remained (Ezekiel 11:14–21; 33:23–29).* Two of the nine disputation speeches in Ezekiel, Ezek 11:14–21 and 33:23–29, are critical for our discussion because they present both sides of the controversy between the two communities. The first passage dates from before the Destruction, the

---

14. Ibid., 11.

second took shape in its wake.[15] In both, Ezekiel quotes the position of Those Who Remained in order to refute it—from an exilic point of view. Both parties utilize strategies of division, and reflect an acute interest in the question of *continuity* with Israel's past history.

The disputation of **11:14–21** is in fact the second disputation speech in ch. 11. The chapter closes a combination of prophecies in chs. 8–11, given to the prophet במראות אלהים ("in visions of God," 8:3).[16] Led in these visions through the Temple courts, the prophet sees Jerusalem's abominations (ch. 8). In retaliation for its idolatry and lawlessness (חמס, v. 17; and 9:9), Ezekiel describes Jerusalem's impending punishment (ch. 9), which causes him to fling himself upon his face and cry aloud, אהה אדני יהוה המשחית אתה את כל שארית ישראל בשפכך את חמתך על ירושלים ("Ah, Lord God! Are You going to annihilate all that is left of Israel, pouring out Your fury upon Jerusalem?"). God answers in the affirmative. Indeed, the iniquity in Jerusalem causes Him to act with no compassion whatsoever (vv. 9–10), and so Jerusalem's punishment is to be carried out (v. 11). The two disputations in ch. 11 continue this line of thought. The first refutes the assertions of officials in Jerusalem (11:3), and prophesies total calamity upon its inhabitants (11:1–13). This prophecy gains additional force with the sudden death of the Jerusalem official Pelatiah son of Benaiah (v. 13).[17] In a dramatic reaction, the prophet again throws himself upon his face and cries out for the second time, אהה אדני אלהים כלה אתה עשה את שארית ישראל ("Ah, Lord God! You are wiping out the remnant of Israel!," v. 13). The second prophecy quotes the inhabitants of Jerusalem after the 597 B.C.E. exile, yet prior to the 586 destruction and second exile, arguing against the Jehoiachin Exiles (v. 15). The prophet refutes the Jerusalemites words with an important prospect of restoration to his community of Exiles. In the following discussion I argue that the juxtaposition of the two disputations one after the other places the second, vv. 14–21, as a reply to the prophet's repetitive cry. Prior to the Destruction, Ezekiel identifies the (new) "remnant of Israel" as the Exiles.[18]

---

15. I will deal with the various issues of dating in the ensuing discussion.

16. The literary structure of Ezek 8–11 is detailed in Greenberg, *Ezekiel 1–20*, 192–205.

17. The name of the official פלטיהו is in itself significant, as the name means "Yahweh has delivered"; see Block, *Ezekiel 1–24*, 338.

18. So Greenberg, *Ezekiel 1–20*, 193. The proximity of these two passages does not exclude the initial independence of each (i.e. 11:1–13 and 14–21). Yet the possibility of their initial independence should also not preclude Ezekiel from having intentionally joined these passages. Both disputations serve as integral components

Ezekiel 33:23–29 brings us to the months after the fall of Judah
(v. 21). The inhabitants of Jerusalem are now the inhabitants of the ruins
of that city (ישבי החרבות האלה על אדמת ישראל, v. 24). Nevertheless, they
still hold to prestigious exclusive perspectives, which are fiercely refuted
by the prophet in a judgment prophecy of total calamity (vv. 25–29).

(a) *The People Who Remained*. The two quotations that Ezekiel
refutes in these disputations share the same final clause. Their generic
characteristics enable us to trace the Jerusalemite side of this ideological
conflict:

רחקו מעל יהוה לנו היא נתנה הארץ למורשה

Keep far from the LORD;
the land has been given as a possession (NJPS: "heritage") to us. (11:15)

אחד היה אברהם ויירש את הארץ ואנחנו רבים
לנו נתנה הארץ למורשה

Abraham was but one man, yet he was granted possession
of the land. We are many;
surely, the land has been given as a possession to us. (33:24)

The pronouncement, "the land has been given as a possession (NJPS:
'heritage') to us" (לנו [היא] נתנה הארץ למורשה), constitutes a statement
of in-group definition by Those Who Remained in the land. It states the
exclusive rights of those left in Jerusalem and Judah to possess the land,
in contradistinction to those exiled from it; presence in or absence from
the land is taken as the factor which determines inheritance. Tracing the
traditional background of this argument leads us to consider pentateuchal
concepts of the land.

The concept that God gave the land to His people to possess, לרשתה,
is a major theme in Deuteronomy.[19] Yet the phrase נתן (ארץ) למורשה,
which is shared by Ezek 11:15 and 33:24, more closely resembles

in the larger prophetic unit of chs. 8–11, and thus should be dated prior to the
Destruction of Jerusalem. So Zimmerli (*Ezekiel 1*, 256, 260, 264), who connected the
editorial work with either Ezekiel or his disciples; see also Joyce, "Dislocation and
Adaptation," 46–50. Eichrodt (*Ezekiel*, 142–43), on the other hand, on the basis of
comparison with Ezek 33:23–29 and the words of consolation in 11:16–21, argued
that the conflict indicated in 11:14–21 is post-587. Block (*Ezekiel 1–24*, 342–46)
took a kind of middle way, suggesting that this passage represents a pre-586 prophecy which put in its current location by a pro-Exiles redactor, though he does not
exclude the possibility that the prophet himself was responsible for the juxtaposition.

19. Note Deut 4:5, 14; 5:28; 6:1; 7:1; 11:31; 12:1; 23:21; 25:19; 28:21, 63;
30:16, 18; 32:47. Yet, several Priestly passages use לרשת as well, such as Gen 28:4;
Lev 20:24; 25:46; Num 33:53.

Exod 6:8.[20] Exodus 6:2–8, a Priestly unit that emphasizes the pattern of promise and fulfillment, builds the bridge between the patriarchs and the Exodus generation; the land that was promised to Abraham, Isaac and Jacob (vv. 3–4) will now be given to the sons of Jacob, who are to be saved from servitude in Egypt.[21]

By evoking this tradition, the Jerusalemites give a new interpretation to this theme of promise and fulfillment.[22] They claim to hold a divine "contract" for the land, announcing (implicit in the passive נִתְּנָה) that God has given *them* the rights to the land. It is the inhabitants of Jerusalem (and only they themselves) who continue to hold to that ancient promise to Abraham; they are the true descendants of those sons of Jacob, the true people of God. Thus, by way of *annexation*, the inhabitants of Jerusalem appropriate to themselves alone past traditions concerning the promise of the land (whether derived from the patriarchal stories and the Exodus traditions or from its distillation in Exod 6:2–8). By mobilizing these traditions, they can mount a theological argument of divine legitimization for their continuing existence as a community within the land.

The opening clauses of the quotations each suggest a different strategy of division. The saying in Ezek 33:24 makes a positive statement concerning the in-group, that is, concerning the continuity and status of Those Who Remained, while Ezek 11:15 quotes a denigrative accusation against the out-group (those afar off, i.e., the Exiles), delegitimizing the existence of the Babylonian group by using Deuteronomic conceptions of exile.

20. The noun מוֹרָשָׁה appears nine times in the Hebrew Bible, once each in Exod 6:8 and Deut 33:4, and seven times in Ezekiel. In addition to the two citations under discussion, the term occurs in prophecies to the nations (25:4, 10), and in the prophecy of consolation to the mountains of Israel (36:2, 3, 5).

21. For the central position of Exod 6:2–8 in the Priestly redaction of the Pentateuch, see Martin Noth, *Exodus* (OTL; Philadelphia: Westminster, 1962), 56–62; Lyle Eslinger, "Knowing Yahweh: Exod 6:3 in the Context of Genesis 1–Exodus 15," in *Literary Structure and Rhetorical Strategies in the Hebrew Bible* (ed. L. D. de Regt, J. de Waard, and J. P. Fokkelman; Assen: Van Gorcum, 1996], 188–98). Its literary context as the introduction to the plagues was discussed by Moshe Greenberg, *Understanding Exodus* (New York: Behrman, 1968), 146–48.

22. The Priestly unit of Exod 6:2–8 was probably known both to the people in Jerusalem and to Ezekiel (the diachronic relative order thus places the prophet after this Priestly passage). See Risa Levitt Kohn, *A New Heart and a New Soul: Ezekiel, the Exile and the Torah* (JSOTSup 358; Sheffield: Sheffield Academic, 2002), 38, 43–44, 66–67, 98–104; in contrast to Johan Lust, "Exodus 6,2–8 and Ezekiel," in *Studies in the Book of Exodus: Redaction, Reception, Interpretation* (ed. M. Vervenne; Leuven: Leuven University Press, 1996), 209–24.

Claims of the in-group occur mainly in Ezek 33:24, which reads: אחד
היה אברהם ויירש את הארץ ואנחנו רבים ("Abraham was but one man, yet
he was granted possession of the land. We are many"). To find Abraham
mentioned in the words of the inhabitants of Jerusalem is in itself quite a
surprise, since outside of the book of Genesis, Abraham is mentioned
only rarely, and this is the only occurrence of his name in Ezekiel.[23]
What is of even more interest is to trace the exact features adapted by the
Jerusalemites from the Abraham stories. In this *Qal VaHomer* argument—אחד היה אברהם ואנחנו רבים—the promise of the land is only
implicitly hinted at.[24] Weight is given to Abraham's actual possession of
the land (ויירש את הארץ), and it thus recalls Exod 6:4 and Gen 17:8, but
even more so Gen 15:7. After the Destruction of Jerusalem, God's
covenant with Abraham gained new relevance. Those Who Remained
counted themselves direct descendants of Abraham, and being many,
they undoubtedly have been permitted to remain in order to continue
inhabiting/inheriting the land.

This line of reasoning accords with the religious-national argument of
"the merit of the forefathers" (זכות אבות), which characterizes the closing
clause of this quotation as well. It commemorates the past constitutive
connection between God and the patriarch Abraham. Emphasizing the
ongoing kinship bond between Abraham and the present community in
Jerusalem, Those Who Remained claim the *continuity* of their own
residence in the land with the line of Abraham's earlier descendents,
and thus their rightful possession of that land. This, then, constitutes a
central argument of divine legitimization presented by Those Who
Remained.

Configuration of the out-group. The call "Keep far from the Lord"
(רחקו מעל יהוה, Ezek 11:15), which according to MT is an imperative,
commands the Exiles to distance/separate themselves from God.[25] The

---

23. Other occurrences outside of Genesis appear in the repeated patriarchal
formula, together with Isaac and Jacob (Exod 3:6, 15; Deut 1:8; 1 Kgs 18:36; Ps
105:6, 8–10, 42, etc.), and alone in "the retinue of Abraham's God" (Ps 47:10; 2 Chr
20:7); and as the chosen forefather (Neh 9:7). Only seven times does Abraham
appear in all the prophetic literature (Jer 33:26, where the name is part of the triple
patriarchal formula; with Jacob, Mic 7:20; three times in Isa 41:8; 63:16 [with
Israel/Jacob]; with Sara, 51:2; and once in Isa 29:22).

24. Compare Isa 51:1–2, where Abraham appears to be central to the Exilic
community of the second half of the sixth century B.C.E. See the discussion on
pp. 118–19.

25. Interpreting the imperative, Greenberg (*Ezekiel 1–20*, 189) adduced the close
connections between the cult and the concept of the land as God's land, as appears,
e.g., in Josh 22:24–27. Compare to the *BHS* suggestion that we read the verb in the

use of the imperative to a community that had already been physically distanced suggests the demand that the Exiles "let go" of God theologically and emotionally. The inhabitants of Jerusalem use the traditional concept of exile to establish their argument. That is, there is an essential connection between residence in God's land and worship of God, one that is opposed to an equally essential connection between residence in foreign lands and the worship of foreign gods (as in Deut 4:25–28; 28:36, 64; 1 Sam 26:19; see also Jer 5:19; 16:10–13). Being outside of God's land means that the Deportees are outside of God's domain. This implies practical consequences for worship—the Jehoiachin Exiles must now worship other gods; furthermore, according to Those Who Remained, the Jehoiachin Exiles have been deprived of their religious-national, land-linked identity as the people of God. This argument demonstrates the use of a traditional concept of exile, which would have been well-known to both Exiles and non-Exiles, in order to delegitimize the existence of the community of the Jehoiachin Exiles.[26]

To conclude, the anonymous quotations in Ezekiel suggest that, following the Jehoiachin exile (Ezek 11:15), and then the Destruction (33:24), Those Who Remained sought to accomplish their reidentification as God's people by using ideological strategies of separation from the exiled Judeans. Utilizing the arguments of *continuity* and *annexation*, they applied past traditions and established concepts to their community in Jerusalem, and thus constructed a newly legitimate status for themselves as the people of God;[27] at the same time, they reinforced their singular status by using arguments that showed their sister community in exile to be the out-group, and thus *not* legitimate heirs to Abraham.

It is of great significance that, although still resident in the land, even if temporarily estranged from their actual property (Jer 42:12), the community of Those Who Remained had an interest similar to that of the Jehoiachin Exiles in rebuilding an exclusive identity, understanding

Perfect, רְחַק, followed by Zimmerli, *Ezekiel 1*, 229; Brownlee, *Ezekiel*, 163; Joyce, "Dislocation and Adaptation," 51; Block, *Ezekiel 1–25*, 341, 347–48. Although the perfect form suits the causative perfect הרחקתים in the reply (v. 16), it presents a weaker, less polemical, statement. Commentators (such as Block, *Ezekiel 1–25*, 348–49) adopted this reading to explain the economic interest of Those Who Remained in taking over the Exiles' property. But, beyond its conjectural character, this suggestion reduces the importance of the ideological arguments, to which Zimmerli had already pointed (*Ezekiel 1*, 261).

26. See Rom-Shiloni, "Deuteronomic Concepts of Exile," especially 119–22.

27. The position of Those Who Remained is further elaborated upon by Jeremiah (Jer 32:6–15; 42:9–17, etc.), see pp. 323–33, below.

themselves as the legitimate heirs to Israel of the past.[28] Moreover, it is significant that, like the Exiles themselves, they crafted that claim to legitimacy by excluding from the people of God those from whom they had been separated.

(b) *The Jehoiachin Exiles*. Ezekiel's empathy to the Jehoiachin Exiles is clearly marked by the three terms that present them as his own people: אחיך אחיך אנשי גאלתך וכל בית ישראל כלה ("your brothers, your brothers, men of your kindred, all of that very house of Israel," Ezek 11:14).[29]

The refutation of the Judean argument in **Ezek 11:16–21** is structured to respond to both halves of the quotation; thus it retains responses to both the in-group and out-group arguments. First, Ezekiel answers the imperative "Keep far from the Lord" (רחקו מעל יהוה, v. 15); he acknowledges that God Himself has distanced the exiles כי הרחקתים ("I have indeed removed them far," v. 16). Then, in reply to the Jerusalemites' claim לנו היא נתנה הארץ למורשה ("the land has been given as a possession to us," v. 15), Ezekiel promises that God will give the land to the Exiles ונתתי לכם את אדמת ישראל ("and I will give you the land of Israel," v. 17).[30] In its general content, the refutation contradicts the implicit message of abandonment and doom in the quotation with a prophecy of consolation that defines the *Jehoiachin Exiles* as the people with whom God dwells, and hopes for *their* restoration (vv. 17–20). In contrast, annihilation is going to be the fate of those who hold to abominations (v. 21).

Describing Ezekiel's in-group. In v. 16 God declares כי הרחקתים בגוים וכי הפיצותים בארצות ("Indeed it was I who distanced them and dispersed them"). In accordance with the Deuteronomic concept of exile, Ezekiel ascribes the deportation to God (see Deut 28:36: יולך יהוה אתך ואת מלכך אל גוי, "The Lord will drive you, and the king you have set over you, to a nation [unknown to you or your fathers, where you shall serve other gods, of wood and stone]"). However, in contrast to Deut 4:25–28; 28:36, 64, Ezekiel redefines the relationship between God and His people

28.   Oded Lipschits, "Demographic Changes in Judah between the Seventh and the Fifth Centuries B.C.E.," in Lipschits and Blenkinsopp, eds., *Judah and the Judeans in the Neo-Babylonian Period*, 323–76.

29.   For the MT and the LXX version, οι ανδρες της αἰχμλωσίας σου (אנשי גלותך), see Block, *Ezekiel 1–24*, 341, 346. Note also בני עמך in Ezek 3:11 and 33:30.

30.   This relationship of statement and response between v. 15 and v. 17 was suggested already by Eliezer of Beaugency, *Kommentar zu Ezechiel und den XII kleinen Propheten von Eliezer aus Beaugency* (ed. S. Poznanski; Warsaw: Mekitze Nirdamim, 1909), on Ezek 11:17. Such literal, structural, and thematic accord between quotation and counter-speech often appear in the disputation speeches; see Graffy, *A Prophet*, 105–19.

in exile, and thus focuses his refutation on the divine legitimization of the Exiles' community. Although they have been exiled to foreign lands, the Exiles are not destined to serve foreign gods; they have not been expelled from the presence of God.[31] On the contrary, those expelled are themselves the objects of restoration. *They* will be gathered from among the peoples and receive the inheritance of the land (v. 17). Upon their return, *they* will purify the land from its detestable things and abominations (v. 18), and God will transform *their* hearts (v. 19) in order to renew the covenant relationship exclusively with *this* community of His people (v. 20).

Defining the out-group. Verse 21 poses a syntactical difficulty with regard to its implicit subject ואל לב שקוציהם ותועבותיהם לבם הלך ("But as for them whose heart is set upon their detestable things and abominations").[32] Designating the "others" as "those holding to" שקוצים and תועבות sets v. 21 in opposition to v. 18. Since upon their return, the Repatriates are expected to "do away" with those illegitimate cults that are still prevalent in the land, it is indeed plausible that "those holding to them" (v. 21) designates Those Who Remained. Through this implicit identification, the prophecy marks a cultic distinction between the Jehoiachin Exiles and Those Who Remained.[33] This distinction is among the first signs of an exilic process of differentiation between the Exiles and Those Who Remained, in which the latter are accused of worshipping other gods in God's land.[34]

Ezekiel's innovative conception that exile is *not* a sign of divine rejection gains further strength in the words ואהי להם למקדש מעט בארצות אשר באו שם (v. 16), a phrase that has garnered many interpretations. Two major paths have been taken in interpreting היה להם למקדש מעט. According to the first, מקדש has its usual meaning of "sanctuary," and

---

31. So Eliezer of Beaugency, *Kommentar zu Ezechiel*, on Ezek 11:16.

32. Greenberg (*Ezekiel 1–20*, 191) identified the oppositional community in Ezek 11:14–21 according to the contradictory phrases הלך בחקותי (v. 20) and לב (v. 19); see also Eliezer of Beaugency on Ezek 11:18.

33. A similar dichotomy is implicitly suggested also in Jer 29:16–20, in the contrast between the disobedient king and people in Jerusalem (תחת אשר לא שמעו, vv. 16–19), and the demand presented to the Exiles community to change its ways (ואתם שמעו, v. 20). Ezek 20 suggests yet another interpretation, in which evaluative distinction is done among the Exiles (vv. 35–38).

34. This categorization will eventually play a major role in the Persian-period contest between the Repatriates, designated as זרע הקדש in the later texts, and the בני הנכר or עמי הארצות, the residents of Judah, who, as we have seen, are presented as foreigners (e.g. Ezra 4:2–3; 9:1–2; Neh 9:2–3; 10:29, etc.). See above, especially on pp. 34–36.

מעט, already in the early translations (and subsequently by traditional commentators), is to be interpreted as an adjective that signifies diminution.[35] According to a second path of interpretation, suggested by most of the critical commentaries, מקדש is to be taken as metonymy for the presence of God, and מעט is interpreted as an adverb that minimizes His presence with the Exiles.[36] Although מקדש in this metonymical sense is a *hapax*, Ezekiel coins this phrase to proclaim that exile does not cause separation from God.[37] God continues to be present in the life of the Exiles, though in a reduced fashion compared to His previous presence in His Temple. Ezekiel advocates here that in exilic circumstances (and even prior to the Destruction of His Temple), God has a dynamic presence, adjusting His appearances to His people's different dwelling places.[38]

---

35. Linguistically, although מעט comes after the noun it describes, it can be an adjective, as in other rare instances, all occurring in late books: Eccl 9:14; Dan 11:34; Ezra 9:8; Neh 2:12. See the LXX (and the Vulgate), the Peshitta, and the Targum, which identify the concrete reference for this small temple as the contemporary synagogue. The Targum, ויהבית להון בתי כנישתא תנין לבית מקדשי ואנון כזעיר במדינתא דאתגליאו לתמן ("therefore I have given them synagogues, second only to My Holy Temple, because they are few in number in the countries to which they have been exiled" [trans. Samson H. Levey, *The Targum of Ezekiel* (Edinburgh: T. & T. Clark, 1987), 41]) presents a double translation of מעט—first, referring back to the Temple, and second, to the Exiles.

36. According to this interpretation, מעט is an adverb of measure (and not of time), as in 2 Kgs 10:18; Zech 1:15. Note the translations of George A. Cooke, "and I became to them a sanctuary in small measure" (*Ezekiel* [ICC; Edinburgh: T. & T. Clark, 1936, repr. 1985], 125); Zimmerli, "and I have been to them (only) a little for a sanctuary" (*Ezekiel 1*, 126); so also Greenberg, who translated the phrase as "reduced presence" (*Ezekiel 1–20*, 190); and cf. Joyce's suggestion that the figurative use of מקדש מעט presents "the motif of Yahweh himself becoming a 'sanctuary'" ("Dislocation and Adaptation," 54).

37. מקדש occurs 73 times in the Hebrew Bible, none of them in this abstract sense. It usually designates either the Temple itself (so 29 times in Ezekiel: 12 times in chs. 1–39, and 17 in chs. 40–48); a holy artifact (such as the tithe, Num 18:29); the tabernacle vessels (Num 3:38); or finally, the holy precincts of the tabernacle (Exod 25:8) or the Temple (Lam 1:10; similarly the plural: מקדשים, Ezek 21:7; Jer 51:51).

38. This concept in v. 16 of God's presence with the Exiles accords with Ezekiel's perception throughout (cf. Joyce, "Dislocation and Adaptation," 56–58). God is immanently present in the Temple on the one hand (Ezek 9–10, and 43:1–7), just as he has dynamic and transcendent presence in the lands of the Dispersion (Ezek 1:1–3:15; 11:16–21, etc.). See John F. Kutsko, *Between Heaven and Earth: Divine Presence and Absence in the Book of Ezekiel* (Winona Lake: Eisenbrauns, 2000), 77–100, especially 96–99.

In his refutation Ezekiel crafts a new concept of exile. In opposition to the exilic layer of Deuteronomy (Deut 4:29–31; 30:1–10) and the Holiness Code (Lev 26:39–45), Ezekiel's innovation establishes *God* (not the people) as the initiator of the restored relationship with the Exiles (Ezek 11:16–21; 36:22–32).[39] In this polemical context, the accent on the divine initiative illustrates further Ezekiel's identification with the community in exile.[40] This ideological innovation constituted the new status of the Exiles as away from the land of Israel, but not distanced from God, and as separated from Those Who Remained in Judah. Hence, Ezekiel's consolation prophecy reveals the prophet's vital contribution to the evolution of an exilic ideology during the first years of the exile.

In **Ezek 33:23–29** the prophet confronts a declaration of rights by Those Who Remained in ruined Jerusalem: לנו נתנה הארץ למורשה ("the land has been given as a possession to us," v. 24). In contrast to the disputation in Ezek 11:14–21, in these verses the prophet does not explicitly set his prophecy of doom against a prophecy of consolation directed to the Exiles.[41] This silence about the Exiles is spurred by the quotation itself, which does not mention them (in contrast to 11:15). This feature could therefore be explained as simply another sign of the formal and thematic accord maintained between the quotation and the refutation.[42] Yet, the lack of reply or comment on the central argument of Those Who Remained, with its reliance on the Abraham tradition, seems significant. To confront Jerusalemite reasoning, Ezekiel chooses a different ideological argument altogether, based on the Priestly and Holiness Code legal conceptions. In two extreme accusations (vv. 25–26), Ezekiel

---

39. The importance of the divine transformation of the heart in Ezekiel's prophecies of consolation was noted by Greenberg, *Ezekiel 1–20*, 341, and *Ezekiel 21–37*, 735–38, and thoroughly discussed by Thomas M. Raitt, *A Theology of Exile: Judgment/Deliverance in Jeremiah and Ezekiel* (Philadelphia: Fortress, 1977), 132–34, 147–50, 175–84. Ezek 6:8–10; 20:43–44; 36:31 (like 16:59–63, which I consider as non-Ezekelian) present the people's regret and repentance as a *reaction* to, not a *stimulus* for, God's initial salvific actions.

40. Compare Greenberg's explanation of this idea as resting on a pessimistic outlook on the probability of the people's repentance (*Ezekiel 21–37*, 735–38).

41. Rimon Kasher suggested (*Ezekiel 25–48* [Mikra LeYisra'el; Jerusalem: The Hebrew University/Magnes; Tel Aviv: Am Oved, 2004 (in Hebrew)], 641) that the juxtaposition of 33:30–33 to our passage (vv. 23–29) is meant to give the last word to the Exiles, who are here called בני עמך and even עמי (v. 31); this itself is meant to convey a degree of consolation.

42. Graffy, *A Prophet*, 105–29. Compare Greenberg (*Ezekiel 21–37*, 688), who argued that the disputation in Ezek 33:23–29 confronts a perspective held by Edom (Ezek 36:2). I would rather focus on the intra-Judean conflict.

names cultic, social, and sexual sins committed in the land of Judah, as an introduction to the rhetorical question: והארץ תירשו ("yet you expect to possess the land?!").[43]

Michael Fishbane and Moshe Greenberg explained the concentration on the people's sins as the prophet's furious reaction, recalling traditions of Abraham's righteousness. But there is no trace of any such tradition in Ezekiel's refutation. It rather seems that, lacking an adequate response based on the Abraham traditions, Ezekiel shifts the entire question into the realm of legal obligation.[44] The three capital crimes of which Ezekiel accuses Those Who Remained, as well as the question והארץ תירשו, allude to the Holiness Code's concept of land and exile. According to Lev 18 and 20, idolatry, bloodshed, and sexual offenses defile the land to the point that it vomits out its inhabitants (Lev 18:24–30; 20:22), causing God to drive out its inhabitants in total abhorrence (Lev 20:23).[45] Ezekiel's cry והארץ תירשו (Ezek 33:25, 26) echoes the promise of the land: ואמר לכם אתם תירשו את אדמתם ("You shall possess their land," Lev 20:24). Yet, by posing it as a rhetorical question directed against those in Jerusalem, the prophet abolishes the promise for "those who live in these ruins in the land of Israel" (Ezek 33:24).

Moreover, Ezekiel applies to the community left in Judah the threats of removal from the land found in Lev 18:24–30. This passage from the Holiness Code catalogues the fates of אנשי הארץ ("the people who were in the land," v. 27), or the Canaanite peoples (20:23, MT גוי, but plural in the Versions), in order to deter Israel from the calamitous results of following in their ways.[46] The Canaanite peoples of the land were

43. In contrast to the commentators who understand והארץ תירשו as a rhetorical question, the NJPS translates this phrase as an indicative sentence, perceiving it then as clear mockery or sarcasm. Gershon Brin ("The Date and Meaning of the Prophecy against 'Those Who Live in These Ruins in the Land of Israel' [Ezekiel 33:23–29]," in *Texts, Temples, and Traditions: A Tribute to Menahem Haran* [ed. M. V. Fox et al.; Winona Lake: Eisenbrauns, 1996], *29–*36 [in Hebrew]) saw the element of sarcasm and condemnation already present with the demonstrative pronoun האלה (in 33:24).

44. See Fishbane, *Biblical Interpretation*, 375; and Greenberg, *Ezekiel 21–37*, 689–90.

45. See *b. Men.* 13.2. See also the discussion of the sins and their relationship to the Holiness Code in Greenberg, *Ezekiel 21–37*, 684–85; note too Jan Joosten, *People and Land in the Holiness Code: An Exegetical Study of the Ideational Framework of the Law in Leviticus 17–26* (SVTP 67; Leiden: Brill, 1996), 169–92.

46. Baruch J. Schwartz, *The Holiness Legislation: Studies in the Priestly Code* (Jerusalem: The Hebrew University/Magnes, 1999 [in Hebrew]), 222–37; Jacob Milgrom, *Leviticus 17–22* (AB 3A; New York: Doubleday, 2000), 1571–78.

expelled because of their "abhorrent practices" (חקות התועבות, 18:30), which were mainly of a sexual nature (Lev 18:6–23). But the prohibitive speech of 18:24–30 does not limit itself to the threat of expulsion of the people from the land; it warns of further calamity (v. 29).[47] Accordingly, in contrast to the argument of Those Who Remained, that they should possess the land in *continuity* with past history and the promise to Abraham, Ezekiel does not even bother to predict their exile, but goes on to foretell their total annihilation by sword, beast, and pestilence, in accord with Leviticus' more dire projections (Ezek 33:27). Furthermore, the prophet widens the scope of his prophecy to include complete desolation of the land (vv. 28–29).[48]

Based on Lev 18:24–30, then, Ezekiel establishes two counter-arguments against Those Who Remained in Jerusalem. First, he draws an analogy between Those Who Remained and the (Canaanite) peoples of the land, thus characterizing them as "other" and rejecting the possibility that Those Who Remained might have any kinship with the community of the Jehoiachin Exiles in Babylon. According to the prophet, the inhabitants of Jerusalem are excluded from the inheritance of the land, they equal the Canaanite peoples of the land who were expelled and extinct. Second, Ezekiel initiates a rhetorical opposition between the Jehoiachin Exiles and the empty land, an opposition that will be carried on and further developed by Deutero-Isaiah and Zechariah.[49] In Ezekiel's prophecy these two arguments are first linked together.[50]

To summarize: Ezekiel develops a claim of divine delegitimization of the continuous existence of Those Who Remained in Judah. Further-more, he emphatically reflects an assumption of the superiority and

47. Schwartz (*The Holiness Legislation*, 228–37) suggested that Leviticus makes a clear distinction between expulsion and calamity. Yet, in terms of the fate of Israel (18:29), it seems rather that in three passages (Lev 18:24–30; 20:20–24; Num 33:50–59) expulsion does mean annihilation, even if there is no reference to the vehicle of execution. Thus, these passages differ from Lev 26's perspective on exile.

48. Total calamity and an empty land characterize other judgment prophecies against Jerusalem, see pp. 173–81, below. Milgrom (*Leviticus 17–22*, 1573–74) argued that in the Holiness Code the land "automatically regurgitates its inhabitants in the process of cleansing itself," and thus, in contrast to the Priestly perception, the land is not irrevocably impure. Ezekiel then reflects here the Priestly position in prophesying that the sins require the desolation of the land itself (as in Ezek 6:11–14).

49. See the discussions on pp. 49–61, 106–8, above.

50. Compare to the Persian-period sources, which illustrate the separation of these two arguments: the prophetic sources utilize the opposition between the Exiles and the empty land, whereas Ezra–Nehemiah utilizes the opposition between the Repatriated Exiles and the peoples of the land(s). See above, pp. 41–45.

exclusivity of the Jehoiachin Exiles, and reveals that this outlook was in place from the very start, from 597 B.C.E. and on.[51]

As an advocate of the Jehoiachin Exiles, Ezekiel formulates a concept of exile that enables *continuity* of Judahite existence *outside* the Land of Israel. He clearly knows and deviates from both Deuteronomy's and the Holiness Code's conceptions of land and exile. Furthermore, in his prophecy of restoration (11:16–21), Ezekiel supplies divine legitimization to this community of Exiles, seen now as the exclusive remnant of the people of God. In opposition, the prophet delegitimizes the community in Jerusalem, accusing it of various cultic sins (11:21; 33:25–26) that estrange them from the land, which thus remains empty and desolated.[52] These strategies of division create explicit differences of superiority and inferiority between the groups, the one considered Israel, the other analogized as the people of the land.

(2) *Implicit Disputations: Separate Histories, Separate Futures for the Two Judean Communities*. In his social-anthropological studies, Fredrick Barth mentioned the importance given to questions of origin in the evolution of a group's present identity.[53] Having outlined the rival arguments in this conflict, we can now proceed to Ezekiel's observations on the history of the God–people relationship, and thus to his conception of the two communities' possibilities for present and future existence.

In two passages, Ezek 16:1–43 and 20:1–38, I suggest that Ezekiel expresses his perspective on the distinctive origins and future of each of the two Judahite communities.

The two prophecies have several characteristics in common. First, they each open with the call to the prophet to accuse the protagonists of abhorrent practices: בן אדם הודע את ירושלים את תועבתיה ("O mortal,

---

51. This separation is explicitly suggested in Jer 24:1–10 (see below, pp. 233–37); and appears implicitly also in the diverse descriptions of the Jehoiachin Exile in 2 Kgs 24:8–17, in comparison to the general reference to the 586 destruction and exile in 2 Kgs 25. For the exilic perspective of 2 Kgs 24–25, see Seitz, *Theology in Conflict*, 215–21.

52. Religious misbehavior as a delegitimating device to determine hierarchical differentiation between groups is also implemented in the historiography; see the various denigrations of the Northern Kingdom, accused of following "the ways of Jeroboam son of Nevat and the sins he caused Israel to commit," down to the time of its destruction and exile (1 Kgs 12:25–33; 13:33–34; 15:26, 34, and constantly through the book of Kings; finally, see 2 Kgs 17:21–22, which suggests a somewhat different yet still denigrating perspective).

53. Barth, *Ethnic Groups*, 29.

proclaim Jerusalem's abominations to her," 16:2), and התשפט אתם
התשפוט בן אדם את תועבת אבותם הודיעם ("Arraign, arraign them, O
mortal! —Declare to them the abhorrent deeds of their fathers," 20:4).[54]
The former statement is aimed at Jerusalem, while the latter is directed
toward the Jehoiachin Exiles. A second common denominator is structural: both passages start with a retrospective which goes back to the
initial constitution of the relationship between God and his people (16:1–
14; 20:5–26),[55] proceed to the present generation in a chronological
contraction that skips over intervening history to the present generation
(16:15–34; 20:30–33), and look to the future (16:35–43; 20:34–38). The
third similarity is thematic: in both prophecies the prophet lays out his
agenda concerning the question, "Who are the people of God?," asserting
that God's people may be drawn from only one of the two communities,
either the Jehoiachin Exiles or Those Who Remained in Judah. However,
in other features the two passages differ.

Literary genre. **Ezekiel 16:1–43**, the metaphoric story of the
abandoned baby, the beautiful bride, and the harlot wife, is told in the
structural framework of a judgment prophecy. The first part consists of a
long description of the sinful wife's guilt and ingratitude (vv. 1–34); it is
followed by a passage describing her punishment (vv. 35–43).[56]

In contrast, **Ezek 20:1–38** is construed as a disputation speech, though
with special structural features.[57] As is typical of the genre, the core of

54. An even closer parallel to the opening of Ezek 20:4 appears in Ezek 22:1:
ואתה בן אדם התשפט התשפט את עיר הדמים והודעתה את כל תועבותיה ("Further, O
mortal, arraign, arraign the city of bloodshed; declare to her all her abhorrent
deeds!"). Yet, the passages differ, first, in the grammatical person of the address; and
second, in their content. Ezek 22:1–12 deals with Jerusalem's present iniquities and
does not present a retrospective history of the God–people relationship. Third, in
terms of their rhetorical style, explicit apodictic charges shape Ezek 22 (similar to
Ezek 16), in contrast to Ezek 20's reliance on historical traditions concerning the
covenant (cf. Zimmerli, *Ezekiel 1*, 454–55).

55. Ezek 20:27–29, 39–44 are secondary, see Rom-Shiloni, "Facing Destruction," 200–201.

56. Ezek 16:1–43 is one of five different passages in Ezek 16 and 23 which
use the family metaphors of adoption and marriage in diverse ways. On their initial
independence as a unit and their literary nature as metaphorical stories (not allegory), see J. Galambush, *Jerusalem in the Book of Ezekiel: The City as Yahweh's
Wife* (SBLDS 130; Atlanta: Scholars Press, 1992), 10–11.

57. In a previous study I suggested a different division for ch. 20 than is
commonly followed (Rom-Shiloni, "Facing Destruction," 194–204). In the present
chapter, I adduce only the necessary points for the present argument. Most commentators have divided ch. 20 into two initially independent units: a historical speech
(vv. 1–31) and a disputation speech (confined to vv. 32–44). So Eichrodt, *Ezekiel*,

the disputation is the refutation of the elders' despairing words, quoted in v. 32: נהיה כגוים כמשפחות הארצות לשרת עץ ואבן ("We will be like the nations, like the families of the lands, worshiping wood and stone").[58] The elders of Israel approach the prophet with a reflection or a question in which they seek to interpret the dissonance between the traditional concept of exile and their present existence in Babylon. The Deuter-onomic concept, which they cite, indeed threatens that exile will doom them to worshipping wood and stone (ועבדתם שם אלהים מעשה ידי אדם עץ ואבן, "there you will serve manmade gods of wood and stone," Deut 4:28 and 28:36, 64). This assertion challenges the Exiles' continued existence as the people of God.

The furious rejection of the elders' inquiry is accentuated by an *inclusio* repetition, which frames the retrospective speech in the dispu-tation's introductory section:[59]

הלדרש אתי אתם באים חי אני אם אדרש לכם נאם אדני יהוה

Have you come to inquire of Me? As I live, I will not respond to your inquiry—declares the Lord God. (20:3)

ואני אדרש לכם בית ישראל חי אני נאם אדני יהוה אם אדרש לכם

Shall I respond to your inquiry, O house of Israel? As I live—declares the Lord God—I will not respond to you. (20:31)

In the course of his speech the prophet first proclaims the abhorrent deeds of "their fathers" (vv. 4–26). Returning to his contemporaries (vv. 30–32a), Ezekiel then quotes their words (v. 32b) and disproves them with a unique prophecy of deliverance, which describes God as reigning over the people: ביד חזקה ובזרוע נטויה ובחמה שפוכה ("with a strong hand, and with an outstretched arm, and with overflowing fury," vv. 33–38). Ezekiel's special perspective on the relationship between

276–84; Zimmerli, *Ezekiel 1*, 404, 413–14; L. C. Allen, *Ezekiel 20–48* (WBC 29; Waco, Tex.: Word, 1990), 5; and also Graffy, *A Prophet*, 65–66. In contrast, Greenberg (*Ezekiel 1–20*, 376–81) and Yair Hoffman ("Ezekiel 20: Its Structure and Meaning," *Beit Miqra* 20 [1975]: 480–86) argued for the unity of the chapter.

58. So Zimmerli, *Ezekiel 1*, 414. For further discussion of the speech and its traditional background, see Rom-Shiloni, "Facing Destruction," 194–98.

59. In addition, all the literary features of the introductory section of a dispu-tation speech are present: (1) the prophetic formula ויהי דבר יהוה אלי לאמר (v. 2; as in Ezek 11:14, etc.); (2) the essential features preceding the quotation: the verb אמר, and the identification of its subject, אתם (v. 32); (c) a twofold rejection of the exiles' concern—once in the *inclusio* and once in the immediate context of vv. 32 and on. Cf. Graffy, *A Prophet*, 105–29.

God and His people is thus the focus of this disputation presented in both his *retrospective* accounting and in his *prospective* articulation of the ongoing relationship during the exile.[60]

Future prospects. The difference in genre emphasizes the distinctly opposite content of the two prophecies. Ezekiel 16:1–43 prophesies judgment and calamity against Jerusalem, while Ezek 20:1–38 forecasts consolation and hope for the Exiles.

Metaphors to describe the God–people covenant relationship. The contrast in content, particularly between the future prediction to Jerusalem and that delivered to the Jehoiachin Exiles, caused Ezekiel to use different metaphors to designate contrasting perspectives on the God–people covenant relationship.

The metaphor in **Ezek 20** is the well-known political metaphor which designates God as King and the people as His vassals.[61] The retrospective speech (vv. 4–31) depicts four periods (covering three generations) in a graduated pattern of three and four: (a) the servitude in Egypt—the first generation of the fathers (vv. 5–10); (b) the Exodus and journey through the desert of this first generation (vv. 11–17); (c) the second generation in the desert (vv. 18–26); (d) Ezekiel's contemporary generation in Babylon (vv. 30–31), where the historical retrospective reaches its climax.[62] In repeating God's rejection of the Exiles' fears and assumption, the prophet straightforwardly reproves his contemporaries in exile: הבדרך אבתיכם אתם נטמאים ("do you defile yourselves in the manner of your fathers?," v. 31).[63]

In order to characterize the God–people relationship, Ezekiel describes the first three periods using repetitive components. (a) God has benefited his people by choosing them and constituting a covenant relationship with them by means of an oath (20:5–6), and has further committed them

---

60. So Block, *Ezekiel 1–24*, 613. For other proposals concerning the possible content of Ezek 20, see Hoffman, "Ezekiel 20," 473; Greenberg, *Ezekiel 1–20*, 387–88; and Kasher, *Ezekiel 1–24*, 385.

61. To mention only selected comparative studies on vassal treaties and the biblical covenant concept, see Delbert R. Hillers, *Treaty Curses and the Old Testament Prophets* (2d ed.; BibOr 16; Rome: Pontifical Biblical Institute, 1964); Moshe Weinfeld, "The Covenant of Grant in the Old Testament and in the Ancient Near East," *JAOS* 90 (1970): 184–203; idem, "Beriṯ—Covenant vs. Obligation," *Bib* 56 (1975): 120–28; Bruce K. Waltke, "The Phenomenon of Conditionality Within Unconditional Covenants," in *Israel's Apostasy and Restoration: Essays in Honor of R. K Harrison* (ed. A. Gileadi; Grand Rapids: Baker, 1988), 123–40.

62. Contra Greenberg, *Ezekiel 1–20*, 377–78.

63. Translated thus by ibid., 362.

to his covenant through specific commands (vv. 7, 11–12, 18–20, 25–26).[64] Yet, (b) they have sinned against him in their disobedience (vv. 8, 13, 21, 24). (c) God should have punished them with a calamitous judgment: ואמר לשפך חמתי עליהם לכלות אפי בהם ("then I resolved to pour out My fury upon them, to vent all My anger upon them there," vv. 8b, 13b, 21b; למען אשמם, "that I might render them desolate," v. 26). However, (d) "for the sake of His name, that it might not be profaned in the sight of the nations," God repeatedly refrained from such a course of action (ואעש למען שמי לבלתי החל לעיני הגוים, vv. 9, 14, 22) and instead, (e) reduced the judgment against them (vv. 10, 15–17, 22–26). Thus, following the political metaphor, covenant as initiated by God the King includes specific commitments and stipulations; and the vassals' disobedience brings the sovereign time and again to punish the rebels.

Ezekiel selected these four eras from the people's history in order to emphasize two main points to his fellow Exiles:

1. The geographical horizon—the common denominator of the depicted eras (with the exception of the secondary verses, vv. 27–29) is existence outside the Land of Israel.[65] This special geographical point of view in Ezek 20:1–32 has been overlooked by scholars. In contradistinction to the traditional perception of the exile as a period of distance and separation from God, Ezekiel points out the fact that God had initially established the relationship with his people outside the Land of Israel, in an exilic environment.[66]

---

64. The divine initiative and hierarchy governing the conditions of the covenant parallel Neo-Assyrian treaties, which usually refrain from specifying the sovereign's obligations towards his vassal(s); see Simo Parpola and Kazuko Watanabe, *Neo-Assyrian Treaties and Loyalty Oaths* (SAA 2; Helsinki: Helsinki University Press, 1989), xiv–xv. The sovereign–vassal relationship differs in the Neo-Hittite treaties, as presented by George Mendenhall, "Covenant Forms in Israelite Tradition," *Biblical Archaeologist* 17 (1954): 50–76; and Moshe Weinfeld, *Deuteronomy and the Deuteronomic School* (Winona Lake: Eisenbrauns, 1972; 2d ed. 1992), 68, 70–74.

65. For the secondary nature of vv. 27–29 and 39–44, see Zimmerli, *Ezekiel 1*, 405, 412; Rom-Shiloni, "Facing Destruction," 200–201. Compare Greenberg, *Ezekiel 1–20*, 378; Hoffman, "Ezekiel 20," 482; Block, *Ezekiel 1–24*, 641–45; and Kasher, *Ezekiel 1–24*, 385–86, all of whom considered vv. 27–29 part of the original speech.

66. Ezek 20 joins other covenant traditions which are set outside the Land of Israel (the only exception to this convention is Josh 24). See David Sperling, "Joshua 24 Re-examined," *HUCA* 58 (1987): 119–36, especially 133–36.

2. God's commitment to the covenant: Ezekiel accentuates the fact
    that God initiated the covenant relationship with His people in
    Egypt (v. 5); at the same time, however, the prophet makes the
    exceptional claim that disobedience to God and to His ritual
    demands had started at this very first stage (vv. 7–8), and had
    persisted ever since (vv. 13, 21, 30).[67] Time and again the people
    deserved to be punished with total calamity (vv. 8b, 13b, 21b),
    but God decided unilaterally not to destroy them, for the sake of
    His own prestige in the face of the foreign peoples (vv. 9, 14,
    22).[68] Although the divine oath had changed as a consequence of
    the people's sins (vv. 6, 15, 23), God never retracted it; and the
    people's behavior did not abrogate the everlasting continuity of
    his commitments.

In Ezekiel's prophecy of consolation (vv. 33–38) these two central
lessons bridge the intervening centuries and connect the present
generation of the Exiles in Babylon to the earlier or former generations
in Egypt and in the desert.[69]

Hence, the prophet vigilantly bypasses the inherited concept of exile
by invoking a different conception of covenant, based on Priestly (especially Exod 6:2–8) and Deuteronomic Exodus traditions.[70] Accordingly,
he perceives the Exiles as the direct successors to the first generation in

---

67. The theme of the practice of idolatry prior to settlement in the land connects
Ezek 20 to Ps 106 (and Josh 24:14). Cf. George W. Coats, *Rebellion in the Wilderness* (Nashville: Abingdon, 1968), 227–28, 233–34; Block, *Ezekiel 1–24*, 615–16.

68. Fishbane (*Biblical Interpretation*, 366) argued that this pattern in Ezek 20
appears to allude to Exod 32:9–14.

69. Various allusions to the Exodus in vv. 33–38 illustrate this connection:
והבאתי אתכם אל מדבר (v. 34); והוצאתי אתכם מן (vv. 33, 34); ביד חזקה ובזרוע נטויה (v. 34);
מסרת הברית (v. 37); העמים (v. 35). Note also the even more explicit allusion, במדבר
ארץ מצרים (v. 36). For allusions in vv. 33–38 (as also vv. 5–6 and elsewhere) to the
Priestly tradition in Exod 6:2–8, see Michael A. Fishbane, *Text and Texture: Close
Reading of Selected Biblical Texts* (New York: Schocken, 1979), 131–32; idem,
Biblical Interpretation, 366–67. Nevertheless, Ezekiel's words differ considerably
from that tradition: (a) he does not mention the fathers as the recipients of the
promise to the land (Exod 6:2, 8; and see Greenberg, *Ezekiel 1–20*, 364); (b) unparalleled in Exod 6, Ezekiel requires immediate obedience of God's demands (Ezek
20:7); (c) Ezekiel describes the salvation using idioms of wrath aimed at the people.
Cf. *b. Rosh Hashanah* 32b, and Greenberg's discussion of חמה שפוכה in Ezekiel
(*Ezekiel 1–20*, 371–72).

70. Cf. Levitt Kohn, *A New Heart*, 98–103. For different evaluations of the
function of the wilderness traditions in Ezekiel's speeches, see Eichrodt, *Ezekiel*,
279–80; and Coats, *Rebellion*, 240–41.

Egypt. Ezekiel thus refutes the desperate fears of the Elders, accentuating the idea that the Exiles continue to have hope for continuity in their relationship with God. Although in exile, they are still God's people, and He is their King.

Ezekiel 16:1–43 integrates two metaphors from the family sphere, the adoption and the marital metaphors, in which God is Father and then Husband, and the city is first His daughter and then His wife.[71] This passage in Ezekiel has attracted vast scholarly attention; I will restrict myself to the covenant concept that it presents in three main points: initiation of the covenant relationship, its violation, and finally the wife's/the city's judgment.

(i) *Initiating covenant relationship, 16:1–14*: Initiation of the covenant relationship appears as a two-stage process, designated by the repetition on "When I passed by you and saw you" (ואעבר עליך ואראך, vv. 6, 8). First, Jerusalem—a baby born in the land of Canaan (ומלדתיך מארץ הכנעני, v. 3) to an Amorite father and a Hittite mother and abandoned at birth—is adopted by God (vv. 4–7).[72] Second, when the young girl reaches maturity, God establishes the covenant relationship with her through marriage: ואשבע לך ואבוא בברית אתך נאם אדני יהוה ותהיי לי) ("and I entered into a covenant with you by oath—declares the Lord God; thus you became Mine," v. 8).[73] As in marital commitments, the hierarchical relationship between the two parties in this covenant is clear. God, the husband, initiates the relationship, and the result is that He owns the bride, Jerusalem (ותהיי לי, v. 8).[74] Throughout vv. 8–14 ותהיי לי is the only phrase which hints at the bride's obligation of loyalty towards her

71. The marriage metaphor with the people or the city as God's wife was thoroughly treated by Galambush, *Jerusalem*. For the adoption metaphor in the God–people relationship, and the comparative use of adoption terminology in the diplomatic relationships, see Shalom M. Paul, "Adoption Formulae: A Study of Cuneiform and Biblical Legal Clauses," *MAARAV* 2 (1979–80): 173–85. The two family metaphors are integrated in Jer 3:4 as well, and the common terminology was treated by Weinfeld, *Deuteronomistic School*, 80–81; Greenberg, *Ezekiel 1–20*, 254.

72. Meir Malul, "Adoption of Foundlings in the Bible and Mesopotamian Documents: A Study of Some Legal Metaphors in Ezekiel 16.1–7," *JSOT* 46 (1990): 97–126. On Jerusalem's genealogy, see below, p. 166.

73. An oath does not appear as a component in the marital ceremony (but see Ruth 3:13; and the use of "covenant" to designate marriage in Mal 2:14; Prov 2:17). Thus Greenberg (*Ezekiel 1–20*, 278) considered ואשבע לך to be the tenor intruding into the metaphoric vehicle. Yet, God taking an oath is also uncommon (Deut 4:31; 28:9), and thus Zimmerli (*Ezekiel 1*, 349) designated this as a unique feature in Ezekiel's use of the metaphor.

74. The phrase היה ל[ו] ל designates a change of status for the subject in relation to the object (BDB, 226).

husband. In contrast, the story focuses on an impressive list of the benefits God as Husband has given her (vv. 9–13). The description reaches the point where the bride is prepared for the position she ought to undertake, as God's wife: ותצלחי למלוכה ("and <you> became fit for royalty," v. 13). Likewise her beauty results from her patron: כי כליל הוא בהדרי אשר שמתי עליך ("for it was perfected through the splendor which I set upon you," v. 14). This description clarifies that the metaphors drawn from the family sphere are subordinate to the metaphor of God as King. Nevertheless, the family metaphors function independently in Ezekiel, and together with the political metaphor, they even function to help the prophet to present his counter-positions regarding the two Judahite communities.[75]

(ii) *Violation of the covenant, 16:15–34*: In complete disregard of the terms of the marriage/the covenant, the wife/Jerusalem, in total ingratitude, has given to other gods what she had received as bride-price from YHWH (vv. 15–22), and further betrayed Him with human "foreigners," "lovers" (vv. 23–34). The figurative sexual description reaches its apex as the adulteress is parodied for behavior unheard of even among prostitutes, ויהי בך הפך מן הנשים בתזנותיך ואחריך לא זונה ובתתך אתנן ואתנן לא נתן לך ותהי להפך ("You were the opposite of other women: you solicited instead of being solicited; you paid fees instead of being paid fees. Thus you were just the opposite!," v. 34).[76]

The adulterous nymphomaniacal behavior is construed in constant transitions between the vehicle of the metaphor and its tenor.[77] The wife/Jerusalem is accused of adultery; the accusation is formally separated into two paragraphs (vv. 16–22, 23–34), which stand for sins taken from two spheres. In the religious sphere, adultery involves building cultic sites (vv. 16, 24–25), producing figurines (v. 17), serving them various offerings (vv. 18–19), and the most severe of all, sacrificing God's sons and daughters to them (vv. 20–21; as also 23:37).[78] In the political sphere, adultery means counting on foreigners from among the

75. The two metaphorical systems operate interchangeably in Ezekiel and Jeremiah, yet they function independently according to the particular message of each prophet. This polemical usage is specific to Ezekiel. For a fuller discussion, see Dalit Rom-Shiloni, *God in Times of Destruction and Exiles: Tanakh (Hebrew Bible) Theology* (Jerusalem: The Hebrew University/Magnes, 2009 [in Hebrew]), 323–75.

76. Galambush, *Jerusalem*, 98.

77. So Peggy L. Day, "The Bitch Had It Coming to Her: Rhetoric and Interpretation in Ezekiel 16," *Biblical Interpretation* 8 (2000): 231–54.

78. במות טלאות (v. 16), along with גב and רמה (vv. 24, 31), are all designators of cultic sites; see Greenberg (*Ezekiel 1–20*, 280–82), and his discussion of the unique language and style of this passage (pp. 296–97).

Egyptians (16:26), the Assyrians (v. 28), and the Babylonians (v. 29).[79] Both spheres add up to the general accusation against the wife/the city for not remembering her youth, ולא זכרתי (ק: זכרת] את ימי נעוריך ("you did not remember the days of your youth," vv. 22, 43).[80]

The story remains faithful to the marital metaphor in detailing the sins. Varied forms of the roots זנה and נאף dominate the terminology of sin.[81] Even the general term תועבות, "abominations" (16:22, 36), which in Deuteronomic sources refers to cultic, moral, and sexual offenses, appears (as if through the lens of the Holiness Code's writer) to concentrate on sexual misconduct.[82] The adulterous behavior illustrated so vividly through the marital metaphor portrays Jerusalem's sins of disloyalty as a profound betrayal of the old covenant with God. Yet, in contrast to Ezek 20, and to the general usage of the political metaphor, there is no mention of disobedience to God's laws and rules (compare Ezek 20:11, 13 etc).[83]

(iii) *Judgment, 16:35–43*: The judgment upon the wife/the city continues this metaphorical narrative. In contrast to her initial salvation from disgrace and helplessness, an act of salvation which had brought her to prestigious status among the peoples (v. 14), and in retaliation for her sins (vv. 15–34), the wife is now accused of adultery and murder.

---

79. The political sphere is the focus of attention in Ezek 23:1–35, 36–49; whereas the religious sphere in Ezek 23:1–35 plays only a role (vv. 7, 30 and 14). This is then one major difference between the metaphorical passages in Ezekiel. See Galambush, *Jerusalem*, 110.

80. זכר is an important component of political and covenant terminology throughout the biblical literature (historiography, law, prophecy, and poetry). The command to remember refers to God's salvation from the bondage in Egypt (Deut 7:18 and 16:3), to his leadership in the wilderness (8:2), and to his constant beneficial involvement (8:18; note also Isa 62:6; Neh 4:8). These objects of remembrance are all rooted in the Exodus traditions, and exemplify God's roles as warrior who has saved his people in times of distress (as in Exod 13:3). See Hermann Eising, "זכר," *TDOT* 4:67–69. Since in Ezek 16:1–43 Ezekiel ignores the Exodus traditions in any explicit way, זכר in vv. 22, 43 must be understood as another implicit allusion.

81. For זנה, זנות, and תזנות (an Ezekelian *hapax*, which appears twenty times in Ezek 16 and 23), as well as other unique features of the language and style of Ezek 16, see Greenberg, *Ezekiel 1–20*, 296.

82. תועבות (and the phrase חקות התועבת in v. 30) in Lev 18:24–30, according to Schwartz (*Holiness Legislation*, 222–23), bears a general and abstract meaning in order to convey the implications of this impurity and abominations for the national fate. For the difference between the uses of תועבות in Deuteronomic and Priestly sources, see Milgrom, *Leviticus 17–22*, 1581.

83. This is, then, another unique feature of Ezek 16:1–43, in comparison with the other uses of the marital metaphor in Ezekiel. Compare to Ezek 16:59–63, which opens with a phrase resembling the vassal oath (אשר בזית אלה להפר ברית, v. 59).

Hence, she is doomed to return to a state of shame and helplessness, via total destruction (vv. 39–41).[84]

Jerusalem is accused of two capital crimes and sentenced accordingly: ושפטתיך משפטי נאפות ושפכת דם ("I will inflict upon you the punishment of women who commit adultery and murder," 16:38; and 23:45, 37). The juxtaposition of the two crimes, adultery and sacrificial murder, alludes to Lev 20.

This Holiness Code passage is the second (in addition to Lev 18) to contrast the commands of God with the abominable laws of the foreign Canaanite peoples (20:22–23; and see also 18:1–5, 26). The (detestable) laws (חקות הגוי in 20:23,[85] or חקתיהם in 18:3; and כל התועבת האלה, vv. 26, 27) are specified in the cultic sphere as the sacrifice of children to Molech (20:2–6), and in the moral sphere as sexual offenses (20:9–21). Leviticus 20 names two sets of punishments, one after the other. The first, in the third person singular (or plural) is activated against individual sinners (20:1–21). The second, in the second person plural, is extended to the entire people (vv. 22–24) and articulates the clear, conditional threat that disobedience to God's commands will result in the land vomiting out its inhabitants (v. 22).[86] Since the people of Israel inherited/possessed the land of those who had lost it *because* of their sins (v. 24), a constant threat hangs above the heads of those who live in God's land.

The allusive connections to the Holiness Code's concepts of land and exile seem to me to be the keys to understanding Ezekiel's choice of this specific marital metaphor with regard to God–Jerusalem relationship.[87] Leviticus 20 supplies the legal basis for the complete delegitimization of the Jerusalemites as the people of God, and predicts that community's eventual physical calamity.

---

84. Block (*Ezekiel 1–24*, 500–503) presented this "ironical twist" in Jerusalem's fortune. I accept Day's observation ("The Bitch," 237–54), that the lovers' participation in the harlot's execution is another example of the tenor in this section as well (compare to the adultery laws, in Lev 20:10; Deut 22:22–24). Nevertheless, this intrusion of the tenor does not exclude the basic line of thought in this passage, which rests on the different judgments directed at sexual offenses in the Holiness Code (Lev 20).

85. [הגוי] חקות in Lev 20:23 appears in the plural form in the versions, cohering with the plural forms at the end of the verse, עשו ואקץ בם, and in accordance with 18:24 (however, 18:28 uses the singular). See Milgrom, *Leviticus 17–22*, 1759.

86. Schwartz (*Holiness Legislation*, 135–44) presented the literarily independent position of each of the two chapters; and see Milgrom, *Leviticus 17–22*, 1577, 1765–68.

87. Compare Galambush's suggestion (*Jerusalem*, 103–5) that the thematic key to this metaphoric passage is Jerusalem's impurity, and specifically the sanctuary's defilement, which prepares the ground for God's abandonment of his city.

Just as Ezekiel refutes the words of the Jerusalemites in Ezek 33:24–29 by making allusions to Lev 18 and 20,[88] so here the prophet adapts these same central themes in the judgment prophecy of Ezek 16:1–43. The same analogy conveys the prophet's views concerning the origin of Jerusalem, its sins, and its punishment.

On the subject of Jerusalem's origin, Ezekiel goes even further than 33:24–29, not only identifying Jerusalem and her conduct with the denigrated "practices of the nation that I am driving out before you" (חקות הגוי אשר אנכי משלח מפניכם, Lev 20:23), but arguing in addition that Jerusalem is "by origin and birth" Canaanite: "By origin and birth you are from the land of the Canaanites—your father was an Amorite and your mother a Hittite" (16:3). The three major Canaanite "peoples of the land"—the Canaanites, the Amorites, and the Hittites—serve as Jerusalem's ethnic and religious milieu.[89] In utilizing the adoption metaphor Ezekiel identifies the city with these peoples, an identification which has a decisive impact on her past and present misconduct, and subsequently on her future judgment.[90] Her adoption and the tremendous benefits poured upon her by God cannot erase this initial "biography."

88. See the discussion on pp. 153–56, above.

89. Ezekiel uses *מכורות in this meaning of "land of origin" in Ezek 21:35; 29:14. "Canaanite, Amorite, and Hittite" is the repeated trio naming the major Canaanite peoples whom God is to drive out of the land (Exod 33:1–2) or annihilate (Exod 23:23), and from whom the people of Israel are admonished to keep separate, and whom they are to ban (as in Deut 7:1–5; 20:17). According to Tomoo Ishida ("The Structure and Historical Implications of the Lists of Pre-Israelite Nations," *Bib* 60 [1979]: 461–90), these three nations open the repetitions of the "six peoples of the land" pattern; they are listed in two alternative orders: Canaanite, Amorite, Hittite (Exod 32:2; Josh 11:3), and Canaanite, Hittite, Amorite (Exod 3:8, 17; 13:5; Judg 3:5; Neh 9:8). Ishida argued that the "six peoples" list has become a "quasi-canonical formula" in the biblical literature (ibid., 489).

90. Greenberg (*Ezekiel 1–20*, 274) suggested that the pagan peoples of Canaan are mentioned here in order to reprove the people. Modern scholars had focused on associating the three nations with the Jebusites, the pre-Israelite inhabitants of Jerusalem (Greenberg quoted Benjamin Mazar, *Jerusalem Through the Ages* [Jerusalem: Israel Exploration Society, 1968 (in Hebrew)], 4), but this step seems completely unnecessary. Ezekiel's rhetorical choice of this trio intends to recall the three major Canaanite peoples, and has nothing to do with the actual history of Jerusalem; and see Block (*Ezekiel 1–24*, 475), who recognized the polemical nature of Jerusalem's genealogy. On the medieval Jewish interpretation of this verse, and on Ezekiel's attitude toward Jerusalem, see Dalit Rom-Shiloni, "Jerusalem and Israel, Synonyms or Antonyms? Jewish Exegesis of Ezekiel's Prophecies against Jerusalem," in *After Ezekiel: Essays on the Reception of a Difficult Prophet* (ed. A. Mein and P. Joyce; London/New York: T&T Clark International, 2010), 89–114.

The sins of Jerusalem parallel those of the Canaanite peoples. In the language of Lev 20, Jerusalem follows the very same abominations.[91] Condemned as a harlot and as "cultic murderer," Jerusalem's sins are unforgivable and her punishment irrevocable.

Finally, in pronouncing Jerusalem's judgment, Ezekiel deviates from Lev 20. According to the latter, God expelled the Canaanites from the land, an expulsion which ended in their extinction (Lev 20:23, and so already 18:28). In his words to Jerusalem Ezekiel does not foresee displacement from the land as part of Jerusalem's punishment. The prophet rather combines Lev 20's two sets of punishments.[92] The individual death penalty of the murderer and the adulteress becomes the only retaliation to Jerusalem's offenses, forecasting total calamity within the land, not exile.[93]

Table 1. *Ezekiel as Advocate and Opponent*

In-group Legitimization	*Out-group Delegitimization*
Ezekiel as the Jehoiachin Exiles' Advocate	Ezekiel as Opponent of Those Who Remained in Jerusalem
Ezek 20:1–38	Ezek 16:1–43
את תועבת אבותם הודיעם "Declare to them the abhorrent deeds of their fathers" (Ezek 20:4)	הודע את ירושלים את תועבתיה "Proclaim Jerusalem's abominations to her" (Ezek 16:2)
* *The God–People Relationship*: Illustrated by the political metaphor of God as Sovereign and the people as his vassals (i.e. 20:33)	* *The God–People Relationship*: Illustrated by family metaphors (adoption and marriage)

91. Condemnation of the Canaanite peoples for sexual misconduct has its roots in several stories in the book of Genesis, namely, the story of Ham, Canaan's forefather (Gen 9:22–27), Dinah's rape (Gen 34), and the story of Sodom and Gomorra (Gen 19); and see Schwartz, *Holiness Legislation*, 157–62.

92. Milgrom (*Leviticus 17–22*, 1759) considers vv. 22–23 a separate unit appended to the list in ch. 20 under the influence of ch. 18.

93. The similarities between Lev 20 and Ezek 16:35–43 with regard to the penalties are scant and doubtful, mainly because vv. 39–43 present rapid changes from the metaphoric vehicle to its realistic tenor. Nevertheless, two of the death penalties appear in both: being pelted with stones for the sacrifice of sons to the Molech (רגם באבן, Ezek 16:40, as in Lev 20:2), and being burned in fire for sexual offenses (שרף באש, Ezek 16:41, as in Lev 20:14). See Greenberg, *Ezekiel 1–20*, 287. Block (*Ezekiel 1–24*, 503) mentioned only Deut 22:23–24 as being alluded to in Ezek 16:40; and see also Peggy L. Day, "Adulterous Jerusalem's Imagined Demise: Death of a Metaphor in Ezekiel XVI," *VT* 50 (2000): 285–309.

* *Constitution of the Covenant Relationship*: God had chosen Israel in Egypt (vv. 5–6), and established the covenant on a divine oath and obligation of the people to obey his rules and to worship God exclusively	* *Constitution of the Covenant Relationship*: God had adopted a deserted new-born baby of Canaanite origin. As she reached maturity God married her and brought her up to be "worthy of kingship" (vv. 1–14)
* *Violation of the Covenant*: The people disobeyed God's commandments throughout the several phases of their history: (1) the servitude period in Egypt (vv. 5–10, esp. 8); (2) the first generation in the desert (vv. 11–17, esp. 13); (3) the second generation in the desert (vv. 18–26, esp. 21); (4) Ezekiel's contemporary generation of Exiles (vv. 30–31)	* *Violation of the Covenant*: Jerusalem has become an adulteress woman. Being unfaithful to God, she committed adultery with other gods (in the religious–cultic sphere, vv. 15–22) and with human "foreigners" (in the political sphere, vv. 23–34)
* *Retaliation*: Although God intended to annihilate His people time and again (vv. 8, 13, 21), He refrained from doing so for the sake of His prestige among the nations (vv. 9, 14, 22); and though judgment aggravated, it repeatedly lessened the calamitous verdict (vv. 10, 15–17, 23–26) In this context, God destined the people to exile (v. 23) But in contrast to the Deuteronomic preexilic concept of exile (such as Deut 4:25–28; 28:36), which the Exiles paraphrase (v. 32), Ezekiel proclaims that the covenant relationship between God and the Jehoiachin Exiles continues. God is still their King, and they are His people (v. 33)	* *Retaliation*: Jerusalem is judged for her sins. Being of Canaanite origin, and following Canaanite practices, she is sentenced as adulteress and cultic murderer: משפטי נאפות ושפכת דם "the punishment of women who commit adultery and murder" (v. 38) Echoing Leviticus 18 and 20, Jerusalem is doomed to total death within the land (vv. 35–43)
* *Restoration*: The covenant relationship will be reaffirmed in the wilderness of the peoples, the wilderness of the land of Egypt, after which the Exiles will be led to the land of Israel (vv. 34–38)	* *Restoration*: No exile, no restoration

Using the two metaphors to describe the God–people relationship, Ezekiel differentiates sociologically between the past and the future fates of the two communities in exile and in the Land of Israel, respectively (see Table 1).

For the in-group, the political metaphor of Ezek 20:1–38 enables Ezekiel to emphasize the *continuity* of the political covenant in the relationship between God and the Jehoiachin Exiles, the constitution of which took place outside the Land of Israel, in Egypt. God is the initiator and preserver of the covenant, despite the people's repeated disobedience. As was proven before, God is committed to His people, and thus the continuity of the covenant relationship is guaranteed for the future as well: God is the Jehoiachin Exiles' King.

Continuity functions as well in Ezekiel's arguments *against the out-group*. The family metaphors in Ezek 16:1–4 allow Ezekiel to confine Jerusalem to the land, in Canaan. From her origins, through her constant misconduct, to her punishment, Jerusalem resembles the Canaanite peoples, the previous peoples of the land, whom God had expelled. But, in Ezekiel's extreme position, Jerusalem is not even doomed to exile, only to death, to total calamity within the land.

Ezekiel uses these lines of *continuity* argumentation, and specifically *annexation*, recalling constantly different pentateuchal historical and legal traditions and conceptions, to reconstruct his group's beliefs even as he establishes strategies of division and creates two distinctive histories of the God–people relationship. Relying on the Exodus traditions, Ezekiel legitimates the Exiles' ongoing existence as the people of God, with whom the covenant is expected to be restored in "the desert of peoples" (Ezek 20:36) and who will be led back to the Land of Israel. In contrast, the prophet delegitimitizes the homeland community by referring back to the legal and historic traditions related to the Settlement, which demand clear separation from the Canaanite peoples.

Construing this similarity between Those Who Remained and the Canaanite peoples is a tactic Ezra–Nehemiah later uses during the Persian period (compare Ezra 9:1–2, 10–14; Neh 10:29–31; 13:23–27).[94] Ezekiel can thus be considered the founding father of this particular separatist ideological strategy.

c. *Ezekiel against Jerusalem (Ezekiel 1–24)*
On the basis of the delegitimizing arguments against Jerusalem already adduced, it is time to broaden the scope of the investigation to the whole first part of the book of Ezekiel, chs. 1–24. The spotlight is trained on the

94. See the discussion of Ezra–Nehemiah, pp. 41–45, above.

prophecies of judgment against Jerusalem, with their two components of guilt and punishment.[95] Since, by the historical sequence, the partial exile of 597 B.C.E. preceded Jerusalem's destruction, the question for the prophet and his peers was: What is and what should be the role of exile in determining the relationship of the two separate Judahite communities in the first decades of the sixth century B.C.E.? Ezekiel's answer to this question can be found in his reconception of the linear concept of exile. The traditional conception essentially follows the three-step sequence, iniquity–death/destruction–exile; but Ezekiel adds selective possibilities for the restoration of the exiled community.

In Ezekiel's prophecies of judgment one often recognizes the prophet's distinction between the object of the prophecy and the audience to which his prophecy is addressed. This distinction is of paramount importance with regard to the evaluation of the prophecies against Jerusalem.[96]

Indeed, the commissioning prophecy (1:1–3:15) labels Ezekiel's audience, his fellow Exiles, as a בית המרי ("a rebellious breed," 2:5, 6, 8). The Exiles are descendants of generations of rebels against God, המה ואבותם פשעו בי עד עצם היום הזה ("they as well as their fathers have defied Me to this very day," 2:3), and the circumstances of exile have not yet, and are not expected to, change their "brazenness of face and stubbornness of heart" (קשי פנים וחזקי לב, 2:4). Traces of condemnation of the Exiles' ongoing disobedience are also found in Ezek 14:1–11; 20:1–32; 33:30–33. Nevertheless, throughout this first part of the book, judgment is not aimed against the Exiles.[97] Judgment in Ezekiel's prophecies focuses on Jerusalem, and to a lesser extent on the land of Israel (7:1–27), the mountains of Israel (6:1–10), and several peripheral areas in southern Judah (21:1–5, 6–10). The few prophecies of consolation which appear in the first section of the book (and throughout) focus on the Jehoiachin community in exile (17:22–24; 20:1–38, 39–44).[98]

---

95. Another judgment prophecy outside chs. 1–24 is Ezek 33:23–29, discussed above.

96. Commentators have of course discussed Ezekiel's harsh judgments against Jerusalem, but have not generally attributed this harshness to the prophet's social inclinations and his pro-Exile polemical tendencies; see, for instance, Greenberg, *Ezekiel 1–20*, 15–17; Zimmerli, *Ezekiel 1*, 56–59.

97. An exception is the prophecy against the peace prophets (13:1–16), and likewise the rebuke of the elders in Babylon, in 14:1–11, which nonetheless calls them to repent (v. 6), and sets the future goal as restoration of God's covenant relationship with them (v. 11; see also 18:21–32).

98. Ezek 16:59–63, however, prophesies hope and restoration to Jerusalem. See the discussion below, pp. 187–92.

This distinction between Jerusalem and the Exiles complicates Ezekiel's message.[99] Jerusalem in Ezekiel's prophecies is the distant object of judgment, the fortunes of which the immediate audience in exile is anxious to learn about (for instance, see Ezek 8–11, with the *inclusio* of 8:1–3 and 11:22–24; 14:21–23; 33:21–22, 30–33, etc.). While it is reasonable to assume that during the first years in exile and certainly prior to Jerusalem's destruction, the Exiles still identified with the Jerusalemite community in the homeland, it seems that Ezekiel wants to draw clear lines of difference between the communities with respect to their misdeeds and thus to their respective fates.[100] The following discussion thus fills out our perception of Ezekiel's construction of Jerusalem as the out-group.

(1) *Jerusalem's Guilt.* Ezekiel rebukes Jerusalem with both metaphoric and factual lists of sins. Disobedience against God, with idolatry as its major expression, occupies most of the prophet's attention (5:5–9; chs. 8; 16; and 23). Highly accentuated are moral misdeeds, generalized as חמס ("lawlessness," 7:11; 8:17), מֶטָה ("crime," 9:9), and דמים ("bloodshed," 9:9, etc). Both spheres, the moral and the cultic, are joined in the lists of Ezek 18:1–20 and 22:1–16, and indicated under the general (and frequently used) term תועבות ("abominations": 5:9; 7:3, 4, 8, 9; 9:4; 12:16; 16:2, 47, 50; 18:13, 24; 20:4; 22:2; 23:36; 33:26, 29; 36:31). At times this term stands for particular transgressions committed in Jerusalem: sins of idolatry (5:11; 6:9, 11; 8:6 [×2], 9, 13. 15, 17; 11:18, 21; 14:6; 16:36; 18:12; 43:8); other cultic misconduct (44:6–7, 13); and sexual offenses (16:22, 51, 58; 22:11). In addition, beyond the metaphoric stories of chs. 16 and 23, the emphasis on religious and moral misdeeds perpetrated in Jerusalem and in the land of Judah/Israel is phrased by means of "an implied or latent personification" of the city as the

99. Scholars have often treated the main *genres* in Ezekiel as distinguished chronologically; that is, judgment is said to precede 586, while consolation is said to postdate 586, and even to postdate Ezekiel himself (see Zimmerli, *Ezekiel 1*, 62–65). Consequently, the few consolation prophecies within chs. 1–24 were suspected of being late and secondary. But see Mein (*Ezekiel and the Ethics of Exile*, 177–215, 216–56, especially 233–40) who observed the theological tension and shift within Ezekiel between the human (Jerusalemite and Exilic) responsibility for occasioning judgment and the full divine responsibility for salvation. Note also Joyce's criticism in "Dislocation and Adaptation," 47–49, and *Ezekiel*, 26–27. The sociological framework (supported by ideological and theological arguments) suggested here concurs with this scholarly track and renders unnecessary this sort of attempt at chronological categorization.

100. Compare Greenberg, *Ezekiel 1–20*, 16.

perpetrator (5:7–17; 22:1–6; 24:1–14).[101] This rhetorical strategy governs the terminology of sin, which is taken from the sexual/marital spheres. Abominations are labeled with a term that designates sexual promiscuousness, זמה ("depravity," 22:9, 11; 24:13);[102] they are detested like menstrual blood, נדה ("unclean thing," 7:19, 20) and טמאת הנדה ("the impurity of a menstruous woman," 22:10; 36:17).[103] Blood occupies a major place in Jerusalem's transgressions and in the description of her state of defilement. In Ezek 16:1–43 the blood of birth appears first, then the menstrual blood, and at last the bloodshed of cultic murders in the sacrifice of children. This narrative provides the metaphorical content for the notion of the city's impurity, טמאה ("defilement," 5:11; 22:15; 24:11, 13 [×2]; 36:25, 29),[104] and contextualizes her shame and disgrace (5:14, 15; 22:16). In Ezek 22:1–16, Jerusalem is even called עיר הדמים ("city of bloodshed," 22:2), with reference to both cultic and social capital crimes, as well as sexual offenses (22:9–12), all of which add up to her shame and disgrace (5:14, 15; 22:16).[105] Jerusalem is, then, constantly identified with the adulteress wife and murderer of the metaphoric story of Ezek 16:1–43.

By way of comparison, neither the marital metaphor nor barely any of the associated terms appear in the restricted references to the Exiles'

---

101.   See Galambush, *Jerusalem*, 130–41, especially 130.

102.   Out of its 29 occurrences in the entire Hebrew Bible, זמה appears 13 times in chs. 16 and 23 of Ezekiel, and once in 22:9. Although זמה has the general meaning of "wicked plan, intention" (as in Isa 32:7; Job 31:11), its three occurrences in Leviticus refer to sexual offenses (18:17; 19:29; 20:14). This legal usage is adopted by Ezekiel, and also reflected in Jer 13:27 in parallel to נאופים, in a prophecy which uses the marital metaphor as well. Singurdur O. Steingrimsson (*TDOT* 4:89–90) recognized Ezekiel's use of זמה to specify particularly the sins of Jerusalem and Judah.

103.   Greenberg, *Ezekiel 1–20*, 152.

104.   The verb טמא appears in reference to sexual offenses in Ezek 18:11; 22:11, and 33:26. Otherwise in Ezekiel it refers to idolatry, and has the metaphorical sense of cultic defilement (14:11; 20:7, 18, 30–31; 22:4; 36:17–18; 37:23); cf. Gunnel André, "טמא," *TDOT* 5:337–40.

105.   In opposition to the honor and prestige of the wife, shame and disgrace result from the woman's exposure and nakedness and thus are part of the harlot's punishment (16:37–41). This is further elaborated in the two appended passages which directly present this message, using the noun כלמה ("shame," 16:52, 54, 63), with בוש as the verb (16:63). Curiously, the variety of nouns and verbs from the roots זנה and נאף, which dominate the language of Ezek 16 and 23, do not appear in other prophecies against Jerusalem. זנה, however, is mobilized against the Exiles in 20:30 (see above) and 6:9.

guilt or misconduct.[106] Both תוֹעֵבוֹת and the verb טמא occur in the context of an accusation of idolatry (14:6, 11), but only general disobedience and greed for materialistic profits (בצע) are specified as the offenses of Ezekiel's audience (33:31–32). The only exception is the rhetorical question in Ezek 20, which the prophet addresses to his generation of Exiles: הבדרך אבותיכם אתם נטמאים ואתם שקוציהם ואחרי זנים אתם ("do you defile yourselves as your fathers did and go astray after their detestable things?," vv. 30–31). It seems that Ezekiel purposely uses these extreme terms, which usually designate sinful Jerusalem, in order to shock his audience in exile and accentuate the absurdity of their thought (in v. 32). Nevertheless, the prophet makes a chronological distinction between the Exiles (אתם) and all earlier generations (אבותיכם). Ezekiel's generation has the opportunity for, and will be led by God to, transformation (vv. 33–38).

(2) *Jerusalem's Punishment.* The conception of Jerusalem's guilt helps Ezekiel conceptualize the Destruction as justifiable *talio* punishment. In addition, in his projections for retaliation against Jerusalem, Ezekiel develops different configurations—the three elements of the traditional conception of exile—iniquity, destruction, and exile; adding a fourth potential facet, that is, restoration.

Iniquity–Destruction. In addition to the passages already discussed (16:1–43; 33:23–29), most of the prophecies of judgment against Jerusalem and Judah foresee total destruction within the land or on its borders (6:1–7, 11–14; 7:1–27; 11:1–13; 12:17–20; 21:1–5, 6–12, 13–22, 23–32; 22:17–22, 23–32; 23; 24:1–14). In these passages, the expected three-part sequence is fragmented, and includes only the first two elements. No mention is made of deportation or of the possibility that the Jerusalemites might join the Jehoiachin Exiles in Babylon. These prophecies exemplify Ezekiel's interpretation and adaptation of the Deuteronomic preexilic concept of exile, which understands dislocation as annihilation and does not perceive the possibility of existence outside the Land of Israel (cf. Deut 6:10–15; 8:19–20; 11:13–17, etc).[107]

Iniquity–Destruction–Exile and Death. The sign-acts in **Ezek 4:1–5:4** present another variation of this concept of exile. The prophetic unit in chs. 4–5 brings together commands to symbolize both the siege of Jerusalem (4:1–3, 4–8, 9–11, 16–17) and its destruction (5:1–4), intertwined

---

106. This then differentiates the two communities in their responsibility for their individual fates. Compare Mein (*Ezekiel and the Ethics of Exile*, 233–40), who argued that responsibility for the disaster was shared between the communities.

107. See Rom-Shiloni, "Deuteronomic Concepts," 103–9.

with references to existence in exile (4:12–15).[108] Struggling with what seems "heterogeneous" and thus secondary to Greenberg,[109] and has been called "a redactional conflation" of separate sign-acts by Block (following Friebel),[110] scholars have sought to trace references to the linear sequence of siege–destruction–exile in this passage; accordingly, they have re-differentiated the sign-acts and held their verbal interpretations to be secondary expansions.[111]

Three basic sign-acts demonstrate different stages in the siege of Jerusalem: the first two commands, to incise upon a tile a model of the besieged city and to place an iron griddle so as to block it off, show forth the setting of the siege and its prolongation (4:1–3); the order to eat rationed food illustrates the misery of famine in the town (4:9–11, 16–17); and finally, shaving the hair and destroying it in three parts demonstrate the city's fall and the total destruction of its inhabitants (5:1–4).

In Ezekiel's schematic style, the inhabitants of Jerusalem are to be divided in three groups (5:1–2). One third will be burnt by fire within the city; the second will be stricken by sword all around it; the third will be scattered to the wind (vv. 2, 12), and God will unsheathe a sword after them (v. 2). Similarly, in the interpretative prophecy, 5:5–17, one third will die within the city from pestilence and famine, another shall fall by the sword around about it, and the third will be scattered in every direction, and God will unsheathe the sword after them (v. 12). In

---

108.   This division is based on the repetition of the imperative clauses [בן ואתה] אדם [קח לך] ("And you [O mortal], take," 4:1, 3, 9; 5:1). Accordingly, Ezek 4:4–8 as a whole is considered a secondary addition (or even amalgamation of interpretations), which according to Zimmerli (*Ezekiel 1*, 155, 163–65, 168) may have been appended even in the prophet's life time. Greenberg (*Ezekiel 1–20*, 118) argued that references to exile are to be found in 4:6, 12–15; Friebel (*Jeremiah's and Ezekiel's Sign-Acts*, 209–24, among others), added 5:2–4. Indeed, 4:4–8 raises tremendous interpretive difficulties which have not yet been solved (cf. Greenberg, *Ezekiel 1–20*, 104–6; Zimmerli, *Ezekiel 1*, 163–64). To add another difficulty, these verses point to the city's iniquity, in contrast to the other sign-acts which all refer to the punishment. Friebel (*Sign-Acts*, especially 218–19) convincingly argued against Greenberg's differentiation between 390 years of iniquity, and 40 years of punishment/exile. Unfortunately, I do not find traces of exilic circumstances in either 5:2–4 or 4:6, and thus will concentrate below only on 4:12–15 as addressed to Ezekiel's immediate audience in Babylon (contra Friebel, *Sign-Acts*, 247).

109.   Greenberg, *Ezekiel 1–20*, 118; and see Zimmerli, *Ezekiel 1*, 154–55.

110.   So Block, *Ezekiel 1–24*, 168–69; following Friebel, *Sign-Acts*, 195–202.

111.   Zimmerli (*Ezekiel 1*, 168) has argued that even the expansions could have been added by the prophet himself, and in any case the additions are not later than 547 B.C.E. (based on the understanding that the 40 days designate 40 years of exile from 586 B.C.E. on).

both descriptions, the division into three illustrates the totality of this annihilation.

The intriguing phrase is the one concerning the third part: והשלשית אריק אחריהם תזרה לרוח וחרב אריק אחריהם ("and a third scatter to the wind, and I will unsheathe the sword after them," vv. 2, 10, 12; and 12:14). זרה לרוח, which at face value describes dislocation, differs from the common agricultural imagery behind the phrase זרה בארצות (e.g. Ezek 6:8; 36:19, etc.). The latter, which Ezekiel uses regularly in the phraseology of exile, evokes the image of the scattering of seeds as part of sowing, and thus promises resettlement and continuity. זרה לרוח, however, in Ezek 5 and 12 applies to the separation of the wheat from the chaff, where the latter is scattered to the wind, being of no further use or significance.[112]

Moreover, the scattered people are further doomed to be pursued to the death by God, who will unsheathe the sword against them (וחרב אריק אחריהם).[113] The change into the first person with God as the agent is commonly interpreted as an intrusion of the tenor, which illustrates the clear influence on Ezekiel of Lev 26:33: ואתכם אזרה בגוים והריקתי אחריכם חרב ("and you I will scatter among the nations, and I will unsheathe the sword against you").

Leviticus 26:27–39 describes the consequences of disobedience, in a picture of destruction that includes famine (vv. 27–29, and already in v. 26), destruction of cultic places and cities (vv. 30–31), desolated land (vv. 30–32), and dispersion (v. 33). Verses 36–39 add that even this dislocation does not bring peace to the deportees, but rather increased fear, and eventually, death:

ולא תהיה לכם תקומה לפני איביכם ואבדתם בגוים ואכלה אתכם ארץ איביכם
והנשארים בכם ימקו בעונם בארצת איביכם[114]

> You shall not be able to stand your ground before your enemies, but shall perish among the nations; and the land of your enemies shall consume you. Those of you who survive shall rot over their iniquity in the land of your enemies. (Lev 26:37–39)

112.　This same agricultural imagery may elucidate the calamity that has befallen Israel (Jer 15:7), or the fate of Israel's enemies (Isa 41:14–16). See also Jer 13:24.

113.　הריק חרב with God as agent appears also in Ezek 12:14 and Ps 35:3 (הריק חנית, "spear"); with human agents in Ezek 28:7; 30:11; and Exod 15:9. Cf. ריק, *HALAT*, 1228. The sword as an additional means of annihilating the deportees appears also in Jer 9:15 and Amos 9:4.

114.　ימקו בעונם in Lev 26:39, according to Milgrom (*Leviticus 23–27* [AB 3C; New York: Doubleday, 2001], 2326–27), comes from מקק and means "to rot," as in Isa 34:4; Zech 14:12; Ps 38:6; and in Rabbinic Hebrew. This negative prospect of suffering in exile is mentioned in Ezek 4:17; 24:23.

The allusions to Lev 26 have led scholars to highlight further similarities between Ezek 5:3–4 and the concept of the remnant in Lev 26:40–45.[115] According to the Holiness Code's point of view, a remnant of the deportees, from their various places in exile, will repent and restore the relationship with God. Corresponding to this concept, Ezek 5:3–4 is said to project a hope in the few who will survive the exile.[116] Yet, this interpretation cannot be accepted. The sign-act in Ezek 5:3 involves the preservation of a small amount of hair to be treasured in the prophet's skirt, and thus raises the expectation of salvation. But although hope was given to that remnant at first, v. 4 excludes every optimistic possibility. The prophet is commanded to throw some of them (the strands of hair) to the fire, which will inflame the whole House of Israel. Hence, those few scattered survivors from Jerusalem will become dangerous to the whole House of Israel, that is, the already resettled Judean community in exile. This interpretation gains further strength from the context. First, in the sign-act itself, the three thirds constitute a whole, and the consuming fire does not permit the possibility of survivors. Second, the verbal interpretation in 5:5–17 follows the division into three and repeats the threats of the scattering to the wind and the unsheathed sword (v. 12), but never mentions any remnant of survivors from Jerusalem (vv. 13–17). Hence, 5:3–4 do not suggest an optimistic prospect for a Jerusalemite remnant in exile. On the contrary, these verses close the sign-acts with an additional intensification of the forecast of Jerusalem's total annihilation.

These dramatic sign-acts describing Jerusalem's destruction, from siege to fall, were expanded with a salient comment concerning the Exiles.[117] Ezekiel 4:9–17 present a sign-act focused on rationed food and drink while under siege in Jerusalem (vv. 9–11), which is verbally interpreted in vv. 16–17.[118] In between the sign-act and its interpretation intrudes a passage which focuses on eating defiled bread while among the nations (vv. 12–15).[119]

---

115.   For the clear allusions of Ezek 4–5 to Lev 26, see Greenberg, *Ezekiel 1–20*, 109; Block, *Ezekiel 1–24*, 194; and Milgrom, *Leviticus 23–27*, 2348–52.

116.   So Friebel, *Sign-Acts*, 241–42; Block, *Ezekiel 1–24*, 194–95; and Greenberg (*Ezekiel 1–20*, 108–9 and 126), who, while accepting that the verses foretell calamity, still (based on מהם) talked about the preservation of a remnant which would continue to suffer persecution in exile.

117.   See n. 128, below.

118.   Ezek 4:9–11 continues the situation of siege; it continues to apply to the circumstances where the prophet still lies on his side for 390 days (v. 9b; see v. 5). Cf. Friebel, *Sign-Acts*, 224–26.

119.   See Friebel, *Sign-Acts*, 199–200.

This expansion (vv. 12–15) does not cohere with the surrounding sign-acts. First, it does not continue the narrative thread of the previous verses, but rather introduces a different issue altogether. Second, it clearly has no relevance to Jerusalem, and does not contribute to the logical development of the sign-acts referring to the siege of the city and subsequent calamity. Rather, the dialogue starts with a command to eat a "barley cake" (עגת שערים) baked over human excrement (בגללי צאת האדם, v. 12). This is explained as a symbol of the unclean (טמא) bread that the Exiles will eat among the peoples (v. 13). The prophet arises to protest, claiming that he has never been defiled (v. 14). Since Ezekiel has already been at least five years in exile, this comment is of particular interest. In addition, Ezekiel does not restrict himself to bread, and talks of eating meat.[120] In reply God changes the human excrement to cow's dung (צפיעי הבקר), over which the prophet is then allowed to prepare his bread (ועשית את לחמך עליהם, v. 15). The dialogue, which starts with clear denigration of the circumstances of exile, reaches, through Ezekiel's protest, a point of compromise.[121]

This divine concession is of paramount importance for the ongoing daily life of the Exiles as the people of God, since it contrasts the accepted concept of exile known, for instance, from Hos 9:3, and replaces it with divine approval.[122] Yet, in its present context, this message is almost implicit, as vv. 16–17 change the geographic setting again, and return to Jerusalem. The city is doomed to suffer famine, that is, a lack of bread and water, which will continue until the inhabitants suffer the total absence of both, and starve to death: "they shall stare at each other, heartsick over their iniquity" (ונשמו איש ואחיו ונמקו בעונם, v. 17).[123]

---

120. Friebel (ibid., 249) explained the jump from eating a barley cake baked on human excrement to eating unclean meat of נבלה וטרפה as an analogical expansion of "derived uncleanness" and not as an inherent defilement.

121. Zimmerli (*Ezekiel 1*, 171) raised the question of whether v. 15 should be understood as part of the general interpretation of the sign-act or only as a personal concession, and indeed took the former option. Amazingly, the positive compromise and the general comforting message it holds for the Exiles was overlooked by scholars, who in interpreting this sign-act did not refer to the significant point that Ezekiel, while being in exile, declares that he has never eaten defiled food. It seems that 4:12–15 should add to the other examples of adaptation to living in exile (Diaspora) which Joyce has pointed out ("Dislocation and Adaptation," 56–58).

122. The concept that the exilic arena includes eating defiled food is reflected also in Dan 1:8; note also the general references to foreign lands as defiled in Josh 22:19; Amos 7:17.

123. Translation by Greenberg, *Ezekiel 1–20*, 99.

To conclude: with a fairly pessimistic perspective, chs. 4–5 perceive both the siege over Jerusalem and the exile as long-term punishments justified by the people's sins.[124] Jerusalem's misery is beyond encouragement; the siege will end in famine and in the death of all of the city's inhabitants, either in the city itself or in its periphery. In the sequence iniquity–destruction–exile (and restoration), according to Ezek 4–5, Jerusalem will suffer immensely in the course of its destruction, and the few survivors that will be dispersed to the wind will suffer further calamity. Thus, for the Jerusalemites, exile still means annihilation. In contrast, 4:12–15 establishes the prophet as mediator between God and the community to which Ezekiel belongs, that is, that of the Jehoiachin Exiles, striving to find a solution that will normalize life for them away from God's land.

This differentiation of fates, shown through the juxtaposed and implicitly reversed sign-acts, suggests that Ezekiel is here interpreting Lev 26. The prophet seems to be aware of the difference between Lev 26:33–39 and 40–45, and their juxtaposition.[125] The first passage predicts annihilation (Lev 26:33–39), which the prophet applies to Those Who Remained in Jerusalem from the 597 exile till the city's destruction in 586 B.C.E. The second promises settlement and restoration of the covenant with God, even in exile (Lev 26:40–45), if accompanied by the necessary practical and spiritual changes of repentance that the prophet helps to phrase. Thus, despite the contextual proximity of the two different fortunes foreseen for those expelled, Ezekiel distinguishes them sociologically, and thus differentiates between two possibilities for existence in exile. Hence, the traditional sequence iniquity–destruction–exile and finally restoration is not automatically applied by Ezekiel, and it does not designate a uniform fate for all segments of the community. Rather, exile can mean annihilation for Those Who Remained, just as it can signify continuation and restoration for the Jehoiachin Exiles.

---

124.   This general statement is not to cover over the interpretive difficulties in the phrase נשא עון and the years 390 and 40 for the House of Israel and that of Judah respectively. For נשא עון, see Zimmerli, *Ezekiel 1*, 164; and for distinguishing the respective meanings of iniquity and punishment for Israel and Judah, see Greenberg, *Ezekiel 1–20*, 105; Block, *Ezekiel 1–24*, 176–79.

125.   Milgrom (*Leviticus 23–27*, 2287–90, 2304) has shown that in parallel to the five units of blessings in Lev 26:3–13, vv. 27–39 close a five-unit pattern of curses ordered in increasing severity. This literary argument leads up to the thematic change in vv. 40–45, with the Exiles' confession of sins, and God's response in promises of restoration. Hence, form and content establish the secondary appendix nature of these verses of consolation (pp. 2329–30). Furthermore, Milgrom has convincingly argued that Ezekiel knew MT Lev 26:3–39.

Looking at these chapters from the perspective of the internal conflict between the communities illuminates yet a further rhetorical technique that Ezekiel uses time and again in chs. 1–24—the intertwining and juxtaposing of prophecies against Jerusalem with side comments or complete passages of hope addressed to the Jehoiachin Exiles.[126]

Iniquity–Destruction–Exile–Exclusion. Notwithstanding Ezekiel's tendency to negate the existence, beyond 586 B.C.E., of Those Who Remained in Jerusalem, the prophet does present several prophecies in which survivors from Jerusalem reach the community in Babylon. **Ezekiel 12:15–16** and **14:21–23** give a didactic mission to those survivors from Jerusalem, who are designated as אנשי מספר, a small number of people (12:6), or פלטה המוצאים בנים ובנות, survivors of sons and daughters (14:22). In the first passage they are to tell of their abominations to the nations (12:16). The second configures the refugees as object-lessons for the Exiles, so that the account of the survivors' ways and deeds will console the Exiles, showing them that the Jerusalemites have been properly and justifiably punished (14:22–23).[127]

Although they appear to contradict Ezekiel's prophecies of Jerusalem's total annihilation, these two prophecies still uphold the Jehoiachin Exiles' superiority. Even after 586 B.C.E., and in the setting of exile, the Jerusalemite survivors are clearly marked and denigrated as the ongoing reminder of Jerusalem's iniquities and unworthiness. These passages indicate the enduring hostility and at the very least the patronizing view of the Jehoiachin Exiles, accentuating the distinctions in prestige and rank between the Judean communities (as presented above in Ezek 11:14–21; 33:23–29, etc.).[128]

This sequence of iniquity–destruction–exile and restoration recognizes the existence of survivors from Jerusalem in Babylon after 586, but does not legitimate their integration into the community of the Jehoiachin

---

126. Other examples of this intertwining of prophecies against Jerusalem and pro-Exiles appear within the editing of chs. 8–11, and specifically the contrast between the two disputations in 11:1–13 and 11:14–21. See also 6:1–7, 11–14, with vv. 8–10 referring to hope in a remnant in exile.

127. So Zimmerli, *Ezekiel 1*, 312–13; Block, *Ezekiel 1–24*, 451.

128. Ezek 22:13–16 prophesies exile for the Jerusalemites, and is considered a secondary addition by the prophet or his school (so Zimmerli, *Ezekiel 1*, 455, 459). An argument for its secondary character is the prospect of exile predicted for the inhabitants of Jerusalem, and not annihilation within the city, as in Ezek 5:1–17; 16:1–43, etc. Yet, it still coheres with Ezekiel's general perspective, which does not accept the 586 Exiles into the established exilic community, but forecasts its further calamity in exile.

Exiles. This remarkable sectarian attitude exemplifies the severity of the conflict between the two Judean communities. In Ezekiel's evaluation of exile, this linear sequence applies only to Jerusalem. Being in exile prior to Jerusalem's destruction, the 597 B.C.E. Jehoiachin Exiles are not counted among the community that will suffer destruction, expulsion, and extinction. Thus Ezekiel transforms the interests of his fellow Exiles from Jerusalem to their own community in exile. Restoration is confined to those Jehoiachin Exiles (as explicit in Ezek 11:14–21; 20:1–38).

(3) *The Desolated Land of Judah.* One repeated component in Ezekiel's prophecies of judgment against Jerusalem is the portrait of the damage executed on the ecological substance of the land, which adds to the fatal blows aimed at the population of Judah. Ezekiel prophesies that the land will become empty of both man and beast: והכרתי ממנה אדם ובהמה ("and I will cut off from it man and beast," 14:13, 17, 19). The destruction of the urban landscape and the agricultural life will bring wild beasts to occupy the ruins and thus hasten the land's desolation והיתה שממה מבלי עובר מפני החיה ("and it became a desolation with none passing through it because of the beasts," v. 15). Desertedness and desolation in both rural and peripheral urban areas is the image with which Ezekiel concludes several of his prophecies against Jerusalem and the Land of Israel (Ezek 6:14; 12:19–20; 15:8; 21:1–5; 33:28–29; 38:8).

This description further influences Ezekiel when he comes to illustrate restoration in the land. The empty, desolate mountains of Israel will revive in preparation for accepting the gathered Exiles, who are called עמי ישראל ("My people Israel," 36:5–12). No mention at all is made of the existence of any of Those Who Remained in the land throughout the exile. The annihilation of man, beast, and the land itself designates a definite and total end to one era, and prepares the way for the restoration of the Exiles as the sole community of God's people in the days to come.[129] These prophecies exemplify the extreme degree to which Ezekiel transfers exclusive significance to the community of the Jehoiachin Exiles. The prophet not only excludes the Jerusalemite community, but further intensifies this exclusion through the emphasis on the uninhabited desolation of that land.

---

129. Transformation in the ecological state of the land from destroyed to restored appears also in Jer 32:42–44; 33:10–11, 12–13; and in Isa 35; 51:3, etc.

The theme of the empty land, which has its origin in descriptions of total destruction effected by God/the gods in biblical and Mesopotamian sources alike, is utilized in Ezekiel's message as a rhetorical argument in the disputation between the communities.[130] Without further delving into the scholarly debate over the theme of the empty land in the exilic and postexilic literatures, suffice it to say that Ezekiel can be identified as one of the first to utilize this argument, already by the very early years of the sixth century.[131]

(4) *Juxtaposition of the Contrasting Fates.* The socio-ideological transfer of the community's hopes from Jerusalem to Babylon is implicitly illustrated also by the use of the literary technique of juxtaposition in several prophecies in chs. 1–24. As presented above, Ezek 11 (or even chs. 8–11 as a whole), with its two disputations, is one such example; another is **Ezek 24**, which ends the first part of the book.[132] After the horrific judgment upon "the city of blood" in 24:1–14, the prophet's clear differentiation between the communities reaches its apex, in the most painful sign-act the prophet is commanded to perform, **Ezek 24:15–27**.[133] The prohibition against mourning his wife, the delight of his eyes,

---

130. Desolation of the landscape functions as a common motif in biblical descriptions of destructions. See, for instance, Ezekiel's prophecies against the nations (Ezek 25:5, 13; 35:3–4, 7–9), and Jeremiah's prophecies of judgment against Israel and the nations (e.g. Jer 9:9–11; 51:26, 62, etc.), as well as Lamentations (Lam 1:7; 2:15, 16; 5:18). This motif is well attested in the lists of curses found in Neo-Assyrian political treaties (cf. Hillers, *Treaty Curses*). It is also found in the Mesopotamian laments over the destruction of cities and temples; see Frederick W. Dobbs-Allsopp, *Weep, O Daughter of Zion: A Study of the City-Lament Genre in the Hebrew Bible* (BibOr 44; Rome: Pontifical Biblical Institute, 1993), 66–72; Piotr Michalowski, *The Lamentation Over the Destruction of Sumer and Ur* (Winona Lake: Eisenbrauns, 1989), ll. 300–330.

131. Ezekiel's polemical use of this motif in this conflict mitigates against Robert P. Carroll's late dating for the ideological contention over the theme of the empty land ("The Myth of the Empty Land," 79–93); followed by Hans M. Barstad, *The Myth of the Empty Land: A Study in the History and Archaeology of Judah During the "Exilic" Period* (Symbolae Osloenses Fasc. Suppl. 28; Oslo: Scandinavian University Press, 1996).

132. See Kasher, *Ezekiel 25–48*, 641.

133. Block ("Ezekiel's Boiling Cauldron: A Form-Critical Solution to Ezekiel XXIV 1–14," *VT* 41 [1991]: 12–37) emphasized the anti-Jerusalemite perspective of 24:1–14, suggesting it is an "unannounced disputation address" in which Ezekiel refutes the Jerusalemites' sense of superiority based on the fact that they have remained in the inviolable city (see also his commentary: *Ezekiel 1–24*, 769–83, followed by his discussion of 24:15–27, on pp. 785–94).

and Ezekiel's exact implementation of that command, establish Ezekiel himself as a portent for the Exiles (והיה יחזקאל לכם למופת, vv. 24, 27). The delight of their eyes and the desire of their hearts is God's Temple in Jerusalem, which is a source of pride and glory (גאון עזכם, v. 21). The Jehoiachin Exiles are not to mourn its physical destruction, nor the death of sons and daughters in Jerusalem (v. 25; cf. 14:21–23). The prohibition against mourning the homeland community denotes the Exiles' final separation from the Jerusalem community, as Margaret Odell said in characterizing mourning:

> the act of mourning appears to have little to do with the expression of grief; rather, it is concerned with establishing and severing ties between the living and the dead. Prohibitions against mourning reflect an attempt to dissociate from the deceased.[134]

Indeed, this passage completes the prophecies of judgment in Ezekiel with the clearest message contrasting the death of Jerusalem with the ongoing life of the Exiles. They, the Jehoiachin Exiles, are the living remnant of the people of God, and none other.

Ezekiel's negative attitude towards Jerusalem is further accentuated by the disappearance of Jerusalem from the prophet's messages of future consolation. Jerusalem is not mentioned in the second unit of the book, ch. 25 and on;[135] and restoration is restricted on the one hand to the scattered (exiled) people (chs. 34; 36–37), and on the other hand to the desolate mountains of Israel, which will revitalize with the return of the people of God (36:1–15).

(5) *Summary and Conclusions*. In closing, I want to suggest some of the factors that may have motivated Ezekiel to establish this binary opposition between the two Judahite sister communities, which were forcibly separated by the Babylonian policy of exile in 597 B.C.E.

Ezekiel's references to Jerusalem and its fate constitute, first of all, a response to his immediate audience in exile. During the first years of dislocation, before the city's destruction, the Exiles seem to have expressed interest and concern regarding their homeland, the city of God, the Temple, and the fortunes of their fellow Judahites (as can be gathered

---

134. Margaret S. Odell, "Genre and Persona in Ezekiel 24:15–24," in Odell and Strong, eds., *The Book of Ezekiel*, 195–220 (201). Compare to Block (*Ezekiel 1–24*, 794), who suggested that the order to refrain from mourning designates the Exiles' recognition of "the dawn of a new age."

135. One exception is Ezek 36:38, where the memory of Jerusalem's past is mentioned.

for instance from Ezek 24:15–27; and see also Ps 137). The prophet in reply structures an ideological separation of the communities.[136]

In addition, the severe prophecies of judgment against Jerusalem hold central position in Ezekiel's theology. The prophet comes to an understanding of God's role in the defeat, exile, and destruction, and justifies God in his measures against Jerusalem, by declaring the city's sinfulness and guilt. Thus, a concern with theodicy motivates Jerusalem's condemnation.

Beyond all this, I believe, Ezekiel understands the ideological necessity of redefining the religious-national identity of the Exiles. The prophet had to reconcile well-known and cherished pentateuchal conceptions of land and exile with the fact of the partial exile which took place eleven years prior to the Destruction of Jerusalem. If Deuteronomic and Priestly traditional concepts had remained unaltered, the historical circumstances would have endangered the existence of the Jehoiachin Exiles as a continuing Yahwistic community. As the inhabitants of Jerusalem had claimed (Ezek 11:15; 33:24, as also Jer 22:24–30), and as the Elders of Israel of the Jehoiachin Exiles express in their grief and despair (Ezek 20:32), the Exiles could have been doomed to annihilation via assimilation into their exilic culture.

From the disadvantageous situation of expulsion, Ezekiel steps forward with a competing agenda, through which he builds a distinct identity for the Jehoiachin Exiles as the *exclusive* community of the people of God. By establishing arguments of legitimacy in support of his fellow Exiles and delegitimatizing arguments against Those Who Remained in Jerusalem, Ezekiel crafts an exilic ideology which enables *continuity* of national existence in exile and promises restoration to the Exiles.

Ezekiel's main structural strategy is the *annexation* to his Exilic community of historical and legal traditions from the Pentateuch, which are presumably known to his fellow Exiles as well. Ezekiel sets his arguments on solid ground, as he presents innovative perspectives which are all rooted in Israel's past. This explains his immediate influence on his contemporaries, and his ongoing impact on the exilic community, as this may be seen in the prophecy and historiographic literature of the late sixth and fifth centuries B.C.E.

136.   This is where I part ways with Mein (*Ezekiel and the Ethics of Exile*, 234), who does not identify antagonism between Ezekiel and the Jehoiachin Exiles on the one side, and Those Who Remained on the other.

To summarize Ezekiel's major contribution for generations that followed, I will highlight here the arguments that comprise Ezekiel's conception of exile, on the one hand, and of the exclusive status of the Jehoiachin Exiles community, on the other.

(i) *Past traditions*. Legitimization of the Jehoiachin Exiles rests on the Exodus traditions, which relate God's constitution of the covenant relationship with his people in Egypt and in the desert, away from the Land of Israel. The exilic arena thereby becomes an advantageous context for the future restoration of the covenant (Ezek 20:1–38). This in turn accounts for the centrality of the Exodus traditions in the later exilic literature, for instance in Deutero-Isaiah.

However, when it comes to the delegitimization of Those Who Remained as the out-group, the prophet equates them with the "people of the land," by drawing on the Settlement traditions and invoking the general pentateuchal legal demands to keep separate from the Canaanite peoples. Ezekiel dwells on the supposed ongoing adherence of Those Who Remained to despised local abominations (Ezek 16:1–43), to suggest that their existence in the Land of Israel will end in expulsion and annihilation, in accordance with the conceptions of the Holiness Code (Lev 18:24–30 and 20:22–24). This tactic of categorizing Those Who Remained as of foreign (Canaanite) origin endures all the way to Ezra–Nehemiah's denigrations of the local community in Yehud.

(ii) *Present status*. Ezekiel differentiates between the communities with respect to their religious and moral qualities in various ways. The Jerusalem community's trespasses include capital offenses, both religious and moral, which determine their doom: total calamity, according to both Deuteronomic and Priestly /Holiness Code legal traditions. At the same time, the concentration on Jerusalem's offenses alleviates the burden from the Jehoiachin Exiles. Since Ezekiel does not consider his fellow Exiles obedient or virtuous either, Jerusalem's present sins serve as a warning for the Exiles (14:1–11; and, implicitly, Ezek 18:1–20). By comparison with the community in Jerusalem, the Exiles enjoy higher prestige. As a community they are certainly not doomed to annihilation (14:11).

(iii) *Future prospects*. Passages of hope within chs. 1–24, as well as the prophecies of consolation (chs. 34–37), express the legitimization of the (Jehoiachin) Exiles as the future restored community. The God–people relationship will resume with them, in exile (20:32–38). God's dynamic presence will constantly accompany the Exiles (11:16). In the future restoration God will regather *them* into the Land of Israel, *their* land (11:17), and transform *their* hearts to promise eternal obedience (11:18; 36:26–27). The covenant formula which constituted the covenant relationship between God and the children of Israel (Lev 26:11; Deut 26:17), will apply in future to *this* community of Exiles (11:20; as also 34:30; 36:28).

The prospect of the Exiles' restoration in the land appears in literary proximation to several prophecies of judgment against Jerusalem and Judah, in the description of the desolation of cities and land (e.g. 6:11–14). Hence, the idea that the land lays barren and awaits the returnees is already part of Ezekiel's message of hope to his community of Exiles (36:4–15).[137]

In opposition, delegitimization of Those Who Remained in Jerusalem leads Ezekiel to adapt the linear sequence of iniquity–destruction–exile and potential restoration as presented in the pentateuchal legal codices. But Ezekiel either cuts the sequence, portraying the Jerusalemites' catastrophe as involving neither exile nor survivors (as in 5:1–17, etc.), or treats refugees from the destroyed Jerusalem as nevertheless doomed to complete annihilation in the lands of their exile (5:1–4). In any case, survivors of the 586 destruction are not to join the Jehoiachin Exiles in Babylon (12:15–16; 14:21–23). Hence, Ezekiel maintains a separatist exclusive stance against Jerusalem both before its destruction and in the aftermath of the disaster. No reconciliation is offered to those few refugees of the past sister community.

Ezekiel's sociological identification with the Jehoiachin Exiles has caused the prophet to set clear ideological distinctions between the two Judahite communities. With his rhetorical skills and his innovative adaptations of pentateuchal traditions to accommodate the complicated reality of his time, Ezekiel has established himself as the first major speaker for the Exiles in Babylon.

2. *Editorial Strands in Ezekiel:*
Inclusive Outlooks within Exclusive Substrata

Ezekiel's stance of extreme exclusivity on behalf of the Jehoiachin Exiles seems, however, not to have persisted. Already within the book of Ezekiel, it is possible to identify ideological modifications that illustrate what Zimmerli called the "successive development of a kernel element... in new additions at a somewhat later time."[138] While I am usually inclined

---

137. For a later strand within the consolation prophecies in Ezekiel see below, pp. 192–96.

138. Zimmerli discussed the "process of literary editing" in Ezekiel in the introduction to his commentary (*Ezekiel 1*, 68–74), and regularly referred to it in his interpretation.

to accept Moshe Greenberg's holistic reading of Ezekiel,[139] and while I appreciate Paul Joyce's emphasis on "the marked homogeneity of the Ezekiel tradition" (and I clearly agree that the book reached its final form within the sixth century), I do find the diverse references to issues of group identity in Ezekiel to be a fruitful arena within which to locate the distinct layers of this successive literary development.[140]

The prophet's followers, disciples, or tradents seem to have altered Ezekiel's extreme exclusivist stance. Two substantial modifications to the prophet's group-identity definitions may be discerned as secondary layers in Ezekiel:[141] (1) the possibility of reinstitution of the covenant relationship with Jerusalem and its inhabitants (16:59–63), and (2) an inclusive attitude towards the Exiles that encompasses both the Jehoiachin group and those who came subsequently to Babylon (Ezek 34–37).[142]

139.   Greenberg, *Ezekiel 1–20*, 18–27.

140.   Joyce, *Ezekiel*, 7–16, quotation from p. 12. Indeed, Zimmerli (*Ezekiel 1*, 68–70) contributed important insights on "the school of Ezekiel" even before he noted the possibility that "a great part of the transmission in the 'school' and the 'updating of tradition' of many oracles took place in Ezekiel's house by the prophet himself" who conducted "the secondary work of learned commentary upon and further elaboration of his prophecies, i.e., with a kind of 'school activity'" (p. 71). These observations rule out most of his earlier observations, as aptly and repeatedly shown by Greenberg.

141.   For even later strands in Ezekiel, see William A. Tooman (*Gog of Magog: Reuse of Scripture and Compositional Technique in Ezekiel 38–39* [FAT 2/52; Tübingen: Mohr Siebeck, 2011]), who argued that, typologically, the Gog prophecies in Ezek 38–39 are akin to Second Temple era "rewritten scripture." Tooman dated this expansion upon Ezekiel to the late Persian period at the earliest, following the return and resettlement of the Babylonian Exiles (pp. 271–72); but then he suggested that the author was most likely an individual of the Hellenistic period, not necessarily (though probably) of Priestly circles, who had clearly mastered the Torah, Prophets, and Psalms, and considered them authoritative (pp. 273–74). In his discussion, Tooman (pp. 73–75) aptly defined these chapters' unique perspectives on the resettlement and the restoration (see particularly 38:8–12), comparing them with Ezekiel's own prophecies of consolation and those of his immediate followers (Ezek 11; 16; 20; 28; 34–37, and even chs. 40–48).

142.   The above-mentioned points concerning the reinstitution of the covenant relationship with Jerusalem and its inhabitants (16:59–63) and the inclusive consolation prophecies of chs. 34–47, are by no means exhaustive in terms of the growth of traditions in the book of Ezekiel. Ezek 40–48 may provide a great wealth of evidence on the book's literary development. From the perspective of group identity issues, Ezek 40–44 is of special interest, as it opens a new frontier in reference to the future Temple personnel. See Jon Levenson (*Theology of the Program of Restoration of Ezekiel 40–48* [HSM 10; Missoula, Mont.: Scholars Press, 1976), who attributed these chapters to the Ezekiel School (p. 131). He nevertheless understood

6. Ezekiel and His Book

The secondary nature of these passages may be substantiated on literary grounds. The ideological differences between these passages and the extreme exclusivity outlined above may thus be adduced as another significant marker of distinction between authors within the book of Ezekiel.

a. *Reinstitution of the Covenant Relationship with Jerusalem (Ezekiel 16:59–63)*

As noted above, Ezekiel draws clear distinctions between the two communities in his prophecies of judgment and consolation: Jerusalem is destined for calamity, the Exiles are to be delivered (Ezek 11:14–21; 20:1–38, 39–45; 34; 36; 37). There is only one exception to this representation in Ezekiel, to which I now turn.

I have already discussed the prophecy of judgment against Jerusalem in Ezek 16:1–43, a prophecy that opens with Jerusalem the adopted baby, who grows to be God's wife, and then His adulterous woman, before she is sentenced to death (vv. 1–43).[143] A second prophecy is attached in vv. 44–58, which seemingly follows upon the metaphoric story, but then deviates significantly from it.[144] In terms of its imagery, this passage employs the marital metaphor of the earlier verses, but not the adoption one. This structures the thematic difference between the two passages: vv. 44–58 do not refer to the initiation of the God–Jerusalem relationship (compare to 23:2–4; and to the role of the adoption and the marital metaphors in 16:1–15). The two passages also differ greatly in their terminology. While זנה and נאף govern vv. 1–43, they are completely absent from vv. 44–58, which uses the general terms: דרכים, חטאת, תועבות (vv. 47, 50, 51, 52). The only exception is זמה, which appears

the conflict to reflect an early "intra-Aaronite struggle" (p. 133), recounted from the Zadokite perspective. The excluded party, according to Levenson, are the Levites who served as altar clergy, who are now accused of abomination: "The Zadokite stratum has escalated the Deuteronomistic polemic by reporting the identity of the intruders as not only non-Levitical but non-Israelite as well" (p. 137). Levenson noted that those excluded are called בני נכר and not גרים, who appear favorably in Ezek 47:21–23 (p. 155 n. 42).

143. Ezek 16:1–43 was discussed earlier, see pp. 156–69, above.

144. The five independent units in chs. 16 and 23 (16:1–43, 44–58, 59–63; 23:1–35, 36–49) differ in their utilization of the family metaphors (the adoption and marital metaphor in ch. 16, but only the marital metaphor in ch. 23), just as they are distinct in their language, literary, and ideological characteristics; see the commentaries on these passages. Galambush (*Jerusalem in Ezekiel*, 10–11) characterized those units as metaphoric stories.

side by side with תועבות in the closing verse of this unit (v. 58).[145] The
final difference between the passages may be seen in the execution of
judgment. Jerusalem's judgment in 16:1–43 is brought upon her in the
form of warlike measures executed by her lovers (vv. 27, 37–41). There
is no mention of such agents in vv. 44–58, where judgment is indicated
only by the Ezekelian phrase נשא כלמה (vv. 52 [×2], 54), and as the
shame and disgrace brought upon her by Aram and Philistia (v. 57).[146]
Ezekiel 16:44–58 is rather closer to 23:1–35 in its portrayal of the relationship between God and Jerusalem. In both metaphorical passages, the
sisters illuminate the sins of Jerusalem, angered far beyond her sisters
(16:47–48, 51–52; 23:11). The prophet's tendency to denigrate Jerusalem is accentuated throughout this passage; the prophet abstains from
calling Jerusalem by name, while he does repeatedly name her sisters,
Samaria and Sodom (16:46, 48, 49, 53, 55, 56). The prophecy closes
with an accusation that justifies the city's judgment (v. 58).

The third section of ch. 16 closes this prophetic unit with a sudden
twist.[147] Ezekiel 16:59–63 prophesies hope and restoration to Jerusalem.
Although it draws on the language and literary style of vv. 1–43, as well
as that of vv. 44–58,[148] this passage differs from its predecessors in
several aspects.[149] In terms of its theme, vv. 59–63 continue the topic of

---

145.   זמה occurs only twice in Ezek 16:1–43 (vv. 27, 43). Compare its four
occurrences in 23:1–35 (vv. 21, 27, 29, 35), and three in 23:36–49 (vv. 44, 48, 49),
See Greenberg, *Ezekiel 1–20*, 294.

146.   נשא כלמה is an expression peculiar to the book of Ezekiel. Beside its
occurrences in 16:52 (×2), 54, and 63, it appears in consolation prophecies (34:29;
36:6, 7, 15; 39:26) and in prophecies against the nations (32:24, 25, 30) and once in
chs. 40–48 (44:13). Contra Zimmerli (*Ezekiel 1*, 351), who argued that נשא כלמה,
like נשא עון, illustrates the sins of Jerusalem, I would argue that the phrase designates judgments brought upon the Exiles, who suffer disgrace from the nations
surrounding them (so in Jer 51:51; Ps 44:16). It frequently occurs in prophecies of
salvation that put forth the annulment of disgrace as part of the reinstitution of the
covenant (34:29; 36:5, 6).

147.   Blenkinsopp (*Ezekiel*, 79) and Block (*Ezekiel 1–24*, 511–22) divided the
chapter differently, and found that the promise of restoration starts in v. 53. But as
Block noted, vv. 53–58 continue to denigrate Jerusalem and actually suggest "a
backhanded rebuke to Jerusalem" (512–15, quotation from p. 514). Indeed, the only
phrase upon which it is possible to base such a proposition is ושבית [ק: ושבות]
שביתיך בתוכהנה ("and your fortunes along with theirs," v. 53).

148.   See Greenberg, *Ezekiel 1–20*, 295–97.

149.   Although he recognized its secondary nature, Joyce (*Ezekiel*, 134–35)
nevertheless held that the recognition formula in v. 62 attests to the congruence of
this redactional levels with what is assumed to be the prophet's own work. Joyce

Jerusalem's disgrace and shame that was the focus of vv. 44–58; it is much closer to these verses than to the adulterous behavior elaborately described in vv. 1–43. Yet, these closing verses suggest a new (even surprising) theme of restoration of the covenant relationship, in full reversal from the portrayals of the God–Jerusalem relationships vv. 1–43, 44–58. This unit clearly contradicts the judgment prophecy of vv. 1–43, which pronounces judgment upon Jerusalem according to her misdeeds משפטי נאפות ושפכת דם ("the punishment of women who commit adultery and murder," v. 38), and relates execution of that punishment (vv. 36–43), concluding with the proclamation, הא דרכך בראש נתתי ("I will pay you back for your conduct," v. 43). This line of denunciation for sexual sins continues in vv. 44–58, and closes with the accusation, את זמתך ואת תועבותיך את נשאתים ("You yourself must bear your depravity and your abominations," v. 58). Verses 59–63, on the other hand, present a unilateral reinstitution of the covenant that includes a unique statement of God's general absolution of Jerusalem's misdeeds (v. 63: בכפרי לך לכל אשר עשית, "when I have forgiven you for all that you did").

Verse 63 thus presents a third and final conclusion to this chapter, a highly significant reversal of its two previous ones:

v. 43:	וגם אני הא דרכך בראש נתתי נאם אדני יהוה ולא עשיתי
	[ק: עשית] את הזמה על כל תועבתיך
v. 58:	את זמתך ואת תועבותיך את נשאתים, נאם יהוה
v. 63:	בכפרי לך לכל אשר עשית נאם אדני יהוה

In most of its occurrences in the Hebrew Bible, כיפר is contextualized in ritual.[150] כיפר על / בעד, "make atonement," is an element of the ritual (liturgical) practices conducted by Moses (Exod 32:30), by the High priest (as in Lev 16:30), or by other priests (Lev 4:35 and passim), on behalf of individuals or the community. These rituals are implemented in order to resolve tensions and restore the orderly relationship between God and His people; that is, atonement expunges the people's sins, purifies the people and subsequently calms God's anger (Ps 78:38). Thus, in the majority of its occurrences, כיפר is the human ritual action, conducted in the hope that God will forgive (see ונסלח לו/להם, Lev 4:20, 26, 31, 35). This is the sense of the term in Deut 21:8, the only other example of the phrase כיפר ל with God as agent in the Hebrew Bible. Ezekiel 16:63 is among the few instances that at face value are detached from

---

also considered the portrayal of consolation as a genuine divine initiative to be of Ezekiel's composing; see below.

150. See Bernard Lang, "כפר," *TDOT* 7:288–303.

the ritual arena, and have God as the agent. In only a few additional instances, God is the agent of כיפר (Deut 32:43; Jer 18:23; Pss 65:4; 78:38; 2 Chr 30:18). The divine propitiation is requested or promised in critical, life-threatening situations.[151] It seems that at the close of Ezek 16, בכפרי לך לכל אשר עשית makes a statement that indeed holds out this meaning of absolution: God here atones Jerusalem for all those ritual sins described in 16:15–25, summarized under זמה and תועבת (vv. 43, 58). Thus, I understand the choice of כיפר ל in Ezek 16:63 to be a genuine reversal and a far-reaching correction initiated by God, annulling the accusations addressed previously at Jerusalem. The unilateral divine initiative of consolation, including a general transformation of the people's hearts with no prior demand for repentance, is typical of Ezekiel (see 11:19–20; 36:24–27), and indeed it stands as a sign of the general homogeneity of the book.[152] But the twist here from fierce accusation and prospects of annihilation to divine absolution of the entire range of cultic sins is remarkable and singular within the book.

An even more significant difference is the hope expressed for Jerusalem. Beyond its special place in the context of Ezekiel 16, this closing coda is unique by comparison with all the other prophecies in Ezekiel that address Jerusalem and are clearly judgment prophecies against the city and its inhabitants. Verses 59–63 proclaim an exceptional prophecy of consolation to Jerusalem, exceptional because consolation prophecies in Ezekiel are otherwise reserved for the Exiles (11:14–21, and chs. 34–37).

Another major difference that distinguishes vv. 59–63 as secondary involves the deployment of the metaphors for the God–people covenant relationship. This closing coda presents a mixed usage of both metaphorical spheres, adding to the dominant marital metaphor phraseology typical of the political covenant metaphor of the Suzerain treaties (e.g. בזית אלה להפר ברית, "you have spurned the pact and violated the covenant," v. 59; cf. the appearance of this phrase in its political context in Ezek 17:11–21).[153] This addition creates an otherwise unprecedented combination with the family-marital metaphors of vv. 1–43. This amalgamation of the different metaphoric spheres is bridged over by the reversal of the two repeating phrases: זכר and ימי נעוריך (see vv. 22, 43).

---

151.   Lang, *TDOT* 7:300–301"; and see Cooke, *Ezekiel*, 181.

152.   See Joyce, *Ezekiel*, 26–27; and Mein, *Ezekiel and the Ethics of Exile*, 202–15.

153.   It has been suggested that the repetition of אלה and ברית at the close of ch. 16 and in ch. 17 illustrate editorial activity motivated by proximity. See Zimmerli, *Ezekiel 1*, 71.

In this new context, it is God who will indeed remember His ancient covenant and renew it as eternal (v. 60), just as it will be the city of Jerusalem that acknowledges God (v. 62).

An additional argument for the secondary nature of this passage is its unique lexemes. The covenant terminology found here is restricted to this passage in Ezekiel: ברית עולם ("eternal covenant," which otherwise occurs only in 37:26); הקים ברית (vv. 60, 62); זכר ברית (vv. 60, 61, 63).[154] The verb כיפר, "make atonement," otherwise appears in Ezekiel only in ritual contexts within chs. 40–48 (Ezek 43:20, 26; 45:15, 17, 20). Likewise, the phrase פתחון פה ("open the mouth," v. 63) appears only here.[155]

Therefore, ch. 16 as a whole indeed illustrates what Zimmerli called "the development of tradition in the book of Ezekiel."[156] It illustrates the different positions held by Ezekiel and it closes with a passage by a later generation of tradents who either do not carry on the earlier exclusive attitudes towards Jerusalem, or consider Jerusalem to be a metonymy for their (now) repatriated Babylonian community.

Margaret S. Odell has put forth a highly interesting proposal concerning the function of shame in the Hebrew Bible, and specifically in Ezek 16:59–63.[157] Shame (conveyed via the roots בוש and כלם) designates the loss of status (individual or group alike). Specific attention is paid to the initiator of this experience, which may either be the people/person themselves (as in Num 12:14), or some powerful other entity (as in 1 Sam 25:7), including one's enemies (see Ps 44:16–17) or God Himself (Ps 44:10). Indeed, shame was "a fact of life among the exiles."[158] But here is where I think Odell's reading may be broadened. Could not shame have been felt under the change of status that came with Neo-Babylonian subjugation of the land of Judah (compare Ezek 36:6: יען כלמת גוים נשאתם, referring to the "mountains of Israel" after the Destruction)? And likewise, could not shame have been felt as a

---

154. The string (יהוה) זכר ברית (עולם) is unique to Priestly sources (Gen 9:15, 16; Lev 26:42, 45) and is evoked by Pss 105:8; 106:45; 111:5. הקים ברית את occurs in the blessing of Lev 26 (v. 9). The two phrases appear together in Deut 8:18, but זכר is the people's obligation, and הקים ברית is God's. Cooke (*Ezekiel*, 180) aptly pointed out that Ezekiel does use the phrase כרת ברית in Ezek 17:13; 34:25; 37:26.
155. For פתחון פה (v. 63), see Block, *Ezekiel 1–24*, 518–19.
156. Zimmerli, *Ezekiel 1*, 334.
157. Margaret S. Odell, "The Inversion of Shame and Forgiveness in Ezekiel 16:59–63," *JSOT* 56 (1992): 101–12; and see Block, *Ezekiel 1–24*, 519–20.
158. Odell ("Inversion of Shame and Forgiveness," 105) very aptly concluded that "the expression of shame is the opposite of what we would consider the feeling of unworthiness; rather, it is the expression of an individual's outrage that others do not acknowledge and respond to his or her claims."

reflection of the status of the land and the Repatriates during the early Persian period in Yehud? I thus accept Odell's thematic reading of this passage, and especially her suggestion (following Greenberg) that the prohibition of (or the limitation on) shame in פתחון פה מפני כלמתך con-cerns the annulment of rituals of complaint addressed to God, as she paraphrases: "You will no longer have complaints (lit. mouth opening) that are necessitated by your shame."[159] This may be understood as another and different perspective on the questions concerning fasts and mourning procedures addressed to Zechariah (7:1–7) and to Deutero-Isaiah (Isa 58) by the Repatriates in Persian Yehud.

The last possibility seems to be the most reasonable context for this addition in 16:59–63. The closing coda of ch. 16 adapts Ezekiel's earlier harsh prophecy against Jerusalem; in its attempt to invert judgment and seek assurance of forgiveness, this non-Ezekelian passage sets aside Jerusalem's iniquity. With that final addition, the tradents suggest a plan for the reinstitution of the God–people covenant relationship, under-standing Jerusalem as metonymy for the Repatriated community of their time.[160]

b. *An Inclusive Attitude toward the Exiles (Ezekiel 34–37)*
A second point of difference between the prophet and his followers, as I have noted, concerns the relationship to the Jehoiachin Exiles. The distinction seems to leave its marks mainly on the prophecies of con-solation in Ezekiel. While some of those are specifically addressed to the Jehoiachin Exiles (11:14–21; and implicitly 33:24–29), most of these prophecies do not specify the addressees as a special community among the Exiles.[161]

Hence, chs. 34–37 differ significantly from chs. 1–24, 33 (and 25–32) not only in their overall content (consolation vs. mainly judgment in the remainder of the book), but primarily in their conceptions of group identity.[162] Building on Ezekiel's projections of consolation, a second strand of tradents added what seems to be a very delicate modification of

159. Ibid., 106.
160. On the medieval Jewish interpretation that understands Ezekiel's attitude toward Jerusalem as a metonymy for the entire people of Israel, see Rom-Shiloni, "Jerusalem and Israel, Synonyms or Antonyms?"
161. See the discussion on pp. 144–56, above.
162. Greenberg (*Ezekiel 21–37*, 705) aptly showed the nature of the prophecies of consolation in Ezek 34–37 as reversals of the prophecies of judgment, following the lines of the blessings of Lev 26:1–13, 40–45; just as Ezekiel's portrayals of the Destruction adapt the curses of Lev 26:14–39.

the prophet's messages. Yet this modification represents a crucial step forward in the crafting of Babylonian exilic ideologies. Therefore, I propose that we need to analyze the messages of consolation in Ezekiel by allowing the possibility of literary and thematic developments within "the marked homogeneity of the Ezekiel tradition."[163]

As discussed above, chs. 1–24 draw clear lines of demarcation between Jerusalem and the Jehoiachin Exiles, the "people of your kindred" (or with the LXX: "of your Exile," 11:14). Chapters 34–37, however, supply no clues to determine whether distinctions between the exilic groups— the Jehoiachin Exiles of 597, the 586 Exiles from Jerusalem, or the 582 Exiles (following Jer 52:28–30)—are being maintained. In clear difference from the polemic between the Babylonian Exiles and Those Who Remained, the grain of the explicit polemic between the earlier and later exilic communities evaporates (compare to Ezek 12:15–16; 14:21–23).

Nevertheless, a dynamic of exclusivity still directs the formation of group identity. This later layer of the book retains the restriction that prophecies of consolation are directed only to the Exiles, to those who are away from the land, who are eventually to be gathered and brought back there.

The in-group designations within these prophecies of consolation refer to the addressees as the people, the entire people, of God.[164] The people are called ישראל (Ezek 34:2), עמי בית ישראל (in 34:30), עמי ישראל (in 36:12), (כל) בית ישראל (in 36:10, 16, 22, 32, 37; 37:11). Similar names are given to the land that is the target of return: הרי (מרום) ישראל (Ezek 34:13, 14; 35:12; 36:1, 4, 8), נחלת בית ישראל (in 35:15), אדמת ישראל (in 36:6; 37:12; אדמתם, in 36:16). We are told that it is the Exiles who have been designated by the nations as עם יהוה אלה (in 36:20), who were deported from His land (ומארצו יצאו). Hence, lines of *continuity* govern those prophecies of consolation. A clear equation is suggested between the Exiles and Israel, the community, the people, who are the objects of restoration in the land. Furthermore, time and again the prophecies repeat phrases of entirety, such as כל בית ישראל כלה ("the whole House of Israel," 36:10).

---

163. See Joyce, *Ezekiel*, 12; and compare Kasher (*Ezekiel 1–24*, 125–32), who did recognize the diversity in the messages of consolation, yet harmonized these passages as all belonging to the prophet (and even suggested that they reflect an early pro-Jerusalem perspective [p. 125]).

164. Mein (*Ezekiel and the Ethics of Exile*, 220–22) aptly accentuated the communal (rather than the individual) message of the salvation oracles in Ezekiel.

The close and caring relationship between God and His dispersed people is metaphorically portrayed in Ezek 34, where the people are God's flock, צאני (Ezek 34:6 [×2], 7 [×4], etc.). This flock comprises the descendants of a long line of God's people under evil leadership; as a consequence of the neglect of these leaders their flocks were dispersed among the nations (34:1–10). They are now promised that they will be lead by God, the true shepherd (34:11–16, 17–25), who will establish for them a Davidic shepherd, ruler, נשיא (vv. 23–24).[165]

Thematically, the consolation prophecies of chs. 34–37 respond to the Exiles' despair concerning their further existence in exile (37:1–14, esp. v. 11; see also 20:32; 33:10).[166] The prophecies as a group address the covenant relationship with God, now that the people face dislocation from the land and the reality of exile. Each passage within the consolation prophecies contributes its own angle on a different facet of this broader topic:[167] the status of the (dispersed) Exiles as the people of God (34:1–16, 17–24; 36:16–32), and the covenant relationship, which is explicitly discussed in 34:25–30; 37:26–28, and clearly is behind all the other passages. When mentioned, the people's obedience is guaranteed by the divine transformation of the heart and the spirit (36:26–27; note also 11:19–20) which accompanies the reinstitution of the covenant relationship; note the repetition of the covenant formula (36:28; and 11:20).[168] These topics are frequently connected with the prospect of restoration in the land. Once God gathers them back, He will lead the House of Israel to the mountains of Israel—which are portrayed as waiting in complete desolation for this divine restoration (35:12–15; 36:4–15, 29–32, 33–37). The empty land will revive in preparation for

165. Ezek 34 is one remarkable instance of the literary evolution within Ezekiel, and yet illustrates the difficulties in discerning the layers of this evolution. See Zimmerli (*Ezekiel 2*, 213, 220, 222), who referred vv. 25–30 to the prophet's disciples, still located within Babylon; and compare Greenberg's literary approach (*Ezekiel 21–37*, 705–709), by which he argued for the chapter's unity.

166. Another desperate quotation occurs in the disputation in Ezek 33:1–18. However, I consider ch. 33 as a closure to chs. 1–24, since, like ch. 11, it holds two disputation speeches, the first prophesying hope for the Jehoiachin Exiles (repeatedly called בני עמך, vv. 2, 12, as in the earlier chapters), and the second predicting annihilation to those who live on the ruins of Jerusalem (vv. 23–29).

167. Tova Ganzel ("The Descriptions of the Restoration of Israel in Ezekiel," *VT* 60 [2010]: 197–211) presented an overview of Ezekiel's conceptions of consolation. She based her argument for the literary unity of the prophecies on the notions of thematic diversity and the possibility of progression of ideas within the works of a single author—but these in themselves do not testify to literary unity.

168. See Raitt, *A Theology of Exile*, 128–36, 174–76, 182–84; and Mein, *Ezekiel and the Ethics of Exile*, 221–22.

the Returnees (36:8–12, 29–30, 34–35).[169] All these lines of consolation reverse the earlier judgments: they draw on the blessings of Lev 26 (vv. 1–13), and they further mobilize national traditions of the two kingdoms (37:15–28), including references to the Davidic rulership (34:24; 37:24).

These passages clearly use the three exilic arguments of exclusivity: *continuity*, *entirety*, and *annexation* of earlier traditions and national conceptions. Thus, I am unable to accept H. G. M. Williamson's conclusions concerning Ezekiel's vision of restoration. Following Zimmerli, Williamson considered Ezekiel to present an idealistic and utopian description of return and the reunion of Israel as one people.[170] But while "Israel" indeed governs the designations of the people in Ezekiel (Zimmerli found 185 occurrences of the name Israel versus only 15 of Judah), there needs to be a more critical analysis of its use within the book. Utilizing "Israel" does not necessarily mean holding to inclusive positions. On the contrary, this same tactic reinforces the exclusive stances in the book (of both the prophet, and his tradents). "Israel" is a divisive, exclusivistic designation, used by the Babylonian Exiles to mark themselves as the sole community continuing the national designations, and annexing to themselves the national traditions, as those who carry on the national existence.

Concerning designation of an out-group. Being cautious about employing *argumentum ex silentio*, I will restrict my comments to just noting that these prophecies do not mention any specific Judean Diaspora settled in Babylon or elsewhere. They seem to utilize only the general formulae הגוים אשר באו שם ("but when they came to those nations," in 36:20); or the phrase ואפיץ אותם בגוים ויזרו בארצות ("I scattered them among the nations, and they were dispersed through the countries," 36:19) and its reversal ולקחתי אתכם מן הגוים וקבצתי אתכם מכל הארצות ("I will take you from among the nations and gather you from all the countries," 36:24).[171] Of stronger value is the silence concerning any remnant in Judah that might conceivably function as an out-group. Since the prophecies do portray the land as completely empty and desolate, they simply do not give room for the existence of a Judean community in the land of Israel.

169. See the discussion of the empty land, on pp. 180–81, above.

170. Williamson, "The Concept of Israel in Transition," 143–44; Zimmerli, *Ezekiel 2*, 563–65.

171. This is a remarkable Ezekelian phrase that runs through the judgment prophecies against Israel, the prophecies against the nations, and the consolation prophecies as well (see Ezek 11:16; 12:15; 20:23, 41; 22:15; 29:12 [against Egypt]; 30:23, 26 [against Egypt]; 39:29 [ארצות / עמים]).

These messages within Ezek 34–37 show once more the homogeneity of the Ezekiel tradition—that is, they may represent the prophet's words and conceptions, just as they might reflect later revisions and sporadic additions that might have been added within a relatively close time span, still within the sixth century, and probably earlier than the Edict of Cyrus.[172]

These conceptions seem parallel to the Babylonian exilic ideologies of Deutero-Isaiah and Zechariah. But in fact these passages might offer the missing link between Ezekiel and those early Persian-period prophets.

In terms of in-group definitions, the consolation prophecies in Ezek 34–37 appear to broaden Ezekiel's message of restoration. They are no longer occupied with the struggle against Those Who Remained in the land, but rather focus on consolidating the identity of the Exiles. On that end, they show inclusive orientation that encompasses all the various exilic groups. Thus, they no longer give preeminence to the Jehoiachin Exiles.

Concerning polemic against any out-groups, while these prophecies let go of Ezekiel's struggles against Those Who Remained, they still keep hold of Ezekiel's second track of exclusivity, maintaining the dichotomy between the Exiles and the empty land. Either prior to, or even contemporaneous with, early Persian-period prophecy, this second strand in Ezekiel carries on the exclusivity of the Exiles as a group, but for the first time configures it as *exclusive inclusivity*. This non-Ezekiel strand clearly maintains the Exiles' exclusive prestige as Israel, the people of God, עם יהוה אלה, the one community entitled for restoration.

3. Conclusions

In closing this long discussion of the book of Ezekiel, I want to stress that the role of the prophet (and his followers) in structuring and developing the Babylonian ideology of exile cannot be overestimated.

This chapter elucidated two ideological strands within the book. The first, which I have traced back to the prophet himself, is the voice of extreme exclusivity, the voice that declares the Jehoiachin Exiles to be the prestigious, one-and-only legitimate community of Judeans. The second strand, which may be traced through minor modifications within the prophecies of consolation (chs. 34–37), broadens the in-group circle to include all Exiles, regardless of their time of deportation. Thus, this second strand suggests an inclusive perspective, but it is important to note that the in-group is still *restricted* to those in the exilic community.

---

172. Mein, *Ezekiel and the Ethics of Exile*, 258.

The book of Ezekiel throughout shows no dramatic change in regard to its portrayal of the out-group, those left behind in Jerusalem. According to both strands, the Jerusalemites are represented either as the "people of the land"—that is, non-Judahites (non-Yahwistic)—or simply as nonexistent in relation to a portrait of the land as totally destroyed and emptied of its people.

Thus, Ezekiel's successors transform the prophet's conception of the exilic people of God, but maintain his in-group/out-group split between the exilic and Yehud-based Judean groups. Both aspects of this development are significant: as we have seen, the various elements of this transformed conception are drawn upon in different ways by Deutero-Isaiah and subsequent writers descended from the exilic community, even following the return to the land.

Chapter 7

JEREMIAH AND HIS BOOK:
TWO ANTAGONISTIC PERSPECTIVES

1. *Jeremiah: Between Jerusalem and Babylon*

Judean perspectives were already introduced above in Ezekiel's disputation speeches (Ezek 11:15; 33:24), where the prophet quotes anonymous voices in Jerusalem, prior to the city's destruction and in its aftermath. The present chapter focuses on the prophet Jeremiah, who indeed is said to be one of Those Who Remained in Jerusalem following the Jehoiachin Exile (597 B.C.E.), remaining even after the final Destruction of Jerusalem (586 B.C.E.). Jeremiah thus represents the "opposition" to Ezekiel's positions on group-identity issues.

But, as has been widely recognized, the book of Jeremiah contains these two opposing polemic perspectives in one and the same prophetic collection.[1] In contrast to the expectations raised by Jeremiah's biographical and ideological data as presented below, prophecies in Jeremiah proclaim a hope for restoration exclusively to the Jehoiachin Exiles' community (i.e. Jer 24); and in still other consolation prophecies (mostly in chs. 30–33), the addressees are unspecified Babylonian Exiles.[2]

Hence, Judah and Babylon are two locations that correspond to two very different, major layers of the book: the Jerusalemite–Judahite layers of Jeremiah's pronouncements (and those of his tradents in Judah), and the Babylonian exilic layers added by tradents or redactors in Babylon. Accordingly, the prophecies address (at least) two distinct audiences.

---

1. Ernst W. Nicholson, *Preaching to the Exiles: A Study of the Prose Tradition in the Book of Jeremiah* (New York: Schocken, 1970), 117; Seitz, *Theology in Conflict*, 228–35; Carolyn Sharp, *Prophecy and Ideology in Jeremiah: Struggles for Authority in the Deutero-Jeremianic Prose* (London: T&T Clark International, 2003), 157–70; Mark Leuchter, *The Polemics of Exile in Jeremiah 26–45* (Cambridge: Cambridge University Press, 2008), 1–25.

2. Among the redactional references to exile are Jer 16:14–15; 23:7–8; 24; 29:8–14, 16–20; passages in chs. 30–33, among them 32:36–41; 32:42–44; chs. 50–51 (with the exception of Jer 51:46–52), etc. These are discussed below, pp. 241–44.

Carolyn Sharp aptly opened her discussion of the book with reference to the oversimplified nature of these kinds of categorizations, which create an opposition between the "authentic" and the "compositional-redactional" layers of the book.[3] Indeed, the following discussion locates at least three major strands of composition in the book of Jeremiah, all of which date from the sixth century.[4]

The earlier levels of "Jeremiah's words" comprise what may be assumed to be authentic prophecies as well as pro-Judahite layers of compilation and redaction. The portrayal of Jeremiah as a historical personage seems to me easily in keeping with the historical milieu of Judah in the late seventh and early sixth centuries B.C.E. Nevertheless, it seems that Judean tradents of Jeremiah interpreted and elaborated his pronouncements over time; thus I would not insist on trying to recover the prophet's *ipsissima verba*.[5] For the sake of this discussion, suffice it to recognize that native Judean perspectives are clearly discernable; their Judean provenance may be validated by the interweaving of the biographical details concerning the prophet with the prophetic messages.

A second primary stratum, which often mounts an ideological opposition to the first, contains probably several distinct strands of exilic additions and redactions (among them Deuteronomistic elements). They all reveal clear Babylonian exilic ideological tendencies, sharing perspectives with Ezekiel and Deutero-Isaiah.[6]

---

3. Sharp, *Prophecy and Ideology in Jeremiah*, xi–xvi.

4. With reference to the timeframe, I incline to earlier datings rather than later ones. Among the earliest, Seitz (*Theology in Conflict*), Lundbom (*Jeremiah 1–20*, 100–101), and Leuchter (*Polemics of Exile*, 1–17) found the compilation of Jeremiah (according to Lundbom, even its two major textual versions represented by the MT and LXX) to have been completed by the first half of the sixth century (ca. 570 or 560 B.C.E.). I find more adequate the suggestions of Nicholson (*Preaching to the Exiles*, 116–35) and Alexander Rofé ("The Arrangement of the Book of Jeremiah," *ZAW* 101 [1989]: 390–98), among others, who allow for additional decades of literary evolution within the sixth century, until ca. 520 B.C.E. For later datings, see for instance, Albertz (*Israel in Exile*, 312–27, table on p. 321), who proposed a gradual Deuteronomistic growth of the book until 525–520, with additional materials added in the fifth and even the fourth/third centuries B.C.E.

5. For a study of the relationships between the prophet, his book, and later exilic tradents responsible for chs. 26–52, see Leuchter, *Polemics of Exile*, 145–65. But while Leuchter was mainly interested in scribal activity, the current discussion highlights the differences between earlier and later tradents on the issue of identity (and see n. 6 below).

6. Compare to Albertz (*Israel in Exile*, 322–27) who, following Winfried Thiel, (*Die deuteronomistische Redaktion von Jeremia, 1–45: Mit einer Gesamtbeurteilung der deuteronomistischen Redaktion des Buches Jeremia* [2 vols.; WMANT 41, 52;

Finally, and more complicated to discern, are traces to Repatriates' revisions and adaptations of Jeremian prophecies of consolation (i.e. prophecies of the earlier Judean layer). These adaptations further substantiate the suggestion that the Repatriates continued to maintain Babylonian exilic ideological positions even after the return to Persian Yehud.

Hence, to rephrase the issue of the complexity of the book of Jeremiah: the social and geographical differences that distinguish Jeremiah from Ezekiel operate within the book of Jeremiah itself. Concerning the conceptions of land and exile, and the definition of group identities, the book reveals two literary complexes: a pro-Judahite cluster and a pro-*golah*, that is, Babylonian exilic, one. Groups of tradents within Jeremiah represent each of these two communities.

Thus, compiled and edited first in Judah (and in Egypt), then in Babylon, and then returning to its home base in Judah but with a different tradent community, the book of Jeremiah contains a wide variety of perspectives sometimes in contradiction to the prophet's own earlier pronouncements. This is then where questions of literary evolution meet the challenge of group-identity issues. These geographical and social distinctions seem crucial to the present discussion, as they account for the coexistence of two contradictory conceptions of exile in Jeremiah, reflecting two different sets of group identity definitions.[7]

Neukirchen–Vluyn: Neukirchener Verlag, 1973, 1981], 2:113–15), argued that the three Deuteronomistic editions of the book of Jeremiah evolved in the land of Judah in the early postexilic period. Furthermore, Albertz (p. 325) considered the polemic in Jer 40–44 to be between the Deuteronomistic residents of Judah and those tempted to emigrate to Egypt following the assassination of Gedaliah. I find this argument untenable; see below.

7. This is where I part company with Leuchter (*Polemics of Exile*) on several central points: (1) I assume a much more complicated and a longer process of literary evolution in Jeremiah (but still within the sixth century). (2) Leuchter denied the possibility of a Judahite growth of the Jeremianic traditions, arguing there were simply no literate persons to carry on this tradition (pp. 7–8). I find that notion improbable and a clear oversimplification; literary creativity has long been recognized in Judah following 586 B.C.E. (see pp. 10–11, above). (3) Leuchter (pp. 6, 8, and passim) understood Jeremiah himself to direct hopeful messages to the Jehoiachin Exiles; he argued for tensed relationships between the groups at times, and for inclusive trends among the Babylonian Exiles at others (pp. 60–65). Furthermore, he did not recognize the political motivations of the Babylonian and Judahite communities in this internal struggle, but argued that the Supplement chapters demonstrate only one side of the dispute, that of "the Babylonian Judeans," who have Jeremiah's support (see pp. 8, 135, 145). Accordingly, he held that group-identity polemics in the Supplement illustrate the dichotomy between the Babylonian Exiles and the

Along these lines, this chapter first delineates the message(s) of Jeremiah (and his Judean tradents) as a distinct prophetic strand in the book; second, it addresses the Babylonian exilic (and editorial) levels of the book to present the clear Babylonian orientation that governs the development of the Jeremianic tradition first in Babylon and then back in Yehud.

a. *Jeremiah as a Judean Voice of Those Who Remained*
Biographical details in the book of Jeremiah tell about the prophet who had prophesied in Jerusalem during the last decades before its fall.[8] He remained in the city throughout the siege (Jer 21:1–10; 37–38) until Jerusalem's destruction (Jer 39), and was given the choice, and chose, to remain in Judah under the governorship of Gedaliah (40:1–6); then, however, although he protested, he was taken to Egypt along with Baruch the scribe (43:1–7), and presumably died there.

Jeremiah's personal choice to remain in Judah underscores his constant message regarding subjugation to Babylon, loss of the land, and exile. This message may be traced in three different prophetic contexts: in his prophecies against the last Davidic kings; in his repeated calls to accept subjugation to Babylon; and in his hopeful message to the Remnant of Judah.

(1) *Prophecies against the kings of the House of Judah (Jer 22:1–23:6)*: Jeremiah specifies exile as the fate of two kings, Shalum son of Josiah (22:10–12, see 2 Kgs 23:31–35) and Coniah (Jehoiachin) son of Jehoiakim (Jer 22:24–30, see 2 Kgs 24:8–17).[9] Exile in these judgment prophecies is worse than death. Jeremiah 22:10 reads:

Exiles in Egypt (pp. 126–36, 152–56). (4) He also relied on the rather oversimplified assumption that the "polemics of contemporaneous circles of literati" may be categorized as "a countertradition of lexemes and ideas" (p. 9, and see Leuchter's comment in p. 201 n. 49). Above all, (5) Leuchter put a much greater emphasis on struggles over scribal authority than on issues of identity (as, for instance, pp. 120–23). The discussion below argues against these claims.

8. William L. Holladay, *Jeremiah 2* (Hermeneia; Philadelphia: Fortress, 1989), 25–35. It is not necessary for the purposes of the present study to pinpoint the year Jeremiah may be presumed to have started his prophetic career; on which, see the commentaries.

9. It is of interest that if indeed Jer 23:5–6 refers to Zedekiah, his own exile is not mentioned. That, of course, poses a challenge to the hopeful (some would say Messianic) message that these verses suggest. I thus concur with Jack L. Lundbom (*Jeremiah 21–36* [AB 21B; New York: Doubleday, 2004], 170–76), who assigned this prophecy to Jeremiah himself, arguing that the prophet articulates the hope for

אל תבכו למת ואל תנדו לו בכו בכו להלך כי לא ישוב עוד וראה את ארץ מולדתו

Do not weep for the dead and do not lament for him; weep rather for him
who is leaving, for he shall never come back to see the land of his birth!

Once exiled, these two leaders and their company will terminate their
lives in their new locations, never to return to their longed-for homeland
(vv. 10–12, 26–27).[10]

(2) *Repeated calls to accept the subjugation to Babylon*: Drawing on the
same basic conception (that exile is worse than death), Jeremiah urges
Zedekiah to accept Babylonian rulership (Jer 27:10–15; 37–38), calls the
people to surrender to the Babylonians (21:8–10; repeated in 38:2), and
debates with Hananiah the prophet concerning the permanence of the
Babylonian regime over Judah (ch. 28). Jeremiah is accused by officials
of weakening the moral resistance of the Judean army; he is even accused
of treason (37:12–16; 38:1–6; as also 26:7–11). On the Babylonian
withdrawal of the siege, Jeremiah is caught leaving town and accused
of deserting to the Babylonians (37:11–16).[11] As though to confirm these
accusations, following the destruction of the city, Nebuzaradan, the
Babylonian official who destroyed Jerusalem, grants Jeremiah the special
privilege of choosing his future place of residence. Given the choice,
Jeremiah indeed chooses to remain in the land, in Mizpah, with Gedaliah
son of Ahikam (40:1–6).[12]

These incidents, and the suspicions thrown at the prophet by his
contemporaries, seem to have affected scholars of Jeremiah as well, who
thus tend to portray the prophet as a collaborator with the Babylonians
and as holding politically to a pro-Babylonian agenda. This dynamic has

an ideal Davidic ruler (as also in Jer 30:8–9; and the parallel verses in 33:14–16).
But Lundbom further cautioned that messianic messages should not be read back
into Jeremiah, and found these verses, and especially the play on Zedekiah's name,
to be "a sharp censure of Judah's last king" (p. 175).

10. Jeremiah's position against Jehoiachin contrasts sharply with that of Ezekiel
(Ezek 17); see above, pp. 143–44. See Wilhelm J. Wessels, "Jeremiah 22, 24–30: A
Proposed Ideological Reading," *ZAW* 101 (1989): 232–49.

11. For this accusation and the meaning of לחלק משם בתוך העם, see Israel
Eph'al, "You Are Defecting to the Chaldeans," *ErIs* 24 (1994): 18–22 (in Hebrew).

12. John Hill ("Jeremiah 40:1–6: An Appreciation," in *Seeing Signals, Reading
Signs: The Art of Exegesis; Studies in Honour of Antony F. Campbell, SJ for His
Seventieth Birthday* [ed. M. A. O'Brien and H. N. Wallace; London: T&T Clark
International, 2004], 130–41) presented Jer 40:1–6 as "a key text" to the new begin-
ning in Judah after the Destruction, a highly important passage that articulates
Jeremiah's separation from the 586 deportees, and his choice to remain with
Gedaliah in the land.

also led to the sociological reconstruction of a political struggle during the last decades of Jerusalem, a struggle between two antagonistic parties led by opposing prophetic opponents—the "rebellious party" of the royal court, accompanied by priests and the "peace prophets," over against Jeremiah and the Shafanides.[13]

I disagree with this sociopolitical reconstruction. I find Jeremiah's position on the issue of subjugation to Babylon to be theologically grounded, as so well-articulated in Jer 27.[14] If anything, Jeremiah's position is actually a clear pro-Judah/pro-land one, which is based on the combination of three major theological conceptions.[15] First, Jeremiah understands God to be the Lord of History, who has given Nebuchadnezzar His servant governance over the entire region (27:4–8). It is quite remarkable that at this crucial time of subjugation, the Judean prophet portrays the Babylonian emperor as but a vassal of YHWH, the Judahite deity.[16] Adjunct to this conception, however, and not less important, are Jeremiah's conceptions of the primacy of the land and of the meaning of exile. These two intertwined conceptions prompt the prophet's understanding that subjugation to Babylon is the only way to assure the nation's continuing existence in the land. Or, to put it differently, Jeremiah's conception of exile, as a personal and national calamity and virtual death sentence, causes him to stand fiercely against aspirations of rebellion against Babylon, which would most certainly bring death and the loss of the land (27:11–13).

(3) *Jeremiah's message to the Remnant of Judah*: This same line of thought governs Jeremiah's words to Those Who Remained after 586 B.C.E., whom he calls the "Remnant of Judah."[17] He urges the Remnant

---

13. This political dichotomy was reconstructed in detail by Shmuel Yavin, "Families and Parties in the Kingdom of Judah," *Tarbiz* 12 (1951): 241–67 (in Hebrew), and is carried on within the commentaries. For a historical reconstruction see also Nahum M. Sarna, "The Abortive Insurrection in Zedekiah's Day (Jer. 27–29)," *ErIs* 14 (1978): *79–*96.

14. See the discussion of Jer 27:9–15 on pp. 212–14, below.

15. For Jeremiah's theopolitical perceptions, see Yair Hoffman, "Reflections on the Relationship between Theopolitics, Prophecy and Historiography," in *Politics and Theopolitics in the Bible and Postbiblical Literature* (ed. H. G. Reventlow, Y. Hoffman, and B. Uffenheimer; JSOTSup 171; Sheffield: JSOT, 1994), 85–99.

16. See Ziony Zevit, "The Use of עבד as a Diplomatic Term in Jeremiah," *JBL* 88 (1969): 74–77.

17. שארית יהודה designates the community that remained, in Jer 40–44. It occurs in words of God or of the prophet (Jer 42:15, 19; 44:7, 12, 14, 28), in the author's words (40:11; 43:5), and in the speech of Johanan son of Kareah (40:15). A similar term is שארית העם (Jer 41:10); and see below, p. 228.

of Judah to remain in the land, reiterating the death sentence that awaits outside it (42:9–17).[18]

This contextual framework suggests that for Jeremiah, the loss of the land was the worst possible foreseeable judgment that could fall upon the last kings of Judah (and the entire people). Exile, for Jeremiah, meant personal and national annihilation. Thus, the utilization, by Jeremiah and his tradents, of Deuteronomic conceptions of land and exile, merits particular consideration.

b. *Jeremiah's Conceptions of Land and Exile: The Ideological Foundation of Judean Exclusivity*
(1) *The Theological Challenge of Exile: Four Deuteronomic Perspectives on the Loss of the Land.*[19] Biblical sources in general, and Deuteronomy in particular, treat exile from a theological perspective. Exile is not (only) a historical consequence of war, a standard element of a calculated imperial international policy, but a divine judgment upon a disobedient people (2 Kgs 17:18–23; 24:20).[20] Hence, the concept of exile is one among many examples in Deuteronomy and in the Deuteronomistic History, wherein the metaphor of political suzerainty has been transferred to the relationship between God and His people. Parallel to the human-political sphere, exile is presented theologically as a divine judgment threatened or executed against the disloyal people in reaction to their cultic misconduct and their transgressions against the covenant to which they were committed by God (as, for instance, in Deut 4:25–28).[21] God is the agent of exile, who acts with justification, according to His previously announced warnings (as in Deut 8:1, 19–20) and according to the stipulations of His treaty with the people (Deut 28:1, 15, 69).

18. The same concept drives Jeremiah's moral and social message in 7:3–15, which also seems in accord with the Deuteronomic concept of the land in Deut 16:20.

19. The following discussion was originally written for my "Deuteronomic Concepts of Exile Interpreted in Jeremiah and Ezekiel," which included materials from both Jeremiah and Ezekiel. In the present context, I focus only on Jeremiah; I dealt with Ezekiel's usage of Deuteronomic conceptions of exile also in my "Facing Destruction," 197–98.

20. This theological construct does not distinguish the people of God from those of other nations (cf. 2 Kgs 17:11), and so also it is generally brought into play in the prophecies to the nations, such as Ezek 25:6–7; 30:20–26, etc.

21. This fully corresponds to the overall Deuteronomic concept of the God–people relationship, see Weinfeld, *Deuteronomy and the Deuteronomic School*, 59–157.

Exile challenges the concept of the gift of the land, which had become central throughout the Israelite religion as one of the three points in the triangular relationship of God–People–Land.[22] According to the Deuteronomic concept, the land is under God's sovereignty; thus, He allows his people to live in it, He gives them the land as possession (as in Deut 1:8).[23] Yet, the land is a conditional gift, which either benefits the obedient people with long-term existence upon it (Deut 11:8–9), or brings calamity (and exile) upon the disobedient, upon the people that violates God's covenant (Deut 11:8–9, 16–17):[24]

ושמרתם את כל המצוה אשר אנכי מצוך היום למען תחזקו ובאתם וירשתם את
הארץ אשר אתם עברים שמה לרשתה: **ולמען תאריכו ימים על האדמה אשר
נשבע יהוה לאבתיכם לתת להם ולזרעם** ארץ זבת חלב ודבש:...
השמרו לכם פן יפתה לבבכם וסרתם ועבדתם אלהים אחרים והשתחויתם להם:
וחרה אף יהוה בכם ועצר את השמים ולא יהיה מטר והאדמה לא תתן את יבולה
ואבדתם מהרה מעל הארץ הטבה אשר יהוה נתן לכם:

Keep, therefore, all the Instruction that I enjoin upon you today, so that you may have the strength to enter and take possession of the land that you are about to cross into and possess, **and that you may long endure upon the soil that the LORD swore to your fathers to assign to them and to their heirs**, a land flowing with milk and honey...

Take care not to be lured away to serve other gods and bow to them. For the LORD's anger will flare up against you, and He will shut up the skies so that there will be no rain and the ground will not yield its produce; **and you will soon perish from the good land that the LORD is assigning to you**.

22. Daniel I. Block, *The Gods and the Nations: Studies in Ancient Near Eastern National Theology* (ETSMS 2; Jackson, Mo.: Evangelical Theological Society, 1988), 5–6, 98–123; Moshe Weinfeld, "Inheritance of the Land—Privilege versus Obligation: The Concept of the 'Promise of the Land' in the Sources of the First and Second Temple Periods," *Zion* (1984): 115–37 (in Hebrew).

23. Gerhard von Rad, "The Promised Land and Yahweh's Land in the Hexateuch," in *The Problem of the Hexateuch and Other Essays* (trans. E. W. Trueman Dicken; Edinburgh: Oliver & Boyd, 1966), 79–93. Joosten (*People and Land in the Holiness Code*, 169–92) correctly emphasized the "feudal relationship" between God, people, and land as a concept shared throughout the Pentateuch. See Exod 15:17; see also in the Priestly and Holiness Legislation sources (Exod 6:2–8; Josh 22:19; Lev 25:23) and in Deuteronomy (Deut 1:8; 6:10, 18, 23).

24. Patrick D. Miller, "The Gift of the Land: The Deuteronomic Theology of the Land," *Int* 23 (1969): 451–65; Norman C. Habel, *The Land Is Mine: Six Biblical Land Ideologies* (OBT; Minneapolis: Fortress, 1995), 36–53; and references to the entire biblical literature, in Weinfeld, "Inheritance of the Land," 115–26.

This concept of the land as a conditional gift, with its accompanying threats of dislocation, is fundamental to the Deuteronomic concepts of exile. In this framework, exile is positioned in opposition to the concept of the Land.

Dislocation and exile denote the loss of the land in ten relatively short passages in Deuteronomy (Deut 4:25–31; 6:10–15; 8:19–20; 11:13–21; 28:20–26, 36–37, 63–64; 29:21–27; 30:1–10, 15–20).[25] The literary and thematic contours of these passages suggest that the conditional gift will be taken away if the people violate the covenant. Dislocation is divine retaliation for the transgressions of disloyalty, disobedience, and the worship of other gods. But beyond this common denominator, these passages do not present a unified perspective on exile.

In the study of Deuteronomy, references to exile have played a major role in arguments for the literary-historical differentiation of layers within the book. Scholars have separated the book diachronically into preexilic and exilic layers, perceiving the latter as contemporary with the exilic strand of the Deuteronomistic literature (Dtr[2]) and with the prophetic literature of the sixth century B.C.E., mainly the books of Jeremiah, Ezekiel, and Deutero-Isaiah.[26]

The present study illuminates four independent perspectives on exile, found in Deuteronomy. A semantic survey illustrates the diversity: thirteen verbal phrases designate dislocation in these texts; three indicate the divine initiative in causing calamity and displacement within the land (אבד, כילה מעל פני האדמה, נשמד / השמיד); and eight specify expulsion (גרש, הוליך, הדיח [נידח], ניהג, ניסה מעל, נתש מעל אדמתו, הפיץ, השליך).[27] Thematically, these phrases convey the different perspectives on exile as they accord with four stages in the process of dislocation resulting from defeat in war: (a) total calamity within the land; (b) deportation and dispersion; (c) continuing existence in exile; and (d) restoration in the land (see Table 2).

---

25. The passages mentioned refer only to the dislocation of the people of Israel from its land. Hence, references that mention only the positive part of this conditional promise (such as למען תחיה וירשת את הארץ אשר יהוה אלהיך נתן לך, Deut 16:20) are not included here; nor is the poetic reference to the expulsion of the Canaanite peoples in Deut 33:27.

26. Gerhard von Rad, *Deuteronomy* (trans. D. Barton; OTL; London: SCM, 1966), 50–51, 183–84; Jon D. Levenson, "Who Inserted the Book of the Torah?," *HTR* 68 (1975): 203–33; A. D. H. Mayes, "Deuteronomy 4 and the Literary Criticism of Deuteronomy," *JBL* 100 (1981): 23–51; Walter Brueggemann, *Deuteronomy* (AOTC; Nashville: Abingdon, 2001), 17–24.

27. By way of comparison, the Holiness Legislation mentions exile only in Lev 18, 20, and 26, and uses only four verbal phrases: אבד, זרה, נעזב מ, שילח.

Table 2. *Four Perspectives on Exile in Deuteronomy*

Passages in Deut	(a) Calamity within the land	(b) Dispersion	(c) Exile Existence in exile	(d) Restoration in/from exile
4:25–31	+ (25–26)	+ (27–28)	+ (27–28)	+ (29–31)
6:10–15	+			
8:19–20	+			
11:13–21	+			
28:20–26	+			
28:36–37		+	+	
28:63–64		+	+	
29:21–27		+	(+)	
30:1–10				+ gathering and return
30:15–20	+			

(a) *Total calamity within the land.* Five of our target passages describe the loss of the land as the final calamitous punishment of the sinful people (Deut 6:10–15; 8:19–20; 11:13–17; 28:20–26; 30:15–20).[28] No exile, and certainly no prospect of continuing existence outside the land of Canaan, is assumed in the following phrases: כי אבד תאבדון מהר מעל האדמה (6:15); עד השמדך ועד אבדך מהר ... עד כלתו אתך מעל האדמה אשר ... הארץ ... לא תאריכן ימים עליה כי השמד תשמדון והשמידך מעל פני (4:26); עד השמדך ... עד אבדך ... אתה בא שמה לרשתה (28:20–26, 47–57; and see Deut 8:19–20; 11:17; 30:18).

Although usually not the focus of scholarly attention, these phrases constitute an independent perspective on the loss of the land; the writers of these phrases describe that process as dislocation within the land itself and perceive annihilation, not exile, as the final consequence.[29] Lexical as well as thematic arguments establish the independence of this

28. Deut 4:26 adds to this list as well. On the nature of Deut 4:25–31, see below, pp. 209–10.

29. So Peter C. Craigie, *Deuteronomy* (NICOT; Grand Rapids: Eerdmans, 1976), 139 n. 4, 189–90. Compare this point of view with the common understanding of these phrases as mere hyperbole, actually referring to exile. So David Z. Hoffman (*Deuteronomy* [trans. Z. Har-Sheffer; Tel Aviv: Nezach, 1959 (in Hebrew)], 75, 102), and Jeffrey H. Tigay (*Deuteronomy* [JPS Torah Commentary; Philadelphia: Jewish Publication Society, 1996], 52–53, 262). The present discussion avoids this line of interpretation, which seems to harmonize the sources.

perspective. The analogy drawn between Israel and the foreign peoples in Deut 8:19–20 confirms that the term אבד should be understood according to its literal meaning of annihilation (and likewise the other verbal phrases quoted above). Thematically, the catalog of curses in Deut 28 mobilizes two distinct descriptions of defeat in war that lead to the loss of the land.[30] According to the first, defeat is portrayed as either widespread death in the land of Canaan (Deut 28:25–26) or as subjugation to an enemy in the homeland (28:30–34, 47–57). This subjugation causes the loss of the personal and everyday components of economical and social independence (28:30–34, 49–57) and leads to calamity (עד השמידו אתך, in v. 48; or עד השמדך, in vv. 45, 51, 61); these passages make no mention of deportation.[31] A second description of defeat in Deut 28 depicts deportation to foreign and unknown lands as end result (vv. 36–37, 62–68), without describing any other concurrent measures of subjugation in the homeland.[32] It is clear from the distinctiveness of these two descriptions that concept (a) is an independent and self-contained conception designating the loss of the land.

(b) *Deportation and dispersion.* Five passages describe expulsion from the land (Deut 4:27–28; 28:36–37, 63–64; 29:21–27; 30:1–10), using the following phrases: ויתשם יהוה מעל אדמתם (Deut 29:27); וישלכם יולך יהוה אתך ואת מלכך אשר תקים עליך אל גוי (in 29:27); אל ארץ אחרת (in בגוים אשר ינהג יהוה אתכם שמה (in 28:36), אשר לא ידעת אתה ואבתיך בכל הגוים אשר הדיחך (in 28:37); בכל העמים אשר ינהג יהוה שמה (4:27); והפיץ יהוה אתכם בעמים (in 30:1); יהוה אלהיך שמה (in 4:27–28 and in 28:64); מכל העמים אשר הפיצך יהוה שמה (in 30:3). These phrases illustrate

---

30. Hillers (*Treaty Curses*, 32–40) emphasized the compositional character of the list of curses in Deut 28, and the tendency to combine traditional curses together. Hence, the logical progression of defeat–subjugation–exile in Deut 28:25–26, 27–37, and 58–68 illustrates the final editorial/compilational stage of this chapter, shaped by a variety of literary and ideological considerations (so Tigay, *Deuteronomy*, 271, 489–92, 494–97).

31. Compare Deut 20:5–7, as well as the blessings in 28:8, 11; see Craigie, *Deuteronomy*, 345; Tigay, *Deuteronomy*, 267–71.

32. Deut 28:62–68 bring together the two themes of annihilation in the land (להאביד אתכם ולהשמיד אתכם, v. 63a) and exile (והפיצך יהוה בכל העמים, v. 64). ונסחתם מעל האדמה joins the two descriptions, since נסח has both meanings (KBL[3], 702): "tear down," designating destruction (Prov 15:25); and "tear away," within the semantic field of exile, like ויסחך מאהל (Ps 52:7, where חתת and נתץ designate destruction and שרש and נסח expulsion and uprooting; compare its Akkadian equivalent *nasāhu*, *CAD* N II, 3–4). This complex of meanings also appears in Prov 2:21–22, with נסח in parallel to כרת, and in opposition to נותר ב and שכן.

exile using either agricultural language (השליך, נתש) or pastoral images of scattering (הוליך, ניהג, הדיח, הפיץ).[33] As can be gathered from the repeated plurals, בגוים (מקצה הארץ ועד קצה הארץ) בכל העמים (with the exception of 28:36, גוי), exile was presumed to be to a wide range of locations, without specific direction or destination.

(c) *Continuing existence in exile.* These same five passages present a picture of continuity of life in exile (Deut 4:27–28; 28:36–37, 63–68; residence in exile is the background of 29:21–28 and 30:1–10). The first three passages refer to two aspects of life among the peoples. First, exile is the place where the people will worship other gods of wood and stone (4:28; 28:36, 64). Second, the Exiles' lives will be full of distress because of shame, mockery, vulnerability, and fear (28:37, 64–67).[34]

(d) *Restoration.* The prospect of restoration appears in only two units in Deuteronomy (Deut 4:29–31; 30:1–10). Yet, these passages do not portray the restoration in similar ways. Deuteronomy 4:29–31 begins with the people's initiative to renew the connection with God and to repent. This repentance guarantees God's beneficent response in accordance with the forefathers' covenant (ברית אבתיך, v. 31), but there is no mention of ingathering of those afar off and their return to the land of Israel. Deuteronomy 30:1–10, on the other hand, starts and closes with repentance (vv. 1–2, 8, 10), and goes on to give a detailed description of God's deeds in response: the divine deeds include ingathering and resettlement in the land (vv. 3–5), transformation of the heart to assure obedience (v. 6), and following the people's complete submission to God, this passage promises blessings for human proliferation and agricultural prosperity (vv. 7–9).

With the exception of Deut 4:25–31, these ten Deuteronomic passages distinctly differ, offering visions of calamity, exile, and restoration.[35] This distinction, then, intensifies the literary questions concerning the amalgamated and complex nature of Deut 4:25–31.[36] But beyond these

33. The agricultural meaning of נתש ("pull out") is still retained in Jer 24:6; 42:10; 45:4; Ezek 19:12 (KBL[3], 737); השליך ("to throw, dispose of," KBL[3], 1528) has a wider usage, but in reference to plants it appears in Ezek 28:17, and along with נתש in Ezek 19:12.

34. Spiritual distress in exile characterizes Pss 42–43; 137, and others.

35. Deut 28:63–64 presents an example of the fusion of concepts (a), (b) and (c).

36. Opinions differ as to the extent of the exilic intrusion into Deut 4. Possibilities include: vv. 29–31, as argued by George A. Smith, *Deuteronomy* (CBC; Cambridge: Cambridge University Press, 1950), 67–69; vv. 25–31 (or possibly 25–40), suggested by Martin Noth, *The Deuteronomistic History* (trans. and ed. D. J. A. Clines; JSOTSup 15; Sheffield: Sheffield Academic, 1991; 2d ed. 1957), 14. See Mayes,

differences and their possible literary implications, several shared concepts in the four Deuteronomic perceptions of exile should be noted:

Theological significance: Exile is one component of the Deuteronomic
description of the loss of the land; it is a counter-concept to that of the
land as a gift. The loss of the land is the most severe way God punishes
His people for violating His covenant.

Scope: The loss of the land is complete and final. Whether it denotes
uprooting within the land or exile from it, the loss of the land designates
dislocation of all the people. None of the texts mentions a remnant that
will survive in the land of Canaan. According to the above-mentioned
passages in Deuteronomy, the survivors of exile, if any, remain in
foreign lands.

Future prospects: The four Deuteronomic concepts of exile demonstrate two major lines of thought concerning the future of the triangular
God–People–Land relationship. According to perceptions (a), (b), and
(c) the loss of the land designates a terminal break in both the physical
existence of the people and in their relationship with God, with no hope
or expectation of return or religious-national continuation. The people
are either doomed to death within the land (a), or to suffer further physical annihilation in exile (b), which will reduce the people to a scant few;
put them under emotional stress from the surrounding peoples in the new
places of settlement; and end in religious extinction, that is, the worship
of other gods in foreign lands. Dislocation cuts off those exiled from
their religious-national identity as the people of God (c).[37] Only perspective (d) states that out of this ongoing distress there might emerge a
modest hope for restoration of the covenant relationship with God, either
still in exile, or as part of an overall return to the land.

Hence, Deuteronomy presents two clashing visions for the future,
calamity and restoration, which on the face of it indeed reflect a chronological gap in the literary evolution of the book. While references to
uprooting and exile as a final and total punishment could certainly be
preexilic reflections based on the recent experiences of Neo-Assyrian
exiles from the Northern Kingdom and the whole region,[38] prospects for
restoration of the covenant with God in exile (and for the return to the

---

"Deuteronomy 4," 23–51; Moshe Weinfeld, *Deuteronomy 1–11* (AB 4A; New York:
Doubleday, 1991) 216–17; Dennis T. Olson, *Deuteronomy and the Death of Moses:
A Theological Reading* (Minneapolis: Fortress, 1994), 29–37.

37. So Tigay (*Deuteronomy*, 53), who specified the danger as "religious
assimilation."

38. The Neo-Assyrian exile of 701 might also influenced Deuteronomy; see
Stohlmann, "The Judaean Exile," 147–76.

land of Israel) could only denote a (Neo-Babylonian) exilic or even postexilic layer within the book of Deuteronomy (i.e. Deut 4:25–31; 30:1–10; as well as 29:21–27).[39]

(2) *The Deuteronomic Perspectives on Exile/Loss of the Land Utilized in Jeremiah.* Jeremiah appears to know of these four Deuteronomic perspectives on annihilation, exile, and restoration, which he either accepts or refutes. This general statement applies not only to the "authentic" Jeremian prophecies, but also to the redactional Deuteronomistic/Babylonian levels of the book. In addition, the independence of each of these four Deuteronomic perspectives is borne out by the distinctive uses to which they are put in Jeremiah.[40] However, there is a substantial difference between the prophetic book and Deuteronomy in terms of their respective conceptions of exile. While Deuteronomy (in its four perspectives) conceives of annihilation or exile as an encompassing event that includes the people as a whole and omits any mention of a remnant in the land, the book of Jeremiah, in most of its passages, testifies to a different historical reality, in which exile was experienced as a partial event: an event that divided the people in Judah into two communities—Exiles and Those Who Remained in the homeland.[41] This significant distinction establishes clearly the direction of borrowing, as both the Jeremian and the editorial passages elaborate and adapt the Deuteronomic references to exile to suit their individual contexts.[42] The prophetic tradition's acquaintance with these Deuteronomic conceptions of annihilation and exile is recognized in common phraseology, literary allusions, and thematic resemblances.

39. The exilic dating of Deut 29:21–27, based on its exilic perspective on the land of Canaan (הארץ ההיא, vv. 21, 26) and its references to Jeremiah, is widely acknowledged (so Tigay, *Deuteronomy*, 282; and Robert M. Polzin, *Moses and the Deuteronomist: A Literary Study of the Deuteronomic History*. Part One. *Deuteronomy, Joshua, Judges* [New York: Seabury, 1980], 69–71, 72). In addition, this passage illustrates the Exiles' physical and mental separation from and antagonism toward the land and the People Who Remained there (this may be seen in the use of the third person plural in the verbal forms and suffixes in vv. 24–27). Nevertheless, in contrast to Deut 30:1–10, this passage does not project restoration.

40. Mayes ("Deuteronomy 4," 50–51) had used this path in his presentation of the exilic layer in Deuteronomy. Yet Mayes did not discuss the differences within the book concerning the concepts of exile.

41. On the notion of partial exile, see the discussion and references in the Preface, pp. xiv–xvi.

42. This direction of borrowing was recently proposed also by Georg Fischer, "Fulfillment and Reversal: The Curses of Deuteronomy 28 as a Foil for the Book of Jeremiah," *Semitica et Classica* 5 (2012): 43–49.

Common phraseology. More than all other prophetic books of the eighth and seventh or sixth and fifth centuries B.C.E., the book of Jeremiah holds the record for the variety of *verbal phrases* used to denote exile. Jeremiah uses eleven verbs, five of which are also found in Deuteronomy: אבד (Jer 27:10, 15) designates calamity; השליך (Jer 7:15; 22:28) suggests dislocation in an image taken from agriculture; הוליך (Jer 52:26, and 32:5), הדיח (and נידח, 27:10, 15, etc.), and הפיץ (as in Jer 9:15; as also פזר, Jer 50:17) are pastoral images. In addition, Jeremiah uses verbs that do not occur in Deuteronomy: זרה, which is taken from agricultural imagery (see Lev 26:33; in reference to exile זרה is used in Jer 15:7; 31:10; 49:32, 36; 51:2), as well as verbs taken from the political realm—namely, גלה (Jer 20:4 and elsewhere),[43] הטיל (Jer 16:13; 22:26, 28), ריחק (Jer 27:10), and שילח (Jer 24:5; 29:20).[44]

Literary allusions and thematic resemblances. Poetic and prose prophecies in Jeremiah utilize all the above mentioned Deuteronomic conceptions of exile.[45]

(a) *Total calamity within the land.* **Jeremiah 27:9–15** is one of almost two dozen prophetic units in Jeremiah which describe death and destruction as the final and conclusive judgment upon Jerusalem, with no dispersion in view.[46] The danger Jeremiah sees in the false prophecy,

43. Hans J. Zobel, "גלה," *TDOT* 2:476–88.

44. Ezekiel uses six of the same verbs, three from Deuteronomy—הוליך (Ezek 36:12); הדיח (Ezek 4:13); הפיץ (as in Ezek 11:16, etc.)—and three which are not Deuteronomic: גלה (Ezek 39:18); זרה (as in Ezek 5:2, 10, 11, etc.); ריחק (Ezek 11:16). Within prophecies of the eighth–seventh centuries, גלה occurs most prominently in Amos, referring usually to political-human measures (as in 1:5, 8, etc.), and once to God as the agent of exile (5:27). גלה occurs also in Isaiah (e.g. 5:13); as well as in the Twelve: in Hosea (10:5) and Micah (1:16). Other verbs occur in Isaiah: זרה (30:24); נידח (in 11:12; 16:4); and ריחק (in 6:12; 26:15); and elsewhere in the Twelve: עקר, גרש (Zeph 2:4); נידח (Joel 2:20; Mic 4:6; Nah 1:9; Zeph 3:19); הפיץ (Nah 1:8). In Persian-period prophecy, Deutero-Isaiah uses גלה (Isa 49:21), זרה (41:16), נידח (56:8), שילח (45:13; 50:1); and Zech 1–8 uses זרה (Zech 2:2, 4 [×2]).

45. Many of the following prose passages were considered editorial (non-Jeremian) because of their resemblances to Deuteronomy. This well-known scholarly position may be seen in the commentaries. In this context I call attention to the exegetical techniques utilized in these prophecies as definite markers of the allusive-interpretive status of these passages in relation to Deuteronomy. Therefore, unless otherwise specified, the following passages join other prose and poetic examples throughout the book of Jeremiah, which there is no need (or good reason) to classify as editorial. See Dalit Rom-Shiloni, "Actualization of Pentateuchal Legal Traditions in Jeremiah: More on the Riddle of Authorship," *ZABR* 15 (2009): 254–81.

46. A variety of verbs with God as subject illustrates the widespread calamity: איבד, החרים, כילה, הכרית, השבית, שיחת, שיכל, התם (Jer 5:12–14; 7:16–20, 30–34; 9:9–10; 11:15–17; 13:12–14; 14:10–12, 15–16; 16:1–9; 21:3–7; 36:29); similarly,

לא תעבדו את מלך בבל ("do not serve the king of Babylon," 27:9, 14), is that it will bring calamity upon Judah. Rebelling against the Babylonians means rebelling against God, and it is God who will punish the disobedient vassals of Babylon (v. 8). God's judgment will include uprooting the people from the land, which in Jeremiah's prophecy implies annihilation:

> כי שקר הם נבאים לכם למען הרחיק אתכם מעל אדמתכם והדחתי אתכם
> **ואבדתם**...
> כי לא שלחתים נאם יהוה והם נבאים בשמי לשקר למען הדיחי אתכם **ואבדתם**
> אתם והנבאים הנבאים לכם

> For they prophesy falsely to you—with the result that you shall be
> banished from your land; I will drive you out **and you shall perish**...
> I have not sent them—declares the LORD—and they prophesy falsely in
> My name, with the result that I will drive you out **and you shall perish**,
> together with the prophets who prophesy to you. (Jer 29:10, 15)

The verb אבד appears here in the sense of "to perish," as in the Deuteronomic passages of perspective (a), where it refers to the loss of the land (Deut 4:26; 8:19; 11:17; 28:20–26; 30:18).[47] This meaning reinforces Jeremiah's presentation of the opposition between two ideas. On the one hand, continuous existence in the land depends directly on subjugation to Babylon:

> והגוי אשר יביא את צוארו בעל מלך בבל ועבדו והנחתיו על אדמתו נאם יהוה
> ועבדה וישב בה

> But the nation that puts its neck under the yoke of the king of Babylon,
> and serves him, will be left by Me on its own soil—declares the LORD—
> to till it and dwell on it. (Jer 27:11)

On the other hand, rebellion against Babylon will bring neither exile nor dispersion, but rather death in the land:

there are a number of prophecies where the catastrophe is brought about by human enemies within the land, and exile is not mentioned at all (Jer 5:10–11, 15–17; 6:1–5, 6–8; 8:16–17; 12:7–13; 16:16–18; 21:8–10; 34:20–22; 37:3–10).

47. The verb אבד in this sense occurs in Jer 6:21; 12:17; 15:7; metaphorically in Jer 4:9; and in prophecies against the nations (10:15 and 46:8; 51:18, 55; in the Hiphil, Jer 25:10; 49:38); note the parallelism of אבד/נכרת (Jer 7:28). Within the semantic field of physical destruction, אבד in Jeremiah designates the ecological catastrophe of the land; see Jer 9:11 (and compare with destruction of cultic places in Deut 12:2; 2 Kgs 19:18; Isa 37:19). Compare to Lev 26:38, ואבדתם בגוים ואכלה אתכם ארץ איביכם ("but [you] shall perish among the nations; and the land of your enemies shall consume you"), which draws on the other meaning of אבד ("be lost," "wander"); see Milgrom, *Leviticus 23–27*, 2273, 2326. Other occurrences of this latter meaning are Deut 22:3; 26:5; Jer 23:1; 50:6; Ezek 34:4, 16; and Deut 32:28; Jer 18:18; Ezek 7:26.

הביאו את צואריכם בעל מלך בבל: ועבדו אתו ועמו וחיו למה תמותו אתה ועמך
בחרב ברעב ובדבר כאשר דבר יהוה אל הגוי אשר לא יעבד את מלך בבל

Put your necks under the yoke of the king of Babylon; serve him and his
people, and live! Otherwise you will die together with your people, by
sword, famine, and pestilence. (Jer 27:12–13)

Jeremiah interprets political realities in light of the theological concept
of loss of the land as a divine punishment. He prophesies to Zedekiah
and to the people an irrevocable and final death penalty, and in so doing,
he adapts Deuteronomic perception (a) to suit his historical situation.
However, Jeremiah deviates from Deuteronomy by not mentioning the
religious-cultic sins that repeatedly exemplify the people's disobedience
in Deuteronomy (Deut 6:12–15). By positing rebellion against Babylon
as disobedience to God, Jeremiah expands the concepts of obedience
and disobedience beyond the Deuteronomic perspective. In Jer 27, transgression and disloyalty result from the refusal to accept the central
theological tenet of God as Lord of History (27:4–8), for which Jeremiah
considers calamity and loss of the land a suitable punishment.[48]

   (b) *Deportation and dispersion.* Without mention of specific destina-
tions or of any future existence as a people in exile, the use of deportation
and dispersion languages characterizes several prophecies of doom in
Jeremiah.[49] **Jeremiah 9:11–15** for instance, goes even further in describing dispersion as a complement to calamity:

לכן כה אמר יהוה צבאות אלהי ישראל הנני מאכילם את העם הזה לענה
והשקיתים מי ראש: **והפיצותים בגוים אשר לא ידעו המה ואבותם** ושלחתי
אחריהם את החרב עד כלותי אותם:

Assuredly, thus said the LORD of Hosts, the God of Israel: I am going to
feed that people wormwood and make them drink a bitter draft. **I will
scatter them among nations which they and their fathers never knew**;
and I will dispatch the sword after them until I have consumed them.
(Jer 9:14–15)

Jeremiah 9:15 alludes to Deut 28:36: יולך יהוה אתך אל גוי אשר לא ידעת
אתה ואבתיך ("The LORD will drive you, and the king you have set over

---

48. Weinfeld ("Inheritance of the Land," 124–26) listed moral and social misconduct (Jer 7:5–15), as well as failure to keep the Sabbath (17:21–27), as the specific sins that Jeremiah considers to be reasons for the loss of the land in addition to
the general transgression of the covenant. I suggest that the failure to acknowledge
God as Lord of History should be added to this list of conceptual and specific sins.
49. In this category are prophecies in which God is the agent of destruction (Jer
7:1–15; 9:11–15; 10:19–21; 15:1–4, 5–9), and in which human enemies direct the
catastrophe (Jer 18:13–17).

you, to a nation unknown to you or your fathers").[50] Hence, Jeremiah extends the descriptions of Deut 28:36–37, 63–64, and 29:21–27 regarding the fate of those exiled, which is only vaguely referred to in Deuteronomic concept (b). Jeremiah explicitly describes God's efforts to finish the calamitous measures taken against the people, who are doomed to slaughter among the nations ושלחתי אחריהם את החרב עד כלותי אותם ("and I will dispatch the sword after them until I have consumed them").

Another clear allusion to this Deuteronomic perception—exile as death on foreign and unknown land, without possibility of return—characterizes Jeremiah's repetitive prophecy to Jehoiachin, **Jer 22:24–30**:[51]

והטלתי אתך ואת אמך אשר ילדתך **על הארץ אחרת אשר לא ילדתם שם** ושם תמותו ועל הארץ אשר הם מנשאים את נפשם לשוב שם שמה לא ישובו

I will hurl you and the mother who bore you **into another land, where you were not born**; there you shall both die. (Jer 22:26)

העצב נבזה נפוץ האיש הזה כניהו אם כלי אין חפץ בו מדוע הוטלו הוא וזרעו **והשלכו על הארץ אשר לא ידעו**

Is this man Coniah a wretched broken pot, a vessel no one wants? Why are he and his offspring hurled out, and cast away **in a land they knew not**? (Jer 22:28)

(c) *Existence in exile.* In two prophecies, **Jer 16:10–13** and **5:19**, which are similarly built in a question and answer pattern, Jeremiah offers an interpretation of Deut 28:36 and 64. In a manner unparalleled in Deuteronomy (though it may be inferred), Jeremiah presents a full correlation between sin and punishment (מידה כנגד מידה) in his reply to the people's wondering about the reasons for their distress:

ואמרת אליהם על אשר עזבו אבותיכם אותי נאם יהוה וילכו אחרי אלהים אחרים ויעבדום וישתחוו להם ואתי עזבו ואת תורתי לא שמרו

say to them, "Because your fathers deserted Me—declares the LORD—and followed other gods and served them and worshiped them; they deserted Me and did not keep My instruction. (Jer 16:11)

---

50. Less direct is the echo of Deut 28:64, אלהים אחרים אשר לא ידעת אתה ואבתיך עץ ואבן, in Jer 9:15. עם אשר לא ידעת appears in Deut 28:33 regarding an enemy that subjugates the people in their homeland. The unknown character of the enemy is further elaborated in 28:49–50.

51. For a discussion of the imagery in כלי אין חפץ בו and העצב נבזה נפוץ, see Moshe Held, "Rhetorical Questions in Ugaritic and Biblical Hebrew," *ErIs* 9 (1969): 71*–79*.

והטלתי אתכם מעל הארץ הזאת על הארץ אשר לא ידעתם אתם ואבותיכם
ועבדתם שם את אלהים אחרים יומם ולילה אשר לא אתן לכם חנינה

**Therefore I will hurl you out of this land to a land that neither you
nor your fathers have known, and there you will serve other gods,**
day and night; for I will show you no mercy. (Jer 16:13)

The same line of thought appears in Jer 5:19:[52]

והיה כי תאמרו תחת מה עשה יהוה אלהינו לנו את כל אלה ואמרת אליהם
כאשר עזבתם אותי ותעבדו אלהי נכר בארצכם כן **תעבדו זרים בארץ לא לכם**

And when they ask, "Because of what did the LORD our God do all these
things?" you shall answer them, "Because you forsook Me and served
alien gods on your own land, **you will have to serve foreigners in a land
not your own.**"

In this paraphrastic way, Jeremiah maintains the concept of exile as
calamity. Explained from the national-religious point of view, Jeremiah
illustrates the Deuteronomic perception in a logical equation, thus YHWH
is to the Land of Israel as the foreign gods are to foreign lands:

Yahweh : Land of Israel = Foreign gods : Foreign lands

Worshipping foreign gods in God's land will cause God to expel His
people to an unknown land where worshipping other gods is expected
(5:19; 16:13). The literal and thematic connections between Jer 16:13
and Deut 28:36, 64 are clear: הארץ אשר לא ידעתם אתם ואבותיכם (Jer
16:13) alludes to אל גוי אשר לא ידעת אתה ואבתיך (Deut 28:36); and
ועבדתם שם את אלהים אחרים (Jer 16:13) repeats ועבדת שם אלהים אחרים עץ
ואבן (Deut 28:36, 64). Hence, exile designates a clear break between God
and the Exiles, with no prospect of restoration, אשר לא אתן לכם חנינה
("for I will show you no mercy," Jer 16:13).[53]

The two prophecies in 5:19 and 16:13 share another feature, which is
their failure to mention any warlike measures preceding the described
exile. This gives rise to two different assumptions concerning the dating
of these prophecies, namely, that they may be linked either to the period
between the Jehoiachin exile and the Destruction (597–586 B.C.E.),[54] or

---

52. The words אלהי נכר and עבד זרים are two unique phrases, brought together in
Deut 32:12, 16; Ps 81:10; see also Jer 2:25. Cf. William Holladay, "Jeremiah and
Moses: Further Observations," *JBL* 85 (1966): 17–27, especially 20–21.

53. The word חנינה is a *hapax legomenon* translated as "compassion," "mercy."
The LXX reads the verb in the plural (יתנו) suggesting that the foreign gods are the
subject (see Robert P. Carroll, *Jeremiah* [OTL; Philadelphia: Westminster, 1986],
342–44).

54. Holladay (*Jeremiah 1* [Hermeneia; Philadelphia: Fortress, 1986], 474–75,
and 190–91 for 5:19) bases his assessment of the Jeremianic authenticity of these

to that of the Babylonian exile (after 586 B.C.E.), because the existence of the nation is no longer presumed.[55]

I am inclined to accept the first suggestion. Thus I see in Jeremiah's words a special emphasis on the calamity awaiting the Jehoiachin Exiles (in accordance with Jer 22:24–30). This observation, then, may represent one of Jeremiah's major contributions to the conception of exile. The prophet reaffirms the traditional Deuteronomic concept in the context of his theological explanation, and applies it against the Jehoiachin Exiles in the period prior to the Destruction.

(d) *Restoration in exile or from exile*. Restoration appears in Jeremiah only in (later) prophecies that present exilic perspectives; as for instance, in **Jer 16:14–15**:[56]

לכן הנה ימים באים נאם יהוה ולא יאמר עוד חי יהוה אשר העלה את בני ישראל
מארץ מצרים: כי אם חי יהוה אשר העלה את בני ישראל מארץ צפון ומכל
הארצות אשר הדיחם שמה והשבתים על אדמתם אשר נתתי לאבותם:

Assuredly, a time is coming—declares the LORD—when it shall no more
be said, "as the LORD lives who brought the Israelites out of the land of
Egypt," but rather, "as the LORD lives who brought the Israelites out of
the northland, and out of all the lands to which He had banished them."
For I will bring them back to their land, which I gave to their fathers.

This prophecy of consolation interrupts a succession of prophecies of doom, and reoccurs with slight variations in Jer 23:7–8. Literary intrusion is but one argument for identifying the prophecy as not Jeremian. Although Jer 16:14–15 does not explicitly allude to the Deuteronomic conception (d) (see pp. 210, 212, above), it clearly parallels exilic perspectives and phraseology.[57] The projected restoration emphasizes two components: ingathering from a northern land and from all the other lands of expulsion, and reestablishment in the land given to the forefathers. Furthermore, salvation is portrayed as an even greater event than

---

prophecies on (1) the unique use of the verb הטיל in the phrase הטיל את על הארץ אחרת, which is similar to Jeremiah's prophecy against Jehoiachin (22:24, 28; compare Ezek 32:4, where טול serves to describe the judgment without involving dispersion); (2) the attitude to foreign gods (as in Jer 2:28); and (3) the admonition to the present generation (Jer 7:26). Thus, he dated the prophecy to 598 B.C.E.

55. So William McKane, *Jeremiah 1–25* (ICC; Edinburgh: T. & T. Clark, 1986), 371–72.

56. Exilic perspectives characterize passages that were mentioned above, n. 35.

57. Deuteronomistic sources present the phrase (יהוה) השיב (את העם) אל האדמה אשר נתן לאבתם in 1 Kgs 8:34; and as a threat of dislocation in 1 Kgs 21:8. In Jer 24:10, the reference to the land (האדמה) given to them and to their forefathers designates the calamity expected for Those Who Remained.

the Exodus. While the Exodus in Jeremiah appears only as part of the historical retrospective on the God–people relationship,[58] the analogy to a future second Exodus from the north as a central component of consolation parallels the message of the exilic prophets, Ezekiel (20:32–38), and, with greater emphasis, Deutero-Isaiah (as in Isa 48:20–21; 52:11–12).[59] Jeremiah 16:14–15 appears as a corrective to Jer 16:10–13. It may be part of a contribution added to the book by exilic Deuteronomistic redactors (like Jer 24; 29:16–20), or even by non-Deuteronomistic authors from among the Exiles (like Jer 32:36–41).[60]

Thus, the book of Jeremiah presents all four Deuteronomic perceptions on loss of land and exile. The diverse attitudes to the loss of the land in Jeremiah add an ideological argument to the distinction between literary layers in this book. By adding (1) the biographical data regarding the prophet; to (2) Jeremiah's prophecies against Jehoiachin and the Jehoiachin Exiles (Jer 5:19; 16:10–13; 22:24–30); and (3) persistence of the idea that settlement in the land should be maintained by the People Who Remained in Jerusalem under Zedekiah before the Destruction (27:9–15) as well as in its aftermath (40–43), we can now supplement Jeremiah's pro-land/pro-Judah ideology with (4) his overall conception of exile.

Jeremiah uses the Deuteronomic concepts (a), (b), and (c) to promote a pro-Judah perspective; therefore, as he proclaims that exile means death and calamity. This is a constant ideology to which Jeremiah subscribes both before and after the Destruction—the Judeans should insist on staying in the land. Leaving the land of Judah would bring annihilation, as he prophesies to Shallum and to Jehoiachin (Jer 22:10–12, 24–30), to Zedekiah (27; 37:19–23), and later to "the Remnant of Judah" leaving for Egypt (Jer 42:13–17).[61] This ideology illustrates an exclusive

58. The phrase העלה מארץ מצרים occurs in Jer 2:6; 11:7.

59. The second Exodus is usually considered a central motif in Deutero-Isaiah. Cf. Westermann, *Isaiah 40–66*, 21–22; Yair Hoffman, *The Doctrine of the Exodus in the Bible* (Tel Aviv: Tel Aviv University Press, 1983), 60–66 (in Hebrew).

60. Cf. Holladay, *Jeremiah 1*, 474, 621–23; Carroll, *Jeremiah*, 344–45. The exilic contribution to the concept of restoration, with clear connections to Ezekiel and to Deutero-Isaiah, may further be seen in Jer 32:36–41; see Dalit Rom-Shiloni, "The Prophecy for 'Everlasting Covenant' (Jeremiah 32:36–41): An Exilic Addition or a Deuteronomistic Redaction?," *VT* 53 (2003): 201–23.

61. Jer 29:1–7, Jeremiah's letter to the Jehoiachin Exiles, implicitly reverses Deut 4:25–28, as presented by Adele Berlin, "Jeremiah 29:5–7: A Deuteronomic Allusion," *Hebrew Annual Review* 8 (1984): 3–11. The prophet inverts the threat ונשארתם מתי מספר בגוים, and encourages the Exiles to settle down, and to multiply: ורבו שם ואל תמעטו (Jer 29:6). Yet Jeremiah does not prophesy to the Exiles restoration and return to the homeland. Hence, although Jer 29:1–7 deviates from the

land-bound tendency, similar to the short quotations of Those Who Remained in Ezekiel (11:14; 33:24). The strength of Jeremiah's ideology is his reliance on Deuteronomic land and exile conceptions, which give his prophecies extra forces of legitimization through the arguments of exclusivity, and in particular the arguments of *continuity* and *annexation* of legal-conceptual traditions adapted for the current circumstances

In contrast, the restoration passage, Jer 16:14–15, which thematically parallels the exilic Deuteronomic concept (d), seems to be a later non-Jeremian "correction" or adaptation. In accordance with Ezekiel, this exilic strand in the book of Jeremiah suggests that hope for restoration rests with the Jehoiachin Exiles (as clearly, for example, in Jer 24:5–7; 29:10–14).

The entire polemic between the Judean communities of the sixth century B.C.E. may thus be recognized in the book of Jeremiah through the prism of the utilizations of these conceptions of land and exile. In his adaptation of these Deuteronomic conceptions, Jeremiah (and possibly his Judah tradents) may not only be counted as one of Those Who Remained under Zedekiah in Jerusalem prior to its fall, but should be considered the theological and ideological advocate of this community of Judeans in the land. Jeremiah thus serves in a similar position to that of Ezekiel among the Jehoiachin Exiles; that is, Jeremiah may be among the constructors of the Remainees' group identity under the new circumstances of their ongoing Judean existence in the land. Judgment prophecies in Jeremiah put forth the notion that exile means calamity; thus, Those Who Remained are the sole survivors of the people of God, by the virtue of their continuous residence in His land.

Jeremiah's own awareness of his pivotal role in strengthening the exclusive status of Those Who Remained may be further illustrated in the prophecies of consolation addressed to the people in Jerusalem, in the symbolic act and prophecy on the occasion of redeeming or actually purchasing the field in Anathoth (Jer 32:6–15), and mainly in Jeremiah's prophecy to "the Remnant of Judah" before their descent to Egypt (Jer 42:7–17; and chs. 40–44). And yet, these passages are but small part of the complicated and highly ideological prophecies of consolation in the book of Jeremiah, which bring the two sides of the divide into close proximity.

previous prophecies of annihilation suggested above, it does not conform to the exilic passages in Jeremiah (Jer 29:10–14, etc.), which prophesy restoration of the relationship with God and return to the land, under the clear influence of Deut 4:29–31 and 30:1–10. For the authenticity, i.e., the connections of this passage with the earlier and Judean context of vv. 3–7, see Carroll, *Jeremiah*, 555–56.

2. *Prophecies of Consolation in Judean and Babylonian Contexts:*
Jeremianic Prophecies, Secondary Layers, and Transforming Perspectives

Prophecies of consolation in Jeremiah appear in several units of the book (Jer 3:14–17, 18; 16:14–15; 23:7–8; ch. 24; chs. 30–33; and passages within chs. 50–51; in addition, 29:16–20, chs. 40–44 are also discussed). Some may be assumed to be Jeremian in origin, or at least Judean in their geographical location and Neo-Babylonian in their dating; the others must have been the product of the prophet's Babylonian followers and editors of the book. Among the latter are prophecies that may be addressed to the community of Babylonian Repatriates in Yehud. Thus, they reflect Babylonian exilic ideologies that may be dated to the Neo-Babylonian and even to the early Persian period.

These prophecies have attracted a great deal of scholarly attention. Textual, linguistic, literary, thematic, historical, redactional, and comparative criteria have been employed to distinguish strands within those prophecies. The major distinction has been between early prophecies, which are said to be among the earliest in Jeremiah's career, and (later) prophetic passages that resemble Ezekiel, Deutero-Isaiah, even Nehemiah, in style and themes. The two (or even more) prophetic strands were placed side by side by the redactors of Jeremiah.

In addition to the standard methods, I propose to examine these prophecies utilizing sociological categories of group-identity analysis, differentiating between in-group and out-group perspectives, looking at exclusivistic strategies and arguments. This avenue of study shows that group-identity markers are indeed major components in the prophecies of consolation within Jeremiah. Each of the prophetic passages of consolation independently utilizes elements which contribute to building self-identities and/or counter-identities, that is, designations, arguments, and strategies which create a framework of exclusivity.

Hence, the complicated picture within the book of Jeremiah validates my assumption that making claims about identity was not an innovation of the Persian period. On the contrary, the book of Jeremiah is unique within biblical literature in its attestation to the existence of antagonistic identity claims throughout the sixth century. The claims of Those Who Remained in the land after the Jehoiachin exile and following the Destruction may be overtly heard, as well as implicitly discerned, side by side with the claims of various exilic groups in Babylon, and the even later assertions of Babylonian Repatriates back in Yehud.

Moreover, the book of Jeremiah's attestations to this early exilic period (597–586 B.C.E., and on) is actually the only evidence of explicit confrontations between the two communities. Yet much more common in the book are re-identifications of the in-group within each of the communities.

The following discussion thus differentiates the prophecies of consolation in Jeremiah into those that are pro-Judah (in two distinct contexts within the prophet's activity) and those that are pro-*golah* (in three different Babylonian-exilic strands). While the pro-Judah passages seem to be genuinely Jeremian (or to come from his tradents) within Judah, the Babylonian exilic passages parallel Ezekiel, Deutero-Isaiah, and Nehemiah. Thus, they seem to belong to the secondary editorial Babylonian strands of Jeremiah.

a. *Pro-Judean Prophecies of Consolation: Inclusive Constructions of the In-group*
Pro-Judahite prophecies of consolation stem from two different periods within the prophet's activity. First, early in his career Jeremiah prophesied to Northern Israel, encouraging them to join Judah (incorporate into Zion). To the later period belong his prophecies to the Remnant of Jerusalem/Judah, which were delivered initially after the Jehoiachin Exile (597 B.C.E.), and then again and with even greater force after the Destruction (586 B.C.E.).

(1) *Incorporating the Northern Kingdom within Zion.* The Book of Consolation (Jer 30–31) contains several prophetic passages that address the former Northern Kingdom of Israel: **Jer 30:5–9, 10–11; 31:2–6, 7–9, 10–14, 15–22**.

Jeremiah 30:5–9 is directed toward the remnant left in the land in the aftermath of the Assyrian conquest of Samaria. Jeremiah 31:2–6 uses the designations "Jacob"/"Israel" (30:7; 31:2), and do not mention a change in the geographical residence of those so designated. Rather, the passage describes an agricultural restoration of the land (31:4–5). These passages, furthermore, call *betulat Israel* "to go up to Zion" (31:6), where they will serve "David their King," now restored to his kingdom (30:9). The other prophecies (30:10–11; 31:7–9, 10–14, 15–22) refer to Jacob/Israel, Ephraim, or *betulat Israel*, as living in exile. They are joyfully called to return to "here" (הנה, in 31:7–8); either back to the land (30:10–11; 31:7–9, 10–14, 15–22), or specifically to Zion (31:10–14). God will reinstitute the close relationship of fatherhood with Ephraim,

His firstborn (31:9), transform their grief into joy (31:12–13), and resettle them in their land (30:10, including their cities, 31:21). The people, on their part, will acknowledge their sins (31:18–19), and enjoy God's "full bounty" (31:14).[62]

One remarkable characteristic of these prophecies is their social/national viewpoint. The prophecies envision the return of Jacob, Israel, Ephraim, from "the northland" (31:8) to the land; to the hills of Samaria (31:5); to Zion; to David as King; to Yahweh as God. It is significant that this vision of unity is presented without using the national name of the Southern Kingdom. "Judah" (as a matter of course) occurs throughout the book of Jeremiah to designate the kings of Judah (54 times in the singular, and 10 in the plural), the people (called simply יהודה, in 2:28; or by the phrase איש יהודה, which occurs 11 times, as in 3:3–4; similarly בית יהודה, in 11:10, etc.), and the cities of Judah (22 times, as in 1:15; 9:10). In all these occurrences "Judah" refers to the kingdom and/or its people. It is thus remarkable that "Judah" does not appear as the incorporating community within the above-mentioned passages of consolation, which designate only the land, Zion, David, and God as the targets of return. These passages portray a restoration limited to agricultural rural life, evidently not as a political revival of the Northern Kingdom of Israel, nor as a confederation of the two Kingdoms. Rather, this former Northern community, designated by its ancient premonarchic ancestors (Jacob, Ephraim, Rachel), is to incorporate back into the community that presently *is* the people of God, and thus once again be considered "my people" (עמי, 31:14).

As presented earlier, *incorporation* (A + B = A) is a sociological strategy suggested by a community which considers itself dominant. While it is certainly an inclusive strategy, it maintains a clear hierarchal relationship between itself and its subordinate communities, and demands full acceptance of its own theology, worship, and political institutions— in this case, those of the dominant community of Judah.[63] Hence, these prophecies seem indeed to reflect a preexilic era, when Judah was at its full political strength, possibly during Josiah's reign.[64]

62. This difference between location in Judah and location in exile in the prophecies directed to Northern Israel seems to be a criterion by which to divide the passage into 30:5–9, 10–11. Compare to Bob Becking, *Between Fear and Freedom: Essays on the Interpretation of Jeremiah 30–31* (Leiden: Brill, 2004), 135–64.

63. On *incorporation* as an inclusive assimilatory strategy, see Horowitz, "Ethnic Identity," 110–40.

64. Marvin Sweeney, "Jeremiah 30–31 and King Josiah's Program of National Restoration and Religious Reform," *ZAW* 108 (1996): 569–83. The above mentioned annotations cause me to accept only partially Sweeney's observations on this earlier

(2) *In-group Exclusive Conceptions of Those Who Remained.* The prophecies to Those Who Remained in Jerusalem after the Jehoiachin exile (597 B.C.E.) and after the final Destruction of Jerusalem (586 and following), reveal Jeremiah's deep awareness of this issue of group-identity, and his genuine contribution to the reshaping of Judean identity under circumstances of crisis.

(a) *Redemption and Possession of the Field in Anathoth (**Jeremiah 32:6–15**)*. This family story, initially autobiographical in nature, tells how Jeremiah is called to purchase his uncle's (or cousin's) field in Anathoth. But as it develops, the story turns into a symbolic deed that gains national significance and divine authorship: ואדע כי דבר יהוה הוא ("then I knew that it was indeed the word of the LORD," v. 8, and v. 15). Five points deserve discussion.

(i) *Time and place.* If the opening verses of ch. 32 (vv. 1–5) may serve as the historical context, this story takes place in the summer of 587 B.C.E., and the places are Jerusalem and Anathoth.[65] Throughout this passage (vv. 6–15) there is not a single mention of exile, or of a Babylonian arena and audience.[66]

(ii) *The relationship between Jeremiah 32:6–15 and the law of redemption in Lev 25:25–34:* Jeremiah is asked to redeem his uncle's(/cousin's) field, a request that at face value works in accordance with the Holiness Code's law of redemption (Lev 25:25–28) and with the story of Ruth (3:9–13; 4:1–12). Yet, in contradistinction to both these sources, the story leaves vague the familial, economic circumstances leading to the transaction. The only clear point is that Hanam'el and Jeremiah both share the understanding that Jeremiah is the *go'el* (vv. 7–8, 9).[67]

---

strand of Jer 30–31. I do agree with his suggestion that the Judean initiative should be linked to Josiah (580–83).

65. So Lisbeth S. Fried and David N. Freedman brought in Milgrom, *Leviticus 23–27*, 2257–62; Lundbom, *Jeremiah 21–36*, 524. Compare to John Bright (*Jeremiah* [AB 21: Garden City, N.Y., 1965], 238–39) and Holladay (*Jeremiah 2*, 211) who suggested 588 B.C.E.; and compare to the ahistoric interpretation suggested by Carroll, *Jeremiah*, 621–22.

66. Compare to Leuchter (*The Polemics of Exile in Jeremiah 26–45*, 60–65), who considered this passage to have been supplemented by the exilic author of chs. 26–52 to raise hope in the endurance of the covenant relationship between God and the post-587 Exiles, and prospects for their redemption.

67. Fried and Freedman's hypothetical reconstruction should be rejected (see in Milgrom, *Leviticus 23–27*, 2257–62; Milgrom himself expressed a different position on pp. 2195–96). On *go'el* as a theological term, see Robert L. Hubbard, "The *go'el* in Ancient Israel: Theological Reflections on an Israelite Institution," *BBR* 1 (1991): 3–19.

Moreover, a more detailed comparison shows that Lev 25:25–34 discusses six different legal cases of land redemption, yet none of them parallels the case of Hanam'el and Jeremiah; and in fact they differ in two significant aspects.[68] First, according to Lev 25:25, the redeemer is called to action only after the land had been sold to another (a stranger): כי ימוך אחיך ומכר מאחזתו ובא גאלו הקרב אליו וגאל את ממכר אחיו ("If your kinsman is in straits and has to sell part of his holding, his nearest redeemer shall come and redeem what his kinsman has sold").[69] However, according to Jer 32:7–8, when Hanam'el approached Jeremiah, he had not yet sold his field to a third party outside the family.[70] Hanam'el suggests to Jeremiah a preventative measure meant to *guarantee* that the land not be sold to an outside owner, that is, a case not mentioned in Lev 25:25–34.[71]

Second, there is the legal status of the redeemer with regard the land, and Jeremiah's purchase of it. According to the law, the redeemer holds the land only temporarily, until the land returns to its first owner on the Jubilee year (Lev 25:28, 31, 35–38). Milgrom has pointed out an important difference between these passages in the usage of קנה. He suggested that the lack of the verb in the Leviticus context, and the emphasis on it in Jer 32 (and in Ruth 4:1–10), imply that in the case of Hanam'el and Jeremiah "the redeemer possesses the land for himself. And unless the original owner or his heirs exercise their rights of redemption and repurchase the property, it remains with the redeemer for perpetuity."[72] Furthermore, Milgrom added, "Since Jeremiah is the

68. Lev 25:25–34 suggest six different cases in which redemption is possible: (1) when there is a redeemer in the family, the closest relative is obliged to redeem the sold property (v. 25); (2) if there is no redeemer, (a) the first owner may redeem the field himself (vv. 26–27); (b) if he does not have the resources to re-buy the land, the property will remain with the new owner till the Jubilee (v. 28) and then revert to the first; (3) a house within a walled city may be redeemed within one year (v. 29); (4) if the house within a walled city is not redeemed within the first year, it will remain permanently in the hands of the buyer (v. 30); (5) rural houses (outside of walled towns), are treated like fields (v. 31); (6) Levite cities and houses have special status (vv. 32–34).

69. Milgrom (*Leviticus 23–27*, 2191) reconstructed three possible scenarios that this law might address, and argued that the redeemer is obliged to act only if the land is sold to a foreigner (*ger*, according to Lev 25:35–38). Under these circumstances, the first owner is to work as שכיר with the redeemer until the Jubilee, when he will retrieve his land.

70. Lundbom (*Jeremiah 21–36*, 505) conjectured that Hanam'el "has become poor"; this, however, has no explicit basis in the text.

71. See Milgrom, *Leviticus 23–27*, 2193–204.

72. Milgrom, *Leviticus 23–27*, 2195.

redeemer, Hanam'el or his heirs have lost their rights of redemption."[73] Hence, the purchase is a permanent one—a contract was written, signed, and sealed in jars, "so that they may last a long time" (Jer 32:14), commemorating continuous and eternal ownership of properties in the land.

These differences demonstrate that the relationship between Jer 32:6–15 and Lev 25:25–34 is not that of direct literary dependence. Jeremiah 32:6–15, just like Ruth, tells of the practical procedure of land redemption, and thus focus on aspects that are not made explicit in the setting forth of the legal principle in its precedent casuistic nature. The two passages are, however, thematically connected, as they focus on the importance of land redemption by a member within the family.

This specific comparison is nevertheless worthwhile, if only to illustrate the full importance of this symbolic act. One crucial point joins these three passages on redemption—the notion of the continuous possession of the family land. The law sets the process of redemption into a theological context when it aims at keeping property within the father's household, within the family (the tribe), or, on a wider scale, within the nation, following the theological dictum כי לי הארץ ("for the land is Mine," Lev 25:23).[74] Thus, Lev 25 brings together the legal framework of property ownership with the national-religious conception of the land. This conceptual synthesis underlies Jeremiah's symbolic act in its concluding prophecy (v. 15): the law of redemption guarantees *continuity* of personal and national possession of the land, with no gap.[75]

(iii) *Two unique expressions focus on continuity:* They are first uttered by God (v. 7), but then repeated and elaborated by Hanam'el (v. 8): כי לך משפט הירשה ולך הגאלה ("for the right of succession is yours, and you have the duty of redemption").[76] משפט הגאלה ("right of redemption," v. 7) comes from the legal context of the family law concerning the redemption of ancestral lands (as in Lev 25:24);[77] whereas, משפט הירשה

73. Ibid., 2196.

74. Ibid., 2192; and so Yair Hoffman, *Jeremiah 25–52* (Mikra LeYisrael; Jerusalem: The Hebrew University/Magnes; Tel Aviv: Am Oved, 2001 [in Hebrew]), 619.

75. For Jeremiah's utilization of Priestly, and specifically Holiness Code Legislation and conceptions, see Rom-Shiloni, "Actualization," 254–81. This is not to aver that Jeremiah knew Priestly writings in their final form.

76. For משפט in the meaning of "legal claim/right, or procedure," note: משפט הכהנים (Deut 18:3; 1 Sam 2:13); משפט המלך (in 1 Sam 8:9, 11); משפט הבנות (Exod 21:9); משפט יתום ואלמנה (Deut 10:18); and finally, denoting a legal procedure משפט הבכרה (Deut 21:17); for a cultic context, משפט האורים (Num 27:21); and see further in the pair חוק and משפט as in Num 9:14; Exod 15:25.

77. NJPS translates כי לך משפט הגאלה לקנות ("for you are next in succession to redeem it by purchase." Helmer Ringgren ("גאל," *TDOT* 2:350–55) emphasized the

("right of possession," v. 8) transfers the personal-familial story into the national sphere. ירש has the meaning of "take possession of a land which is not legally permitted" (this then contrasts with the legal meanings of both גאל and קנה). Norbert Lohfink explains the Qal form of ירש as "juridical seizure of enemy territory after battle";[78] ירש in this sense serves as a major component of the Deuteronomic/Deuteronomistic conception of the land as handed over to the forefathers and to the people to possess (cf. Jer 32:23). This meaning is indeed drawn upon in Jeremiah in reference to both judgment (8:10) and consolation (30:3; 49:1–2). I suggest that, by adapting this national term to the symbolic act described in Jer 32:6–15, the prophet is asserting the legitimacy, in God's eyes, of the legal procedure through which Jeremiah takes possession of Hanam'el's field.[79] Thus, while Jeremiah combines the two very different and even contradictory terms of גאלה and ירשה, he declares that redemption and possession of the land are both a legal obligation and a formal privilege.

(iv) *The procedure of redemption*: The passage elaborates in great detail (vv. 9–13) how the land is purchased and paid for, and how the ספר המקנה ("deed of purchase") in two copies is signed by Jeremiah in the presence of witnesses, and put in jars. As the legal redeemer from the standpoint of the family law, and by virtue of his immediate agreement to serve in this role (v. 9), he maintains *continuity* in the possession of the land.[80]

(v) *The prophecy:* Verses 14–15 conclude the symbolic action with instructions to preserve the deeds of purchase "so that they may last a long time" (v. 14), and with a prophecy: עוד יקנו בתים ושדות וכרמים בארץ הזאת ("houses, fields, and vineyards shall again be purchased in this land," v. 15). The fairly short final prophecy in Jer 32:15 uses the phrase עוד יקנו (*'od* + *yiqtol* [Niphal form]), which is a unique sixth-century construction, found mostly in consolation prophecies. This construction

obligatory nature of redemption in order to maintain the family possessions (of diverse kinds), regardless of the redeemer's will.

78. Norbert Lohfink, "ירש," *TDOT* 6:368–96 (378); and see Weinfeld, *Deuteronomy and the Deuteronomic School*, 313–16.

79. Compare Lohfink (*TDOT* 6:376), who emphasized the difference between גאלה and ירשה as signifying the difference between "rights and obligations"; and compare Holladay (*Jeremiah 2*, 213–14), who considered the two terms synonymous.

80. Compare William McKane (*Jeremiah 26–52* [ICC; Edinburgh: T. & T. Clark, 1996], 841), who, on the one hand, suggested an intervening period in exile, but on the other, mentioned the possibility that this passage indeed reflects the perspectives of Those Who Remained after 587 B.C.E.

appears to designate both short-term prospects (Zech 1:16, 17; including threats of immediate judgment, as in Ezek 8:6, 13, 14; Jer 2:9) and long-term forecasts that include exile (Isa 49:20; 56:8; Zech 8:20–23). Hence, linguistic criteria fall short of defining the future outlook of Jer 32:15.

Thematically, however, the emphasis on the continuing possession of the land, through both the law of the redeemer (משפט הגאלה) and the divine permission to possess the land (משפט הירשה), with no interruption that might symbolize exile, leads me to infer that the promise of possession in v. 15 has an immediate significance; that is, it applies to Those Who Remained in Judah.[81]

Two points support this conclusion: (1) The conception of uninterrupted, divinely sanctioned, possession of the land, as put forth in this symbolic act, is well-situated in the prophet's biography and in the Jeremian–Judean message prior to the Destruction and in its aftermath, as already sketched out here.[82] It coheres with Jeremiah's commitment to the uninterrupted settlement of the land, a conception that motivates the prophet in his prophecies to Zedekiah during the last decade of Jerusalem and Judah (Jer 27:8–11 and vv. 12–13, as well as 38:14–23). This same commitment to the land stands behind Jeremiah's personal choice to remain in Judah with Gedaliah (40:1–6), and it governs his prophecies to those in Judah who are ready to flee to Egypt in the aftermath of Gedaliah's assassination (42:7–12, see below). (2) Jeremiah's position clearly contradicts Ezekiel's Babylonian exilic perspective. As discussed above, Ezekiel refutes this exact argument, characterizing it as prevalent in the land of Israel (Ezek 11:15; 33:24). The repeated phrase in these verses, לנו [היא] נתנה הארץ למורשה, expresses the Remnant of Jerusalem's claim of their right of possession, which, similar to Jer 32:6–15, evokes pentateuchal conceptions of the land.[83]

Utilizing the conceptually contradictory terms משפט הגאלה and משפט הירשה in this description of his symbolic purchase of the land (Jer 32:6–15), Jeremiah advocates the exclusive status of the Judean Remnant as redeemers and possessors of the land at the eve of the 586 destruction and deportation. Jeremiah's counter-prophecy stands in contradistinction to any claims made by the Jehoiachin Exiles in Babylon. The linguistic

---

81. Compare Lundbom (*Jeremiah 21–36*, 511), who maintained that Jeremiah proclaimed a hopeful message "for the land of Judah," but added that "these words, though spoken to a Judahite audience, nevertheless send a strong message to exiles in Babylon that their stay there will be temporary and that the day will come when houses, fields, and vineyards will again be bought by Judahites in Judah." I do not find this inclusive perspective valid.

82. See the discussion above, pp. 200–219.

83. See the discussion above, pp. 144–56.

and thematic similarities between the passages in Ezekiel and in Jeremiah validate the claim that the two prophets and their communities respectively were in the middle of a live polemical exchange with high theological and political stakes.

This line of consolation in Jeremiah may therefore be considered the expression of an exclusivist in-group ideology of the Judean Remnant during the period 597–586 B.C.E. and on. Like Ezekiel in Babylon, Jeremiah plays as mediator between God and the people. From the perspective of those still living in Judah, he establishes the ideological arguments to legitimize the *continuity* of the settlement of Those Who Remained in Judah, through the *annexation* of pentateuchal conceptions of the land. Implicitly, this strategy also utilizes the argument of *entirety*, promising permanent ownership to the new buyer, and excluding the first owner's right of redemption.

(b) *The Conditional Fate of the "Remnant of Judah" (**Jeremiah** 42:7–22)*. שארית יהודה, the "Remnant of Judah," is a repeated designation in Jer 40–44, one which refers specifically to Those Who Remained in Judah after the Destruction. It occurs in speeches of God and of the prophet (42:15, 19; 44:7, 12, 14, 28); in the additions of the editors/the story-teller (40:11; 43:5), and in the words of Johanan son of Kareah (40:15). A similar term is שארית העם ("the Remnant of the people," 41:10).

As has been thoroughly discussed, chs. 40–44 indeed evince the two antagonistic layers of a Jeremian–Judean foundation and a Babylonian redaction. The Babylonian editorial layer displays the great disappointment at the failure of what could have been a restoration of the Judean community after 586.[84] Thus, these chapters utilize both in-group designations and hopes of consolation that originated with the community that remained in Judah under Gedaliah in Mitzpah.[85] However, these

84. See Gunther Wanke, *Untersuchungen zur sogenannten Baruchschrift* (BZAW 122; Berlin: de Gruyter, 1971), 91–133; Karl F. Pohlmann, *Studien zum Jeremiabuches* (FRLANT 118; Göttingen: Vandenhoeck & Ruprecht, 1978), 123–44, 198–204; Thiel, *Die deuteronomistische Redaktion von Jeremia 26–52*, 62–68. These scholars (and many others) considered the redactional layer to be Deuteronomistic. I would leave the identification of this redactional layer much more open; see the discussion below.

85. For the positive views of this community's future in Jer 40–41 on Those Who Remained, see Hill, "Jeremiah 40:1–6: An Appreciation," 130–41, especially pp. 137–41; Ehud Ben Zvi, "The Voice and Role of a Counterfactual Memory in the Construction of Exile and Return: Considering Jeremiah 40:7–12," in *The Concept of Exile in Ancient Israel and Its Historical Contexts* (ed. E. Ben Zvi and C. Levin; BZAW 404; Berlin: de Gruyter, 2010), 169–88.

same chapters are coupled with passages that denigrate the Judean community as the out-group, by way of both exhortations and judgment prophecies that are customarily identified as coming from the Babylonian-Deuteronomistic tradents of Jeremiah. The latter circle of authors, in fact, is said to have shaped the entire unit so as to close the door on this community in Judah, and to designate the Babylonian-exilic (and then, Repatriate) community in its entirety as the sole legitimate people of God.[86]

Therefore, although the earlier pro-Remnant strand is currently intertwined with further editorial anti-Remnant readings within these very chapters, the two counter-pronouncements concerning the two communities may still be highlighted.[87]

Jeremiah 42:7–22 relates Jeremiah's last-moment attempt to prevent "the Remnant of Judah" from running away to Egypt in what seems to have been a "voluntary exile," motivated by fear of Babylonian reprisals (Jer 41:16–18; cf. 2 Kgs 25:26).[88] Jeremiah pronounces a conditional consolation prophecy (comprised of four oracles, vv. 9b–11a, 11b–12, 15b–17, 18), elaborated by the prophet's words of exhortation (vv. 13–15a, 19–22).[89] Consolation is predicated on the commitment to an ongoing settlement in the land of Judah (see 42:10, in comparison to the prophet's exhortation in v. 13).[90] Should this condition be kept, God promises restoration of life in the land and reinstitution of the relationship between God and Those Who Remained in Judah (vv. 10–12).[91]

---

86. For a summary of the different literary strands of the Gedaliah story, see Lipschits, *The Fall and Rise of Jerusalem*, 339–44, 349–59. Lipschits (354), however, explained this ideological rift on political and economical grounds.

87. Revealing the "early origin of the narrative" was the task recently articulated by Hermann-Josef Stipp, "The Concept of the Empty Land in Jeremiah 37–43," in Ben Zvi and Levin, eds., *The Concept of Exile*, 103–54; see especially 124–32. But Stipp did not go beyond mentioning that an "early origin of the narrative" got its Babylonian ideological proclamation.

88. Other passages that could just as well have been brought forward as revealing the Judean strand or the earlier narrative are indeed 40:1–6, 7–12; see n. 85, above.

89. So Lundbom, *Jeremiah 37–52* (AB 21C; New York: Doubleday, 2004), 128, 136–38.

90. Stipp ("The Concept of the Empty Land in Jeremiah 37–43," 125–26) adduced apt arguments against "the Egyptian theory" as the setting for this story. I believe that Stipp did not give enough weight to the disputation between Jeremiah and his immediate audience of the Remnant of Judah over their conceptions of the land and the exile.

91. והשיב אתכם אל אדמתכם ("and He will bring you back to your own land," 42:12); but the LXX, the Vulgate, and the Peshitta have the first person (thus denoting God as the agent); see Lundbom (*Jeremiah 37–52*, 133) for the apt evaluation of the

This promise is established on two explanatory clauses. The first, כי
נחמתי אל הרעה אשר עשיתי לכם ("for I am appeased for [NJPS: 'I regret']
the punishment I have brought upon you," v. 10), presumes that the toll
of judgment has been paid.[92] The second, כי אתכם אני להושיע אתכם
ולהציל אתכם מידו ("for I am with you to save you and to rescue you from
his hands," v. 11), God proclaims His presence and promises his
assistance to Those Who Remained in confronting the king of Babylon.
However, disobedience to this divine demand of continual residence in
the land of Judah will bring total annihilation upon those descending to
Egypt, who will have no remnant (vv. 13–15a, 15b–17), and no prospect
of return (but see 44:28).

Formally, when Jeremiah opens his words with אם שוב תשבו בארץ
הזאת ("if you remain in this land," v. 10),[93] followed by a pronouncement of consolation (vv. 10–12), he borrows the Deuteronomic admon-
ishment pattern (compare Deut 28:1, 15). Then, Jeremiah continues to
the exhortation—ואם אמרים אתם לא נשב בארץ הזאת ("But if you say,
'We will not stay in this land'," v. 13)—which opens the threat against
disobedience to the divine demand (vv. 13–17).[94]

versions. The LXX's use of first person for both ורחם and והשיב seems harmonistic
(as also the Peshitta and the Vulgate). Another issue under scholarly debate is
whether the root behind והשיב is ישב or שוב, which relates to the problem of the
permission granted to Those Who Remained. According to Bright (*Jeremiah*, 256)
this verse reflects an exilic perspective; but I prefer Wilhelm Rudolph's proposition
(*Jeremiah* [HAT 12; Tübingen: Mohr, 1958; 3d ed. 1968], 254) that it refers to the
uprooting of Judeans south of Jerusalem to the area of Beit Lehem. See Carroll,
Jeremiah, 716.

92. The phrase ניחם על הרעה / אל (v. 10) may be interpreted in two ways:
(1) "God is regretful of His earlier intentions," as in Jer 18:8, 10; 26:3, 13, 19 (and
in the negative, 15:6; 20:16); see also Judg 2:18, etc. (and so interpreted by NJPS).
(2) "God is appeased of His anger, and is changing His first plan," as in 2 Sam
24:16; Ezek 5:13. I prefer the second option, as more appropriate to the current
context. See David N. Freedman, "When God Repents," in *Divine Commitment and
Human Obligation: Selected Writings of David Noel Freedman* (2 vols.; Grand
Rapids: Eerdmans, 1997), 1:409–46. Amos 7:3, 6 demonstrate prophetic intercession
to delay the threat of divine wrath. According to Freedman, only the people's repen-
tance/obedience (rather than God's initiative) insures that the respite is permanent
(p. 410; see pp. 415–16, and the discussion of the Jeremian passages, pp. 428–32).

93. The unique construction אם שוב תשבו (v. 10), combining שוב and ישב, had
attracted attention already by the time of the Versions and was subsequently noted
by commentators. See Holladay (*Jeremiah 2*, 300), who adduced Jer 8:13; 48:9 as
additional examples for an intentional wordplay in Jeremiah.

94. Compare to Carroll (*Jeremiah*, 717–19) who argued for a change in the
prophet's attitude towards the community in the land, and held that Jer 42:7–17
contradicts Jer 21:8–10. He further recognized that 42:10–17 shares the same

Thematically, Jeremiah draws on preexilic Deuteronomic conceptions of land and exile.[95] In this framework, exile represents a final and comprehensive judgment of annihilation (vv. 15–17; and see Deut 4:25–28), whereas remaining in the land promises continuing existence (42:10–12). This position is repeated in other prose passages in Jeremiah that suggest this same conditional promise and threat prior to the Destruction (7:3–7; 11:3–5; 17:22–27; 22:4–5; 25:5–7).[96]

Jeremiah 42:7–22 addresses the Remnant of Judah *after* its fall, and *after* the assassination of Gedaliah, urging them to remain settled in the land, so as to insure restoration within its borders (following the descriptions of return in 40:11–12). God has reversed His plan to destroy Judah totally, and He now calls for a period of grace, of reconciliation, to be granted to the Remnant. The prophecy thus envisions salvation and rescue by God from the king of Babylon within the land,[97] projecting that he (God and/or the Babylonian king) will treat the Remnant with a merciful attitude and restore them to their ancestral properties (v. 11).[98] The one thing the Remnant must *not* do is leave the land of Judah; such a

---

conditional framework as Jer 7:3–7; 11:3–5; 18:7–10; 22:3–5, but he considered all these passages to be non-Jeremian "sermons." I, however, understand those similarities to denote genuine Jeremian pronouncements; see n. 96.

95. See the discussion on pp. 204–19, above.

96. These passages were called "covenant speeches" by James Muilenberg ("The Form and Structure of the Covenantal Formulations," *VT* 9 [1959]: 347–65), and many scholars consider them to stem from the Deuteronomistic editorial level of the book (Quelle C for Duhm, Mowinckel, and others). I am more convinced by the view that these speeches may be Jeremian (as suggested by Bright; Helga Weippert, *Die Prosareden des Jeremiabuches* [BZAW 132; Berlin: de Gruyter, 1973]; Holladay; and Lundbom); see Rom-Shiloni, "Actualization," 267–78.

97. והשיב אתכם אל אדמתכם ("he shall…resettle you back in your own land") refers to resettlement within the land (reading והשיב from ישב Hiphil, in accordance with לא נשב, v. 13), and does not need to refer to exile and return (as may be inferred by reading שוב, as translated by NJPS: "…bring you back to your own land" and the Versions). I would understand this delicate but significant change (from ישב to שוב) to mark the secondary Babylonian reworking of the initially Judean narrative. For detailed discussions of the Versions, see McKane, *Jeremiah 26–52*, 1034–35; and see also Stipp ("The Concept of the Empty Land in Jeremiah 37–43," 127), who nevertheless inclined against the possibility of ישב in preference to שוב as the *lectio difficilior*, thus substantiating the setting of the story within the Babylonian *golah* (p. 128).

98. On the sequence of divine actions and its counterpart in the activity of the human-Babylonian king, ואתן לכם רחמים ורחם אתכם ("I will dispose him to be merciful to you: he shall show you mercy," v. 12), see 43:10, 12 (Lundbom, *Jeremiah 37–52*, 133). The third verbal phrase והשיב אתכם אל אדמתכם ("he shall… bring you back to your own land") leaves the agent vague.

step would be taken as a clear act of disobedience on the part of the people, and would guarantee that God would reinitiate punishment against the people in Egypt (vv. 13–17).[99]

The prophecy thus adds a third identity-building argument, that of *entirety*, to the two arguments of exclusivity already in play (*continuity* and *annexation*). By designating the Judeans Who Remained as שארית יהודה, all that is left, the prophet reinforces this community's self-identity as the sole "real" people of God, those who in accordance with the Deuteronomic conceptions of land and exile, (may) continue to hold to this status here in the land, without the punishment of exile.

This prophecy has been edited, however, by the Babylonian Exiles to reinforce the general proclamation of Jer 40–44 in their current form *against* this Remnant of Judah. That was the point when Jeremiah's exhortation to his fellow Judeans served the Babylonian exilic ideology to delegitimize the very existence of this other Judean community.[100] Babylonian-exilic editing has changed the overall thrust of the passage from pro-Judean to anti-Judean.

These prophecies in Jeremiah—the redemption of the field in Anathoth (32:6–15), and this prophecy to the Remnant of Judah before the descent to Egypt (42:7–22)—are of paramount importance to the current discussion, as they ideologically substantiate the "other" side of the Babylonian-exilic ideologies, and indeed validate the polemical nature of both Ezekiel's and Jeremiah's prophecies.

In both prophecies, and throughout the pro-Judean strand in Jeremiah, the prophet serves as the ideological advocate of Those Who Remained, supplying the arguments to legitimate their continuous existence as the people of God in the land.[101]

---

99. I follow here Freedman ("When God Repents," 428–29) who emphasized that the reversal in the divine plan is temporary and conditional; in Jer 42:10–22 God's intention moves from bad to good (vv. 10–12; for a movement in both directions, see Jer 18:7–10). Gary E. Yates ("New Exodus and No Exodus in Jeremiah 26–45: Promise and Warning to the Exiles in Babylon," *TynBul* 57 [2006]: 1–22) suggested that the migration to Egypt symbolizes an opposing future of "No Exodus" for the Judean community.

100. See Stipp ("The Concept of the Empty Land in Jeremiah 37–43," 126–28), who argued that the original narrative was "not talking *to* the Egyptian diaspora, but *about* them, to a different audience" (p. 126), which, according to Stipp, was the Babylonian *golah*. I would agree with Stipp on this and indeed consider it to be secondary to the initial Jeremian–Judean narrative. For the Babylonian *golah* perspectives on chs. 40–44, see pp. 237–41.

101. Ben Zvi ("The Voice and Role of a Counterfactual Memory," 178–83) argued that the book of Jeremiah provides legitimacy to Gedaliah even when the

It is thus important to note that the People Who Remained were also engaged with issues of identity, with in-group and out-group definitions, and used the same arguments of exclusivity to articulate their own claims to the heritage of Israel. Yet, this voice eventually disappeared—shortly after it was last heard in Jeremiah (and to a lesser extent in Ezekiel).

It is also remarkable to note that in both prophecies (32:6–15; 42:7–22) there are no hints of explicit out-group arguments against the Judean Exiles in Babylon. This may be explained in two ways. First, as part of the genuine pro-Judean strand, this may illustrate the use of the argument of *entirety*, that implicitly excludes anyone not living in the land. But these chapters do hold negative characterizations of the out-group, that however are themselves aimed against the same community of Those Who Remained. Thus, the second and more plausible explanation is that these seem to be clear indications of editorial activity, which may be classed with other additions within Jeremiah that advanced Babylonian-exilic positions. These will be addressed in what follows.

b. *Pro-golah Prophecies of Consolation: Three Exclusive Babylonian Exilic Strands*
As part of the editorial process, prophecies directed to the Remnant of Judah have been positioned side by side with prophecies directed to the Babylonian Exiles (as, for instance, Jer 32:6–15 to the Remnant in Judah, and vv. 36–41, 42–44 to the Exiles; and passages within chs. 30–31, and 33). Hence, an exilic editorial agenda governs the structure of entire units within the book (e.g. chs. 40–44), and pro-*golah* passages reveal the Babylonian exilic ideologies at work in the final redaction of Jeremiah. In fact, with reference to in-group and out-group definitions, three different Babylonian exilic strands may be discerned.

(1) *In-group and Out-group Definitions: The Jehoiachin Exiles' Exclusive Positions in Jeremiah (24; 29:16–20; 40–44).* **Jeremiah 24** presents the clearest example of boundary setting between "us" and "them." This prophecy has long been considered non-Jeremian, and has been presumed to reflect the Babylonian exilic perspective of the editorial strata of the book.[102] I would be much more specific and say

prophet is not mentioned, through the proximity between 40:1–6 and 7–12 and the Nebuzaradan speech (40:2–3).

102.   Philip Hyatt ("Jeremiah, Introduction and Exegesis," *IB* 5:788–89, but compare to 996–98) considered ch. 24 to be Deuteronomistic, presumably written around 550 B.C.E. in Egypt; while Nicholson (*Preaching to the Exiles*, 81–83) correctly moved the Deuteronomistic authorship of this oracle to Babylon. Carroll

that, based on its labeling of "self" and "other," its arguments, and its rhetorical strategies, this chapter illustrates a strand of the Jehoiachin Exiles' exclusivist ideology.[103]

The vision of the two baskets of figs, good and bad, brought before God, symbolizes two groups, according to the divine explanation. The "good" basket is designated as גלות יהודה (NJPS: "the Judean exiles," v. 5), and refers specifically to the Exiles who left with Jehoiachin (v. 1).[104] The "bad" basket indicates a long list of people and groups: צדקיהו מלך יהודה ואת שריו ואת שארית ירושלים הנשארים בארץ הזאת והישבים בארץ מצרים ("King Zedekiah of Judah and his officials and the remnant of Jerusalem that is left in the land, and those who are living in the land of Egypt," v. 8). The list distinguishes royalty from lay people; then שארית ירושלים ("the remnant of Jerusalem") is further divided into two communities:[105] Those Who Remained in the land, and those who

---

(*Jeremiah*, 482–88) argued that the passage was exilic or even postexilic, reflecting the conflict of Ezra's era; Holladay (*Jeremiah 1*, 655) admitted that the chapter contains Deuteronomistic phraseology and a message that diverges from Jeremiah's point of view, but he limited such instances to expansions of specific phrases within vv. 5–7, 8–10, which he held to express the exilic and the postexilic communities' own important message. These expansions were added to an authentic prophecy dated to the reign of Zedekiah, 594 B.C.E. (p. 657). Also adopting this dating was Jeremiah Unterman (*From Repentance to Redemption: Jeremiah's Thought in Transition* [JSOTSup 54; Sheffield: Sheffield Academic, 1987], 55–87). Lundbom (*Jeremiah 21–36*, 222–36) and Mark Leuchter (*Josiah's Reform and Jeremiah's Scroll: Historical Calamity and Prophetic Response* [HBM 6; Sheffield: Sheffield Phoenix, 2006], 179–82) have both argued for the Jeremianic authorship of Jer 24.

103.   Contra Carroll (*Jeremiah*, 483), who indeed thought that this strand in the Jeremiah tradition was meant to function as "propaganda for a particular group of deportees." Yet, he found it to echo the Ezra–Nehemiah traditions that evolved during the reconstruction of Jerusalem; for an opinion that Jer 24 is late and exceptional status, see also Albertz, *Israel in Exile*, 323. I find it unnecessary to project this strand into the later period.

104.   גלות יהודה appears only in Jer 24:4, 5; 29:22; otherwise הגולה is used in clear references to the Jehoiachin Exiles (29:1, 4, 20, 31; as in Ezek 3:11, etc.). Indeed, McKane (*Jeremiah 1–25*, 608–9) considered גלות יהודה to refer to the earliest group, to the Jehoiachin Exiles, *excluding* the 586 deportees and thereby delimiting "the entire, Babylonian, exilic community" (609). Compare בתוך כל גלות ירושלים ויהודה המגלים בבלה ("among all Exiles of Jerusalem and Judah [NJPS: among those from Jerusalem and Judah] who were being exiled to Babylon," Jer 40:1), which refers to the 586 Exiles.

105.   שארית ירושלים is a *hapax*; in the noneditorial levels of the book, within chs. 40–44 this community is called nine times in those chapters שארית יהודה, with the meaning of the Remnant of Judah from Those Who Remained, see pp. 203–4, 228, above.

were resettled in Egypt. All these groups date back to the period immediately prior to the Destruction (597–586 B.C.E.), or shortly after it.

The crucial dichotomy established in Jer 24 between גלות יהודה and שארית ירושלים is constructed upon the three arguments of exclusivity:

Continuity. Galut Yehudah is said to have gained God's favor (... אכיר לטובה, "so will I single out for good," v. 5; ושמתי עיני עליהם לטובה, "I will look upon them favorably," v. 6a), and faces the prospect of regathering in the land (והשבתים על הארץ הזאת, "and I will bring them back to this land," v. 6a), and a transformation, initiated by God, which will lead to reinstitution of the covenant relationship (ונתתי להם לב לדעת אתי כי אני יהוה, והיו לי לעם ואנכי אהיה להם לאלהים, "And I will give them the understanding to acknowledge Me, for I am the LORD. And they shall be My people and I will be their God," v. 7a), in continuity with Israel's past history.[106] This transformation is mentioned, however, as a reaction towards the people's return to God: כי ישבו אלי בכל לבם ("when they turn back to Me with all their heart," v. 7b).[107]

---

106.   Verses 5–6 transform the Jeremian phraseology of judgment in the earlier levels of the book into words of consolation, directed at the Jehoiachin Exiles. The *hapax* phrases, הכיר את ... לטובה (v. 5) and שם עינו על ... לטובה (v. 6, together with 32:42; 39:9), suggest a transformation in God's attitude towards this community of Exiles; compare the earlier and judgmental pronouncements in which the antonyms לרעה ולא לטובה occur (21:10; 39:16; 44:27; and 14:11). This same transformation also appears in the two pairs לא נתש / נטע, לא הרס / בנה (v. 6b), which reconfigure the earlier threats of judgment advanced using the verbs נתק, נתש, הרס, האביד, and their opposites בנה, נטע (Jer 1:10; 18:7–9; and in part, 12:17). Such transformations also occur in prophecies of consolation to the larger community of Exiles (31:28), to the Repatriates (31:38–40), and in Jeremiah's call to the Remnant of Jerusalem (42:10), which is then dramatically transformed back into a judgment against them in 45:4. Thus, I would not consider these phrases Deuteronomistic (concurring with Weippert, *Die Prosareden des Jeremiabuches*, 193–202; and Holladay, *Jeremiah 1*, 36–37, 658; *Jeremiah 2*, 308). On the other hand, however, I would not exclude the possibility that their occurrence in 24:6 is a secondary adaptation of Jeremiah's own phraseology, used now to support the Jehoiachin Exiles in Babylon (and see the notes below discussing other phrases).

107.   כי ישבו אלי בכל לבם (v. 7b; see Jer 3:10 and Deut 30:10; 1 Kgs 8:48), together with כי אני יהוה (because of its parallels in P [Exod 6:2–8], H, and Ezekiel, as in Ezek 20:5–6), are counted by Holladay (*Jeremiah 1*, 658–59) as later additions. Holladay relied on an *ex silentio* argument concerning both these phrases, which do not appear in Jer 31:31–34 (a passage he rightfully considered authentically Judean). Indeed, כי אני יהוה expands the object of knowing YHWH, which occurs in Jer 22:16; and 9:23, and comprises yet another non-Deuteronomistic phrase in this prophecy. Unterman (*From Repentance to Redemption*, 64–67) recognized that the mention of the people's repentance occurs in Jer 24:7 "almost as an afterthought" (p. 66).

At the other extreme, those bad figs, King Zedekiah and the Remnant of Jerusalem, are doomed to total annihilation.[108] The phraseology used in vv. 9–10 brings together several otherwise independent curse motifs for the sake of denigrating this "other" community as doomed both in the land and in Egypt.[109]

Entirety. This denigration and predicted judgment constructs an argument of *entirety*. Since the land of Judah will be completely empty once those afflictions are implemented against the Remnant of Jerusalem, in all of their places of residence (v. 10), *Galut Yehudah* in Babylon represents the *entire* people of God; it is the only community that God will return to the land, the only community with whom God will reinstitute the covenant relationship.

Annexation: *Galut Yehudah* thus annexes to itself several national traditions as referring exclusively to its own future; that is, the conceptions of covenant, land, and the trajectory of exile–redemption.

However, Jer 24:8–10 does not give an indication of counter-arguments against the Jerusalemite position. It does not explain why the Remnant of Jerusalem (including those settled in Egypt) is cursed. This may be compared to Jer 29:16–20.

Nevertheless, he held this phrase to be a major example Jer 24's deviance from Deuteronomistic phraseology and perceptions, and thus to be Jeremian in its authorship. Based on its exceptional phraseology (see pp. 234–35 nn. 105–7, above, and n. 109, below), I include Jer 24 with Jer 32:36–41 as non-Jeremian (and non-Deuteronomistic), early exilic Babylonian passages; see Rom-Shiloni, "Everlasting Covenant."

108.　Among the later additions, Holladay (*Jeremiah 1*, 659) included the reference to "those dwelling in Egypt" (v. 8, influenced by 44:27). But here is one example of the trap into which Holladay has fallen by insisting on the authenticity of this prophecy. I would, however, accept his observation as to the exilic addition of בכל המקמות אשר אדיחם שם ("in all the places to which I banish them," v. 9; see his p. 659). This phrase, indeed, refers to exile as the divine judgment upon this community (preceding a promise of restoration), in contradistinction to the calamitous fate predicted for the Remnant of Jerusalem (including those who voluntarily migrated to Egypt, v. 10).

109.　Among these expressions: משל ושנינה is a *hapax* in Jeremiah, otherwise appearing only in late Deuteronomistic passages (Deut 28:37; 1 Kgs 9:7); שמה ושרקה (as in Jer 19:8; 25:9); לקללה ולחרפה (in other references to the land of Judah, as in 44:8); לחרבה לשמה (in 25:11; and note לחרבה לשממה in 44:6); שמה (in 2:15; 4:7); and several expressions that bring together four of these terms: לחרבה לשמה לשרקה ולקללה (in 25:18) and והייתם לאלה ולשמה ולקללה ולחרפה (in 42:18; 44:12). The opening phrase ונתתים לזועה (*Qere*: לזעוה) occurs in both Jer 24:9 and 29:18 in reference to the Remnant, and once in a judgment prophecy it refers the total destruction within the land (15:4; following Deut 28:25).

While ch. 24 expresses most clearly the antagonism between Judean groups of the first decades of the sixth century, one fragmentary prophetic passage, **29:16–20**, should also be addressed here.[110] The prophecy builds on the same imagery and dichotomy. It names the king and the people of Jerusalem as אחיכם אשר לא יצאו אתכם בגולה ("your brothers who did not go out with you into exile," v. 16, in parallel to 24:8–10), as the "bad figs," doomed to annihilation. It mentions quite similar list of curses to the one brought in ch. 24 (vv. 17–18; compare to Jer 24:9–10), and it further adds an explicit accusation, which is absent in Jer 24—a reference to the people's sin of disobedience to the words of God delivered by His prophets (v. 19). But the prophecy is cut off just as it moves to address כל הגולה אשר שלחתי מירושלים בבלה ("the whole exilic community which I banished from Jerusalem to Babylon," v. 20). In the current editorial sequence, v. 20 functions as the introduction to the coming judgment upon the prophets serving in Babylon, Ahab son of Koliah and Zedekiah son of Ma'aseiah (vv. 21–23), and upon Shema'iah son of the Nehelamite (vv. 24–32). But, based on the parallel established in Jer 24, it is much more reasonable to think that vv. 16–20 were secondarily interpolated into their present context (note the natural flow between v. 15 and 21), and originally contained a different, favorable prophecy addressed to the Jehoiachin Exiles.

These stylistic and ideological characteristics construct a divisive rhetoric that is close to Ezekiel's ideology and his exclusive preference for the Jehoiachin Exiles. As in Ezek 11:1–13, 14–21; 33:23–29, the argument of exclusivity entails a dichotomy of self and other, which is portrayed as a matter of life and death for the groups involved (Jer 24:5–7 vs. vv. 8–10; 29:16–19 vs. v. 20).[111]

Chapters 40–44 (together with 45:1–5) present a thoroughly edited story of the Remnant of Judah, told in its present form by Babylonian exilic authors.[112] This masterful editorial work highlights the transition

110.   On the interpolative nature of 29:16–20, see Holladay, *Jeremiah 2*, 135; Carroll, *Jeremiah*, 559, who holds that these verses support the 597 Exiles; and Sharp, *Prophecy and Ideology*, 108–11, who argued for competing editorial voices in this chapter.

111.   Contra the argument of Holladay (repeated twice in *Jeremiah 1*, 656), that this prophecy's main concern is "that those who stay at home should not feel superior." This is much too mild a description of the antagonism suggested in this chapter, and certainly that of vv. 8–10.

112.   These chapters were studied from distinctively different angles by Wanke, *Untersuchungen zur sogenannten Baruchschrift*, 91–133; Pohlmann, *Studien zum Jeremiabuches*, 198–204; and Leuchter, *The Polemics of Exile in Jeremiah 26–45*, 120–41, among others.

in the Remnant's fortunes from restoration (40:7–12) to annihilation (40:13–45:5),[113] and advances several counter-arguments delegitimizing Those Who Remained as the Remnant community.[114]

Continuity. The main problem that characterizes the Remnant of Judah, now all living in the land of Egypt according to this narrative, is their ongoing disobedience. The demand to listen/obey and the fact of the Remnants' ongoing disobedience is highlighted by the pairing שמע / לא שמע); this disobedience is directed against both Jeremiah the prophet (see 42:1–43:7, especially 43:2–3) and YHWH Himself (43:4–6; as also 42:13–15, 20–22; 43:4; 44:5, 15–19, 23).[115] With their settlement in the land of Egypt, the Remnant adds yet another dimension to their disobedience (ch. 44). In continuity with their ancestors they worship other gods (44:2–6, 7–10), bringing the inevitable divine judgment of total calamity upon themselves (vv. 11–14). Their response to Jeremiah further justifies their fate (vv. 15–19), and elicits a second threat of total annihilation (vv. 27–30). Closing with what is definitely a salvation prophecy, announced to Baruch (45:1–5), this last passage portrays Baruch as the sole survivor of YHWH's total punishment: כי הנני מביא רעה על כל בשר נאם יהוה ("for I am going to bring disaster upon all flesh—declares the LORD," 45:4–5).[116] Thus, this Babylonian exilic perspective uses a negative construction of *continuity* as a counter-argument against the Judean community now in Egypt.

---

113.   Note the contradiction between the promise of 42:10 and the final threat in 45:4. Hence, while 45:1–5 is usually treated as a colophon (to either chs. 26–36, 26–44, or even to chs. 1–44) or a piece of personal guidance (Holladay, *Jeremiah 2*, 307–11), it seems rather to be more tightly connected in rhetorical terms, making an important thematic statement on the issue of identity to close chs. 40–44 (see Carroll, *Jeremiah*, 747–50).

114.   These counter-arguments indeed start already within chs. 37–39, in reference to the reign of Zedekiah. For a discussion of chs. 37–43, where ch. 44 is understood as a secondary Deuteronomistic expansion, see Stipp, "The Concept of the Empty Land in Jeremiah 37–43," especially 122.

115.   See Stipp (ibid., 129–30), who aptly defined this repeated terminology as "deuterojeremianic" and challenged the scholarly trend to refer these chapters to the Deuteronomistic redaction based on this meager data.

116.   הנני מביא רעה על כל בשר alludes to the story of the Deluge, casting Noah as sole survivor (Gen 6:13). כל בשר occurs also in Jer 12:12; 25:31, as an indicator of total calamity; thus I would suggest that all these passages allude to the totality of destruction brought on by the Deluge, emphasizing the magnitude of the coming destruction. In a different context, note the divine epithet, אלהי כל בשר ("the God of all flesh," 32:27).

Entirety. As a further expression of their disobedience, the "other" Judean community(/ies), that is, Those Who Remained in Judah post-586, have all fled to Egypt, leaving Judah empty and desolate. Throughout these prophecies of total calamity to the Remnant of Judah, the editorial presentation accentuates the exclusive positive status of the Babylonian exilic community. The Babylonian Exiles have thus become established as the sole people of God.[117]

Strategically, these chapters do not point toward an explicit confrontation between the two groups; they do not supply positive in-group arguments to establish claims of the Babylonian Exiles.[118] Rather, they focus on out-group argumentation against the "other" community. The final redaction of Jer 40–44 reworked the originally pro-Judah texts in such a way that we can still detect the positive "in-group" statements of the Remnant of Judah in these passages (see 40:1–6; 40:7–41:18; 42:1–22), but the overall rhetorical flow denigrates this very community as an illegitimate community, doomed to annihilation. The Babylonian editorial layers advance the great disappointment at what could have been a restoration of the Judean community after 586 (40:7–12).[119] In their counter-presentation of Those Who Remained, the rhetoric builds the emotional tension—if only this community had followed the recommendation of Gedaliah (40:9–10); if only they had obeyed God according to Jeremiah's prophecies (note the sequence of their commitment in 42:1–6;

---

117.   This same perspective appears in 2 Kgs 25; see vv. 21 and 26. See Stipp, "The Concept of Empty Land in Jeremiah 37–43," 131–32, 150–54.

118.   Stipp (ibid., 132–36) enumerated the evidence for a positive stance towards the Babylonian regime in Jer 37–43. His main argument for considering this stance as part of the Babylonian exilic strand of these chapters was that while such arguments were not necessary for the non-Exiles to articulate, they would have been vital for an exilic spokesperson under the direct eye of the powerful Babylonian regime, soon after 587 B.C.E. Stipp (pp. 153–54) thus thought of these chapters as reflecting a debate within the Babylonian Exiles themselves, urging the Exiles to accept favorably the rulership of their Babylonian overlords so to allow the survival of the people.

119.   Ben Zvi ("The Voice and Role of a Counterfactual Memory," 183–88) pointed out that "counterfactual, alternate memory" of the Babylonian Judahites might have governed further rereadings of these chapters by subsequent Babylonian Exiles. In addition, he mentioned that as consequence of these rereadings the literati among the Exiles faced questions of causality, according to which they laid full responsibility for the current circumstances on human agents. They indeed raised multiple conceptual questions concerning the meaning of exile, remnant, and so on (pp. 186–88). It is surprising, then, that Ben Zvi did not consider these rereadings as part of an internal polemics between the Judean and the exilic groups.

the prophetic exhortation, 42:7–22; their disobedience, 43:1–7, espe-cially v. 4; and their additional ongoing cultic disobedience in Egypt, 44:7–14, 16–19, 23). Finally, if only they had not enhanced their long standing religious-cultic disobedience in Egypt (44).[120] But, of course, they did not. On the contrary, they did all they possibly could to disobey God, and thus brought their own calamitous judgment upon themselves (44:26–30). These chapters gradually shut down on any hopes for the restoration of this community of the Remnant of Judah, placing great emphasis on showing how the community of Those Who Remained had "with its own hands" worked to fulfill Jeremiah's prophecies of judg-ment against them. Hence, through their own agency, Judah was left completely empty of Judeans, waiting desolate for returnees from Babylonian.[121] These defamatory statements clear the way to confirming the Jehoiachin Exiles as the one and only community of the people of God. Thus, the explicit paradigm of Jer 24 is implicitly employed by the editors of chs. 40–44 (45).

To sum up: these passages in Jeremiah may be classified with similar passages known from Ezekiel, reflecting the initial stages of polemic prior to the Destruction and in the early years after it, namely, 597–586 B.C.E. and following.

The author of Jer 24, like Ezekiel, had to emphasize that while the Jehoiachin Exiles had indeed been removed from the land (Ezek 11:16; Jer 24:5), they (and only they) should be considered the recipients of the promise of future return and restoration in their land; they (and they alone) are the (entire) people of God, those with whom God will reinsti-tute the covenant relationship. The Babylonian Exiles lay claim to arguments of *continuity* and *entirety*, and they *annex* national covenant traditions in the service of these claims.

In their overall edited format, chs. 40–44 argue for the illegitimacy of the Remnant of Judah, by using counter-claims of *continuity* in their disobedience. These chapters bring their story to an end, with Judah desolate and empty of all Judeans, and the people in Egypt doomed to total annihilation (and to worshiping foreign gods on foreign land). I

---

120. For Jer 44 as a Deuteronomistic attempt to defend the religious dogma of the great Josianic reform, see Yair Hoffman, "History and Ideology: The Case of Jeremiah 44," *JANES* 28 (2001): 43–51.

121. Stipp ("The Concept of the Empty Land in Jeremiah 37–43," 151) con-sidered this depiction of the empty land to be the climax of Jer 37–43. He further suggested (p. 152) that 42:11–12 reflects the Exiles' expectation of restoration following Babylonian permission to return. Instead, I see that hopeful message to be a secondary Babylonian exilic modification of an initial Jeremian proclamation directed towards Those Who Remained.

believe this study, at this point, shows that these texts are motivated by an internal polemic, one which rests on this essential need within each of the two Judean communities to redefine their Judahite identity.[122]

With these arguments and counter-arguments those passages represent the earliest stage of a shift in the center–periphery relationship among the Judean communities by the early sixth century B.C.E. The center clearly moves early to Babylon, in the very first decades of the exile.

This explicit (at times only implicit) polemic between the Babylonian Exiles and Those Who Remained in Judah is, however, fairly limited in Jeremiah. Much more prominent are emphases on in-group definitions. In-group perspectives of Those Who Remained were presented above; these passages are the place to locate in-group definitions stemming from the Babylonian exilic community in the book of Jeremiah.

(2) *Inclusive Babylonian Exilic Perspectives*. A distinct strand among the prophecies of consolation in the book of Jeremiah may be understood in the framework of the Babylonian exilic situation. Without mounting an explicit polemic against the Judean communities, the following prophecies address the Exiles in Babylon: Jer 3:18; 16:14–15; 23:7–8; 29:10–14; 30:12–17; 32:36–41; 50:17–20, 33–34; 51:20–24. A special group of consolation prophecies are those embedded within the prophecies against Babylon, where a proclamation of salvation for God's people is combined with a call for revenge and a description of the city's future fall (50:28; 51:1–6, 7–10, 11–14, 34–44, 45–53). All of these prophecies share the following characteristics:

1. A promise of ingathering of the dispersed, from the land in the north, or specifically from Babylon, and a prospect of resettlement back in the land of their fathers (3:18; 16:14–15; 23:7–8; 29:10–14; 50:17–20, 28; 51:1–6, 7–10, 45–53).

2. The land to which the Exiles are to return is described as empty and desolate. The people of God are far away from the land (51:50–51); restoration thus consists in reinstituting Zion after a period of forsaken neglect: נדחה קראו לך ציון היא דרש אין לה ("they called you 'Outcast,' that Zion whom no one seeks out," Jer 30:17; and implicitly in 32:36).[123] Throughout these prophetic

122. Contra more "practical" explanations that focus on political and economical causes of the internal Judean struggle; see Lipschits, *The Fall and Rise of Jerusalem*, 349–59, especially 354.

123. Jer 30:12–17 shows close parallels to Deutero-Isaiah's metaphoric treatment of Zion as a woman (see Isa 49:14–21, 22–26). This adds to the element of reversal characteristic of the consolation prophecies within Jeremiah (compare

passages there is no mention of any Judean population within the land of Judah which these returnees shall rejoin.

3. Very prominent among these prophecies are their phraseological and thematic resemblances to Ezekiel and Deutero-Isaiah on the one hand (Jer 16:14–15; 30:12–17; 32:36–41),[124] and their similarities to Deuteronomistic (exilic) phraseology on the other (29:10–14; 32:36–41).[125]

Nevertheless, once these prophecies are considered as a group, their diverse rhetorical style and themes are apparent.[126] This diversity may be the result of a relatively long period of literary evolution involving a number of exilic authors.[127] Their timespan may extend from the first decades of the sixth century down to its second half (597–586 B.C.E. and following; 570–538 B.C.E.), still within the Neo-Babylonian period. But, in addition, diversity of authors may also stem from different exilic groups or literary circles involved in the evolution of the book of Jeremiah in Babylon and active throughout that period, within which the Deuteronomists were only one component.

Jer 22:20–22); yet in contrast to the feminine metaphor deployed in Jer 30:12–17, Jeremiah usually designates the people as בתולת בת עמי (as in Jer 2:17–37; 14:17). Another similar technique of reversal is the renaming of Zion, which in Deutero-Isaiah gains the names: עיר יהוה ("the city of YHWH"), חפצי-בה ("I delight in her"), דרושה ("Sought out"), all in opposition to her previous name עזובה ("Forsaken") (see Isa 60:14; 62:4, 12; compare also Jer 30:16 and Isa 42:24).

124. The combination of שוב, נדח, קבץ, all in the Hiphil, and the phrase הושיב לבטח, illustrates the phraseological and thematic resemblances between this strain as it occurs in Jeremiah, Ezekiel, and Deutero-Isaiah, while highlighting the uniqueness of the Jeremian exilic idioms; see Rom-Shiloni, "Everlasting Covenant."

125. Allusions to Deuteronomic/Deuteronomistic phrases may be found in Jer 29:10–14 in reference to Deut 30:1–10. Note also the application of the Deuteronomistic phrase לבלתי סור מעל to designate disobedience (Jer 32:40; see 2 Kgs 10:31; 15:15, 18; compare the Deuteronomic phrase סור מן הדרך, as in Deut 9:12, 16; Judg 2:17), etc.

126. Compare, for instance, the different phraseology concerning the return to the land, which appears as the land given to the forefathers: הארץ אשר הנחלתי את אבותיכם (Jer 3:18, alluding to Deut 3:28; 19:3; 31:7; Josh 1:6; see Isa 49:8; Zech 8:12; and compare to Jer 12:14); והשבתים על אדמתם אשר נתתי לאבותם (Jer 16:15, see 1 Kgs 8:34: והשבתם אל האדמה אשר נתת לאבותם; and only partially in 23:8: וישבו על אדמתם); the land from which the people was expelled: והשבתי אתכם אל המקום אשר הגליתי אתכם משם (29:14); or simply "this place," והשבתים אל המקום הזה (32:40). והשבתים לבטח

127. In "Everlasting Covenant," 211–15, I discussed ten *hapaxes* that occur in Jer 32:36–41, which demonstrate the independent stance of the Babylonian-exilic author of this passage.

Looking at the sociological categorizations which contribute to a community's identity, each of these prophecies utilizes the three arguments of exclusivity in relation to the Babylonian Exiles: *continuity*, *entirety*, and the *annexation* of national traditions.

I will restrict myself here to but one example. **Jeremiah 16:14–15** (and with slight yet significant differences, **23:7–8**) seems to be a prophetic passage interpolated into two different contexts.[128] The prophecy promises the ingathering of the people from the land in the north, מארץ צפון (NJPS: "out of the northland," v. 15) and ומכל הארצות אשר הדיחם שמה ("from all the lands to which He had banished them," v. 15), and utilizes the three major in-group arguments. *Continuity* is seen in the designation of the present Exiles, the addressees, as בני ישראל, the national name of the people saved previously from Egypt. *Continuity* with and *annexation* of ancient national traditions is further emphasized by the analogy drawn between the first Exodus and this second projected one, which is to outshine the first.[129] Jeremiah 16:15, והשבתים על אדמתם אשר נתתי לאבותם, not only closes this new Exodus with the picture of resettling the people in the land, but explicitly alludes to the return as bringing "the people back to their land, which I gave to their fathers" (16:15, compare to the shorter וישבו על אדמתם, in Jer 23:8).[130] The two

128.   On the interpolation of this passage in Jer 16:14–15 and its role as a corrective to Jer 16:10–13, see Holladay (*Jeremiah 1*, 474, 621–23), who thought the verses fit better in ch. 23, in a context of consolation prophecies. Holladay dated the two passages to the fifth century, based on the occurrence of זרע בית ישראל ("the offspring of the House of Israel," 23:8), see n. 130, below.

129.   This second Exodus has been recognized as a major theme of consolation in Ezekiel (20:32–38) and especially in Deutero-Isaiah (Isa 48:20–21; 52:11–12). Yates ("New Exodus and No Exodus in Jeremiah 26–45") has indeed emphasized the place of the Exodus within Jer 30–33. However, he did not make a delicate enough distinction between different elements within the Exodus traditions. I suggest that we need to maintain a distinction between the Exodus–Desert traditions which refer to salvation from bondage and the journey in the desert (as invoked in Jer 16:14–15), and the Exodus–Desert traditions concerning the covenant, which are linked in Jeremiah with "the day that I freed them [i.e. your fathers] from the land of Egypt," and which appear in prophecies of judgment (e.g. Jer 7:22; 11:4; 34:13).

130.   The phrase יהוה השיב [את העם] אל האדמה אשר נתן לאבתם ("Yнwн brings [the people] back to the land which He gave to their fathers") occurs in Deuteronomistic verses within Kings (1 Kgs 8:34; 2 Kgs 21:8), and in Jer 24:10, which is closer to 2 Chr 6:25. This slight yet significant difference between Jer 16:14–15 and 23:7–8 may be classed with another difference: the phrase זרע בית ישראל (in 23:8), in contradistinction to בני ישראל in 16:14–15 and in 23:7. While the phrase זרע אפרים occurs in Jeremiah (Jer 2:21; 7:15), it is nevertheless much more common in exilic and postexilic literature, and thus is an indicator of late passages within Jeremiah,

implicit arguments of *continuity* and *annexation* lead also to the third, *entirety*. These general references to the people (in Babylon) as the entire people of God, in its past and in its present/future, with no mention of any other national component residing elsewhere, points to the self-perception of the exilic community as the entire people of God.

These prophecies share Deutero-Isaiah's basic group identity perceptions—they treat all the Babylonian Exiles as a single inclusive group and do not attribute any special status to the 597 Jehoiachin Exiles; however, these Exiles (and only they) are *the* people of God. This is, therefore, an exilic strand, different from that of Ezekiel and from Jer 24 (as also 29:16–20, and the editorial layer of chs. 40–44). We may locate this strand in the exilic era (ca. 570/mid-sixth century to 538 B.C.E.), the period when the redaction of the Deuteronomistic literature is thought to have taken place, specifically, the book of Kings, as well as the Babylonian chapters of Deutero-Isaiah (Isa 40–48).

(3) *Repatriate Ideology in Jeremiah?* The most intriguing group of prophetic passages of consolation within Jer 30–33 are several prophecies that resemble, in phraseology and even more in theme, the inclusive Judean perspectives of the Remnant of Judah. The main characteristic shared by these prophecies is their omission of any mention of exile, of any period of separation from the land; in consequence, they lack any mention of gathering the dispersed and returning to Zion. They are very clearly Judean in their geographic outlook.

The prophetic passages in this category are Jer 30:18–22; 31:23–26, 27–30, 31–34, 38–40; 32:42–44; 33:1–9, 10–11, 12–13, 14–22. These prophecies are commonly held to apply to one of two sets of circumstances: either to the period following 586 B.C.E., the era Jack R. Lundbom termed "Jeremiah's Mizpah sojourn (586–582 B.C.E.),"[131] or to

---

such as זרע בית ישראל in Jer 31:36–37 (and Ezek 44:22). Note זרע ישראל in Isa 45:25; 2 Kgs 17:20; Ps 22:24; Neh 9:2; 1 Chr 16:13; in the concatenation of phrases: זרע יעקוב ודוד עבדי ... זרע אברהם ישחק ויעקב (Jer 33:26, and see v. 22). For other similar phrases, note זרע יעקב (Isa 45:19; Ps 22:24); זרע בית יעקב (Ezek 20:5); זרע אברהם (Isa 41:8; Ps 105:6; 2 Chr 20:7); זרע (ה)קדש (Isa 6:13; Ezra 9:2).

131. Lundbom, *Jeremiah 21–36*, 494. But in *Jeremiah 37–52* (pp. 584–85), Lundbom categorized those passages mentioned above as belonging either to the period he termed, "After the Fall of Jerusalem and Second Judahite Exile in 586 BCE" (30:18–21; 31:23–26, 27–30, 38–40; 33:10–11, 12–13, 14–22); or to "Around the Fall of Jerusalem in 586 BC," 32:42–44; 33:1–3, 4–9.

a much later timeframe, namely, the first generation of the Repatriates' transplantation back to Yehud during the Persian period.[132]

I want to suggest a third possibility: these passages represent original prophecies of Jeremiah directed to the Remnant of Judah that were adapted, expanded, and re-read through the lens of the Babylonian Repatriates in Yehud. These secondary rereading(s) added elements that may be compared to similar elements in Persian-period prophetic (and historiographic) literature. The interesting point is that while this adaptation retained the Judean geographical perspective of the earlier Jeremian prophecies, it fused with them perspectives otherwise known from Babylonian-exilic ideologies.[133]

In studying these prophetic passages, the following characteristics emerge as common denominators:

1. The people addressed: While several of these prophecies focus on Jerusalem and the cities of Judah (31:23–26; 32:42–44; 33:10–11, 12–13) and envision the revival of pastoral life in this area (31:24; 33:13), other passages invoke a vast national united audience: עמי ישראל ויהודה (30:3);[134] יהודה וישראל (Jer 33:7), or בני ישראל ובני (31:27, 31; 33:14), as also בית ישראל ובית יהודה יהודה יחדו (50:4–5); and זרע ישראל (31:36, 37).

2. The situation of the land: Both within the city and in its periphery, restoration takes place after a period when the land was empty of man and beast (32:42–44; 33:10–11, 12–13). The empty, desolate land is a distinct Babylonian exilic feature (as, for instance, Jer 30:17; 32:36).

132. This latter opinion governs most of the commentaries on Jeremiah. To give but one example, Holladay (*Jeremiah 2*, 165–67, 224, 228–31) considered Jer 31:23–25, 26, 38–40; 33:12–13, 14–26 to be Persian, but he did not suggest late contexts for 30:18–22; 33:1–11 (pp. 157, 222–24).

133. The suggestion that earlier prophecies have been readapted to new conditions through secondary redactional processes has, of course, been raised by scholars of Jeremiah, and most profoundly by McKane in his commentary. In reference to the consolation prophecies, see Barnabas Lindars, "'Rachel Weeping for Her Children'—Jeremiah 31:15–22," *JSOT* 12 (1979): 47–62. Lindars suggested that in this passage, Jeremiah himself turned to Hosea's prophecies that had been addressed to Northern Israel, which he then readdressed and adapted to Judah following the Destruction (pp. 56–57). Similarly, Lindars recognized later additions to those Jeremianic prophecies, which he characterized as having affinities to other poetic passages in Jeremiah and Deutero-Isaiah, with "little sign of the work of the Deuteronomic editor" (p. 55). See also Sweeney, "Jeremiah 30–31," 582–83.

134. Compare to Jer 3:18, בימים ההמה ילכו בית יהודה על בית ישראל ויבאו יחדו, which does envision reunification and return from exile.

3. The general perspective on restoration: The repeated phrase in these passages, שב (השיב) שבות (כבראשונה), refers to the people's restoration within the land designated as Judah and Israel (33:7–9), "the tents of Jacob" (30:18), or simply "the land" (33:11).[135] These passages use the phrase שב שבות, but do not mention exile as the point of departure; nor do they describe the journey back to the land.[136] It is interesting, though, that these prophecies give substance to restoration by mentioning the destruction of material culture (e.g. the houses of the city, including the royal buildings, 33:4), but the portrait of reversal and restoration focuses on changes in the human beings—the empty and desolate land becomes a place of lively voices of joy, of marriage, and of renewal of worship within the House of YHWH (33:11; and see Isa 65:19).

4. The pattern of the prophecies: These prophecies follow (thus, borrow) the pattern governed by the construction *ʿod* + *yiqtol* discussed above, which I suggested implies restoration within the land in the near future.[137] This pattern characterizes prophecies in chs. 30–31 (30:8–9; 31:2–6), and 32–33 (32:15; 33:10, 12).

5. The process of restoration: The actual restoration is described as rebuilding the city (30:18–22; 31:38–40) and as restoring agriculture in the rural periphery (31:23–26; 33:12–13).[138]

---

135. Jer 30:1–3, as introductory verses to the Book of Consolation, establish the semantic and contextual distinction between two phrases, ושבתי את שבות עמי והשבתים אל הארץ אשר נתתי לאבותם וירשוה and ישראל ויהודה, and join them together. The first phrase signifies restoration within the land, the second refers to regathering the people from exile. On the cumulative nature of these introductory verses, see Sweeney, "Jeremiah 30–31," 571, 577–78. Contra Sweeney (577–82), the addition of chs. 32–33 establishes yet another nuance to the basic meaning of שב שבות, "restore to its previous condition" (referring mostly to the agricultural life in the land), occurs in Hos 6:11; Amos 9:14; Zeph 2:7, and in the above-mentioned passages in Jeremiah (for a detailed discussion of this phrase, see Meir Weiss, *Amos* [2 vols.; Jerusalem: The Hebrew University/Magnes, 1992], 1:299–300, 2:553–54). Exilic (and postexilic) interpretations are responsible for the slight "Jeremian" flavor, meaning, the prospect of the restoration of Judah alone.

136. שב שבות occurs often with a small yet significant change of the *Qere* to שבית, "captivity, exile," in Jer 29:14; Pss 85:2; 126:4. But see Ezek 16:53; 39:25; and Lam 2:14, where the *Qere* suggests a correction to שבות. Deut 30:3 designates a third stage, where שב שבות becomes part of the "languages of return" as it opens the chain of actions that denote deliverance from exile (as also Joel 4:1; Zeph 3:20).

137. See pp. 226–27, above.

138. According to Holladay (*Jeremiah 2*, 199) the setting of Jer 31:38–40 "is doubtless in the time of Nehemiah."

Idioms of healing function as imagery for restoration in the land
(33:1–9; and already in 30:12–17).[139]

6. Renaming: Restored Zion gains new names: יברכך יהוה נוה צדק
הר הקדש ("the LORD bless you, Abode of righteousness, O holy
mountain!," 31:23); וזה אשר יקרא לה יהוה צדקנו ("and this is what
she shall be called: 'the LORD is our Vindicator'," 33:16).[140]

7. Special thematic components of restoration: (a) A central topic
within these prophecies is the covenant between God and His
people, which is mobilized from two different (perhaps even
contradictory) perspectives. First, the covenant formula, והייתם לי
לעם ואנכי אהיה לכם לאלהים, sets the goal for the future reinstitution of the covenant relationship (30:22, 25; 31:1, 31–34). But
second, the ongoing (present) existence of Israel/Judah as God's
people is guaranteed through the analogy established between
the universal covenant, which ensures cosmic order, and the
covenants God had established with His people, His Davidic
king, and the Levitical priests (31:35–37; 33:14–22). (b) The
prophecies emphasize divine justice by focusing on the qualities
of benevolence and mercy (33:6, 8, 11), and point to the people's penitence (33:1–9; 50:17–20).[141] (c) The prophecies give a
special importance to publicizing God's name among the nations
(33:9). This feature is otherwise unknown among the prophecies
of Jeremiah,[142] but is well-recognized in Ezekiel (Ezek 36:16–
32) and in Deutero-Isaiah (Isa 48:9).

It is almost impossible to differentiate early and late themes in this list
of characteristics. The decisive argument in favor of a notion of secondary adaptations of Jeremian prophecies by Babylonian Repatriates is
this mixture of (at least) two layers within prophetic passages of consolation. The above-mentioned passages contain expansions of prophetic

---

139. The imagery of medical remedies is well-attested within the communal
laments found in Jeremiah (Jer 8:15, 22; 10:19; 14:19) and once in a personal lament
(15:18), as well as these two consolation prophecies (30:12–17; 33:1–9).

140. Compare Jer 30:17: כי נדחה קראו לך ציון היא דרש אין לה ("though they
called you 'Outcast, that Zion whom no one seeks out'"); see also Isa 60:14;
62:4, 12.

141. Mercy and benevolence do not characterize God's behavior towards his
people during the crisis era (see Jer 13:14; 16:5). This is another example of the
reversal of or movement between judgment and consolation in Jeremiah. רחם in a
positive context occurs in Jer 12:15 as well.

142. The one exception in Jer 14:7–9 is a fragment of a communal lament which
Jeremiah quotes and incorporates into his prophecy.

pronouncements, or even two diverse (at times contradictory) outlooks described above as separate perspectives, the one referring to the Remnant of Judah, while the other invokes Babylonian exilic perceptions of group identity and restoration.[143] I will again restrict the discussion here to but two of these prophetical passages.

Jeremiah 33:10–11, 12–13 describe the change within "this place," bringing together a prophetic pronouncement and several expansions (Table 3):

Table 3. *Secondary Adaptation in Jeremiah 33*

אשר אתם אמרים חרב הוא <u>מאין אדם ומאין בהמה</u>	10aβ	כה אמר יהוה עוד ישמע במקום הזה	10	
הנשמות <u>מאין אדם ומאין יושב ומאין בהמה</u>	10bβ	**בערי יהודה ובחצות ירושלים**		
קול אמרים הודו את יהוה צבאות כי טוב כי לעולם חסדו מבאים תודה בית יהוה	11aβ	קול ששון וקול שמחה קול חתן וקול כלה	11	
		כי אשיב את שבות הארץ כבראשנה אמר יהוה	11b	
כה אמר יהוה צבאות עוד יהיה **במקום הזה** החרב <u>מאין אדם ועד בהמה</u> ובכל עריו נוה רעים מרבצים צאן	12			
בערי ההר בערי השפלה ובערי הנגב ובארץ בנימן **ובסביבי ירושלים ובערי יהודה** עד תעברנה הצאן על ידי מונה אמר יהוה	13			

10	Thus said the LORD: Again there shall be heard **in this place** in the towns of Judah and the streets of Jerusalem	10aβ	which you say is ruined, <u>without man or beast</u>
		10bβ	that are desolate, <u>without man, without inhabitants, without beast</u>

---

143. An example of such a contradiction may be found by comparing Jer 32:5–16 with vv. 42–44. The latter passage functions as an *inclusio* for vv. 5–16 and is patterned as an adaptation of that earlier prophecy said to the Remnant of Judah under Zedekiah prior to the Destruction. Like Jer 33:10–11 and 12–13 (to be discussed below), this passage transfers restoration to the empty land to this new context, utilizing the formula שב שבות this new context.

the sound of mirth and gladness, the voice of bridegroom and bride	11aβ	the voice of those who cry, "Give thanks to the LORD of Hosts, for the LORD is good, for His kindness is everlasting!" as they bring thanksgiving offerings to the House of the LORD
For I will restore the fortunes of the land as of old—said the LORD.		
	12	Thus said the LORD of Hosts: **In this ruined place,** <u>without man and beast,</u> and in all its towns, there shall again be a pasture for shepherds, where they can rest their flocks.
	13	**In the towns** of the hill country, in the towns of the Shephelah, and in the towns of the Negeb, in the land of Benjamin **and in the environs of Jerusalem and in the towns of Judah,** sheep shall pass again under the hands of one who counts them—said the LORD.

This consolation prophecy (vv. 10–11), which promises the return of joyful sounds to Jerusalem and to the cities of Judah, the sounds of bride and groom, reverses well-known Jeremian prophecies of judgment (7:34; 16:9; and 25:10).[144] The syntactical pattern of *ᶜod* + *yiqtol* together with שׁב שׁבות, the promise to restore the land "as of old" with no mention of exile and return, identify this prophecy as *originating* among Jeremiah's prophecies of consolation to the Remnant of Judah (as in 32:15).

However, this promise was expanded by four different statements: (1) A description of "that place" through a quotation (10aβ); (2) a second parallel description referring to "the towns of Judah and the streets of Jerusalem" (10bβ); (3) an addition of sounds of rejoicing, which unite with the sounds of worship and thanksgiving in the House of YHWH (11aβ). (4) Moreover, vv. 12–13, which indeed are constructed on the same pattern as vv. 10–11,[145] expand this prophecy further, adding a third (and a fourth) description of "that place," which this time highlights the transformation of the rural areas of Judah (similar to 32:44).

144. The nature of this prophecy as reversal was pointed out by Holladay, *Jeremiah 2*, 224; Carroll, *Jeremiah*, 634–36.
145. See Lundbom, *Jeremiah 21–36*, 534–35.

The arguments for considering these pronouncements as secondary expansions are founded on stylistic grounds:

(1) אשר אתם אמרים חרב הוא מאין אדם ומאין בהמה ("[of] which you say: 'It is ruined! without man or beast'") follows the pattern of 32:36, 43:[146]

> ועתה לכן כה אמר יהוה אלהי ישראל אל העיר הזאת אשר אתם
> אמרים נתנה ביד מלך בבל בחרב וברעב ובדבר

> But now, assuredly, thus said the Lord, the God of Israel, concerning the city of which you say, "It is being delivered into the hands of the king of Babylon through the sword, through famine, and through pestilence." (32:36)

> ונקנה השדה בארץ הזאת אשר אתם אמרים שממה היא
> מאין אדם ובהמה נתנה ביד הכשדים

> And fields shall again be purchased in this land of which you say, "It is a desolation, without man or beast; it is delivered into the hands of the Chaldeans." (32:43)

These three anonymous quotations invoke descriptions of Jerusalem and its surroundings as destroyed and desolate, utilizing prophecies of judgment spoken earlier by Jeremiah.[147] However, the syntactical construction חרב הוא (similar to שממה היא [in 32:43]) is exceptional in Jeremiah. Furthermore, the use of the adjective חרב, "ruined," in this context is itself a *hapax* (33:10, 12); the normally occurring form of the word in Jeremiah is the noun חרבה, "ruin." The latter term is used to describe the fates of the Temple (Jer 22:5), the city (27:17), Jerusalem and the towns of Judah (25:18; 44:2, 6), and the land (7:34; 25:11; 44:22).[148] In addition, the common phrases used in prophecies of judgment in Jeremiah are the verbal phrases: היה שממה (as in 4:27; 50:13), שים שממה (in 6:8; 10:22), נתן שממה (in 15:10; 34:22); these are a bit closer to Jer 32:43: שממה היא, but the syntactical uniqueness remains.

---

146.   Note that the NJPS takes this as indirect rather than direct speech, and therefore misses the parallel between these two verses.

147.   For a discussion of these special quotations in Jer 32, see Rom-Shiloni, "Everlasting Covenant," 208–10.

148.   חרבה occurs eight times in Jeremiah in the singular (noted above), and twice in the plural חרבות (in 25:9; 49:13). Note its similar usage in Ezekiel in reference to Jerusalem (5:14), the mountains of Israel (38:8), the land of Egypt (29:9), Edom (25:13), towns in the Se'ir mountain (35:4); note also its use in the plural חרבות referring to cities (33:24, 27; 36:4, 10, 33; 38:12) and land (26:20).

(2) The impression of extraordinary phraseology is reinforced by this phrase in v. 10aβ, מאין אדם ומאין בהמה, along with the expanded repetition in v. 10bβ, מאין אדם ומאין יושב ומאין בהמה, and the further repeat in v. 12, מאין אדם ועד בהמה. The standard phrase in prophecies of judgment in Jeremiah is the single-phrase construction, מאין יושב (in 4:7; 26:9; 34:22; 44:22), which also appears in prophecies to the nations (46:19; 48:9; 51:29, 37). Hence, the doubled and even tripled constructions of 33:10–12 intensify the impression of that desolation; the construction itself may have been influenced by the Ezekelian phrase אדם ובהמה, "man and beast," which is used in Ezekiel in prophecies of judgment (Ezek 14:12, 17, 19, 21; 25:13; 29:8; 36:11), but only once in Jeremiah (Jer 36:29).

(3) The third expansion (v. 11aβ) adds to the rejoicing sounds of the bride and groom—the private-familial joy in restoring daily life—the sounds of the communal thanksgiving offering and liturgy in the House of YHWH. This expansion finds its equivalent in the liturgy (Pss 100:5; 106:1; 107:1; 136:1–26); while the offering of thanksgiving is recalled in another expansion in Jeremiah (17:26),[149] it otherwise appears only in Second Temple biblical sources (Ezra 3:11; 1 Chr 16:34, 41; 2 Chr 5:13; 7:3, 6; 22:21).[150]

Two major themes were added through those expansions: the emphasis on the land as empty prior to the restoration (vv. 12–13), and the restoration as not restricted to private fortunes and as having its major impact on the worship in the Jerusalem Temple (v. 11; see Ezra 3:11).

Jeremiah 33:10–11, 12–13 seems, therefore, to merge different prophetic pronouncements. The Repatriates' Persian-period expansion is built upon the prophet's earlier proclamation to the Remnant of Judah, which is then adapted to the Repatriates' reality of restoration within the land. The time span between the early exilic period and the last decades of the sixth century, coupled with the prophecy's concentration on in-group perspectives, has facilitated this transformational adaptation.

---

149. Jer 17:26 is to be counted as an editorial expansion of the otherwise authentically Jeremian covenant speech in Jer 17:19–27 (see Dalit Rom-Shiloni, "Law Interpretation in Jeremiah: Exegetical Techniques and Ideological Intentions," *Shnaton* 17 [2008]: 59–79 [in Hebrew]). The other argument to substantiate its secondary and late character is its list of the geographic districts, which is similar to 32:44 and 33:13.

150. Lundbom (*Jeremiah 21–36*, 536) recognized this late context, but nevertheless counted the thanksgiving offering as a possibly ancient institution.

The features that call attention to such secondary rereadings are: reversals of Jeremiah's prophecies of judgment; *hapax* words and syntactical patterns in Jeremiah; and resemblances to Babylonian exilic and postexilic literary compositions, mainly Ezekiel, Deutero-Isaiah, Zech 1–8, and even Ezra–Nehemiah (see, for instance, Jer 31:38–40).[151] The accumulation of such features together in this passage suggests a non-Jeremian, and possibly even a Repatriate, authorship.

3. *Conclusions*

Inclusivity seems to be guiding the in-group approaches within prophecies of consolation in Jeremiah. Yet, teasing out the Jeremian–Judean layers in the consolation prophecies contributes greatly to our understanding of how Babylonian exilic authors, and in a different way their Repatriate counterparts, redefined their in-group identities based on definitions established already by Jeremiah in Judah early in the prophet's career and within the early exilic period (597–586 B.C.E.).

The book of Jeremiah indeed shows the entire spectrum of this polemical interchange. On the synchronic level, Jeremiah suggests that a counter-ideology to that of Ezekiel was already in place by the early sixth century. In terms of diachronic transformations, the book of Jeremiah illustrates in itself the development and the changes within Babylonian exilic ideologies both in Babylon and back in Yehud over the course of the sixth century B.C.E.

This unique and complicated picture of Jeremiah is a fitting lead-in to the concluding chapter of this study.

151.　Another example is Jer 50:4–5 which has several components that reveal its exilic ideological orientation and some that reflect a Judean perspective. Among the Babylonian Exilic characteristics are the formulae בני ישראל המה ובני יהודה יחדו (v. 4), ואת יהוה אלהיהם יבקשו (v. 4), which allude in this context to an exilic situation, where inquiring of YHWH indicates the people's initiative towards repentance (see Deut 4:29 and Jer 29:13); so also the use of ברית עולם (Jer 50:5; and cf. the exilic perspective of Jer 32:36–41). For the Babylonian exilic orientation of this notion of ברית עולם, see Rom-Shiloni, "Everlasting Covenant," 215. For a Judean perspective, note דרך הנה פניהם (Jer 50:5; crying as part of the journey of return draws on Jer 31:9, from the Northern preexilic prophecies). The phrase נלוה אל יהוה (v. 5b) is a *hapax* in Jeremiah, and it invites the people in this context to establish an eternal covenant with YHWH. In this usage the phrase differs from other occurrences of נלוה אל יהוה which appear in cultic contexts (Num 18:2; Isa 56:3, 6), or apply to strangers joining Israel (Isa 14:1). The closest similarity to Jeremiah would be Zech 2:15, where nations attach themselves to YHWH and become His people. But compare Lundbom, *Jeremiah 37–52*, 374–76.

Chapter 8

SUMMARY AND CONCLUSIONS

As this study draws to a close, it is possible now to present its overall scope and the significance of my findings.

I opened the study by pointing out times of exile (597–586 B.C.E. and following) and times of return (538–516, and again 458–432 B.C.E.). This timeframe was the context in which questions of identity captured a central role in Judean theology and ideology. While scholars have focused on the later era, on the explicit conflicts set in Ezra–Nehemiah, the current study established two foundational observations that suggest a different approach. First, the overall question concerning identity is one and the same throughout, during the two formative eras and in between them, over a time span of about 150 years. That question might be phrased: In view of the events and the upheaval that tore the people of God into two communities initially separated geographically, and which then drew them back to geographical proximity, in a period that challenged throughout all traditional understandings of covenantal relationship with God and demanded re-identification of the national-religious identity—which of the two communities could still consider itself and claim to be God's people? The discussions of the specific literary compositions of this period were aimed at locating the ideological argumentations and the different transformations this conflict had undergone over time and place. Second, emphasis was given to the earlier period, to the Neo-Babylonian era, as the formative one that shaped the basic presumptions underlying the later transformations.

In search of ideologies in transition, I have defined Babylonian exilic ideologies as those which, having first taken shape within the earliest exiled community, govern the biblical literature of the sixth and fifth centuries in *both* Babylon and (later) in Persian Yehud. Most of the literary sources at hand illustrate exclusive stances towards non-Babylon-based communities, employing intergroup strategies of *division* that were originally developed by the time of Ezekiel, and that are carried forward in the Babylonian and redactional strands of Jeremiah, in Deutero-Isaiah (chs. 40–48, 49–66), Haggai, Zechariah, and Ezra–Nehemiah.

The investigation has also revealed, however, multiple perspectives on identity obtaining among Those Who Remained in Judah. There, too, we find a dominant strain that understands the Remnant in Judah in exclusive terms. Only to a lesser extent, and restricted to the Neo-Babylonian era, can we discern, in the book of Jeremiah and within Ezekiel, nonexclusive perspectives, which obtained among Those Who Remained.

I structured this discussion along a reverse historical trajectory, moving from the Persian-period sources, about which much has already been said regarding issues of identity formation, to the Neo-Babylonian writings, which have been under-explored in relation to this area. Doing so allowed me to move from what has been presented as a more sharply focused historical picture to one in which the contours of intragroup polemic were assumed to be more faint and amorphous, and to tease out the beginnings of this polemic via its connections with later developments. On the basis of this investigation it is now possible to reconstruct an orderly history of the polemic between the Babylonians and Those Who Remained, from the time of the Jehoichin Exile to the early years of Persian Yehud.

1. *From External Separation to Intergroup Division*

Shared external events and similar internal effects shape the history of Judean communities of the sixth and fifth centuries B.C.E. By the early sixth century Judah had gone through successive forced deportations to Babylon. These external forces brought about the physical division of the community into Exiles and Those Who Remained in Judah. The present study emphasized that this physical division immediately created a crisis of group-identity for each segment of the divided community. Thus, physical division led to socio-ideological division as well, whereby each community set clear barriers between itself as the in-group, and its sister community as the out-group. In the second half of the sixth century, another external force, this time the favorable decree of the Persian king allowing Babylonian Exiles to return to the homeland, brought about the geographical proximity of Repatriates from Babylon and Those Who Remained back in Yehud. Given these shared external circumstances, the intriguing phenomenon is that Judean communities in both locations during the Neo-Babylonian period and the two Yahwistic communities residing side by side in Persian Yehud maintained mutually antagonistic attitudes toward one another.

Considering issues of identity formation from the standpoint of both geographical distance (from Judah to Babylon and vice versa) and diachronic development (over the period of the early sixth to the late fifth centuries B.C.E.), my particular interest has been in the operation of these divisive argumentations in both geographical contexts over time; and in the perhaps preliminary question of how we can retrieve these arguments and counter arguments from the biblical literature of this period—self-legitimization of the in-group community and the delegitimization of out-group community(/ies)—that were set by each of the two antagonistic Judean groups.

The Introduction (Chapter 1) set the terms for this investigation within the social psychology framework of intergroup relations, with a focus on group identity redefinition under circumstances of dislocation and crisis. This study focused on ideological argumentation, the articulation of the "group beliefs" (following Bar-Tal) that each community is said to develop and share. Those beliefs create the community's unity and internal solidarity, and by them the group defines its "groupness" over time, in reference to its past, its present, and even its future prospects. However, a group also distinguishes itself from other groups ("out-groups") by developing feelings of superiority and/or hostility; by initiating strategies of discrimination and (where the relationship may be too close for comfort) delegitimization. Hence, intergroup relations involve the creation and maintenance of boundaries of "otherness" between different but connected groups. In-group definitions tend to develop self-esteem, and negative arguments against an out-group may in fact function to bolster further the in-group identity and self-esteem.

I used this framework of intergroup relations analysis to examine clues to identity in sixth- and fifth-century biblical literature, which to a large extent is dominated by the thought world of the Babylonian Exiles and then the Repatriates; that is, by Babylonian exilic ideologies. Application of the model of intergroup relationships under conflict to the biblical literary evidence made it possible to identify the strategies of in-group and out-group argumentation used in each composition, and thus to trace the redefinitions of group identities as constructed in each literary and historical context. Discussions highlighted the ways in which each of the two Judean communities—the Babylonian Exiles (and later Repatriates), and Those Who Remained—established group boundaries that enabled them to create in-group and out-group definitions; to draw clear lines of inclusivity, and even clearer lines of exclusivity against the other; and to argue that only they could be designated as *the* (true) people of God.

Mobilizing the notion of exclusivity for a context of *internal* intergroup relationships (i.e. among groups of the same nation) required a slight but significant modification in Donald Horowitz's definition of *division* as part of his patterns of identity change among diverse societies. Horowitz suggested that *dissimilation* leads either to *division* (A yields B + C) or *proliferation* (A yields A + B). Yet internal relationships within one nation shows that exclusivity develops as a consequence of intergroup *division*, where A yields "true A" + C.[1]

The process of differentiation was construed by means of three argumentational strategies of exclusivity that are employed throughout the corpus, from Ezekiel down to Ezra–Nehemiah: *continuity, entirety*, and *annexation* of national-religious traditions. Each of these may function in both in-group and out-group claims, and they cover observations concerning the past, present, and future of the in-group and out-group communities.

The utilization of these three arguments of exclusivity for both in-group and out-group argumentation shows that the entire Judean deliberation over group identity following the Babylonian division of the community among both Those Who Remained and among the Babylonian Exiles in their diverse waves of deportation and return, was indeed driven by a dynamic of fierce exclusivity, or at the very least, of exclusive inclusivity; that is, restricted inclusivity that clearly distinguishes the in-group from any out-group.

2. *Continuity and Transformation within Babylonian Exilic Ideologies*

The framework of intergroup relationships proved helpful for observing the internal conflicts between the Exiles and Those Who Remained, over claims to be the true "people of God." Two issues should be separately pointed out. First, different rhetorical even metaphorical configurations of the in-group and the out-group play specific roles in the exclusive definitions of "*the* people of God" vs. "(any) others." Second, the core–periphery relationship between Jerusalem and Babylon is transformed over time, in a way which is observable among the sources. In relation to both issues, sources from the early sixth century contribute unique evidence, otherwise unknown from the literature of the later periods.

In what follows I will reconstruct three stages within the development of Babylonian exilic ideologies during the sixth and fifth centuries, and summarize the intergroup strategies utilized at each stage to construct in-group and out-group definitions.

---

1. On the modification of Horowitz's model of division, see the discussion on pp. 26–29, above.

Table 4. *Shifts of Group Identities within Babylonian Exilic Ideologies*

Period:	Rhetorical Opposition 1	Rhetorical Opposition 2	Core and Periphery	
Early Exilic period (ca. 597–586 and on)	Ezekiel[2] Jehoiachin Exiles (Israel, Jacob) *vs.* Jerusalem (by origin is Canaanite, of the land)	Ezekiel Jehoiachin Exiles *vs.* Jerusalem will become desolate, empty land	Ezekiel Core: Jerusalem Periphery: Babylon Babylon will move to core	
Later Exilic Period (ca. 570 to ca. 530)		Deutero-Isaiah Babylonian Exiles *vs.* empty land	Deutero-Isaiah Core: Babylon Periphery: Jerusalem	
Persian Period (ca. 520 to ca. 430 B.C.E.)	Ezra–Nehemiah Repatriates (Israel, בני הגולה) *vs.* Foreign people(s) of the land(s)	Zechariah (and Haggai) Repatriates *vs.* empty land	Ezra–Nehemiah Core: Babylon Periphery: Yehud	Zechariah (and Haggai) Core: Babylon Periphery: Jerusalem But restored to its core position

a. *Exclusive Definitions of "The People of God" vs. "(Any) Others"*
The Babylonian ideologies employ two different argumentations to designate their "out-group"—that is, to exclude from the people of God any other Judean community besides that of the Babylonian Exiles. The

---

2. This same point of view also characterizes the Babylonian strands in Jeremiah, see pp. 233–52, above.

first argument avers that the inhabitants of the city or the land do not belong to the people of God; they are clearly not Judahite (or Israelite) but foreigners, of either the autochthonic peoples of the land (as in Ezek 16:3; Ezra 9:1–2), or of an amorphous group of different nationalities settled in the land by the Assyrians (Ezra 4:2). The second argument asserts that there is no other Judahite community in the Land. Since the Destruction and the subsequent deportations and, specifically, the emigration to Egypt, the land has been left empty, desolate, and totally barren (Ezek 12:17–20; Isa 49:14–21; Zech 1:7–17).

The study has shown that these two arguments appear independently in different literary sources that represent the Babylonian exilic ideologies, and thus they should be distinguished from one other. The border lines are very clear: the empty land imagery is favored by the prophetic literature, from Ezekiel to Deutero-Isaiah and Zech 1–8, whereas the imagery of the land populated only with foreign, non-Israelite peoples is employed by Ezekiel and later by Ezra–Nehemiah.

The discussion thus traced both of these arguments back to the prophet Ezekiel, who was the first to utilize them in his prophecies against Jerusalem. In Ezekiel's framework, Jerusalem (and its population) is Canaanite in origin (Ezek 16:3); occasionally in his prophecies of judgment, the city (and its inhabitants) is doomed to be empty and desolate (in Ezek 6:14; 33:27–28, etc.). These portrayals, which identify Jerusalem and its inhabitants as the out-group from Ezekiel's perspective, are used throughout the book and serve as well in the prophecies of consolation, where Ezekiel envisions the return of the Exiles to an empty land that is to be revived by God especially for the sake of His people, the Repatriated Exiles (see Ezek 36:8–12).

Ezekiel's double argumentations of exclusivity are thus of paramount importance. They reveal the initial steps of ideological separation of the Exiles from their sister community, and locate them in the first years of the forced political division of the Jehoiachin Exiles and Those Who Remained in Judah, early in the sixth century B.C.E.

Furthermore, analyzing the biblical literature from this point of departure allows us to note the long history of polemical interchange, over the sixth and the fifth centuries B.C.E., between the Babylonian Exiles and Those Who Remained in Judah (Yehud). The early exilic community developed a conception of self-identity as the people of God which excluded all other Judean/Yahwistic communities. Upon the return to Persian Yehud, this exclusive conception was further developed and transformed by Repatriate groups. But it was certainly not initiated at that late point.

I would even argue that the Repatriates as portrayed by Ezra–Nehemiah had no real clue to the initial arguments against Those Who Remained; they simply maintained, and further enlivened, the antagonism they had inherited from those earlier generations in Babylon. In confirmation of this last proposal, three phases, involving three grand transformations, may be discerned in these exclusive Babylonian exilic ideologies.

The earliest phase starts with Ezekiel in Babylon and Jeremiah in Judah, soon after the Jehoiachin exile (597 B.C.E. and on). Ezekiel, as the advocate for the deportees, and as far as our literary sources tell, the first constructor of the Babylonian exilic ideologies, contributed the deportees' side to the struggle. At this early point we also find the perspectives of those living in Judah attested in quotations within Ezekiel and in Jeremiah's pro-Judah voice(s).

In comparison to the Persian-period phase, this initial stage of the internal conflict is characterized by four unique points: (1) the early sources in Ezekiel and Jeremiah testify to a two-sided ideological polemic. Quotations of Judean assertions in Ezekiel and the pro-Judah voices in Jeremiah show us the arguments of Those Who Remained. Their voices will soon vanish from the biblical sources, however, and as of the second phase (see below), the only voices heard in the biblical literature are those of the Babylonian Exiles, and then the Repatriates. (2) Their controversial perspectives place the two contemporary prophets of God on opposite sides of the divide in this crucial debate. Each prophet had a major role in reconstructing the identity of his home community. Each strove to legitimize his community's existence by emphasizing its exclusive status as the current and future people of God. (3) Thematically, the controversy in its initial stage was over differing interpretations of central conceptions in Israelite religion, concerning the relationship between God, His people, and His land, and particularly over conceptions of land and of exile. Both groups share the same national traditions, which are utilized by each prophet as solid arguments to establish his own group's *continuity* with the national past; and (using the strategy of *entirety*) as the sole heir entitled to the anticipated national future of redemption. This *annexation* of the same national traditions illustrates that at this early stage, the two competing groups shared common world views. (4) Finally, the early sixth-century sources show that the exclusionary process involves two synchronic procedures: (a) reidentification of the group by choosing and emphasizing the legitimate exclusive elements, and (b) delegitimization of the other group.

These early sources further illustrate that already as of this stage and throughout the later phases of the conflict, there were no tendencies towards reconciliation between the two Judean groups that had been forced to separate by imperial deportation policy. On the contrary, the two communities developed and continued the above-mentioned ideological arguments that excluded the other (as, for instance, in Ezek 14:12–23; 24:15–27).

The second phase, that of the exilic period (ca. 570 to ca. 530 B.C.E.), is firstly characterized by transformations in (Babylonian) conceptions of the in-group. Among the tradents of Ezekiel, those of Jeremiah, and even more in Deutero-Isaiah (chs. 40–48, 49–66), there appears an expansion of the in-group definition to include all Babylonian Exiles, no matter the time of their deportation, as "true" Israel.

On the other hand, these sources share a complete disregard of any other community of Judeans, and specifically the community in Judah. This disregard is further enhanced by references to the Land of Judah/ Israel as empty and desolate. The *invisibility* of the Judean community in the land (i.e. the out-group) serves well the portrayal of the Babylonian Exiles as the one and only people of God. Hence, of the two rhetorical oppositions used by Ezekiel, only one was carried on within the prophetic literature, and it was greatly elaborated by Deutero-Isaiah. The concept of the empty land has become an argument of exclusion in its implicit testimony to the nonexistence of any other Judean community beside this community of Babylonian Exiles.

In addition, Deutero-Isaiah (in the Jerusalem chapters) evidences an additional step forward, as among his strategies of reidentification, Jerusalem/*bat* Zion is called שבי ירושלים and שביה בת ציון, thus fully and restrictively identified with the Babylonian Repatriates (Isa 52:1–2). Not only does the prophet avoid making reference to any non-Repatriate population in Jerusalem, but he furthermore identifies Jerusalem as the city of those who had been in captivity, the city of the Babylonian Repatriates (52:2, 8–10; and see 45:13; 51:16; 61:1–11).

From the perspective of the last phase of this conflict, the early Persian period (ca. 520 to ca. 430 B.C.E.), we have the benefit of a panoramic retrospective on these long-standing intragroup polemics. At this late era, internal struggles between the Repatriates and Those Who Remained in Judah/Yehud follow two distinct lines of argumentation. The point of departure common to both is the conviction that the Repatriates (and their homeland community of the Babylonian Exiles) is the one and only legitimate community, both in the land (and in the Diaspora). At this point, however, the Persian-period ideologies part company. The prophetic sources follow Ezekiel and Deutero-Isaiah, arguing that the exclusive status of the Repatriates rests on the simple fact that the land has been empty and desolate ever since the Destruction, awaiting the return of the exiled people of God (e.g. Zech 8). Ezra–Nehemiah takes up and transforms Ezekiel's other argument, that all (non-Repatriate Yahwists) inhabitants of the land are "foreigners." Both claims are exclusive.[3] The Persian-period phase thus continues, reuses, and expands earlier arguments of exclusion. It does not seem to have developed any new argumentative strategies. The only innovative element in the internal struggles of the Persian period seems, thus, to be the in-group struggle between the Exiles in the Diaspora and Repatriates in the (new) homeland, as presented by Bedford.[4]

In reference to the characterization of the out-group, there are thus three distinct intergroup dynamics that come into play over these periods. The first phase, the early years of exile, is a time of *separation*. The physical division created the need for each of the two Judean communities to reconstruct their national group identities. The divisive ideological arguments that resulted constitute the crucial beginning of this internal polemic, the time when the initial establishment of these mutually excluding ideological proclamations took place.

The second phase, from around the mid-sixth century and on in Babylon (and in the early years of the return), are dominated by *out-group invisibility*, or a *complete ignorance* of Those Who Remained in the land. But while the out-group becomes fully invisible, as if non-existent, and the land is portrayed as empty, this is a time that shows greater investment in the building up of in-group self-esteem as the chosen people of God (this is mainly seen in Deutero-Isaiah, the Ezekiel School, the Babylonian strands of Jeremiah, and continues to Zech 1–8).

The third and last phase, the times of return and restoration on the early Persian period, shows a much more complicated picture of three dynamics we have met before. The first pertains to the confrontation of Repatriates with Those Who Remained; the two others are within the Repatriates' in-group. On the one hand, the governing dynamic is the ongoing process of *separation* of the Repatriates from any possible remnant community descended from Those Who Remained in the land. This exclusive tendency in its two distinct constructions is shared by the prophetic compositions, the Jerusalem chapters of Deutero-Isaiah, Haggai and Zech 1–8; and by the historiography of Ezra–Nehemiah.

---

3. *Pace* Kessler, "Persia's Loyal Yahwists," 109–10; and see pp. 80–81, 98, above.

4. Bedford, "Diaspora: Homeland Relations in Ezra–Nehemiah."

On the other hand, two other patterns of intergroup dynamics concern the in-group and point to internal tensions. Peculiar to Ezra–Nehemiah is the attention given to *homeland–Diaspora relationships* between the Repatriates and their core community in Babylon. Since this dynamic falls within the category of in-group argumentation, it is built upon *positive acceptance* of further Babylonian Repatriates adjoining their earlier Returnees (although it is not free of exhortations by the new-Repatriates over against earlier ones, as in Ezra 9–10).

Tendencies toward *incorporation* also seem to appear, but they are clearly restricted to the in-group, very limited in fashion and in scope (as they are restricted to individuals). These incorporative tendencies occur in Isa 65–66 and in Ezra–Nehemiah; and as might be expected, such actions are initiated by the supremely dominant community of the Repatriates.[5]

b. *Core–Periphery Relationships: Between Jerusalem and Babylon*
The shift from Jerusalem to Babylon as the core of existence in the perception of the exilic community is one of the dramatic changes brought about by the Destruction and the subsequent Babylonian deportations. During the sixth and fifth centuries these core–periphery relationships became another polemical issue. The return to the land did not unquestionably mean another transformation of perspectives on core and periphery.

One of the areas in which core–periphery relationships play a role is in defining the identity of the "Remnant." The present study argued that the Remnant is a dynamic term, utilized by the in-group with a clearly exclusivist thrust that establishes the prestigious status of the group. It is thus used by both antagonistic parties, each of the communities considering itself to be *the* Remnant.

In fact, the shift from Jerusalem to Babylon as core early in the sixth century seems to be another innovation of Ezekiel and his contemporaries in Babylon (as in Jer 24). In his repeated cries over Jerusalem's annihilation, כלה אתה עשה את שארית ישראל (Ezek 9:8; 11:13), the prophet advances the alternative with the Jehoiachin Exiles (Ezek 11:14–21); that is, that they, the group in Babylon, are now the core of "Israel." According to Ezekiel, the Remnant of Israel, as of the early sixth century, consists of those settled in Babylon. This perception of their own (Babylonian) community as the core is sustained within the Babylonian exilic ideologies down to Ezra–Nehemiah. Its major representatives are

---

5. Beside Ezra 6:19–22, we may mention the list of the Returnees in Ezra 2 (Neh 7) that appears to include nonexilic names and settlements.

the historiographers of the books of Kings, and the prophet, Deutero-Isaiah.

Yet, by the early Persian period another clear distinction develops, one between the historiography of Ezra–Nehemiah and the prophetic literature of Haggai and Zech 1–8. The Babylonian core transplants branches into the land, and it is envisioned that Zion will eventually regain its core position (Zech 2:10–17; but already in Deutero-Isaiah). Nevertheless, Persian-period prophecy (the Jerusalem chapters of Deutero-Isaiah, Haggai, and Zechariah) and historiography (Ezra–Nehemiah) share the perception that hegemony over these definitions of the Remnant is still confined to the Babylonian Repatriates.

This is where definitions of the Remnant demonstrate their weight as another characteristic of exclusivist viewpoints. These exclusivist perspectives of the Remnant may clearly be noticed in Haggai and in Zech 1–8, which independently define their audience as כל שארית העם (Hag 1:12, 14; 2:2; Zech 8:6, 11, 12).

To conclude, a look at the shifts in perceptions of core and periphery further illustrates the dominance of Babylonian exilic ideological perspectives, from Ezekiel through Ezra–Nehemiah, on the formation of the Judean communities over the sixth and fifth centuries. Once Babylon became the core community, it held ideological hegemony among the Repatriates throughout the waves of return. As shown by Bedford, core-periphery tensions evinced in the literature of this period should be seen as developing within the Babylonian community itself. There is no indication that such tensions should be attributed to a struggle between the Babylonian Repatriates and Those Who Remained.

3. *Inclusive Interests: Detecting Voices within the In-group*

By adducing additional literary information within this methodological framework of sociological strategies of intergroup relationships and models of identity change, I have been able to substantiate further the prevalence of tendencies and tactics of *division* in the Babylonian exilic ideologies of the sixth and fifth centuries. There are, however, a few examples of inclusive tendencies within these ideologies as well. The unifying characteristic of these passages is that inclusive attitudes are directed towards (and restricted to) exilic groups alone. Indeed, Deutero-Isaiah forecasts gathering in the dispersed not only from the east and the north (as in Isa 46:11) but from all four corners of the world (43:5–6; 49:12). Yet, all these passages underscore the prophet's perspective as one of the Exiles in Babylon: Zion is the target for return, and those who are away from the (empty) land are the objects of consolation. This is, therefore, a clear illustration of exclusive inclusivity.

Inclusion of foreign individuals (or peoples) from out-group communities is rare. Ezra 6:19–21 seems to be exceptional in its explicit reference to accepting those who separate themselves from the defilement of the peoples of the land. This acceptance, however, is in fact a matter of *incorporation* (A + B = A); that is, the Repatriates, from a distinctively superior point of view, express the willingness to absorb individuals into their own community under the condition that the latter assimilate in all respects into their dominant group. Thus, this inclusiveness is in all respects still exclusive, based on the recognition of the superior, prestigious, and unique status of the Babylonian Repatriated community and its hegemony over the defiled "other."[6]

This same tendency typifies the readiness to accept those designated as בני הנכר in Isa 56:1–6. But it is remarkable that within the general timeframe, by the early Persian period there are no fewer than three different attitudes towards those who wish to "join themselves to YHWH." As a second approach, Ezek 44:4–14 excludes such people from the Temple services; and finally, Ezra–Nehemiah specifies בני הנכר as the "other" group forbidden to intermarry (Ezra 9:1; Neh 10:29). בני הנכר provide an important example of the ideological and sociological complexity at work within the Babylonian exilic ideologies, which were certainly not homogeneous and differed over initiatives toward inclusion within the Repatriated community itself. Thus even *incorporation* was not straightforward in this model of exclusive inclusivity.[7]

4. *Universalism and Exclusivity*

Another topic touched upon in this study was the relationship between universalism and exclusivity.[8] Zechariah 8:20–23 was adduced as one example of inclusive tendencies aimed at non-Judahite peoples that would arrive to seek Yahweh in Jerusalem. Yet, this passage configures

6. Other inclusive language is restricted to the in-group circles of the Babylonian Exiles and Repatriates (e.g. Deutero-Isaiah, Isa 56:3, 6).

7. I therefore find to be somewhat naïve David L. Petersen's suggestion that the innovation of the Second Temple was its function as "a symbol for religious integration" (see "The Temple in Persian Period Prophetic Texts," in *Second Temple Studies*. Vol. 1, *Persian Period* [ed. P. R. Davies; JSOTSup 117; Sheffield: Sheffield Academic, 1991], 124–44, quotation from 138–39). The dynamic in Persian-period Yehud is clearly not one of integration but of incorporation, and the functional difference between the two is highly significant.

8. See pp. 59–60, above.

inclusion as part of the religious-cultic sphere (a conception also known from other prophetic passages, as in Isa 2:2–4 and Mic 4:1–4); it thus does not refer at all to the internal identity deliberations discussed in this monograph. This passage (like others in Deutero-Isaiah that could have been discussed as well) demonstrates the gap between inclusive tendencies toward foreigners in the religious-cultic arena and the lack of such openness and acceptance toward other Judean groups when it comes to sociological issues of group identity. In any event, this inclusive tendency retains the already-mentioned model of identity change, the strategy of *incorporation*. As in the social sphere, *incorporation* in the cultic sphere demands complete acculturation to the community of the Repatriates in Jerusalem. This vision, then, also draws on the superior and prestigious characteristics of Repatriate exclusivity.

5. *Conclusions: Traits of Continuity, Traits of Change*

a. *Traits of Continuity*

Following this presentation of the intergroup transformations and shifts over a period of about 150 years in the struggles between the Babylonian Exiles and Those Who Remained in the Land, it is possible now to note the lines of continuity that tie together the sources discussed.

First, the ideological similarities between different strands of Babylonian exilic ideology (including the transformations within them) add up to a picture of *the permanent and persistent utilization of strategies of division between the Judean communities of Exiles in Babylon and back in the land*. This divisiveness, which I have traced back to Ezekiel, persisted through the sixth and fifth centuries; and, although the different manifestations of it are not homogeneous in all aspects, they certainly manifest explicit shared beliefs. The main governing conception is the exclusive and separatist motivation. Looking at the early community of Those Who Remained in Judah following the waves of Babylonian deportation, similar separatist and exclusive perspectives initially empowered their group-identity reidentification as well (as in Ezek 11:15; 33:24; and Jer 32:6–15). But, since the biblical literature reflects the eventual dominance of the Babylonian Exiles, the voices of Those Who Remained soon vanished. It is of importance to note that an attitude of exclusivity and opposition to Those Who Remained was retained throughout this period. The return to Yehud does not seem to have diminished the antagonism, or to have generated a desire for unity that could have brought these two communities of Judeans back to a shared conception of national identity. On the contrary, the early Persian period, in both its prophetic and historiographic literature, shows the wide gap that had opened between the communities. It illustrates a long tradition of exclusionary and denigrating arguments by the Babylonian Exiles against the legitimacy of (any) other Judean community in the land (or elsewhere). In different ways, this literature crafts and maintains the exclusive identity of the Babylonian communities as the sole heirs to preexilic Israel, using arguments of *continuity* and *entirety*, and the *annexation* of earlier traditions.

The evidence of about 150 years of dislocation, of waves of exile and return, seems strong enough to substantiate the claim that both Haggai and Zechariah, as part and parcel of the Babylonian Repatriate community, maintained these same exclusive boundaries. The audience for their exhortations and their messages of restoration was restricted to this community of Returnees. The lack of explicit proclamations against "others" in these writings does not identify them as inclusivists or as members of the Non-exiled community. Rather, it illustrates that both Zechariah and Haggai are well-versed in the Babylonian exilic ideologies that continued to operate in Persian Yehud upon the return. They either simply did not see, or intentionally disregarded, any other communities of Non-exiled Judeans in the land. Like Ezekiel and Deutero-Isaiah in his Babylonian and then Jerusalem prophecies, the two Repatriated prophets were totally focused on strengthening their own in-group that they completely disregarded any other Judean community (Yahwistic or otherwise) in Yehud, treating all others as if invisible. Recognition of this shared intergroup strategy of *invisibility* of the "other" supports the proposition that exclusivity characterizes Haggai and Zechariah (chs. 1–8) as well.

Second, throughout the study, *Ezekiel has been seen to be the initiator and developer of the Babylonian exilic ideology(/ies)*; that is, this exclusivist ideology has already taken shape as of the early sixth century B.C.E.

Ezekiel's influence on sixth-century literature, and even more on Persian-period literature, has been widely studied. Paul Hanson found Ezekiel to be the "fountainhead of that entire tradition,"[9] the tradition being that of the "Hierocratic party," which Hanson defined as the privileged, conservative, and most powerful social and religious-cultic community. Led by the Zadokite priests, this party, according to Hanson, originated with Ezekiel and subsequently with his school, and was active in the exilic and postexilic periods, thus both in Babylon and in Yehud.

---

9. Hanson, *The Dawn of Apocalyptic*, quotation from p. 228, and see p. 238; the entire discussion is on pp. 220–40.

"Membership" in this party ties together Ezekiel, Haggai, and Zechariah (chs. 1–8), who added prophetic spirit and legitimization to this hierocratic tradition,[10] and Ezra 1–6. A further elaboration of this party's position by Repatriated Levites is attested in Ezra–Nehemiah, and yet a more tolerant spirit characterizes Chronicles. An opposition group, disempowered and thus utopian, was "a prophetic or visionary group," said to advocate change; at first opposition took the form of an open resistance, but this was gradually modified to the expression of eschatological hopes. Among this latter group were Jeremiah, Levitical opponents of the Zadokite priests who allied themselves to the visionary party during the exilic period, and its major advocates, the tradents of Deutero-Isaiah, Trito-Isaiah, and Zech 9–14.[11]

This study, however, has focused on what seems to me to have been *the* major issue at stake, namely, the need for the reformulation of social and national identity in the wake of the Destruction, the dislocation of exile, and also the restoration. From this angle, the basic distinctions between Hanson's two parties seem not to supply a useful line of demarcation.[12] The present analysis has highlighted the prophetic shared beliefs that tie together Ezekiel, the Babylonian editorial strand in Jeremiah, Deutero-Isaiah, Haggai, and Zech 1–8, pointing to the significant distinctions between this ideological trajectory and the identity

10. For Hanson's description of Haggai and Zechariah, see ibid., 240–62, especially p. 246.

11. These socioreligious distinctions were already suggested by Otto Plöger (in *Theocracy and Eschatology*), who was interested in the internal Judean conflict which he also saw as based on religious grounds. Plöger opened his book with a "Historical Introduction" that starts with Antiochus IV Epiphanes, with the Jewish community of Jerusalem of the Seleucid period, and particularly with the movement of the *Hasidim*, which was said to have merged into the Maccabean movement. In tracing the origins of their ideologies, Plöger sought connections with the prophetic literature of the Hebrew Bible (especially Daniel, the Isaiah-Apocalypse [Isa 24–27], Trito-Zechariah [Zech 12–14], Joel), and discussed the "Rise of Apocalyptic." In his concluding remarks (pp. 106–17), Plöger assumed that the internal divisions that had emerged under the political circumstances of the collapse of the Persian empire, might be pushed back to the exilic and postexilic eras, to the rise of eschatological literature within the prophetic writings (which further developed into apocalyptic). Hence, Plöger drew direct connections between the later restrictions put on by theocratic circles for the sake of national exclusivism, and the extreme exclusivism presented by Ezra–Nehemiah.

12. An additional suggestion, that a social affinity existed between Ezekiel and Zechariah (which nevertheless did not preclude significant differences between them), was proposed by Stephen L. Cook, *Prophecy and Apocalypticism: The Postexilic Social Setting* (Minneapolis: Fortress, 1995), 123–65, see especially 148–53.

conceptions of Ezra–Nehemiah (which of course was independently influenced by Ezekiel). Hanson's model of a conservative, ruling, "hierocratic" common denominator over against oppressed, alienated, dissident prophetic elements does not seem to stand before this reading of the evidence. Rather, we may say that prophetic reactions to the physical reality of dislocation (both exile and return) are governed by Babylonian-born shared beliefs that continued to develop over time (with clear transformations) in Babylon and back in Yehud.

Hence, the importance of Ezekiel's contribution to the shaping of Babylonian exilic ideologies on the specific issue of group identity cannot be overestimated. Thomas Renz has suggested that Ezekiel influenced the Babylonian Repatriates through his "vision of a polity focused on Yahweh in the land of Israel."[13] Thus Renz saw Ezekiel's major contribution as shaping the political thought of those who had decided to return.

As already noted, I would broaden this appreciation, and recognize Ezekiel's profound influence first and foremost among his contemporaries in exile, and subsequently on both prophetic and historiographic literature of the Neo-Babylonian and Persian periods:

1. Ezekiel constructed two rhetorical oppositions between the Jehoiachin Exiles and Those Who Remained—the first draws on the analogy of the opposition between the Israelites and the Canaanite peoples of the land (utilizing the Holiness Code's conception of land in Lev 18 and 20); the other rhetorical opposition borrows the theological perception of the total judgment as a punitive divine action that left the land empty and desolate. The metaphor thus presupposes that when the Exiles return, they will be facing an empty land, depopulated of any other ethnic community. Ezekiel manipulated these theological conceptions to articulate a notion of the exclusive status of the Exiles as the entire people of God, in continuity with Israel of the past.

---

13. Thomas Renz, *The Rhetorical Function of the Book of Ezekiel* (Boston: Brill, 2002), 229–47 (238). For specific studies of Ezekiel's influence on Haggai and Zechariah, see Rimon Kasher, "Haggai and Ezekiel: The Complicated relations between the Two Prophets," *VT* 59 (2009): 556–82; idem, "Restoration Programs for the Zion Repatriates: Between Ezekiel and Zechariah," *Beit Mikra* 56, no. 2 (2011): 33–57 (in Hebrew). Kasher followed, criticized, and added to Petersen ("The Temple in Persian Period Prophetic Texts"), who enumerated eight issues of disagreement between the prophets. Kasher has aptly emphasized various distinctions between the earlier and the latter prophets on specific other conceptual issues. But these do not seem to negate their shared basic group identifications.

2. Ezekiel's two definitions of עם הארץ still function in the early Persian period, and help to explain the tension between the positive in-group usage of this term in Haggai and Zechariah (following Ezek 12:19), over against the negative usage of עם הארץ and עמי הארצות in Ezra–Nehemiah (Chapter 4, above). The latter follows Ezekiel's analogical adaptation of Lev 18:27, which opposes the Israelites to אנשי הארץ. Ezekiel adapts this opposition to the confrontation between the Jehoiachin Exiles and the Jerusalem community, which he designates as Canaanite by origin and by birth (Ezek 16:3).
3. It is Ezekiel who shifted the perception of the core of Judean existence to Babylon, prophesying the annihilation of the Remnant in Jerusalem (Ezek 11:1–13, 14–21).

Ezekiel thus had a pivotal role in establishing these fundamental conceptions, which drove Babylonian exilic ideologies over the course of generations.[14] Active as a prophet in the early years of the exile, Ezekiel not only collected the "broken pieces" of that catastrophe, but with great aptitude laid the foundations for the reconstruction of the Babylonian community's self-perception as the (only) people of God. In so doing, he formulated the basics of the "takeover" strategy of this Diasporan community, by which it evolved into the core community of "Judah" within just a few decades. Exilic authors, prophets, and historiographers carried on and developed further Ezekiel's ideological opposition between the (Jehoiachin) Exiles and Those Who Remained in Jerusalem. Trajectories of transformation show that the diverse exclusivist ideologies in play in the Persian period all hearken back to these initial separatist ideologies, already in place from the early years of the Babylonian exile.

Third, a remarkable theme repeats throughout the literary sources discussed, across both time and space—*the genuine interest, common to all groups of Exiles, in the land*. The Babylonian Exiles share an intense interest in that far-off homeland, in what is happening in Jerusalem and Judah. This is the target of their prospects for return and the aim of their hopes for restoration.[15]

14. I would thus broaden Ezekiel's influence beyond that implied by the scholarly tendency to accentuate the Zadokite familial connections. See both Hanson (*The Dawn of Apocalyptic*, 228–40) and Cook (*Prophecy and Apocalypticism*, 148–53). On the question of influence, the work of the prophet as a whole must be considered, not merely the influence of his school and of chs. 40–48; compare Blenkinsopp, *Judaism: The First Phase*, 129–59.

15. Erhard S. Gerstenberger, *Israel in the Persian Period: The Fifth and Fourth Centuries B.C.E.* (trans. S. S. Schatzmann; Biblical Encyclopedia 8; Atlanta: Society of Biblical Literature, 2011), 4–5.

From the literary perspective, this "land orientation" in the exilic literature is indeed remarkable. Biblical compositions of the sixth and fifth centuries B.C.E. are clearly dominated by authors from among the Babylonian deportees and the Repatriated Exiles. Yet, much of this literature is focused on Judean existence in the land, as is discernible in both the historiography (Kings) and the prophetic literature (Ezekiel, the Babylonian editorial strands of Jeremiah, Deutero-Isaiah, Haggai, and Zech 1–8).[16] In fact, besides Esther, the biblical literature does not reflect a Judean existence in exile, which may thus be catalogued as revealing a diasporic orientation.[17]

From the point of view of intergroup relations, two comments are in order: (1) It is important to note that this "land orientation" underlies the entire process of intergroup negotiations among the three Judean groups: the Exiles, the Repatriates, and Those Who Remained. Being in the land or away from it serves as the defining criterion for belonging to one group or the other. (2) It is noteworthy that the Exiles in Babylon continue to negotiate their national status in relation to the Judeans Who Remained in the land of Israel, rather than in relation to the "proximate others" among the diverse national groups present in Babylon, in the much closer vicinity.[18] The Babylonian Exiles follow

16. This distinction between the in-group geographical orientation of the authors and their land orientation (to what is happening in distant Judah) seems to have escaped Gary Knoppers in his recent study ("Exile, Return and Diaspora," 35–38), where he pointed out the astonishing fact that while Exiles are mentioned, there is no reference to the deportees' life "out there" (apart from the closing verses on Jehoiachin in 2 Kgs 25:27–30). Indeed, the focus on Judah is one of the fascinating points that to my mind characterizes the Babylonian exilic ideologies.

17. Compare, however, literary readings of Genesis, specifically of the Joseph stories, and of Esther as novellae set within diasporic contexts, as in W. Lee Humphreys, "A Life-Style for Diaspora: A Study of the Tales of Esther and Daniel," *JBL* 92 (1973): 211–23; Arndt Meinhold, "Die Gattung der Josephsgeschichte und des Estherbuches: Diasporanovelle I," *ZAW* 87 (1975): 306–24; idem, "Die Gattung der Josephsgeschichte und des Estherbuches: Diasporanovelle II," *ZAW* 88 (1976): 72–93; Lawrence M. Wills, *The Jew in the Court of the Foreign King: Ancient Jewish Legends* (HDR 26; Minneapolis: Fortress, 1990); and in a recent Ph.D. dissertation by Oren Biderman, "The Joseph Story (Genesis 37–50): Its Time, Context and Intention" (Tel Aviv University, 2012 [in Hebrew]), 193–209; see further Gerstenberger, *Israel in the Persian Period*, 187–95, especially p. 190.

18. On the possible interactions between the Babylonian Exiles and Babylonians or deportees from other national groups, see Albertz (*Israel in Exile*, 106–9), who mentioned various strategies of survival by which the Babylonian *golah* is assumed to have distinguished its members from other communities in exile. What seems to

the national-religious shared beliefs of Israel when they cling to the land as the essential symbol of the God–people covenant relationships. The dislocation lends the urgency to the reformulating of the Deportees' group identity.

Fourth, the Babylonian exilic ideologies from Ezekiel to Ezra–Nehemiah totally excluded the possibility that any present Judahite community might exist in the land in continuity with preexilic history. By way of the analogy of Israel and the Canaanite peoples developed by Ezekiel, the "peoples of the land" are by definition "not-Israel."

These last two common factors, which originated in exile, were carried back to the land by the Repatriates, struggling to reestablish their status as the only community of the people of God in Yehud. These foundational conceptions are given rhetorical force through the designations of national names, the arguments of exclusivity (*continuity, entirety,* and *annexation* of national traditions), and the divisive strategies and counterstrategies, all of which unite Babylonian exilic ideologies.

These lines of continuity, which run through the entire sixth and fifth centuries (from 597 B.C.E. onwards) support the scholarly model that presumes a context of lively literary creativity, flourishing during the sixth century from soon after the first Babylonian deportations and the subsequent Destruction, in Babylon and probably also in Judah, though this is less evident. The present study has accentuated the way in which Persian-period sources carried these Neo-Babylonian exilic interests, formulated throughout the sixth century, back into Persian Yehud.[19]

The notion of intensive and creative literary activity throughout the sixth century, which is commonly accepted by scholars,[20] was recently thoroughly challenged by Erhard Gerstenberger.[21] He argued that the exilic era (that is, the sixth century B.C.E.) could not have been such a

---

be worth noting is that the exilic biblical literature is hardly interested in these aspects of exilic life. The one topic which gets explicit attention is the matter of other gods; note the polemic on this point in Deutero-Isaiah.

19. *Pace* Williamson ("The Concept of Israel in Transition," 148–52, and his conclusions on 152–53), who laid special weight on the Persian period, which he held to be "a period of accommodation...which in all probability reflects the nature of the temple community in 520 BC...as combining equally those who returned (listed by family association) and those who had remained in the land (listed by domicile...)... 'Israel' may still have been kept sufficiently alive in the memory and in literature to embrace the communities which had been geographically divided." I consider the entire sixth century to be a time of much more active investment in struggles of identity.

20. Albertz, *Israel in Exile*, 203–427.

21. Gerstenberger, *Israel in the Persian Period*, 274–77, 307–8, and passim.

time of "full blossom" in biblical literature. According to Gerstenberger, the post-586 period was a time when "discouragement pervade[d]" both Babylon and Judah, a time when both communities struggled to survive, and were not free to invest the energy needed for producing the biblical literature. Rather, Gerstenberger located the entire literary project of collecting texts and traditions, of revising and adding to earlier materials, and so on, during the Persian period (539–330 B.C.E.), mostly within the Babylonian Diaspora.[22] Gerstenberger advanced the understanding that "The new beginning or, more precisely, the founding of the community of Yahweh since 539 B.C.E., is the premise for the intellectual and theological process of coming to terms with the past."[23]

The current study supplies powerful arguments against theories that consider the Persian period to be the starting point for some or all of the biblical literature. The lines of continuity noticed here as running through the entire sixth century suggest a general course of literary production and transmission that could connect literature written or compiled first in Judah with literary activity in Babylon, that was then carried further by the Repatriates back in Yehud.

Lines of continuity specifically link the prophetic literature from Ezekiel down to Haggai and Zechariah; they may also be noticed in the evolutionary and editorial strands of Jeremiah and Isaiah (as well as Ezekiel).[24] The major connecting bridge seems to be the identity observations, that is, the intergroup relationships that provided evidence to the social connections between the community of the Babylonian Exiles and then the Repatriates, notwithstanding significant transformations over time and place.

b. *Traits of Change*

One of the earliest transformations in the Babylonian exilic ideologies was the expansion of the in-group definitions to include all Exiles in

---

22. Ibid.

23. There seems to be no foundation to Gerstenberger's assumption (ibid., 308), that it takes decades following "the initial shock" for authors to reflect on their situation. His analogy to the experience of Germans following 1945 seems odd to me. Theological reflections of various kinds (like historiographical writings, and rich literature and poetry) were given written form both during the war and immediately following the *Shoah*. There was no interval of "dry years" in between.

24. See Dalit Rom-Shiloni, "What Is 'Persian' in Late Sixth Century BCE Prophetic Literature? Case-Studies and Criteria," in *Discerning Criteria for Dating Persian Period Texts* (ed. R. Bautch and J. Nogalsky; The International SBL Symposium Volume of the Persian Period Seminar; Atlanta, Ga.: Society of Biblical Literature, forthcoming).

Babylon, thus broadening Ezekiel's isolation of the Jehoiachin Exiles as the only people of God. This change may be traced already within the editorial layers of the book of Ezekiel, in the Babylonian strand of consolation prophecies in Jeremiah, and to a much greater extent in Deutero-Isaiah's prophecies. None of the later sources adopt Ezekiel's extreme exclusivity, which opposed the Jehoiachin Exiles to the 586 refugees (פליטה) from Jerusalem (Ezek 14:21–23).

This complicated picture of nuances within Babylonian exilic ideologies leaves several very challenging, unanswered questions concerning the constitution of and the insider relationships within this in-group.[25] What can this later inclusive perspective tell us about the status of the Jehoiachin Exiles within the larger Babylonian communities of Exiles? Could it be that the exclusive status Ezekiel gave them was merely his own limited idiosyncratic perception? The memory of the Jehoiachin Exiles may still be in the background of Zerubbabel's special position (especially in Hag 2:23–27), and it is mentioned as a short note in the patronymics of Mordechai (Esth 2:4), probably by the fourth century B.C.E. Did (or rather, when did) the Jehoiachin Exiles lose their prestigious position as the exclusive exilic group?

It seems that we may indeed assume that as early as the first decades of the Babylonian exiles, a general tendency toward in-group inclusivity overpowered Ezekiel's extreme and exclusive in-group definition, and helped to fuse the several waves of deported Judeans who had arrived gradually in Babylon into a single in-group community. Hence, Ezekiel's extremism remained an exceptional path, not to be followed strictly. Should we thus gather that Ezekiel represents the Jehoiachin Exiles, while even his tradents, and certainly Deutero-Isaiah, give voice to a different subcommunity, perhaps that of the Judean Exiles of 586 B.C.E.? While the evidence is scant, we do have enough data to claim a certain heterogeneity among the later manifestations of Babylonian exilic ideologies on the issue of group identity.

---

25. The question also arises as to the relationship between the Exiles in Babylon and the Judean communities of Exiles in Egypt, and probably in other locations. But, as mentioned in Chapter 1 of this study, the biblical literature is focused on the dichotomy between only two of the Judean communities, the one in Judah (and Egypt), the other in Babylon. One possible explanation (suggested to me by Dr. Ruth Clements in her insightful reading) is that the land orientation might be the factor that was perceived as much more crucial than other topics that might have been relevant to Judean diasporic communities in other locations.

It may indeed be of interest in a future study to explore further the relationship between Ezekiel and Deutero-Isaiah on this issue.[26] Is the latter prophet (and/or the Deutero-Isaiah circle) a descendent of the Jehoiachin Exiles, thus close to Ezekiel? Or could he (/they) be descended from the 586 Judean deportees? If the latter is more likely, then we might find Ezekiel and Deutero-Isaiah to represent distinct prophetic perceptions which might in turn point to an internal conflict among the Exiles in Babylon.[27]

Nevertheless, this diversity within the in-group cannot diminish the centrality of its shared belief in its exclusivist status as the one and only people of God. The Babylonian Exiles and the Repatriates in Yehud share and are linked by a sense of group identity shaped by exclusive inclusivity.

This study has advanced various questions concerning intergroup relationships and their literary expressions in the biblical literature of the sixth and fifth centuries B.C.E. To return to the questions raised in Chapter 1 (p. 8), there still seems to be one question left unanswered.

Sociologists (specifically those specializing in ethno-nationalism) have conducted vast research projects into the modern phenomenon of exilic or diaspora communities. William Safran, for instance, characterized several features as mandatory to a definition of a diaspora community:[28]

(1) The community or its ancestors have been dispersed from a specific, original "center" to two or more "peripheral," or foreign, regions; (2) they retain a collective memory, vision, or myth about their original homeland—its physical location, history, and achievements; (3) they believe that they are not—and perhaps cannot be—fully accepted by their host society and therefore feel partially alienated and insulated from it; (4) they regard their ancestral homeland as their true, ideal home and as the place to which they or their descendants would like to (or should) eventually return—when conditions are appropriate; (5) they believe that they should collectively be committed to the maintenance or restoration

26. Hanson (*The Dawn of Apocalyptic*, 234–35) provided a list of distinctions between them, but then he argued that the tradents of each prophet added similar nuances in terms of their "future orientation toward a restoration" (pp. 236–37).

27. This latter possibility may be substantiated by the many literary allusions to Jeremiah in Deutero-Isaiah; see Sommer, *A Prophet Reads Scripture*, 167–73, 315–31; and Paul, *Deutero-Isaiah 40–48*, 40–1. Compare Williamson ("The Concept of Israel in Transition," especially 143–47), who drew distinctions between Ezekiel and Deutero-Isaiah (chs. 40–55).

28. William Safran, "Diasporas in Modern Societies: Myths of Homeland and Return," *Diaspora* 1 (1991): 83–99 (83–84).

of their original homeland and to its safety and prosperity; and (6) they continue to relate, personally or vicariously, to that homeland in one way or another, and their ethno-communal consciousness and solidarity are fundamentally defined by the existence of such a relationship.

Reading Safran's criteria, it seems that the Hebrew Bible's treatments of exile (and the Jewish history following exile) have paved the way to the modern definitions of exile (and diaspora).

Yet, none of these criteria explain the urgent need in both homeland and Diaspora following 586 B.C.E. to reformulate the identity of each of the Judean communities time and again, so as to create the one and only exclusive community of the people of God. Hence, as I bring this study to its close, I still find it hard to explain the question "why?"

Why did the Judean communities develop such irrevocable internal conflicts when the division itself came from an external force? My conclusions are not far from those of Smith[-Christopher] in *The Religion of the Landless*, yet they are different enough to deserve mention.

I agree with Smith[-Christopher] that the conflicts between the Repatriate community and Those Who Remained were a result of a sociological behavioral process they could not stop, or refrain from. Smith[-Christopher] argued that the circumstances of exile, of living as "a *conquered* minority, *under domination*,"[29] were formative—they created the "permanent separation and separate ('sectarian') consciousness of the exile community."[30] This consciousness brought those Returnees to emphasize and maintain the separatist boundaries between the groups upon return.

On the basis of my examination of the internal conflicts of the sixth and fifth centuries B.C.E., however, I would point out the following. First, the establishment of the conflict between Babylonian Exiles and Those Who Remained is traceable as early as the Jehoiachin exile. It did not take long for the Exiles, in their new locations, to redefine their identity, nor for Those Who Remained to argue for their own exclusive rights in the land. Argumentative tactics that bolstered self-esteem by denigrating the other were quickly developed by both communities. Second, the behavioral dynamic is not only (or not primarily) one of the deportees needing to activate "mechanisms of survival" among dominant communities (in new locations), but rather one of a nation under crisis, physically divided by external forces into two major groups, with each needing to reevaluate and re-create its own social boundaries. Third, "exclusive inclusivity" seems to characterize all the different Judean

29. Smith[-Christopher], *The Religion of the Landless*, 60.
30. Ibid., 203.

voices that participated in the internal conflicts over the sixth and fifth centuries B.C.E. This phrase captures the two extreme options of inclusion and exclusion to portray the fact that even inclusivity may be segmented or restricted to those categorized within the in-group, excluding all others as illegitimate out-groups.

The only explanation I can suggest for the development of such exclusive, or exclusive inclusivistic, positions is the constant ideological necessity to reformulate the shared traditional conceptions of land and of exile, of the covenant with God, and of the national heritage, to confront the diverse fates of the two Judean communities. Under the dramatic circumstances of the sixth and fifth centuries B.C.E., each of these Judean communities had to establish with certainty, in the face of potential theological convictions to the contrary, the *continuity* and the *entirety* of its own community as the exclusive people of God, the people of Israel.

BIBLIOGRAPHY

Ackroyd, Peter R. *Exile and Restoration: A Study of Hebrew Thought of the Sixth Century B.C.* OTL. Philadelphia: Westminster, 1975.

———. "Studies in the Book of Haggai." *JJS* 3 (1952): 1–13.

Ahituv, Shmuel. "New Documents Pertaining to Deportation as a Political System in Ancient Egypt." *Beer-Sheva* 1 (1973): 87–89 (in Hebrew).

Albertz, Rainer. *A History of Israelite Religion in the Old Testament Period.* Translated by J. Bowden. OTL. 2 vols. Louisville: Westminster John Knox, 1994.

———. *Israel in Exile: The History and Literature of the Sixth Century B.C.E.* Translated by David Green. Society of Biblical Literature Studies in Biblical Literature 3. Atlanta: Society of Biblical Literature, 2003 (German original, 2001).

Allen, L. C. *Ezekiel 20–48.* WBC 29. Waco, Tex.: Word, 1990.

Assis, Elie. "A Disputed Temple (Haggai 2,1–9)." *ZAW* 120 (2008): 582–96.

Barstad, Hans M. *The Babylonian Captivity of the Book of Isaiah: "Exilic" Judah and the Provenance of Isaiah 40–55.* Oslo: Novus, 1997.

———. *The Myth of the Empty Land: A Study in the History and Archaeology of Judah During the "Exilic" Period.* Symbolae Osloenses Fasciculi Supplitorii 28. Oslo: Scandinavian University Press, 1996.

———. "On the So-called Babylonian Literary Influence in Second Isaiah." *SJOT* 2 (1987): 90–110.

Bar-Tal, Daniel. "Delegitimization: The Extreme Case of Stereotyping and Prejudice." Pages 169–82 in *Stereotyping and Prejudice: Changing Conceptions.* Edited by Daniel Bar-Tal et al. New York: Springer, 1989.

———. *Group Beliefs: A Conception for Analyzing Group Structure, Processes, and Behavior.* New York: Springer, 1990.

———. *Shared Beliefs in a Society: Social Psychological Analysis.* Thousands Oaks, Calif.: Sage, 2000.

Bar-Tal, Daniel, and Yona Teichman. *Stereotypes and Prejudice in Conflict: Representations of Arabs in Israeli Jewish Society.* Cambridge: Cambridge University Press, 2005.

Barth, Fredrick M. "Introduction." Pages 1–38 in *Ethnic Groups and Boundaries: The Social Organization of Culture Difference.* Edited by F. M. Barth. Bergen: University of Bergen Press, 1969.

Becking, Bob. *Between Fear and Freedom: Essays on the Interpretation of Jeremiah 30–31.* Leiden: Brill, 2004.

———. "Continuity and Community: The Belief System of the Book of Ezra." Pages 256–75 in *The Crisis of Israelite Religion: Transformation of Religious Tradition in Exilic and Post-Exilic Times*. Edited by B. Becking and M. C. A. Korpel. OTS 42. Leiden: Brill, 1999.

———. "On the Identity of the 'Foreign' Women in Ezra 9–10." Pages 31–49 in *Exile and Restoration Revisited: Essays on the Babylonian and Persian Periods in Memory of Peter R. Ackroyd*. Edited by G. N. Knoppers and L. L. Grabbe, with D. N. Fulton. LSTS 73. New York: T&T Clark International, 2009.

Bedford, Peter R. "Diaspora: Homeland Relations in Ezra–Nehemiah." *VT* 52 (2002): 147–66.

———. *Temple Restoration in Early Achaemenid Judah*. JSJSup 65. Leiden: Brill, 2001.

Beilin, Yossi. *His Brother's Keeper: Israel and Diaspora Jewry in the Twenty-First Century*. New York: Schocken, 2000.

Ben Zvi, Ehud. "The Voice and Role of a Counterfactual Memory in the Construction of Exile and Return: Considering Jeremiah 40:7–12." Pages 169–88 in Ben Zvi and Levin, eds., *The Concept of Exile in Ancient Israel*.

Ben Zvi, Ehud, and C. Levin, eds. *The Concept of Exile in Ancient Israel and Its Historical Contexts*. BZAW 404. Berlin: de Gruyter, 2010.

Berlin, Adele. "Jeremiah 29:5–7: A Deuteronomic Allusion." *Hebrew Annual Review* 8 (1984): 3–11.

Berquist, Jon L. "Constructions of Identity in Postcolonial Yehud." Pages 53–65 in Lipschits and Oeming, eds., *Judah and the Judeans in the Persian Period*.

Beuken, Wim A. M. *Haggai–Sacharja 1–8*. SSN 10. Assen: Van Gorcum, 1967.

Biale, David, ed. *Cultures of the Jews: A New History*. New York: Schocken, 2002.

Biderman, Oren. "The Joseph Story (Genesis 37–50): Its Time, Context and Intention." Ph.D. diss., Tel Aviv University, 2012 (in Hebrew).

Blenkinsopp, Joseph. *Ezra–Nehemiah*. OTL. Philadelphia: Westminster, 1988.

———. *Isaiah 1–39*. AB 19. New York: Doubleday, 2000.

———. *Isaiah 56–66*. AB 19B. New York: Doubleday, 2003.

———. *Judaism, the First Phase: The Place of Ezra–Nehemiah in the Origins of Judaism*. Grand Rapids: Eerdmans, 2009.

———. "The 'Servants of the Lord' in Third Isaiah: Profile of a Pietistic Group in the Persian Epoch." *Proceedings of the Irish Biblical Association* 7 (1983): 1–23.

Block, Daniel I. *Ezekiel 1–24*. NICOT. Grand Rapids: Eerdmans, 1997.

———. "Ezekiel's Boiling Cauldron: A Form-Critical Solution to Ezekiel XXIV 1–14." *VT* 41 (1991): 12–37.

———. *The Gods and the Nations: Studies in Ancient Near Eastern National Theology*. ETSMS 2. Jackson, Mo.: Evangelical Theological Society, 1988.

Boda, Mark. "Haggai: Master Rhetorician." *TynBul* 51 (2000): 295–304.

———. *Haggai, Zechariah*. New International Version Application Commentary. Grand Rapids: Zondervan, 2004.

Brett, Mark G. "Interpreting Ethnicity." Pages 3–22 in *Ethnicity and the Bible*. Edited by M. G. Brett. Biblical Interpretation Series 19. Leiden: Brill, 1996.

Bright, John. *Jeremiah*. AB 21. Garden City, N.Y.: Doubleday, 1965.

Brin, Gershon. "The Date and Meaning of the Prophecy Against 'Those Who Live in These Ruins in the Land of Israel' Ezekiel 33:23–29." Pages *29–*36 in *Texts, Temples, and Traditions: A Tribute to Menahem Haran*. Edited by M. V. Fox et al. Winona Lake: Eisenbrauns, 1996 (in Hebrew).

Brown, Rupert. "Social Identity Theory: Past Achievements, Current Problems, and Future Challenges." *European Journal of Social Psychology* 30 (2000): 745–78.

Brownlee, William H. "The Aftermath of the Fall of Judah According to Ezekiel." *JBL* 89 (1970): 393–404.

———. *Ezekiel 1–19.* WBC 28. Waco, Tex.: Word, 1986.

Brueggeman, Walter. *Deuteronomy.* AOTC. Nashville: Abingdon, 2001.

Carr, David M. *The Formation of the Hebrew Bible: A New Reconstruction.* New York: Oxford University Press, 2011.

Carroll, Robert P. *From Chaos to Covenant: Uses of Prophecy in the Book of Jeremiah.* London: SCM, 1981.

———. *Jeremiah.* OTL. Philadelphia: Westminster, 1986.

———. "The Myth of the Empty Land." *Semeia* 59 (1992): 79–93.

Coats, George W. *Rebellion in the Wilderness.* Nashville: Abingdon, 1968.

Cogan, Mordechai. "Judah Under Assyrian Hegemony: A Re-examination of Imperialism and Religion." *JBL* 112 (1993): 403–14.

Coggins, Richard J. *Haggai, Zechariah, Malachi.* OTG. Sheffield: JSOT, 1987.

———. *Samaritans and Jews: The Origins of Samaritanism Reconsidered.* Oxford: Blackwell, 1975.

Collins, John J. *Between Athens and Jerusalem: Jewish Identity in the Hellenistic Diaspora.* 2d ed. Livonia, Mich.: Dove, 2000.

Conrad, Edgar W. *Zechariah.* Sheffield: Sheffield Academic, 1997.

Cook, Stephen L. *Prophecy and Apocalypticism: The Postexilic Social Setting.* Minneapolis: Fortress, 1995.

Cooke, George A. *Ezekiel.* ICC. Edinburgh: T. & T. Clark, 1936. Repr. 1985.

Craigie, Peter C. *Deuteronomy.* NICOT. Grand Rapids: Eerdmans, 1976.

Curtis, Byron G. *Up the Steep and Stony Road: The Book of Zechariah in Social Location Trajectory Analysis.* Society of Biblical Literature Academia Biblica 25. Leiden: Brill, 2006.

Davies, Philip R. "Exile! What Exile? Whose Exile?" Pages 128–38 in *Leading Captivity Captive: "The Exile" as History and Ideology.* Edited by L. L. Grabbe. JSOTSup 278. Sheffield: Sheffield Academic, 1998.

Day, Peggy L. "Adulterous Jerusalem's Imagined Demise: Death of a Metaphor in Ezekiel XVI." *VT* 50 (2000): 285–309.

———. "The Bitch Had It Coming to Her: Rhetoric and Interpretation in Ezekiel 16." *Biblical Interpretation* 8 (2000): 231–54.

Dobbs-Allsopp, Frederick W. *Weep, O Daughter of Zion: A Study of the City-Lament Genre in the Hebrew Bible.* BibOr 44. Rome: Pontifical Biblical Institute, 1993.

Don-Yehiya, Eliezer, ed. *Israel and Diaspora Jewry: Ideological and Political Perspectives.* Comparative Jewish Politics 3. Ramat Gan: Bar-Ilan University Press, 1991 (in Hebrew).

Dor, Yonina. *Have the "Foreign Women" Really Been Expelled? Separation and Exclusion in the Restoration Period.* Jerusalem: The Hebrew University/Magnes, 2006 (in Hebrew).

Duhm, Bernhard. *Das Buch Jesaja übersetzt und erklärt.* HKAT 3/1. Göttingen: Vandenhoeck & Ruprecht, 1892. 4th ed. 1922.

Durham, John I. *Exodus.* WBC 3. Waco: Word, 1987.

Ehrlich, Arnold B. *Jesaia, Jeremia.* Randglossen zur Hebräischen Bibel 4. Leipzig: Hinrichs, 1912.

Eichrodt, Walther. *Ezekiel.* Translated by C. Quin. OTL. Philadelphia: Westminster, 1970.

Elliger, Karl. *Das Buch der zwölf kleinen Propheten.* ATD 25. Göttingen: Vandenhoeck & Ruprecht, 1982.

Eph'al, Israel. "Assyrian Dominion in Palestine." Pages 276–89 in *The Age of the Monarchies.* Vol. 1, *Political History.* Edited by A. Malamat and I. Eph'al. The World History of the Jewish People 4/1. Jerusalem: Masada, 1979.

———. "'The Samarian(s)' in the Assyrian Sources." Pages 36–45 in *Ah, Assyria... Studies in Assyrian History and Ancient Near Eastern Historiography Presented to Hayim Tadmor.* Edited by M. Cogan and I. Eph'al. ScrHier 33. Jerusalem: The Hebrew University/Magnes, 1992.

———. "The Western Minorities in Babylonia in the 6th–5th Centuries: Maintenance and Cohesion." *Orientalia* 47 (1978): 74–90.

———. "You Are Defecting to the Chaldeans." *ErIs* 24 (1994): 18–22 (in Hebrew).

Eskenazi, Tamara Cohn. *In an Age of Prose: A Literary Approach to Ezra–Nehemiah.* SBLMS 36. Atlanta: Society of Biblical Literature, 1988.

Eslinger, Lyle. "Knowing Yahweh: Exod 6:3 in the Context of Genesis 1–Exodus 15." Pages 188–98 in *Literary Structure and Rhetorical Strategies in the Hebrew Bible.* Edited by L. D. de Regt, J. de Waard, and J. P. Fokkelman. Assen: Van Gorcum, 1996.

Fales, Frederick M., and J. N. Postgate. *Imperial Administrative Records, Part II: Provincial and Military Administration.* SAA 11. Helsinki: Helsinki University Press, 1995.

Fensham, F. Charles. *Ezra and Nehemiah.* NICOT. Grand Rapids: Eerdmans, 1982.

Fischer, Georg. "Fulfillment and Reversal: The Curses of Deuteronomy 28 as a Foil for the Book of Jeremiah." *Semitica et Classica* 5 (2012): 43–49.

Fishbane, Michael A. *Biblical Interpretation in Ancient Israel.* Oxford: Clarendon, 1988.

———. *Text and Texture: Close Reading of Selected Biblical Texts.* New York: Schocken, 1979.

Freedman, David N. "When God Repents." Pages 409–46 in *Divine Commitment and Human Obligation: Selected Writings of David Noel Freedman.* 2 vols. Grand Rapids: Eerdmans, 1997.

Friebel, Kelvin G. *Jeremiah's and Ezekiel's Sign-Acts.* JSOTSup 283. Sheffield: Sheffield Academic, 1999.

Fried, Lisbeth S. "The ʿam haʾares in Ezra 4:4 and Persian Administration." Pages 123–45 in Lipschits and Oeming, eds., *Judah and the Judeans in the Persian Period.*

Gafni, Isaiah M. *Land, Center and Diaspora: Jewish Constructs in Late Antiquity.* JSPSup 21. Sheffield: Sheffield Academic, 1997.

Galambush, J. *Jerusalem in the Book of Ezekiel: The City as Yahweh's Wife.* SBLDS 130. Atlanta: Scholars Press, 1992.

Ganzel, Tova. "The Descriptions of the Restoration of Israel in Ezekiel." *VT* 60 (2010): 197–211.

Gelb, Ignace J. "Prisoners of War in Early Mesopotamia." *JNES* 32 (1973): 70–98.

Gerstenberger, Erhard S. *Israel in the Persian Period: The Fifth and Fourth Centuries B.C.E.* Translated by S. S. Schatzmann. Biblical Encyclopedia 8. Atlanta: Society of Biblical Literature, 2011.

Glazer, N., and D. P. Moynihan, eds. *Ethnicity: Theory and Experience*. Cambridge, Mass.: Harvard University Press, 1975.

Goshen-Gottstein, M., ed. *Proceedings of the Ninth World Congress of Jewish Studies, Panel Sessions: Bible Studies and the Ancient Near East*. Jerusalem: The World Union of Jewish Studies, 1988.

Grabbe, Lester L. *Ezra–Nehemiah*. London: Routledge, 1998.

Graffy, Adrian. *A Prophet Confronts His People: The Disputation Speech in the Prophets*. AnBib 104. Rome: Biblical Institute, 1984.

Grauburn, Nelson H. H. *Ethnic and Tourist Arts: Cultural Expressions from the Fourth World*. Los Angeles: University of California Press, 1976.

Grayson, Albert K. *Assyrian and Babylonian Chronicles*. Winona Lake: Eisenbrauns, 1975. 2d ed. 2000.

Green, William Scott. "Otherness Within: Towards a Theory of Difference in Rabbinic Judaism." Pages 49–69 in Neusner and Frerichs, eds., *"To See Ourselves as Others See Us."*

Greenberg, Moshe. *Ezekiel 1–20*. AB 22. New York: Doubleday, 1983.

———. *Ezekiel 21–37*. AB 22A. New York: Doubleday, 1997.

———. *Understanding Exodus*. New York: Behrman, 1968.

Gruen, Erich S. "Diaspora and Homeland." Pages 18–46 in *Diasporas and Exiles: Varieties of Jewish Identity*. Edited by H. Wettstein. Berkeley: University of California Press, 2002.

Gunkel, Herman. "Einleitungen." Pages xi–lxxii in *Die grossen Propheten*, by D. H. Schmidt. Göttingen: Vandenhoeck & Ruprecht, 1923.

Gunneweg, Antonius H. J. "עם הארץ—A Semantic Revolution." *ZAW* 95 (1983): 437–40.

Habel, Norman C. *The Land Is Mine: Six Biblical Land Ideologies*. OBT. Minneapolis: Fortress, 1995.

Halperin, David J. *Seeking Ezekiel: Text and Psychology*. University Park: Pennsylvania State University Press, 1993.

Halpern, Ben, and Israel Kolatt. *Changing Relations Between Israel and the Diaspora*. Study Circle on Diaspora Jewry in the Home of the President of Israel 3/6–7. Jerusalem: The Hebrew University, The Institute of Contemporary Jewry, 1969 (in Hebrew).

Hammack, Philip L. "Narrative and the Cultural Psychology of Identity." *Personality and Social Psychology Review* 12 (2008): 222–47.

Hanson, Paul D. *The Dawn of Apocalyptic: The Historical and Sociological Roots of Jewish Apocalyptic Eschatology*. Philadelphia: Fortress, 1975. 2d ed. 1979.

Haran, Menahem. *Between Ri²shonot (Former Prophecies) and Hadashot (New Prophecies): A Literary-Historical Study on the Group of Prophecies Isaiah 40–48*. Jerusalem: The Hebrew University/Magnes, 1963 (in Hebrew).

Hartman, Louis F. *The Book of Daniel*. AB 23. Garden City, N.Y.: Doubleday, 1978.

Hausmann, Jutta. *Israels Rest: Studien zum Selbsverständis der nachexilischen Gemeinde*. Stuttgart: Kohlhammer, 1987.

Heaton, Eric W. "The Root שאר and the Doctrine of the Remnant." *JTS* 3 (1952): 27–39.

Held, Moshe. "Rhetorical Questions in Ugaritic and Biblical Hebrew." *ErIs* 9 (1969): 71*–79*.

Hill, John. "Jeremiah 40:1–6: An Appreciation." Pages 130–41 in S*eeing Signals, Reading Signs: The Art of Exegesis. Studies in Honour of Antony F. Campbell, SJ for His Seventieth Birthday*. Edited by M. A. O'Brian and H. N. Wallace. London: T&T Clark International, 2004.

Hillers, Delbert R. *Treaty Curses and the Old Testament Prophets*. 2d ed. BibOr 16. Rome: Pontifical Biblical Institute, 1964.

Hoffman, David Z. *Deuteronomy*. Translated by Z. Har-Sheffer. Tel Aviv: Netzach, 1959 (in Hebrew).

Hoffman, Yair. *The Doctrine of the Exodus in the Bible*. Tel Aviv: Tel Aviv University Press, 1983 (in Hebrew).

―――. "Ezekiel 20: Its Structure and Meaning." *Beit Miqra* 20 (1975): 480–86.

―――. "History and Ideology: The Case of Jeremiah 44." *JANES* 28 (2001): 43–51.

―――. *Isaiah*. Olam HaTanakh. Tel-Aviv: Revivim, 1986 (in Hebrew).

―――. *Jeremiah 1–24*. Mikra LeIsrael. Jerusalem: The Hebrew University/Magnes. Tel Aviv: Am Oved, 2001 (in Hebrew).

―――. *Jeremiah 25–52*. Mikra LeYisrael. Jerusalem: The Hebrew University/Magnes. Tel Aviv: Am Oved, 2001 (in Hebrew).

―――. "Reflections on the Relationship Between Theopolitics, Prophecy and Historiography." Pages 85–99 in *Politics and Theopolitics in the Bible and Postbiblical Literature*. Edited by H. G. Reventlow, Y. Hoffman, and B. Uffenheimer. JSOTSup 171. Sheffield: JSOT, 1994.

Hoglund, Kenneth G. *Achaemenid Imperial Administration in Syria-Palestine and the Missions of Ezra and Nehemiah*. SBLDS 125. Atlanta: Scholars Press, 1992.

Holladay, William L. *Jeremiah 1*. Hermeneia. Philadelphia: Fortress, 1986.

―――. *Jeremiah 2*. Hermeneia. Philadelphia: Fortress, 1989.

―――. "Jeremiah and Moses: Further Observations." *JBL* 85 (1966): 17–27.

Horowitz, Donald L. "Ethnic Identity." Pages 111–40 in Glazer and Moynihan, eds., *Ethnicity: Theory and Experience*.

Hubbard, Robert L. "The *goʾel* in Ancient Israel: Theological Reflections on an Israelite Institution." *Bulletin for Biblical Research* 1 (1991): 3–19.

Humphreys, W. Lee. "A Life-Style for Diaspora: A Study of the Tales of Esther and Daniel." *JBL* 92 (1973): 211–23.

Hyatt, J. Philip. "Jeremiah, Introduction and Exegesis." *IB* 5:777–93.

―――. "A Neo-Babylonian Parallel to *BETHEL SAR-ESER*, Zech 7:2." *JBL* 56 (1937): 387–94.

Ishida, Tomoo. "The Structure and Historical Implications of the Lists of Pre-Israelite Nations." *Bib* 60 (1979): 461–90.

Jannssen, Enno. *Juda in der Exilszeit: Ein Beitrag zur Frage der Entstehung des Judentums*. Göttingen: Vandenhoeck & Ruprecht, 1956.

Japhet, Sara. "The Concept of the 'Remnant' in the Restoration Period: On the Vocabulary of Self-Definition." Pages 432–49 in *From the Rivers of Babylon to the Highlands of Judah: Collected Studies on the Restoration Period*. Winona Lake: Eisenbrauns, 2006. Repr. from pages 340–57 of *Das Manna fällt auch heute noch: Beiträge zur Geschichte und Theologie des Alten, Ersten Testaments. Festschrift für Erich Zenger*. Edited by F.-L. Hossfeld and L. Schwienhorst–Schönberger. HBS 44. Freiburg: Herder, 2004.

————. "The Expulsion of the Foreign Women (Ezra 9–10): The Legal Basis, Precedents, and Consequences for the Definition of Jewish Identity." Pages 379–401 in *Teshurah Le-ᶜAmos: Collected Studies in Biblical Exegesis Presented to ᶜAmos Hakham*. Edited by M. Bar-Asher, N. Hacham, and Y. Ofer. Alon Shevut: Tevunot, 2007 (in Hebrew).

————. "Law and 'The Law' in Ezra–Nehemiah." Pages 99–115 in Goshen-Gottstein, ed., *Proceedings of the Ninth World Congress of Jewish Studies, Panel Sessions*.

————. "People and Land in the Restoration Period." Pages 103–25 in *Das Land Israel im biblischer Zeit: Jerusalem-Symposium 1981 der Hebräischen Universität und der Georg-August-Universität*. Edited by G. Strecker. GTA 25. Göttingen: Vandenhoeck & Ruprecht, 1983.

Johnson, Marshall D. *The Purpose of the Biblical Genealogies*. SNTSMS 8. Cambridge: Cambridge University Press, 1988.

Joosten, Jan. *People and Land in the Holiness Code: An Exegetical Study of the Ideational Framework of the Law in Leviticus 17–26*. SVTP 67. Leiden: Brill, 1996.

Joyce, Paul M. "Dislocation and Adaptation in the Exilic Age and After." Pages 45–58 in *After the Exile: Essays in Honor of Rex Mason*. Edited by J. Barton and D. J. Reimer. Macon, Ga.: Mercer University Press, 1996.

Kamionkowski, S. Tamar. *Gender Reversal and Cosmic Chaos: A Study on the Book of Ezekiel*. JSOTSup 358. Sheffield: Sheffield Academic, 2003.

Kasher, Rimon. *Ezekiel 25–48*. Mikra LeYisraʾel. Jerusalem: The Hebrew University/ Magnes. Tel Aviv: Am Oved, 2004 (in Hebrew).

————. "Haggai and Ezekiel: The Complicated Relations Between the Two Prophets." *VT* 59 (2009): 556–82.

————. "Restoration Programs for the Zion Repatriates: Between Ezekiel and Zechariah." *Beit Mikra* 56, no. 2 (2011): 33–57 (in Hebrew).

Kauffman, Yehezkel. *History of Israelite Religion*. Jerusalem: Bialik, 1976 (in Hebrew).

Kessler, John. "Diaspora and Homeland in the Early Achaemenid Period: Community, Geography and Demography in Zechariah 1–8." Pages 137–66 in *Approaching Yehud: New Approaches to the Study of the Persian Period*. Edited by J. L. Berquist. Semeia 50. Leiden: Brill, 2008.

————. "The Diaspora in Zechariah 1–8 and Ezra–Nehemiah: The Role of History, Social Location, and Tradition in the Formulation of Identity." Pages 119–45 in Knoppers and Ristau, eds., *Community Identity in Judean Historiography*.

————. "Persia's Loyal Yahwists: Power, Identity, and Ethnicity in Achaemenid Yehud." Pages 92–121 in Lipschits and Oeming, eds., *Judah and the Judeans in the Persian Period*.

Klein, Ralph W. *Israel in Exile: A Theological Interpretation*. OBT 6. Philadelphia: Fortress, 1979.

Knoppers, Gary N. "Ethnicity, Genealogy, Geography, and Change: The Judean Communities of Babylon and Jerusalem in the Story of Ezra." Pages 147–71 in Knoppers and Ristau, eds., *Community Identity in Judean Historiography*.

————. "Exile, Return, and Diaspora: Expatriates and Repatriates in Late Biblical Literature." Pages 29–61 in *Texts, Contexts, and Readings in Postexilic Literature: Explorations into Historiography and Identity Negotiation in Hebrew Bible and Related Texts*. Edited by L. Jonker. FAT 2/53. Tübingen: Mohr Siebeck, 2011.

————. "Intermarriage, Social Complexity, and Ethnic Diversity in the Genealogy of Judah." *JBL* 120 (2001): 15–30.

Knoppers, G. N., and K. A. Ristau, eds. *Community Identity in Judean Historiography: Biblical and Comparative Perspectives.* Winona Lake: Eisenbrauns, 2009.

Koch, Klaus. "Haggais unreines Volk." *ZAW* 79 (1967): 52–66.

Kogut, Simcha. *Correlations Between Biblical Accentation and Traditional Jewish Exegesis.* Jerusalem: The Hebrew University/Magnes, 1994 (in Hebrew).

Koole, Jan L. *Isaiah III.* 3 vols. Historical Commentary on the Old Testament. Kampen: Kok Pharos, 1997.

Kraus, Samuel. *Isaiah* (1905) in Abraham Kahana's *Torah, Neviʾim, Kethubim with Critical Interpretation.* Jerusalem: Makor, 1969 (in Hebrew).

Kutsko, John F. *Between Heaven and Earth: Divine Presence and Absence in the Book of Ezekiel.* Winona Lake: Eisenbrauns, 2000.

Lang, Bernhard. *Kein Aufstand in Jerusalem: Die Politik des Propheten Ezechiel.* Stuttgart: Katholisches Bibelwerk, 1978.

Lemaire, André. "Toward a Redactional History of the Book of Kings." Pages 446–60 in *Reconsidering Israel and Judah: Recent Studies on the Deuteronomistic History.* Edited by G. N. Knoppers and J. G. McConville. SBT 8. Winona Lake: Eisenbrauns, 2000.

Leuchter, Mark. *Josiah's Reform and Jeremiah's Scroll: Historical Calamity and Prophetic Response.* Hebrew Bible Monographs 6. Sheffield: Sheffield Phoenix, 2006.

————. *The Polemics of Exile in Jeremiah 26–45.* Cambridge: Cambridge University Press, 2008.

Levenson, Jon D. *Theology of the Program of Restoration of Ezekiel 40–48.* HSM 10. Missoula, Mo.: Scholars Press, 1976.

————. "Who Inserted the Book of the Torah?" *HTR* 68 (1975): 203–33.

Levey, Samson H. *The Targum of Ezekiel.* Edinburgh: T. & T. Clark, 1987.

Levitt Kohn, Risa. *A New Heart and a New Soul: Ezekiel, the Exile and the Torah.* JSOTSup 358. Sheffield: Sheffield Academic, 2002.

Lindars, Barnabas. "'Rachel Weeping for Her Children': Jeremiah 31:15–22." *JSOT* 12 (1979): 47–62.

Lipschits, Oded. "Achaemenid Imperial Policy, Settlement Processes in Palestine, and the Status of Jerusalem in the Middle of the Fifth Century B.C.E." Pages 19–52 in Lipschits and Oeming, eds., *Judah and the Judeans in the Persian Period.*

————. "Demographic Changes in Judah between the Seventh and the Fifth Centuries B.C.E." Pages 323–76 in Lipschits and Blenkinsopp, eds., *Judah and the Judeans in the Neo-Babylonian Period.*

————. *The Fall and Rise of Jerusalem: Judah Under Babylonian Rule.* Winona Lake: Eisenbrauns, 2005.

Lipschits, Oded, and Joseph Blenkinsopp, eds. *Judah and the Judeans in the Neo-Babylonian Period.* Winona Lake: Eisenbrauns, 2003.

Lipschits, O., G. N. Knoppers, and M. Oeming, eds. *Judah and the Judeans in the Achaemenid Period: Negotiating Identity in an International Context.* Winona Lake: Eisenbrauns, 2011.

Lipschits, Oded, and Manfred Oeming, eds. *Judah and the Judeans in the Persian Period.* Winona Lake: Eisenbrauns, 2006.

Lipschits, Oded, Gary N. Knoppers, and Rainer Albertz, eds. *Judah and the Judeans in the Fourth Century B.C.E.* Winona Lake: Eisenbrauns, 2007.

Lundbom, Jack R. *Jeremiah 1–20.* AB 21A. New Haven: Yale University Press, 1999.

———. *Jeremiah 21–36.* AB 21B. New York: Doubleday, 2004.

———. *Jeremiah 37–52.* AB 21C. New York: Doubleday, 2004.

Lust, Johan. "Exodus 6,2–8 and Ezekiel." Pages 209–24 in *Studies in the Book of Exodus.* Edited by M. Vervenne. Leuven: Leuven University Press, 1996.

Machinist, Peter. "Palestine, Administration of (Assyro-Babylonian)." *ABD* 5:69–81.

Magdalene, F. Rachel and Cornelia Wunsch, "Slavery Between Judah and Babylon: The Exilic Experience." Pages 113–34 in *Slaves and Households in the Near East.* Edited by L. Culbertson. Oriental Institute Seminars 7. Chicago: The Oriental Institute of the University of Chicago, 2011.

Malul, Meir. "Adoption of Foundlings in the Bible and Mesopotamian Documents: A Study of Some Legal Metaphors in Ezekiel 16.1–7." *JSOT* 46 (1990): 97–126.

Markus, Robert A. "The Problem of Self–Definition: From Sect to Church." Pages 1–15 in *Jewish and Christian Self-Definition.* Vol. 1, *The Shaping of Christianity in the Second and Third Centuries.* Edited by E. P. Sanders. London: SCM, 1980.

Mason, Rex A. *The Books of Haggai, Zechariah and Malachi.* CBC. Cambridge: Cambridge University Press, 1977,

———. "The Prophets of the Restoration." Pages 137–54 in *Israel's Prophetic Tradition: Essays in Honour of Peter R. Ackroyd.* Edited by R. G. Coggins, A. Phillips, and M. A. Knibb. Cambridge: Cambridge University Press, 1982.

———. "The Purpose of the 'Editorial Framework' of the Book of Haggai." *VT* 27 (1977): 413–21.

May, Herbert G. "'This People' and 'This Nation' in Haggai." *VT* 18 (1968): 190–97.

Mayes, Adam D. H. "Deuteronomy 4 and the Literary Criticism of Deuteronomy." *JBL* 100 (1981): 23–51.

Mazar, Benjamin. *Jerusalem Through the Ages.* Jerusalem: Israel Exploration Society, 1968 (in Hebrew).

McKane, William. *Jeremiah 1–25.* ICC. Edinburgh: T. & T. Clark, 1986.

———. *Jeremiah 26–52.* ICC. Edinburgh: T. & T. Clark, 1996.

McKenzie, John L. *Second Isaiah.* AB 20. Garden City, N.Y.: Doubleday, 1968.

Mein, Andrew. *Ezekiel and the Ethics of Exile.* Oxford Theological Monographs. Oxford: Oxford University Press, 2001.

Meinhold, Arndt. "Die Gattung der Josephsgeschichte und des Estherbuches: Diaspora-novelle I." *ZAW* 87 (1975): 306–24.

———. "Die Gattung der Josephsgeschichte und des Estherbuches: Diasporanovelle II." *ZAW* 88 (1976): 72–93.

Mendenhall, George. "Covenant Forms in Israelite Tradition." *Biblical Archaeologist* 17 (1954): 50–76.

Meyers, Carol L., and Eric M. Meyers. *Haggai and Zechariah 1–8.* AB 25B. Garden City, N.Y.: Doubleday, 1987.

Michalowski, Piotr. *The Lamentation over the Destruction of Sumer and Ur.* Winona Lake: Eisenbrauns, 1989.

Middlemas, Jill. *The Templeless Age: An Introduction to the History, Literature, and Theology of the "Exile."* Louisville: Westminster John Knox, 2007.

Milgrom, Jacob. *Leviticus 1–16.* AB 3. New York: Doubleday, 1991.

———. *Leviticus 17–22.* AB 3A. New York: Doubleday, 2000.

———. *Leviticus 23–27.* AB 3C. New York: Doubleday, 2001.

Miller, Patrick D. "The Gift of the Land: The Deuteronomic Theology of the Land." *Interpretation* 23 (1969): 451–65.

Mitchell, Hinckley G. *Haggai, Zechariah, Malachi and Jonah.* ICC. Edinburgh: T. & T. Clark, 1912.

Muilenberg, James. "The Form and Structure of the Covenantal Formulations." *VT* 9 (1959): 347–65.

Murray, Donald F. "The Rhetoric of Disputation: Re-examination of a Prophetic Genre." *JSOT* 38 (1987): 95–121.

Myers, Jacob M. *Ezra–Nehemiah.* AB 14. Garden City, N.Y.: Doubleday, 1965.

Na'aman, Nadav, and Ran Zadok. "Sargon II's Deportations to Israel and Philistia (716–708 B.C.)." *JCS* 40 (1988): 36–46.

Neusner, J., and E. S. Frerichs, eds. *"To See Ourselves as Others See Us": Christians, Jews, "Others" in Late Antiquity.* Chico, Calif: Scholars Press, 1985.

Nicholson, Ernest W. "The Meaning of the Expression עם הארץ in the Old Testament." *JSS* 10 (1965): 59–66.

———. "The Meaning of the Expression עם הארץ in the Old Testament." *JSS* 10 (1965): 59–66.

———. *Preaching to the Exiles: A Study of the Prose Tradition in the Book of Jeremiah.* New York: Schocken, 1970.

Noth, Martin. *The Deuteronomistic History.* JSOTSup 15. Translated and edited by D. J. A. Clines (from the 2d ed., 1957). Sheffield: Sheffield Academic, 1991.

———. *Exodus.* OTL. Philadelphia: Westminster, 1962.

Oded, Bustenay. *The Early History of the Babylonian Exile (8th–6th Centuries BCE).* Haifa: Pardes, 2010 (in Hebrew).

———. "Judah and the Exile." Pages 469–88 in *Israelite and Judean History.* Edited by J. H. Hayes and J. M. Miller. OTL. Philadelphia: Westminster, 1977.

———. *Mass Deportations and Deportees in the Neo-Assyrian Empire.* Wiesbaden: Reichert, 1979.

———. "Observations on the Israelite/Judaean Exiles in Mesopotamia during the Eighth–Sixth Centuries BCE." Pages 205–12 in *Immigration and Emigration within the Ancient Near East: Festschrift E. Lipiński.* Edited by K. Van Lerberghe and A. Schoors. OLA 65. Leuven: Peeters, 1995.

Odell, Margaret S. "Genre and Persona in Ezekiel 24:15–24." Pages 195–220 in Odell and Strong, eds., *The Book of Ezekiel.*

———. "The Inversion of Shame and Forgiveness in Ezekiel 16:59–63." *JSOT* 56 (1992): 101–12.

Odell, Margaret S., and J. T. Strong, eds. *The Book of Ezekiel: Theological and Anthropological Perspectives.* SBLSymS 9. Atlanta: Society of Biblical Literature, 2000.

Olson, Dennis T. *Deuteronomy and the Death of Moses: A Theological Reading.* Minneapolis: Fortress, 1994.

Oswalt, John N. *Isaiah 40–66.* NICOT. Grand Rapids: Eerdmans, 1998.

Parpola, Simo, and Kazuko Watanabe. *Neo-Assyrian Treaties and Loyalty Oaths.* SAA 2. Helsinki: Helsinki University Press, 1989.

Parsons, Talcott. "Some Theoretical Considerations on the Nature and Trends of Change of Ethnicity." Pages 53–83 in Glazer and Moynihan, eds., *Ethnicity: Theory and Experience*.

Patton, Corrine L. "'Should Our Sister Be Treated Like a Whore?': A Response to Feminist Critiques of Ezekiel 23." Pages 221–38 in Odell and Strong, eds., *The Book of Ezekiel*.

Paul, Shalom M. "Adoption Formulae: A Study of Cuneiform and Biblical Legal Clauses." *MAARAV* 2 (1979–80): 173–85.

———. *Deutero-Isaiah 40–48*. Mikra Le-Israel. Jerusalem: The Hebrew University/ Magnes. Tel Aviv: Am Oved, 2008 (in Hebrew).

———. *Isaiah 40–66*. Grand Rapids: Eerdmans, 2012.

Pearce, Laurie E. "'Judeans': A Special Status in Neo-Babylonian and Achaemenid Babylonia?" Pages 267–78 in Lipschits, Knoppers, and Oeming, eds., *Judah and the Judeans in the Achaemenid Period*.

Petersen, David L. "The Temple in Persian Period Prophetic Texts." Pages 124–44 in *Second Temple Studies*. Vol. 1, *Persian Period*. JSOTSup 117. Edited by P. R. Davies. Sheffield: Sheffield Academic, 1991.

———. *Haggai and Zechariah 1–8*. OTL. Philadelphia: Westminster, 1984.

Pfeil, Rüdiger. "When Is a *Goy* a 'Goy'? The Interpretation of Haggai 2:10–19." Pages 261–78 in *A Tribute to Gleason Archer*. Edited by W. C. Kaiser and R. F. Youngblood. Chicago: Moody, 1986.

Piepkorn, Arthur C. *Historical Prism Inscriptions of Ashurbanipal*. AS 5. Chicago: University of Chicago Press, 1933.

Plöger, Otto. *Theocracy and Eschatology*. Translated by S. Rudman. Oxford: Blackwell, 1968. 2d German ed. 1962.

Pohlmann, Karl-Friedrich. *Das Buch des Propheten Hesekiel: Kapitel 1–19*. ATD 22/1. Göttingen: Vandenhoeck & Ruprecht, 1996.

———. *Ezechielstudien: Zur Redaktionsgeschichte des Buches und zur Frage nach den ältesten Texten*. BZAW 202. Berlin: de Gruyter, 1992.

———. *Studien zum Jeremiabuches*. FRLANT 118. Göttingen: Vandenhoeck & Ruprecht, 1978.

Polzin, Robert M. *Moses and the Deuteronomist: A Literary Study of the Deuteronomic History*. Part 1, *Deuteronomy, Joshua, Judges*. New York: Seabury, 1980.

Porter, John. *The Vertical Mosaic: A Study of Social Class and Power in Canada*. Toronto: University of Toronto Press, 1965.

Poznanski, S. ed. *Kommentar zu Ezechiel und den XII kleinen Propheten von Eliezer aus Beaugency*. Warsaw: Mekitze Nirdamim, 1909.

Propp, William C. *Exodus 1–18*. AB 2. New York, N.Y.: Doubleday, 1998.

Rad, Gerhard von. *Deuteronomy*. Translated by D. Barton. OTL. London: SCM, 1966.

———. "The Promised Land and Yahweh's Land in the Hexateuch." Pages 79–93 in *The Problem of the Hexateuch and Other Essays*. Translated by E. W. Trueman Dicken. Edinburgh: Oliver & Boyd, 1966.

Raitt, Thomas M. *A Theology of Exile: Judgment / Deliverance in Jeremiah and Ezekiel*. Philadelphia: Fortress, 1977.

Redditt, Paul L. *Haggai, Zechariah, and Malachi*. NCBC. Grand Rapids: Eerdmans, 1995.

Renz, Thomas. *The Rhetorical Function of the Book of Ezekiel*. Leiden: Brill, 2002.

Rofé, Alexander. "The Arrangement of the Book of Jeremiah." *ZAW* 101 (1989): 390–98.

———. "Isaiah 66:1–4: Judean Sects in the Persian Period as Viewed by Trito-Isaiah." Pages 205–17 in *Biblical and Related Studies Presented to Samuel Iwry*. Edited by A. Kort and S. Morschauser. Winona Lake: Eisenbrauns, 1985.

Rom-Shiloni, Dalit. "Actualization of Pentateuchal Legal Traditions in Jeremiah: More on the Riddle of Authorship." *ZABR* 15 (2009): 254–81.

———. "Deuteronomic Concepts of Exile Interpreted in Jeremiah and Ezekiel." Pages 101–23 in *Birkat Shalom: Studies in the Bible, Ancient Near Eastern Literature, and Postbiblical Judaism Presented to Shalom M. Paul on the Occasion of His Seventieth Birthday*. Edited by C. Cohen, V. A. Hurowitz, B. J. Schwartz, J. H. Tigay, and Y. Muffs. Winona Lake: Eisenbrauns, 2008.

———. "Exiles and Those Who Remained: Strategies of Exclusivity in the Early Sixth Century BCE." Pages 119–38 in *Shay le-Sara Japhet: Studies in the Bible, Its Exegesis, and Its Language Presented to Sara Japhet*. Edited by M. Bar Asher, D. Rom-Shiloni, E. Tov, and N. Wazana. Jerusalem: Bialik Institute, 2007 (in Hebrew).

———. "Ezekiel as the Voice of the Exiles and Constructor of Exilic Ideology." *HUCA* 76 (2005): 1–45.

———. "Facing Destruction and Exile: Inner-Biblical Exegesis in Jeremiah and Ezekiel." *ZAW* 117 (2005): 189–205.

———. "From Ezekiel to Ezra–Nehemiah: Shifts of Group-Identities within Babylonian Exilic Ideology." Pages 127–51 in Lipschits, Knoppers, and Oeming, eds., *Judah and the Judeans in the Achaemenid Period*.

———. *God in Times of Destruction and Exiles: Tanakh (Hebrew Bible) Theology*. Jerusalem: The Hebrew University/Magnes, 2009 (in Hebrew).

———. "Group-Identities in Jeremiah: Is It the Persian Period Conflict?" Pages 11–46 in *A Palimpsest: Rhetoric, Stylistics, and Language in Biblical Texts from the Persian and Hellenistic Periods*. Edited by E. Ben Zvi, D. Edelman, and F. Polak. PHSC 5. Piscataway, N.J.: Gorgias, 2009.

———. "Jerusalem and Israel, Synonyms or Antonyms? Jewish Exegesis of Ezekiel's Prophecies Against Jerusalem." Pages 89–114 in *After Ezekiel: Essays on the Reception of a Difficult Prophet*. Edited by A. Mein and P. Joyce. London: T&T Clark International, 2010.

———. "Law Interpretation in Jeremiah: Exegetical Techniques and Ideological Intentions." *Shnaton* 17 (2008): 59–79 (in Hebrew).

———. "The Prophecy for 'Everlasting Covenant' (Jeremiah 32:36–41): An Exilic Addition or a Deuteronomistic Redaction?" *VT* 53 (2003): 201–23.

———. "What is 'Persian' in Late Sixth Century BCE Prophetic Literature? Case-Studies and Criteria." In *Discerning Criteria for Dating Persian Period Texts*. Edited by R. Bautch and J. Nogalsky. The International Society of Biblical Literature Symposium Volume of the Persian Period Seminar. Atlanta, Ga.: Society of Biblical Literature, forthcoming.

Rothstein, Johann W. *Juden und Samaritaner: Die grundlegende Scheidung von Judentum und Heidentum: Eine kritische Studie zum Buche Haggai und zur judischen Geschichte im ersten nachexilischen Jahrhundert*. BZAW 3. Leipzig: Hinrichs, 1908.

Rudolph, Wilhelm. *Esra und Nehemia*. HAT 1/20. Tübingen: Mohr, 1949.

———. *Haggai, Sacharja 1–8, Sacharja 9–14, Maleachi*. KAT 13/4. Gutersloh: Mohn, 1976.

———. *Jeremiah*. HAT 1/12. Tübingen: Mohr Siebeck, 1947. 3d ed. 1968.

Safran, William. "Diasporas in Modern Societies: Myths of Homeland and Return." *Diaspora* 1 (1991): 83–99.

Sarna, Nahum M. "The Abortive Insurrection in Zedekiah's Day (Jer. 27–29)." *ErIs* 14 (1978): *79–*96.

Sasson, Jack M. *The Military Establishments at Mari*. Studia Pohl 3. Rome: Pontifical Biblical Institute, 1969.

Schramm, Brooks. *The Opponents of Third Isaiah: Reconstructing the Cultic History of the Restoration*. JSOTSup 193. Sheffield: Sheffield Academic, 1995.

Schwartz, Baruch J. *The Holiness Legislation: Studies in the Priestly Code*. Jerusalem: The Hebrew University/Magnes, 1999 (in Hebrew).

Seitz, Christopher R. "The Crisis of Interpretation over the Meaning and Purpose of the Exile." *VT* 35 (1985): 78–97.

———. *Theology in Conflict: Reactions to the Exile in the Book of Jeremiah*. BZAW 176. Berlin: de Gruyter, 1989.

Sellin, Ernst. *Zwölfprophetenbuch*. KAT 12. Leipzig: Deichert, 1922.

Sharp, Carolyn. *Prophecy and Ideology in Jeremiah: Struggles for Authority in the Deutero-Jeremianic Prose*. London: T&T Clark International, 2003.

Sherif, Muzafer. *Group Conflict and Co-Operation: Their Social Psychology*. London: Routledge & Kegan Paul, 1967.

Smith, Anthony D. "Chosen Peoples." Pages 189–97 in *Ethnicity*. Edited by J. Hutchinson and A. D. Smith. Oxford: Oxford University Press, 1996.

———. *The Ethnic Origins of Nations*. Oxford: Blackwell, 1986.

Smith, George A. *Deuteronomy*. CBC. Cambridge: Cambridge University Press, 1950.

Smith, Jonathan Z. "What a Difference a Difference Makes." Pages 3–48 in Neusner and Frerichs, eds., *"To See Ourselves as Others See Us."*

Smith, Ralph L. *Micah–Malachi*. WBC 32. Waco, Tex.: Word.

Smith-Christopher, Daniel L. *A Biblical Theology of Exile*. OBT. Minneapolis: Augsburg Fortress, 2002.

———. *The Religion of the Landless: The Social Context of the Babylonian Exile*. Bloomington: Meyer Stone, 1989.

Snaith, Norman H. "Isaiah 40–66: A Study of the Teaching of the Second Isaiah and Its Consequences." Pages 135–264 in *Studies on the Second Part of the Book of Isaiah*. Edited by H. M. Orlinsky and N. H. Snaith. VTSup 14. Leiden: Brill, 1967.

Sommer, Benjamin D. *A Prophet Reads Scripture: Allusion in Isaiah 40–66*. Stanford: Stanford University Press, 1998.

Sparks, Kenton L. *Ethnicity and Identity in Ancient Israel: Prolegomena to the Study of Ethnic Sentiments and Their Expressions in the Hebrew Bible*. Winona Lake: Eisenbrauns, 1998.

Sperling, David. "Joshua 24 Re-examined." *HUCA* 58 (1987): 119–36.

Stead, Michael R. *The Intertextuality of Zechariah 1–8*. LHBOTS 506. New York: T&T Clark International, 2009.

Steck, Odil H. "Das Problem theologischer Stroemungen in nachexilischer Zeit." *EvT* 28 (1968): 445–58.

Stephan, Walter G., and Cookie W. Stephan. *Intergroup Relations*. Social Psychology Series. Boulder: Westview, 1996.

Stipp, Hermann-Josef. "The Concept of the Empty Land in Jeremiah 37–43." Pages 103–54 in Ben Zvi and Levin, eds., *The Concept of Exile in Ancient Israel*.

Stohlmann, Stephen C. "The Judean Exile After 701 B.C.E." Pages 147–76 in *Scripture in Context*. Vol. 2, *More Essays on the Comparative Method*. Edited by W. W. Hallo, J. C. Moyer, and L. G. Perdue. Winona Lake: Eisenbrauns, 1983.

Stuhlmueller, Carroll. *Rebuilding with Hope: A Commentary on the Books of Haggai and Zechariah*. Grand Rapids: Eerdmans. Edinburgh: Handsel, 1988.

Sweeney, Marvin A. "Jeremiah 30–31 and King Josiah's Program of National Restoration and Religious Reform." *ZAW* 108 (1996): 569–83.

———. "Prophetic Exegesis in Isaiah 65–66." Pages 455–74 in *Writing and Reading the Scroll of Isaiah: Studies of an Interpretive Tradition*. Edited by C. C. Broyles and C. A. Evans. VTSup 71. Leiden: Brill, 1997.

Tadmor, Hayim. "'The People' and the Kingship in Ancient Israel." *Journal of World History* 11 (1968): 3–23.

Tajfel, Henri, and John C. Turner. "The Social Identity Theory of Intergroup Behavior." Pages 7–24 in *Psychology of Intergroup Relations*. Edited by S. Worchel and W. G. Austin. Chicago: Nelson–Hall, 1986.

Talmon, Shemaryahu. "Ezra and Nehemiah." Pages 317–29 in the *Interpreter's Dictionary of the Bible: Supplementary Volume*. Edited by K. Crim. Nashville: Abingdon, 1976.

———. "The Judean ʾam haʾares in Historical Perspective." Pages 71–76 in *Proceedings of the Fourth World Congress of Jewish Studies*. Jerusalem: World Union of Jewish Studies, 1967 (in Hebrew).

———. "Return to Zion: Consequences for Our Future." *Cathedra* 4 (1977): 26–31 (in Hebrew).

Talshir, Tzipora. *Zechariah 1–8*. Olam HaTanakh. Tel Aviv: Davidson–Iti, 1994 (in Hebrew).

Thiel, Winfried. *Die deuteronomistische Redaktion von Jeremia, 1–45: Mit einer Gesamtbeurteilung der deuteronomistischen Redaktion des Buches Jeremia*. 2 vols. WMANT 41, 52. Neukirchen–Vluyn: Neukirchener Verlag, 1973, 1981.

Tiemeyer, Lena-Sofia. "Continuity and Discontinuity in Isaiah 40–66: History of Research." In *Continuity and Discontinuity: Chronological and Thematic Development in Isaiah 40–66*. Edited by L.-S. Tiemeyer. FRLANT. Göttingen: Vandenhoeck & Ruprecht, forthcoming.

———. *For the Comfort of Zion: The Geographical and Theological Location of Isaiah 40–55*. VTSup 139. Leiden: Brill, 2011.

Tigay, Jeffrey H. *Deuteronomy*. Jewish Publication Society Torah Commentary. Philadelphia: Jewish Publication Society, 1996.

Tollington, Janet E. *Tradition and Innovation in Haggai and Zechariah*. JSOTSup 150. Sheffield: Sheffield Academic, 1993.

Tooman, William A. *Gog of Magog: Reuse of Scripture and Compositional Technique in Ezekiel 38–39*. FAT 2/52. Tübingen: Mohr Siebeck, 2011.

Torrey, Charles C. *Pseudo-Ezekiel and the Original Prophecy*. New York: KTAV, 1930. 2d ed. 1970.

Unger, Tim. "Noch einmal: Haggais unreines Volk." *ZAW* 103 (1991): 210–25.

Unterman, Jeremiah. *From Repentance to Redemption: Jeremiah's Thought in Transition.* JSOTSup 54. Sheffield: Sheffield Academic, 1987.

Van Seters, John. *Abraham in History and Tradition.* New Haven: Yale University Press, 1975.

———. *Prologue to History: The Yahwist as Historian in Genesis.* Louisville: Westminster John Knox, 1992.

Vanderhooft, David S. *The Neo-Babylonian Empire and Babylon in the Latter Prophets.* HSM 59. Atlanta: Scholars Press, 1999.

Waltke, Bruce K. "The Phenomenon of Conditionality within Unconditional Covenants." Pages 123–40 in *Israel's Apostasy and Restoration: Essays in Honor of R. K. Harrison.* Edited by A. Gileadi. Grand Rapids: Baker, 1988.

Wanke, Gunther. *Untersuchungen zur sogenannten Baruchschrift.* BZAW 122. Berlin: de Gruyter, 1971.

Watts, John D. W. *Isaiah 34–66.* WBC 25. Waco, Tex.: Word, 1987.

Weinfeld, Moshe. "Berit—Covenant vs. Obligation." *Bib* 56 (1975): 120–28.

———. "The Covenant of Grant in the Old Testament and in the Ancient Near East." *JAOS* 90 (1970): 184–203.

———. *Deuteronomy 1–11.* AB 4A. New York: Doubleday, 1991.

———. *Deuteronomy and the Deuteronomic School.* Winona Lake: Eisenbrauns, 1972. 2d ed. 1992.

———. "Inheritance of the Land—Privilege versus Obligation: The Concept of the 'Promise of the Land' in the Sources of the First and Second Temple Periods." *Zion* (1984): 115–37 (in Hebrew).

Weippert, Helga. *Die Prosareden des Jeremiabuches.* BZAW 132. Berlin: de Gruyter, 1973.

Weiss, Meir. *Amos.* 2 vols. Jerusalem: The Hebrew University/Magnes, 1992.

Welch, Adam C. *Post-Exilic Judaism.* Edinburgh: Blackwood, 1935.

Wessels, Wilhelm J. "Jeremiah 22, 24–30: A Proposed Ideological Reading." *ZAW* 101 (1989): 232–49.

Westermann, Claus. *Isaiah 40–66.* Translated by D. M. G. Stalker. OTL. London: SCM, 1969.

———. *Sprache und Struktur der Prophetie Deuterojesajas.* Calwer Theologische Monographien 11. Stuttgart: Calwer, 1981.

Williamson, Hugh G. M. "The Concept of Israel in Transition." Pages 141–61 in *The World of Ancient Israel: Sociological, Anthropological, and Political Perspectives. Essays by Members of the Society for Old Testament Study.* Edited by R. E. Clements. Cambridge: Cambridge University Press, 1989.

———. "Laments at the Destroyed Temple." *Bible Review* 6, no. 4 (1990): 12–17, 44.

———. "Structure and Historiography in Nehemiah 9." Pages 117–31 in Goshen-Gottstein, ed., *Proceedings of the Ninth World Congress of Jewish Studies, Panel Sessions.*

Wills, Lawrence M. *The Jew in the Court of the Foreign King: Ancient Jewish Legends.* HDR 26. Minneapolis: Fortress, 1990.

Wilson, Robert R. *Genealogy and History in the Biblical World.* New Haven: Yale University Press, 1977.

———. "Genealogy, Genealogies." *ABD* 2:929–32.

Winton Thomas, David. "Haggai." *IB* 6:1035–49.

———. "The Sixth Century BC: A Creative Epoch in the History of Israel." *JSS* 6 (1961): 33–46.

———. "Zechariah." *IB* 6:1051–114.

Wolff, Hans W. *Haggai: A Commentary*. Translated by M. Kohl. Minneapolis: Augsburg, 1988.

Wright, Jacob L. *Rebuilding Identity: The Nehemiah-Memoir and Its Earliest Readers.* BZAW 348. Berlin: de Gruyter, 2004.

Würthwein, Ernst. *Der ʿamm haʾarez im Alten Testament.* BWANT 4/17. Stuttgart: Kohlhammer, 1936.

Yates, Gary E. "New Exodus and No Exodus in Jeremiah 26–45: Promise and Warning to the Exiles in Babylon." *TynBul* 57 (2006): 1–22.

Yavin, Shmuel. "Families and Parties in the Kingdom of Judah." *Tarbiz* 12 (1951): 241–67 (in Hebrew).

Zevit, Ziony. "The Use of עבד as a Diplomatic Term in Jeremiah." *JBL* 88 (1969): 74–77.

Zimmerli, Walther. *Ezekiel 1 and 2*. Translated by R. E. Clements and J. D. Martin. 2 vols. Hermeneia. Philadelphia: Fortress, 1979, 1983.

INDEXES

INDEX OF REFERENCES

Isaiah (cont.)		48:12	104
43:27	104	48:15	116
44:1	120	48:17	105
44:2	120	48:18	106
44:4	133	48:20–22	109, 112
44:5	104	48:20–21	218, 243
44:6	105	48:20	105, 106,
44:9–20	24		112, 118
44:21	104, 105,	49–66	11, 12, 99,
	120		100, 102–
44:23	104		104, 121,
44:24–28	105, 111,		253
	112	49–55	103, 105
44:26–28	107	49:1–6	105
44:26	107, 112	49:3	104, 105,
44:27	112		120
44:28	112	49:5	104
45:1–13	111	49:6	105
45:1–8	108	49:7	105
45:1–7	111	49:8	105, 242
45:2–5	111	49:9–12	106
45:3	105	49:12	106, 109–
45:4	120		11, 263
45:5–6	109	49:13	104
45:8	111	49:14–21	107, 241,
45:9–13	111		258
45:12–13	115	49:14	107
45:13	104, 111,	49:15–21	108
	112, 212,	49:20–23	108
	260	49:20	227
45:15	105	49:21	87, 89,
45:17	105		107, 133
45:19	105, 244	49:21	212
45:20–25	24	49:22–26	241
45:25	105, 244	49:24	113
46:2	113	49:25	113
46:3	87, 88	49:26	105
46:11	109, 110,	50:1–3	106
	263	50:1	114, 115,
46:13	105, 107		212
47:6	106	51:1–2	148
48:1–11	107	51:2	102, 118,
48:1–8	106		119, 148
48:1–2	107	51:3	107, 180
48:1	105	51:4	104
48:2	105	51:9–52:3	114
48:9	247	51:9–11	106, 107

51:11	111, 114
51:12–16	111, 112
51:12	112
51:15	260
51:16	112
51:17–23	106
52	112
52:1–11	111
52:1–10	117
52:1–6	112
52:1–3	114
52:1–2	107, 108,
	112, 260
52:1	112, 113
52:2–3	112
52:2	113, 117,
	260
52:3–6	106
52:3	114–16
52:4–6	112, 115,
	116, 118,
	119
52:4–5	116
52:5	117
52:6	116, 117
52:7–10	107, 112
52:8–10	117, 260
52:10	117
52:11–12	107, 109,
	112, 118,
	218, 243
52:11	108, 112
52:12	105
52:20	107
54	108
54:1–10	107
54:1–4	107
54:2–3	119
54:5	105
54:7–8	115
54:8	105
54:11–17	122
54:12	100
54:15	122
55:2	68
55:3	118
55:5	105

Index of References

INDEX OF AUTHORS

Made in the USA
Monee, IL
09 December 2019

18280213R00188